Recent controversies in political economy

Recent controversies in political economy

Edited by Russell Lewis

London and New York

First published 1992
by Routledge
11 New Fetter Lane, London EC4P 4EE

Simultaneously published in the USA and Canada
by Routledge
a division of Routledge, Chapman and Hall, Inc.
29 West 35th Street, New York, NY 10001

© 1992 The Institute of Economic Affairs

The Institute of Economic Affairs was set up as a research and
educational trust under a trust deed signed in 1955.

Typeset in Scantext Times by Leaper & Gard Ltd, Bristol
Printed and bound in Great Britain by
Mackays of Chatham plc, Chatham, Kent

All rights reserved. No part of this book may be reprinted or
reproduced or utilized in any form or by any electronic, mechanical or
other means, now known or hereafter invented, including photocopying and
recording, or in any information storage or retrieval system, without
permission in writing from the publishers.

British Library Cataloguing in Publication Data

0–415–06163–6 (Hb)
0–415–07979–9 (Pb)

A catalogue reference for this title is available from
the British Library.

Library of Congress Cataloging in Publication Data

Recent controversies in political economy / edited by Russell Lewis.
    p. cm.
  Includes bibliographical references and index.
  ISBN 0–415–06163–6
  1. Privatization—Great Britain.   2. Competition—Great Britain.
3. Housing—Great Britain.   4. Monetary policy—Great Britain.
5. Fiscal policy—Great Britain.   6. Great Britain—Economic
policy—1945–
HD4148.R53   1992
338.941'09048—dc20   91–45321
                                                                 CIP

Contents

List of figures		viii
List of tables		ix
Introduction	Russell Lewis	1

1 Keynesianism 7
Can Keynesianism be falsified?	Brian Snowden and Peter Wynarczyk	7
Keynes' legacy of half-truths	Harold Lydall	9
Futures finally refute Keynes	Robert C.B. Miller	18
Have the Keynesians been vanquished?	Brian Snowden and Peter Wynarczyk	22
Was Keynes a monetarist?	Bernard Foley	26

2 Labour economics 32
Trade unions in a free society	G.R. Steele	32
Breaking into unemployment: the black economy and workfare	Graham Dawson	36
Real wages and employment	Eli Schwartz	40
Institutional reform to tame union power	Charles K. Rowley	46
Trade unions and society: some lessons of the British experience*	Brian Chiplin	52

3 Money and banking 55
Monetary policy since 1971*	Tim Congdon	55
Banking: why should the taxpayer bear the risk?	Forrest Capie	56
Will inflation follow rapid monetary growth?	Gordon Pepper	59
Why Britain needs a monetary anchor	Peter Warburton	62
Deregulating the Securities and Investments Board	Joanna Gray and Cento Veljanovski	67

4 Taxation · 74
More state welfare or lower taxes?	Arthur Seldon	74
Political taxes: abolition, not reform	Barry Bracewell-Milnes	78

*Book reviews

Welfare taxation: opting out to shrink the state	Colin Clark	83
The ethics of tax and expenditure decisions	T. Nicolaus Tideman	86

5 Education 91
Parent power to privatize schools	Michael McCrum	91
Per capita funding: the next step to better schools	John Marks	94
School grants: a bar to consumer sovereignty	Marjorie Seldon	97
School as self-seeking syndicates	Dennis O'Keeffe	100
Dirigisme in Higher Education	J.R. Shackleton	106

6 Housing 112
Removing housing subsidies	Tom Taylor	112
Cutting the cost of housing: why more building land is the answer	Lord Vinson of Roddam Dene	115
Housing: anyone for rent control?	Robert Albon and David C. Stafford	116
Housing reforms to 'create' jobs	Paul Ashton, Patrick Minford and Michael Peel	124
Mortgage subsidy – the myth	John Parry Lewis	131

7 Health 134
The economics of training nurses in the NHS	Keith Hartley and Alan Shiell	134
A policy for the NHS, parts I and II	Patrick Minford	136
Few lessons for the NHS	Ray Robinson	157
How to pay for the NHS	Norman McKenna	159
Rejoinder: few lessons for the NHS	David Green	169

8 Environment 173
Europe's congested air space – time for market solutions	Sean D. Barrett	173
Green for stop	Robert Whelan	178
Roads and transport are private goods	Gabriel Roth	182
Chopping and changing forestry policy	Linda Whetstone	191
Not in my backyard	Richard L. Stroup and Donald R. Leal	194

9 Competition policy 203
Leveraged acquisitions and the market for corporate control	Ken Robbie, Steve Thompson and Michael Wright	203
The economic effects of anti-takeover gimmicks: an American view	Robert W. McGee	210
Monopolies and mergers: an MMC perspective	Sydney Lipworth	218
Can we privatize competition policy?	Graham Mather	222

10 Privatization 226

Privatization – by political process or consumer preference?	John Blundell	226
British Telecom – has privatization delivered competition?	Peter Curwen	234
BR – privatization without tears	David Starkie	239
Privatization and universities	Norman Barry	247
Privatization: let the market decide	Roger Buckland and E.W. Davies	249
Anglican economics	Russell Lewis	253

11 Manufacturing versus services 260

Deindustrialization: myths and realities	Tony Baron	260
Manufacturing or services after 1992?	Peter Lawrence	263
Manufacturing versus services – a false dichotomy?	David Liston, OBE	269
The service sector is also productive	Walter Eltis and Andrew Murfin	276
Why manufacturing industry matters	S. Bazen and A.P. Thirwall	282

12 Europe 288

Demographic trends in the industrial world: Europe's declining population?	David Coleman	288
European Community or imperial superstate?	Norman Stone	297
1992 and beyond: market freedom or collectivist regulation?	Martin Holmes	302
The costs of the CAP	Kenneth Thomson	305
The case for Britain joining the EMS	Nigel M. Healey	311
The argument against joining the EMS	Roy Batchelor	320
The right road to monetary union	John Chown and Geoffrey Wood	324

Index 337

Figures

1.1	American futures, 1972–84	20
3.1	Bank lending to the personal sector, 1980 prices	60
3.2	Structure of city regulation	69
7.1	Project 2,000 proposals	136
7.2	Traps in health reform	138
7.3	Summary of proposals for the NHS	140
7.4	Income support for health	142
7.5	The demand for enhanced insurance under present and proposed systems	148
7.6	Waiting time	155
7.7	Tax relief versus opting-out	156
7.8	High-cost high technology	163
7.9	Example of payment for treatment related to income tax assessment	164
8.1	The electronic loop system	190
10.1	Main privatization forms	228
10.2	Bidding for the use of the rail right-of-way	243
10.3	Passenger services	246
11.1	UK employment: manufacturing and tradeable services	272
11.2	Relationship between productivity and output growth in UK manufacturing and services, 1972–86	278
12.1	The baby boom in the USA (US population–age pyramids)	294
12.2	England and Wales population aged 15–19, 1986–2026	295
12.3	EC Agricultural Fund expenditure, 1980–8	309

Tables

2.1	Average wages, 1986	37
2.2	Average wages, adjusted for wage inflation	39
3.1	UK inflation rate during periods of DM/£ stability, 1976–88	63
3.2	UK exchange rate and visible trade performance, 1977–87	63
3.3	Foreign exchange market comparisons, 1987	64
3.4	Relative money supply growth in UK and Germany, 1971–87	65
7.1	Percentage increase in price of health care, 1980–3	158
7.2	NHS and local authority per-capita spending, England, 1980–1	160
8.1	Market forces in aviation	174
8.2	Airport and airspace charges as a proportion of airline costs	177
8.3	Urban public transport: comparison of institutional alternatives	188
8.4	New planting by Forestry Commission and private woodlands	192
9.1	The UK market for corporate control	208
10.1	Privatization issues, costs and discounts for buyers	250
11.1	Average annual growth rates, 1985–8	263
11.2	Standard industrial classification	264
11.3	UK private sector invisible earnings, 1986	271
11.4	UK financial institutions – net earnings overseas, 1986	273
11.5	Current invisible transactions of major OECD countries	274
11.6	Employment, 1978–88	275
11.7	Employment shifts in the UK, 1971–86	279
11.8	Employment shifts in the UK, 1971–86	280
11.9	UK sectoral shifts expressed as a percentage of GDP, 1971–86	281
11.10	Trends relating to manufacturing and services	283
12.1	Fertility and population in EC countries	290
12.2	Population projections in selected countries, 1985–2025	291
12.3	Gains in economic welfare through CAP reform, 1986	308
12.4	Inflation, 1987	312
12.5	European currencies	316
12.6	Domestic credit expansion (DCE)	318

Introduction

Russell Lewis

The central concern of the Institute of Economic Affairs is the analysis of markets, how they work or fail to work or are prevented from working and how they might be revived. This analysis is presented through a steady stream of publications which, since the Institute was founded more than 25 years ago, have had a powerful impact on the policy thinking both of government and the opposition parties. *Economic Affairs*, the Institute's magazine, pursues the same objectives of market investigation as the Institute's other imprints; but appearing regularly five times a year, and having a wide choice of subjects, it has both greater opportunity and obligation to be topical.

This collection of articles appeared in *Economic Affairs* over the last decade. The volume will be judged, to a large extent, on its success in reflecting and illuminating the issues which have been paramount during the Thatcher era, a period which saw the development of new approaches to the role of government in the economy. It witnessed the final collapse of the old cross-party consensus on issues such as the sanctity of full employment; the secondary role of monetary policy; the validity of corporatism; interventionism; redistributive taxation; education as social engineering; state housing provision; public ownership of basic industries; and the key role of manufacturing in economic growth. More recently remnants of the old-style collectivist thinking have been dealt a new blow with the self-confessed economic failure of the Soviet system and its retreat from Eastern Europe. But ideas of democratic centralism have revived in other directions with calls for draconian economic controls to safeguard or improve the environment, health, safety, women's and minority rights. In the case of the Common Market, economic controls have been proposed to serve the cause of harmonization policies equated, not, as commonsense would commend, with eliminating of competition distortions, but with equalizing economic conditions. The *reductio ad absurdum* of this approach shows that where all economic differences are removed, there is also no scope for trade.

Economic Affairs, as a magazine with numerous short feature articles, is directed not only at specialists but at the wider public. So though it has a large range of distinguished contributors, many from academic circles, it targets the layman as much as the academic, tries to avoid textbook jargon and aims to convey economic information and, we hope, enlightenment, in vigorous everyday language.

Keynesianism may not seem a very promising opening subject for an exercise in popularization: the excuse is that it is a crucial theme. Keynesianism emphasized macro-economics and the grandiose manipulation of consumption and investment, by either fiscal means or through direct public ownership of industry, to attain effortlessly the great goal of full employment. This doctrine has dominated western, and especially Anglo-American, economic policy for most of the post-war period. However, it was essential to abandon these prescriptions if governments were to get to grips with the inflation which has been endemic in the post-war world. The lesson of experience is that the fatal flaw in the Keynesian edifice was the assumption that the trade unions would be perpetually deceived by the 'money illusion'. Keynes believed that while the trade unions would fight to the death against a cut in money wages in hard times they would pay little heed to the fall in the real value of those wages due to inflation. If the unions were like that when the *General Theory* was published, they have more than learnt how to start building their wage demands on the basis of the recent rise in the retail price index. The Keynesian lack-of-effective-demand explanation for unemployment has now withered, so, as Professor Eli Schwartz points out in the chapter on Labour economics, we are brought back to the classical micro-economic approach that attributes dole queues to structural distortions and maladjustments in the economic system.

The question arises about what useful role the trade unions can play in labour relations. There are some who say that, though their role in establishing a market for labour is negative, because they are merely cartels which disrupt market forces, they are nevertheless valuable because they enable workers to participate in a democratic resolution of their problems. Not so, says G. R. Steele of Lancaster University who says 'government of a trade union cannot be democratic, for it lacks the institutions which are vital to a healthy democratic system. It has no organized opposition, no independent judiciary and no free press.'

It is in monetary matters that the biggest turnaround in economic thinking and policy has occurred. Unfortunately the medium-term financial policy to which this led in the first half of the Thatcher era was abandoned by Chancellor Lawson with results we are still living with today. It is to their credit that monetary theorists such as Tim Congdon, Gordon Pepper and Peter Warburton, writing in *Economic Affairs*, criticized the mistakes both of monetary incontinence and of shadowing the deutschemark while they were being made.

Errors in monetary policy were all the more disastrous at a time when it had become the chief means of making short-term adjustments to the economy after the Keynesian idea of steering the economy using changes in taxation went out of fashion. This shift has helped to make more stark the salutary reminder by Dr Barry Bracewell-Milnes that redistributive taxes are political, and are intended to penalize categories of people and activities which the ruling party does not like. They contribute little to revenue, do not help the poor – rather the reverse – and have harmful effects on enterprise and saving.

There is a sparkling contribution made by the veteran Colin Clark not long before he died in which he shows how, by turning the welfare state into a compulsory insurance scheme, income tax could be removed altogether. Such a bold stroke has not yet found favour with most politicians. Despite ample evidence of wastage of resources by state provision, education is still considered too sensitive to return to the private sector. The sustained campaigns by Arthur and Marjorie Seldon on behalf of the voucher scheme to create a schooling market, have still not found favour. But *Economic Affairs* authors like John Marks have pioneered the proposals for independent school trusts which the Government has now adopted.

It must be a matter for regret that Mrs Thatcher chose to throw her reforming zeal behind the ill-fated idea of a local government poll tax instead of reforming some aspect of welfare. Though there has been some freeing of the housing market, rent control still has not been completely abolished, nor have the distortions created by mortgage relief to housebuyers been removed, nor have strict planning controls been greatly reduced. These latter severely hamper labour mobility. Those who are looking for a comprehensive assault on all these obstacles to the creation of a free market in housing will be delighted at the thorough and lucid proposals from Professor Patrick Minford and his colleagues at Liverpool University.

The same authors also put forward a detailed scheme for the reform of the National Health Service. Norman McKenna's ingenious proposals for paying for health provision by charging people according to income is also comprehensive – though whether it would appeal to the numerous health lobbies is another matter. Yet his well-documented plea for a realistic pricing system for health services is on the way to becoming part of the received wisdom, and is one of the operative principles in the government reforms now being implemented, involving the creation of an internal market for NHS services.

Environment issues have evoked almost religious enthusiasms in this age of declining conventional faith and have added a new dimension to many old problems. Unfortunately responses to such issues are all too often more emotive than rational. Robert Whelan's article 'Green for stop' is a useful corrective to anti-growth nostrums and authoritarian prescriptions of the Greens. On the topical problem of congested airspace, Sean Barrett introduces us to SCREAM, the Sufferers Campaign to Resolve the European Aviation Mess, offering a solution to the neurosis-inducing problems against which it protests, through competitive tendering for air traffic control, and the creation of markets in air capacity and competition for airspace. Gabriel Roth gives us fascinating information about how effectively private passenger transport, much of it of the illegal jitney-type, is already serving the public well in cities all over the world – though the prize is surely taken by a bus operator in Dacca who used profits to build a seven-mile-long private road. Linda Whetstone explains cogently why we should finally fell the Forestry Commission.

In the key section on competition my eye was caught by the original suggestion by Graham Mather that competition policy itself should be privatized. If shareholders really want to protect themselves against the short-term policies of the market raider in order to pursue long-term development and ultimately greater profit, then the Stock Exchange should be more flexible about allowing them to choose the structure they want. If that proves to be over-protective of the existing management, the share price will suffer. So the whole process would be self-regulating.

The privatization bonanza of the eighties, has not been entirely triumphal. It is comforting to note that Government has taken aboard the suggestions, made in 1984, by Roger Buckland and E. W. Davies that its marketing technique could be improved – particularly after the campaign to sell British Gas involving the character Sid. Peter Curwen draws attention to the mistake of giving priority to successful flotation at the expense of competition in the case of British Telecom – a controversy still unresolved. Still to come is the sale of British Rail; when it does, David Starkie's ideas about introducing competing train services, using private locomotives and rolling stock while leaving the permanent way in state hands, will come into its own.

Deindustrialization is a frequent cry of critics of the more *laissez-faire* approach to industry in the eighties and early nineties. Yet many of them overlook the fact that much of the plant and equipment in mines and steelworks for instance, taken out of commission was then obsolete. Some of the criticism seems to have been grounded on an old superstition, given credence by Adam Smith, that manufacturing is productive while services are not. The counter to this fallacy provided by Walter Eltis and Andrew Murfin is most valuable, all the more so because it is still viable.

It is appropriate that this collection should end with a series of comments on the European Community, policy on which looks set to be the great talking-point of this decade. The dangers of overregulation from the burgeoning bureaucracy in Brussels and the consequent denial of those market freedoms that form the central tenets of the Rome Treaty are well spelt out by Martin Holmes. Norman Stone reminds us that Habsburg Austria was an earlier and disastrous example of what a mess can be made of a multinational structure through centralization and heavyweight bureaucracy. He explodes the favourite analogy of federalists who see political unity issuing out of economic union in Europe just as Bismarck's

Germany resulted from the Zollverein (a point made by Keynes, incidentally). In fact, says Professor Stone, the customs union made political union less necessary and anyway did not prevent the southern and German Catholic states from declaring war on Prussia.

Many of these arguments are ongoing; *Economic Affairs* intends to keep them going with lively comments on every issue. As usual it is necessary to emphasize that all the views expressed are those of the *authors*. It is a pleasure to introduce such a galaxy of stimulating talent to the reading public to show the practical value of markets in contributing to the good life.

1 Keynesianism

Can Keynesianism be falsified?

Brian Snowdon and Peter Wynarczyk
Source: Economic Affairs, December 1985/January 1986, 6, 2, p. 34.

In *Economic Affairs* October/December 1984, we criticized Professor Charles Rowley's dismissal of Keynesian economics (*Economic Affairs* January/March 1983). We would like to make several points in answer to his rejoinder.

We argued that 'an instant theoretical kill is not possible in the social sciences', which Professor Rowley appears to accept in other disciplines than economics. But he believes that it is the encroachment of ideology in economic affairs which does much to explain the longevity of outmoded ideas. This diagnosis is too simple and the prescription naïve. Professor Rowley appears to advocate 'non-ideological scientific enquiry' as a means to progressive economic knowledge. As an example he points to an alleged growing consensus between monetarists and sophisticated Keynesianism, where differences are based only upon the 'empirical values associated with key relationships in the model'. This piece of Friedmanite psychology is invalid. The differences between the monetarists and some of the sophisticated Keynesians mentioned by Professor Rowley (particularly Keynes and Davidson) are more than empirical. There are deep-seated theoretical differences which reflect the fundamentally different underlying visions of the theorists themselves. These visions by their very nature are irrefutable. Professor Rowley may wish that things were otherwise, but it is invalid to argue as if they are so.

Professor Rowley informs us that his own views on method are Popperian and that 'theory should be exposed ruthlessly to falsification – and should be rewritten when it fails to conform with related evidence'. This argument, which is rather ambiguous, appears to contend that economic theory should be open to falsification without also informing us whether it can be made so. Recent philosophers of science, such as Imre Lakatos, have cast grave doubts upon whether the natural sciences, let alone the softer and more complex discipline of economics, can use the idealistic methodology of falsification. Lakatos demonstrates that Popper's meta-theoretic view of the development of science has itself been falsified and that the history of science is not the history of achievement through falsification.

When Professor Rowley states that if a theory fails to conform with related evidence it should be rewritten, does he mean we should amend the theory to take account of discrepancies or that we should surrender the theory? Economic theory, in attempting to explain and interpret economic events, tend to throw up several competing explanations each of which is, or can be made, consistent with the evidence. Professor Rowley's brand of falsificationist methodology is idealistic and unrealistic – which major tradition of research in economics has been falsified?

We fully accept the naïvety of hydraulic Keynesianism. But this acceptance does not mean that Keynesian macro-economic theories are incapable of explaining the behaviour of macro-economic variables, such as inflation or unemployment, in recent years. Professor Richard Lipsey has provided a persuasive neo-Keynesian account of the emergence of stagflation in the 1970s[1] and Professor John Cornwall of Balhousie University, Nova Scotia, has used the post-Keynesian framework to explain the same events.[2] So appealing to the evidence is not necessarily always going to reveal which is the correct view of how the economy works.

We did not deny that monetarist theory and the New Classical models have provided one explanation in recent years. But it equally cannot account for many important and well-known features of the business cycle. Professor Rowley chose to ignore completely these inconvenient, embarrassing and anomalous aspects which contradict monetarist theory and the new classical models in his reply.

Fundamentalist Keynesians from the very beginning questioned the alleged functional relationships of hydraulic Keynesianism and other formalistic economic models. Keynesian is a rather vacuous word. It has no content unless it is prefixed with an explanatory label. Professor Rowley admits that his concern was essentially with hydraulic Keynesianism. This confession rather dilutes his original dismissal of Keynesian economics (in what appeared to be its entirety). Professor Rowley may dismiss some of the Keynesian some (or all) of the time but he should not conclude from this that he may dismiss all of the Keynesians all of the time. As Phyllis Deane has recently argued:[3]

> The lesson that we should draw from the history of economic thought is that economists should resist the pressure to embrace a one-sided or restrictive consensus, there is no one kind of economic truth which holds the key to fruitful analysis of all economic problems, no pure economic theory that is immune from changes in social values or current policy problems ... the right answers are unlikely to come from any pure economic dogma.

Keynes' legacy of half-truths

Harold Lydall
Source: Economic Affairs, February/March 1986, 6, 3, p. 4.

As we approach the fiftieth anniversary of the publication of *The General Theory* it may be useful to make an appraisal of its effects on theory, policy, and the behaviour of the British economy. British economists and policy-makers became more complete adherents of Keynesianism than those of any other country, except perhaps Australia. But Keynesianism has been in retreat for much of the past decade, with the revival of monetarism and of classical doctrines generally, and as governments have found themselves unable to maintain full employment by Keynesian methods. It is therefore necessary to consider whether there were always some basic errors in the theory as it was expounded by Keynes himself.

The message of *The General Theory*

Keynes created 'macro-economics' which many economists now identify directly with Keynesianism. But macro-economics as such has no 'message', while Keynesian theory does have a clear message. And that message has been passed on, over the past fifty years, to millions of students of economics. It has become part of the background thinking of most educated people in the English-speaking world. In formal terms, the message is conveyed by one or other of two diagrams: the Keynesian cross, relating saving and investment to each other, or the 'IS-LM diagram', suggested by Professor John Hicks, which allows for some of the effects of changes in the money supply. Both diagrams lead to the same conclusion: that, if unemployment occurs, it can be reduced by an increase in net spending by government, or by expanding the money supply, or by a combination of these policies – without undesirable consequences.

But, as we now know, there are two major undesirable consequences of a persistent policy of Keynesian demand-expansion: a balance-of-payments deficit, and growing inflation. Both of these objections are excluded by assumption in the two diagrams described above, which refer to a closed economy, and cannot have a balance-of-payments problem, and which are constructed on the assumption that prices are constant. Of course, most students are told at some point that these diagrams are only first approximations, and that other problems may arise. But everything then becomes more complicated. How much will the balance of payments deteriorate? How much will prices rise? Keynesian theory cannot answer such questions: they are a matter for the econometricians, who themselves have no firm answers. Because the elementary diagrams are so sharp and clear, while the real world effects of reflation are more uncertain, there is a natural tendency for Keynesians to think mainly about the diagrams and to hope for the best about balance-of-payments and inflation problems.

If we go back to *The General Theory* itself, we find two surprising features. The first is that in that book, unlike most of his others, Keynes simply left out the problem of the balance of payments: it was excluded by assumption, so the elementary diagrams are faithful descriptions of what Keynes was saying in that respect. But, on the other hand, Keynes did not assume that one could have a reflation of demand without an increase in prices. On the contrary, he quite explicitly assumed, in line with classical theory, that an increase in total money expenditure (in a closed economy) must lead, in the short run, to a rise in prices, even if money wages were unchanged. This conclusion implies that an increase in employment can be achieved only at the expense of a fall in the real wage.

Employment and the real wage

Thus Keynes did not dispute the classical doctrine that, in the short run, a rise in employment must be accompanied by a fall in the real wage; indeed, he emphasised the point. His differences with his predecessors were not about the aim but about the method of achieving this result. The classical approach was to say that, in a competitive labour market, unemployed workers would agree to work for a lower wage, so bringing down the general volume of wages until there was full employment. Keynes objected to this argument on two grounds. The first was that, in a modern economy, wages are specified in money, not real, terms. If (again, in a closed economy) all money wages fall, prices will fall in roughly the same proportion and real wages will be unchanged. The second objection was that trade unions would put up a fierce and successful resistance to any fall in money wages, because, when each group bargains separately, there is a strong aversion to any fall in relative wages. In a system of decentralized bargaining, if everyone is able to prevent a fall in their own relative position, there cannot be a general fall in money wages.

If it is impossible, or very difficult, to reduce money wages, and if such a reduction has no effects on real wages anyway, the sensible alternative as Keynes saw it was to reduce real wages and raise employment, by expanding total monetary expenditure. But would trade unions accept a fall in real wages achieved in this way? Keynes had no doubt about the answer. He maintained very explicitly that, so long as there was unemployment, trade unions would not respond to the rise in prices caused by an expansion of demand by insisting on a compensating increase in money wages. 'The workers', he wrote, 'though unconsciously, are more reasonable economists than the classical school'.[1] Up to the point of full employment, therefore, an increase in total money spending would lead partly to a rise in output, and hence employment, and partly to a rise in prices; but there would be no rise in money wages. There would be no risk of a self-perpetuating spiral of wages chasing prices, and prices following wages.

Keynes is not the only economist to have had bad luck with a crucial assumption of his theory. Ricardo assumed that technology was constant, and that the capitalist system must eventually grind to a halt. Marx predicted that real wages in Britain would fall steadily and the profit-share increase, so leading to inevitable revolution. Almost exactly at the time when he made that prediction, real wages in Britain were starting on their long upward trend. Keynes' assumption that so long as there is unemployment, trade unions will fail to respond to a rise in prices by demanding a compensating increase in money wages has suffered the same fate. History has proved it to be a fundamental mistake.

The real wage dilemma

The observation that continuous application of Keynesian remedies for unemployment seems to generate continuous, and accelerating, inflation has led to a revival of monetarism, a return to the old quantity theory of money, of which Keynes himself was, of course, an earlier adherent. In the simplest case, this theory says that, if we start from a steady position of output and employment in a closed economy, an increase in the money supply will sooner or later lead to an upward adjustment of prices in exactly the same proportion, with no change in output or employment. More sophisticated versions of the theory allow for the influence of interest rates and price expectations on the demand for money, and hence on the effects of an increase in its supply. But, broadly, the implications of modern monetarist theory are the same as those of the older theory: changes in the money supply which exceed the spontaneous rate of growth of real output have no long-term beneficial effects on employment. They merely lead to inflation.

There is one major difficulty with this theory. How do we know, in practice, what is the equilibrium volume (or what Milton Friedman called the natural volume) of unemployment? We know that the volume of unemployment can change. Twenty years ago it was less than 2 per cent; now it is more than 13 per cent. Which of these, if either, is natural for the UK? Or does the natural volume change over time? If so, what causes it to change? Monetarists tend to assume that whatever is, is natural. If an economy has 2 per cent unemployment with stable prices, and the money supply is then expanded faster than the trend rate of growth of output, prices will rise. And the same applies to an economy which starts from 13 per cent unemployment.

Can this really be true? It is an ominous fact that, even with 13 per cent unemployment (which some people believe to be an underestimate), money wages in the UK are still rising at over 7 per cent per annum and prices at over 5 per cent per annum. How can we account for this?

It seems to me that one element, perhaps the most important element, in explaining the behaviour of wages, prices and unemployment in the British economy of today is the determination of trade unions, irrespective of the volume of unemployment, to resist a fall in the real wages of their members. It is taken for granted today that in its annual wage negotiations a trade union will include as a basic component of its wage demand an increase sufficient to compensate for the previous rise in prices. There are usually other components also, derived from comparisons with other groups of workers or consideration of the amount of profits in the industry, and so forth. But compensation for the previous rise in prices is the rock-bottom minimum; there is a sense of outrage if this demand is not met.

Suppose that it is now the case that most employers are forced by the threat of industrial action to grant an increase in wages at least equal to the preceding rise in prices. Then it is possible to see why the natural rate of unemployment could have been only 2 per cent at one time and 13 per cent today. Consider a situation in which output, prices and productivity are all constant, and where there is a substantial amount of unemployment. If total money expenditure is now increased, either spontaneously or as a result of government policy, the initial effect will be to increase output and employment to some extent and also to raise prices. If money wages were unchanged, real wages would fall. But, if trade unions have the power to insist on compensatory wage increases, inflation accelerates. This acceleration does not prevent the fall in real wages, because prices follow wages with a fairly short time-lag. The main effect of the expansion of money demand is therefore inflation. If employment has increased permanently, it can only be at the expense of a fall in the real wage. And all these consequences follow, irrespective of the initial volume of unemployment. There may be no amount of unemployment which will prevent demand expansion flowing into inflation, so long as trade unions have the power to insist on wage rises to compensate for previous increases in prices. In that case, every actual volume of unemployment is natural in the sense in which Milton Friedman uses the term.

Must prices rise?

Many modern Keynesians would say that the above description of Keynesian theory is inaccurate. They do not try to defend Keynes' assumption that trade unions are willing to accept a fall in real wages when demand is expanding. Rather, they maintain, Keynes made a mistake in accepting the classical doctrine that when money wages are constant, an expansion of demand leads to a rise in prices. This doctrine could be wrong for two reasons. The first is that, because of underlying improvements in technology, managerial efficiency, and the stock of capital equipment, the supply curve is steadily shifting to the right; that is, the competitive price for any given quantity of output is steadily falling. Although the static short-term tendency is for a rise in demand to lead to a rise in prices, if competitive prices are simultaneously shifting downwards, the net effect of demand expansion may be no increase in prices, or even a fall. The second reason is that most, if not all, of modern industry is not operating under conditions of perfect competition, with a rising supply curve, where an increase in demand normally has the effect of raising price, but under conditions of imperfect competition where, up to a point, increased demand is met by increased output without any price increase. The first of these objections is, in my opinion, of considerable importance, and I shall discuss its implications further below. At this point I shall consider only the second objection, on which many Keynesians depend very heavily for the defence of their position.

Now it is clearly true that in most modern industry and services goods are not taken to market and sold at auction to the highest bidder, as in the traditional markets for primary products. Rather, producers fix their prices in the light of their costs and normal mark-ups or, perhaps more realistically, in the light of the costs of their actual or potential competitors. In any case, prices are fixed for a certain period of time and customers are supplied at those prices within a more or less wide range of output. If, then, demand expansion starts at a time when all firms have excess capacity, it may be possible to have a substantial increase in output, and hence employment, without any change in prices. In that case, there will be no fall in the real wage and therefore no wage inflation will be provoked.

The difficulty with this argument is that it requires the assumption that we are living in a closed economy in which all goods and services are sold at fixed prices, and that all suppliers have a good deal of excess capacity. But there are many goods and services, even in our economy, whose prices are quite sensitive to conditions of demand, such as primary products, personal services, land prices, and the building industry. When total demand increases, the rises in the prices of these products feed through either directly to consumer prices, or indirectly via the input costs of other industries. Also, an increase in domestic demand normally leads to a rise in imports, a fall in exports, and a consequent deterioration in the balance of payments. If exchange rates are flexible, this provokes a fall in the value of the pound and hence a rise in the prices of all imports, and even of many exportable goods and services. If, on the other hand, the exchange rate is held fixed, it will usually be necessary quite soon for the government to raise interest rates (which pushes up prices) and eventually bring the expansion of demand to a halt. The alternative policy, supported by some Keynesians, of imposing tariffs or import control would also increase domestic prices and depress the real wage. Further, even if most cost-plus enterprises start with some excess capacity, there are always some that are working close to full capacity. As demand expands, more and more firms are brought up to full capacity operation and they either fail to raise their prices or to meet their customers' requirements – so that there are shortages which lead to an increase in unofficial prices. For all these reasons, there is not really much hope of maintaining fixed prices when demand is expanding, unless there is a substantial simultaneous trend of increasing productivity.

Some Keynesians claim that the success of the Reagan Government in reducing unemployment without provoking a rapid rise in prices is a vindication of Keynesian theory. But there have been rather special reasons for these results. The Reagan Government expanded net government spending while the Federal Reserve Board has simultaneously kept a tight hold on the money supply. The result was a considerable increase in government demand, high interest rates, low private investment, an enormous inflow of foreign capital, a much over-valued dollar, low dollar prices for imports, and hence a favourable effect on consumer prices. The costs of the operation have been a huge accumulation of both internal government debt and foreign debt, and severe competitive pressure on domestic export- and import-competing industries. Whether this combination of policies has been in the best interests of the United States is doubtful. But there can be no doubt about the view that such a combination of policies could not be applied successfully for any length of time in other countries which do not have the same advantages as the United States.

There are exceptions to every law of economics, but it is about as certain as anything can be that an expansion of demand will lead to a rise in prices, unless the underlying upward trend in productivity is sufficient to prevent this. Those Keynesian economists who accept this conclusion have attempted to meet the problem by relying on incomes policy. An incomes policy would be a method of restraining the rise in wages (and possibly other incomes) in response to the increase in prices generated by the expansion of demand, so permitting the demand expansion to continue to reduce unemployment rather than flowing increasingly into inflation. It would, indeed, be a method of forcing trade unions to do what Keynes suggested that they would be willing to do anyway, to hold back on money-wage demands when prices were rising and so permit an expansion of employment. Unfortunately, all previous incomes policies have been badly designed and badly implemented. They have collapsed within a year or two, usually leaving behind a mass of distortions and resentments, so that wages and prices have soon caught up with the trends which they would have followed without the policy. The fault, in my opinion, lies partly in the *ad hoc* emergency nature of these policies, and partly in the fact that they have usually been dependent on voluntary trade union participation. The price for such participation in a so-called social contract has steadily risen, thus shifting power over wide areas of policy away from the elected government to a sectional interest, which is intolerable.

The role of productivity

Even with a tough and effective incomes system the strains which would be imposed on that system by a Keynesian expansion of demand in a country with a low rate of growth of productivity would soon threaten its collapse. This brings us to the most important gap in Keynesian theory. Keynes' theory was essentially short-run. He was concerned with the problem of making full use of existing resources of labour, capital, and technology. To do so he had to assume that workers would accept a fall in real wages. This assumption was plainly wrong, at least in an economy as highly unionised as Britain's. But there is an alternative way out, namely, a sufficiently steady growth of productivity to offset the short-run fall in real wages. Keynes' failure to grasp the importance of this aspect reveals something not only about his theory but also about his whole approach to economics. He was not interested in what we now call micro-economics, the detailed problems of enterprise, management, production, marketing, and so on.[2] Keynes was essentially a macro-economist: that is, an economist who separates himself from what Marshall called the ordinary business of life, who takes the growth of enterprise, technology, and productivity for granted, and concentrates on how to manipulate the levers of fiscal policy, money supply, exchange rates, and the like. But enterprise, technology, and productivity cannot be taken for granted: they can be profoundly affected by the ways in which governments pull the macro-economic levers and in consequence may require specific support from government.

The sharp division of economics since Keynes' *General Theory*, into macro- and micro-economics has been the cause of much confusion in the teaching of the subject. In macro-economics, which is often taught first, students are taught to think in terms of fixed prices: the economy is a simple system linking variables such as national income, consumption, saving, imports and exports. Students are taught that governments can change these variables rather easily, and so produce an ideal combination of employment and balance-of-payments equilibrium. Of course, especially under modern conditions, something has to be said eventually about inflation. But it is not usually related to the conditions of supply and demand for goods and services – the micro-economic side. The teaching of micro-economics itself has become heavily biased towards the consideration of market imperfections. Little or no emphasis is given to the brilliant insights of Adam Smith, and most of the time is spent on cases of market failure. It is scarcely an exaggeration to say that the majority of students have come away from such courses in economics with a belief, based on the micro-economics part, that the market mechanism is full of blemishes, while concluding from the macro-economics part, that governments are marvellous instruments for bringing about growth, equality, full employment and other blessings. It is not surprising, therefore, that so many of our trade-union leaders, politicians, journalists, bishops, and other members of the Establishment, seem sincerely to believe that the fault for unemployment rests entirely on the government. In Keynes' own words, 'Practical men ... are usually the slaves of some defunct economist'.[3]

But if the above arguments are correct the most essential condition for achieving and maintaining high employment in an economy in which real wages are inflexible downwards is a sufficient rate of productivity growth. For the past hundred years productivity in the UK has grown more slowly than in many other countries, and British productivity in manufacturing is now much lower than in Germany, France, Italy and Japan, not to mention North America. This failure is entirely man-made, and it reflects above all the neglect of the nuts and bolts of our economy: enterprise, management, technology, and industrial relations. Despite our early advantage in industrialization, traditional aristocratic attitudes soon sapped its vitality. Industrialists sent their sons and grandsons to public schools to learn Latin and Greek. The London Establishment turned its back on industry and devoted its thoughts to the City and the empire. National education was much neglected and, in its higher reaches, was dominated by Oxford and Cambridge, with their prejudices against the study of anything useful to industry. Even to this day there are no undergraduate courses in accounting and business management in these universities, and scarcely any in the new universities of the 1960s. A professor at the London Business School once told me how, when he went to speak to the sixth form of a well-known public school, the headmaster warned him, 'In this school the word "profit" is a dirty word'.

This kind of attitude has been much reinforced by Keynesianism. Keynesianism is mainly about consumption, and about effortless adjustments in aggregate demand by clever civil servants and central bankers. It is not concerned with the toil and sweat, the enterprise and imagination, the intense devotion to problem-solving and the maintenance of quality, which are the keys to raising production and the standard of life. All of these are taken for granted; and if they are dying out, if the marginal efficiency of capital is declining, so be it – we shall simply get the government to spend more money and get us back to full employment. But the world in which we live is not a world in which we can comfortably settle back into genteel poverty. The oil price rises, while fortunately not directly reducing our own terms of trade, precipitated a world recession which has raised world unemployment and reduced the rate of growth of international trade. Increasing competition in manufactures from continental Europe, Japan and many other countries, especially those in east Asia, have depressed the prices and our sales of these products, and so reduced our effective national productivity. A country which assumed that it could quietly sit back, pull out of the world economy, and concentrate on manipulating government finance would soon bring its people to the edge of disaster. Yet that is still the main message of Keynesianism.

Implications for policy

Any serious attempt to reduce unemployment requires a fundamental shift in our attitudes towards production. At present, many positive steps are being made in this direction; but not enough. The British economy is still being dragged down by long-accumulated attitudes and practices which prevent change, flexibility, cooperation, and a breakthrough into modern ways of working. We need not waste time in finding the culprits for this state of affairs. What matters is to get those who have the power to make changes to effect them. Potential agencies of change are government (inevitably), management, trade unions, and the educational system. Governments cannot go much faster than their electorate, but they can lead. If they understand clearly what is at stake, they can gradually change public understanding and attitudes. Ideally, they should move towards making productivity the main national objective, since productivity is the key to solving all our problems.

A major responsibility rests on management, which alone can take the initiative within enterprises. Management, especially industrial management, needs to receive higher national recognition and respect. It is a disgrace that the media and the educators spend most of their time focusing on failures of management, and give little or no encouragement to good management. But management also has to put its own house in order: it must be both more technically competent, and qualified, and more sensitive to personnel relations. Britain could learn a lot from the Japanese in these respects, as Japan learnt from the British in earlier days.

There are important signs of progress in the attitudes of some trade unions, especially the electricians and the engineers. These and other unions have come to recognize that the crucial determinant of their members' wages and conditions of work is the success of the enterprise in which they work, i.e., their own productivity. The more that the British economy can move in the direction of increased productivity, even eventually in the public sector, the stronger the hope of reducing unemployment.

A dominating influence on attitudes is exercised by the education system. In Britain it has been allowed to drift into a condition in which, instead of supporting national interests, it is largely hostile to them. By a combination of permissiveness, the aristocratic attitude that education should not serve any useful purpose, and the infiltration of socially destructive ideas which denigrate national traditions, the work ethic, morality and loyalty, British schools are helping to produce large numbers of unqualified and unstable young people. Until schools serve their customers better, the future, under any political or economic system, is bleak.

Not all of these faults, of course, can be attributed to the influence of Keynesianism. But Keynesianism was a product of the British disease: it was an attempt to avoid the hard job of reversing the decline in British enterprise, management and productivity by taking the easy way out – more government spending. In so far as they continue to propagate these ideas, British universities, polytechnics and secondary schools will be helping to ensure the continuation of national decline.

Futures finally refute Keynes

Robert C.B. Miller
Source: Economic Affairs, July/September 1985, 5, 4, p. 11.

The macro-economic consequences of large-scale trading in financial futures have received little attention, but the sheer volume of economic activity in this new market suggests that they deserve serious study. Financial futures trading is a development of the last decade, and it has transformed the money markets both in America and Europe. Financial futures are currently traded in Singapore, Canada and Australia, and there are plans to begin in France and Japan.

Financial futures trading is the exchange of currencies, US Treasury Bonds, British government stocks, and even stock-exchange indices such as the Financial Times 100 and the Standard and Poors 500, as if they were ordinary commodity futures, like coffee or sugar. A trader can buy or sell any of them for future settlement at prices fixed in advance. Since settlement has to be made in full only on completion of the contract, it is particularly easy to go short – in effect, selling commodities, shares, currencies or bonds you do not own in anticipation of a fall in prices. Trading has grown rapidly in the last ten years and transactions in Treasury Bonds on the Chicago Board of Trade are now the most numerous of any futures contract in America. From little more than half a million contracts traded in 1976, financial futures trading reached the staggering total of 73 million contracts in 1984, more than half of all futures contracts traded in America. In 1982 trading in financial futures began in London on the London International Financial Futures Exchange (LIFFE) and last year it traded over 2.5 million contracts – about 40 per cent of all London futures trading. Other orthodox physical commodity futures such as coffee, sugar, cocoa and copper are traded on the London Commodity Exchange (LCE) and the London Metal Exchange (LME).

Futures trading in general and financial futures in particular have had their critics, including Lord Kaldor.[1] One of the chief concerns of the critics is that futures trading might divert funds and the attention of investors from the cash and venture capital markets.[2] It is argued that futures trading diverts funds from the cash markets to 'unproductive' activity in the futures markets; the venture capital market is starved, with the result that economic growth is stunted.

But futures trading is a voluntary exchange; losers are equally matched by winners. There will be no change in the supply of loanable funds since, as financial futures trading involves only the shuffling of margin monies amongst participants, capital markets are not deprived of funds. Margin is the term given to deposits made by traders to ensure the completion of the contract. Profits and losses are added or subtracted to this initial margin whenever the trader makes a profit or a loss. A study by a joint group from the US Treasury and the Federal Reserve Board on financial futures markets summed up the argument as follows:[3]

> Cash does not necessarily change hands with futures when the contracts are opened. Existing assets in the investor's portfolio (e.g., US Treasury Bills) may be pledged as margin, or if cash is deposited, the broker and/or the exchange obtains the use of the funds for the duration of the contract. In neither case is there a reduction in the aggregate supply of loanable funds to underwrite real investment activity.

Trading in financial futures evidently does not affect the demand for money. In other words, trading in financial futures will not affect the valuation of cash relative to all other goods and assets, and need have no effect upon the velocity of circulation of money. It follows that it is possible for traders with pessimistic views about interest rates to sell Treasury Bond or gilt futures contracts without in any way increasing liquidity preference, the total demand for cash in terms of all other goods, and 'deflating the economy'. This process is in contrast to ordinary sales of bonds, which would increase the demand for money and deflate the economy as traders exchanged their bonds for cash.

Before the Second World War, Professor Ludwig Lachmann, then working at the London School of Economics, detected what he thought was a serious flaw in the Keynesian system which was only of theoretical interest until the development of large-scale trading in financial futures.[4] Lachmann argued that Keynes' claim that liquidity preference could be altered by changes in expectations about the bond market meant that, with a forward market[5] for bonds, pessimism about the price of bonds did not necessarily lead to an increase in the liquidity preference. Traders could now profit from a fall in bond prices without building up their holdings of cash. As Lachmann put it:[6] 'On an organized forward-market individuals could express their expectations by forward-transactions which do not require any cash'.

Without a forward market in bonds, an increase in bearishness would mean that traders would liquidate their holdings of bonds and replace them with cash. If this view of the future course of interest rates became general, the relative value of bonds and cash would change as the market came to value liquidity more highly: deflation would result.

Lachmann pointed out that this was not true with a forward bond market, for instead of bearishness – fear of higher interest rates setting off an increase in liquidity preference – it might only inspire holders of bonds to protect themselves by selling them on the forward market. It follows that bullishness (optimism that interest rates will fall) and bearishness are not necessarily connected with liquidity preference, which is a quite different phenomenon. Lachmann, an economist of the Austrian school, ascribed changes in interest rates to changes in time preference – the preference for current over future goods. He argued, against Keynes, that as no forward

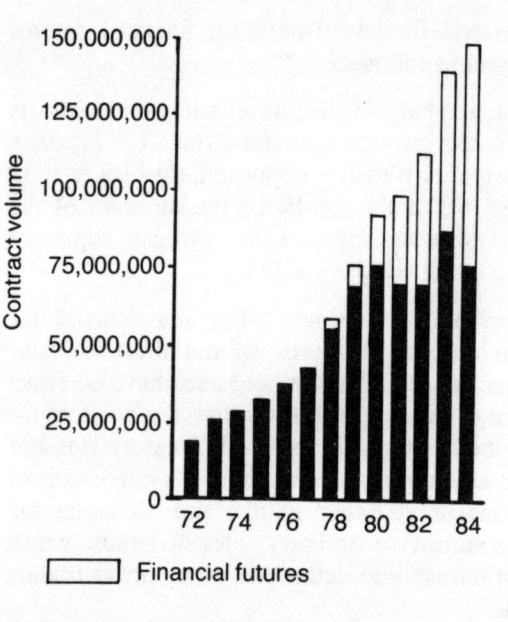

Figure 1.1 American futures, 1972–84

bond market had developed, it implied that the Keynesian mechanism which linked bearishness, liquidity preference and deflation was very weak.

At the time that Lachmann wrote there was no forward market in British government securities or gilts, the bond market foremost in Keynes' mind, and the ideas of such a market was a fiction, intended to illustrate a distinction which Lachmann thought Keynes had ignored. But in the mid-1970s fiction turned into fact. The Chicago Board of Trade developed a futures contract in twenty-year US Treasury Bonds, and currently its volume represents a turn over in excess of $12 billion a day, compared to a cash market trade of half that amount. In Britain, the volume in the LIFFE Long Gilt contract, a British equivalent of the US Treasury Bond futures contract, is equivalent, even after two years' trading, to the volume of trading in gilts on the Stock Exchange.

The development of financial futures on the current scale prompts some interesting questions about Keynesian economics which are not wholly satisfying to Keynesians or their opponents. The American economist Murray Rothbard, writing in 1961[7] before the growth of futures trading began, claimed that because forward or futures trading in bonds had developed, it: 'indicates that traders are not nearly as worried about rising interest rates as Keynes believes. If they were and this fear loomed as an important phenomena, then surely a futures market would have developed in securities'.

The rapid development in the financial futures in the 1970s and 1980s suggests that traders were 'worried about rising rates as Keynes believes'.

One conclusion that could be drawn is that the Keynesian doctrine of liquidity preference and its consequence, that the economy was subject to periodic deflation, were both true to a degree before the development of trading in financial futures. A more likely explanation is that financial futures developed largely as a result of exceptionally volatile interest rates in the 1970s which were themselves the consequence of accelerating inflation inspired by Keynesian thinking.

Whatever the correct explanation of their rapid growth, one consequence of financial futures is clear if Lachmann's argument is correct. The danger of highly destabilizing surges in liquidity preference and consequent bouts of depression is small (at least for the reasons that Keynes suggested). Large-scale futures and forward trading may thus reduce the threat of recurrent recession.

A further consequence of Lachmann's argument is that the market economy appears to have its own defence mechanisms against the sort of instability that Keynes described. If destablizing fluctuations in interest rates and inflation appear, the market is capable of developing its own means of making the inconvenience manageable by making it possible to hedge.[8] It follows that the benign government of Keynesian fantasy is unnecessary even given his assumptions about the character of the volatile bond market. Futures markets provide the wherewithal for traders to hedge against unanticipated price changes by buying or selling futures contracts to profit from the change in prices which would otherwise lose them money. There is also considerable econometric evidence to suggest that the existence of futures markets tends to reduce price fluctuations.[9]

The ability of markets to develop stabilizing mechanisms can be illustrated further by the Cocoa & Sugar Exchange of New York which plans to introduce futures trading on four economic indices. These will include the Consumer Price Index, new car sales, housing starts and an index of corporate earnings allowing traders to insure, or hedge, against unanticipated changes in these indices. For example, a company whose business was closely connected to the sale of cars wished to protect itself against a decline in car sales which it expected, could sell new car sale index futures. If new car sales fell as expected, it would be able to buy back its futures contracts at a profit and protect its earnings. According to the American economist Richard Sandor,[10] who can claim to have invented trading in interest rates when he was employed by the Chicago Board of Trade, a prime requirement for successful trading is volatility in the price of the commodity concerned. It follows that where price volatility appears, it is possible – perhaps even inevitable – that a futures market will develop which will remove much of the resulting inconvenience.

The rapid expansion of futures trading in general and financial futures trading in particular brings substantial advantages. The existence of Treasury bond and gilt-edged futures should make the American and British economies less susceptible to the Keynesian cycle of boom and bust as bearishness about interest rates does not necessarily imply an increase in liquidity preference (the total demand for cash in terms of all other goods) and deflation. In a rather similar fashion the introduction of exotic futures contracts on the New York Coffee Sugar & Cocoa Exchange based on inflation and earnings indices should further stabilize the economy if they have the same success as financial futures.

Large-scale trading in commodity and financial futures has put the final nail into the coffin of Keynesian economics. The growth of futures trading shows that the market economy can respond to the destabilizing actions of government.

Have the Keynesians been vanquished?

Brian Snowdon and Peter Wynarczyk
Source: *Economic Affairs*, October/December 1984, 5, 1, p. 53.

Professor Charles Rowley has claimed that the 'Keynesian macro game is clearly over' and he asks: 'should the vanquished [Keynesians] leave the field'?[1] Apparently the continual series of intellectual battles fought between Keynesians and monetarists in the post-war period has at last resulted in a resounding defeat for the Keynesians. This has been the inevitable outcome of two important factors, one empirical the other theoretical. First, the persistent inflation of the post-war period was a phenomenon Keynesian theory was least designed to deal with. In particular, the progression from inflation to stagflation was inconsistent with a central tenet of orthodox Keynesian consensus, namely the stable Phillips curve, which indicates that higher levels of unemployment should be accompanied by lower rates of inflation. The second development was the theoretical work inspired by Professors Milton Friedman and Robert Lucas of Chicago University which has resulted in the birth of the so-called new classical macro-economics. These developments, with their emphasis on the power of market forces and the importance of inflationary expectations, indicate that unemployment cannot be reduced by systematic reflations of aggregate demand.

In Professor Rowley's view the Keynesian bandwagon has finally ground to a halt. Game, set and match to the neo-classical monetarists? But we claim the game is far from over. We would challenge broadly five contentious issues raised by Professor Rowley.

First, Professor Rowley's suggestion that the Keynesians should leave the field of battle cannot be taken seriously. Knut Wicksell recognized eighty years ago that in economics 'the state of war seems to persist and remain permanent'. Certainly the contemporary state of monetary theory appears like a battlefield with regiments of economists grouped under different banners. It would seem that economic theories, like old soldiers, never die. The current renaissance of classical macro-economics is itself a demonstration of this very proposition, as Professor Rowley readily admits when he states that 'the wheel has turned full circle with the classical dichotomy between the real and monetary economy once again in the ascendant'. Economics has recently witnessed a monetarist counter-revolution, the resurrection of Say's Law and the development of supply-side macro-economics, as well as the renewed interest in the Austrian tradition. Given these recent trends, why should we assume that Keynesianism is a dead or endangered species? An instant theoretical kill is not possible in the social sciences, and recent developments in macro-economics should be enough to convince any student of the history of economic thought that the continual resurrection of economic theories is the normal state of affairs.

It may be useful at this stage to borrow ideas which were first raised within the philosophy of science as a source of useful analogy. Professor Rowley refers to the 'Keynesian paradigm' (framework of analysis) but the application of the work of the philosopher Imre Lakatos, rather than that of the historian Thomas Kuhn, to the history of economic thought would appear to be more appealing in explaining why ideas within economics can make a comeback. Kuhn does not allow a defeated paradigm to return – it is banished and becomes extinct.[2] Thus in claiming the complete demise of the Keynesian paradigm, Professor Rowley is guilty of the same error as many self-assured Keynesians made in the 1950s and 1960s when they assumed that a correct solution had been found to macro-economic problems, rendering the classical approach redundant. Lakatos[3] on the other hand, has argued that theories, or a series of theories (known as a research programme) can make a return; and there is no better example of this than the way in which Professor Friedman and his associates turned a degenerating research programme (the classical version of the quantity theory of money) into a progressive one.

Professor James Tobin of Yale University, one of the world's leading neo-Keynesians, now believes that events have so badly discredited monetarism that 'the stage has been set for a recovery in the popularity of Keynesian diagnoses and remedies'.[4] Does this mean that the new classicists leave the field? Of course not. Macro-economics can only advance by investigating and developing new ideas. We should take heed of J. S. Mill, who noted that 'Both teachers and learners go to sleep at their post as soon as there is no enemy in the field.[5] The new classical school has forced Keynesians to refine their analysis; it will not cause them to leave the field.

Our second criticism relates to Professor Rowley's use of the term Keynesian. Apart from a cursory reference to some modern-day Cambridge heretics, all Keynesians are categorized as if they were a homogenous group of economists. This is far from true.

We would agree with Professor Rowley that events, as well as developments in economic theory, dealt a severe blow to the simplistic hydraulic variety of orthodox Keynesianism which characterized the textbooks until recently. These mechanistic models tended to play down the importance of monetary factors; and placed emphasis instead on the role of fiscal (tax) policy in stimulating aggregate demand in order to increase output and reduce unemployment. Inflation could be predicted from a stable Phillips curve relationship, which was grafted onto this system after 1958. But this variety of Keynesianism should be carefully differentiated from the sophisticated theorizing of neo-Keynesians such as Professors James Tobin and Frank Hahn, and post-Keynesians such as the late Professor Joan Robinson, a close associate of Keynes, who always regarded textbook Keynesianism as a bastardization and misinterpretation of Keynes' own model.

Unlike post-Keynesians, neo-Keynesians do not reject most of the main features of the neo-classical analysis of markets. Neo-Keynesians, for example, accept the neo-classical choice-theoretical framework which views consumers and producers as rational maximizing economic agents making the best use of their available resources. But both groups of Keynesians regard the sluggishness in the response of prices and wages to market forces and the failure of markets to clear as features of market economies which require theoretical explanation. Gradual wage and price adjustment can occur for many reasons, including the prevalence of long-term wage contracts, adjustment costs, decentralized decision-making and the requirement for firms to maintain customer and work-force goodwill. Frequent wage-adjustments would undoubtedly damage employee morale, productivity, and hence long-term profitability. No businessman will require reminding of this latter fact – and yet neo-classical analysis remains immune from such considerations. These characteristics of the labour market also persuaded Keynesians that the macro-economic policies of the present government would result in a substantial loss of output and employment before the inflation rate could be expected to respond. We would interpret the events of the past four years as confirmation of that prediction.

It is incorrect to suggest, as Professor Rowley does, that 'The real balance effect of Pigou, which restored the classical position, was ignored by the advocates of the new religion'. The 'real-balance effect' refers to the direct stimulus to consumer spending (and therefore output and employment) brought about by the effect of falling prices on the real value of wealth holdings. Professor Thomas Wilson has pointed out that, far from neglecting the real balance effect, Keynes had originally invented the concept in the mid-1920s. What is certain is that by 1936 Keynes had decided that wage and price flexibility would not work (in theory or practice) in getting the economy back to full employment; on the contrary, such flexibility could make things much worse. Indeed, it was the stickiness of certain prices (especially money wages) that enabled a decentralized and monetized market economy to function. Both the neo- and post-Keynesian research programmes have continued this Keynes-inspired tradition.

Professor Rowley writes that 'Even during the phase of Phillips curve euphoria, nagging doubts remained among the more perspicacious members of the economics profession, who questioned the absence of any acceptable theory of the labour market that might justify its existence most especially as a long-term relationship'. But it was not only monetarists who remained wary of the stable Phillips curve. Professor Nicholas Kaldor in 1959 was one of the first economists to cast doubt upon the stability of such a relationship.[7] Even earlier, in 1943, Joan Robinson wrote: '... If free collective bargaining, as we have known it hitherto, is continued in conditions of full employment, there would be a constant upward pressure upon money wage rates'.[8]

The stable Phillips curve was as unwelcome to the more perspicacious Keynesians as it was later to become to monetarists.

Our final criticism of Professor Rowley's article relates to the absence of supporting evidence of what is perhaps the most interesting and controversial aspect of the new-classical models. This is the so-called Lucas-Sargent-Wallace (LSW) proposition on the ineffectiveness of policy, which states that Keynesian policies involving the systematic variation of aggregate demand by governments in order to stabilize the economy can have no real effects on output and employment in the short-run or the long-run. Professor Robert Gordon, in a recent survey could find no evidence to support the LSW proposition in the USA for the period 1890–1980![9] The reason for this, according to Gordon, is that prices adjust gradually in the short-run so that production will initially respond to an increase in aggregate demand even if fully anticipated.

The new classical models are also at odds with many well known and conventionally accepted facts associated with the business cycle. For example, in monetarist models we would expect individual spans of unemployment to be of short duration, and the quit rate in the labour market ought to fall in a boom and rise in a recession; real wages should move counter-cyclically. But the evidence does not support any of these propositions. We would also chance our arm and suggest that there are unemployed workers in the UK at present who would be prepared to work at the prevailing wage rate – and yet monetarist theory denies such a possibility. It is with some justification that Professor Frank Hahn has recently noted that: 'to witness the unfolding of policies that it is claimed have the support of the best economic theory, when one knows this to be false, is quite a trial'.[10]

We believe that both aggregate demand and supply factors are important in explaining macro-economic phenomena, such as the amount of unemployment, volume of output and the rate of inflation. Hydraulic Keynesianism and the new classical models are equally naïve in that they both place too much emphasis on one side of the macro-economic equation. A strategy which gives due weight to demand and supply management is required.

Most Keynesians would now accept what Professor Richard Lipsey has called 'the asymmetry'.[11] According to Lipsey, increases in aggregate demand engineered when the economy is close to full employment will lead to an acceleration of inflation. However, reductions in aggregate demand will only have a small retarding effect on inflation in the short-run. For this reason the majority of Keynesians argue the necessity of additional non-demand management instruments, such as incomes policies. Such policies aim to reduce the side-effects on output and employment which a policy of monetary deflation alone will inevitably produce because of the slow adjustment of prices.

If a workable incomes policy proves impossible to design and implement, excessive unemployment and lost output will be the inevitable price paid for controlling inflation.[12] The Keynesian interpretation of the functioning of the UK economy tells a relatively gloomy story about the prospects for inflation control. The new classical models so admired by Professor Rowley assume a degree of price and wage flexibility not present in the UK or any other economy. Only if such flexibility were present and all other monetarist assumptions held would the government's deflationist strategy have been likely to achieve its objectives without the costs of a prolonged and severe recession.

Professor Friedman was wrong when he argued in 1970 that 'the basic differences amongst economists are empirical not theoretical'.[13] The challenge presented by new classical models has rekindled the theoretical debate concerning the inherent stability of market-dominated economies, and the Keynesian research programmes will continue to add to our knowledge and understanding of how such economies function. It would be a sad day indeed if all economists agreed. In such circumstances they might all be wrong!

Was Keynes a monetarist?

Bernard Foley

Source: *Economic Affairs*, April/June 1985, 5, 3, p. 50.

'Worse than any errors or influence bequeathed by Keynes was the licence given to people to defend their own prejudices under the banner of what Keynes would really be for.'[1]

Keynesian orthodoxy dominated the policy-making of the post-war consensus, and until the 1970s monetarists were regarded as a rather endearing group of cranks. Developments within the last decade show the power of the monetarist argument, as the centre of the gravity of both theoretical debate and policy advice has moved decisively away from Keynesianism. Not content with this impressive victory, Rosalind Levačić now wishes to twist the knife by assuring us that Keynes himself was a monetarist.[2]

Her case is not based on the early work of Keynes which was indeed written within the framework of the quantity theory of money. Instead she develops the argument in relation to the fount of what used to be called the Keynesian revolution – *The General Theory of Employment, Interest and Money*.[3]

The argument essentially resolves itself into how Keynes dealt with the issue of real wages. On several occasions she specifically argues that the restoration of full employment requires a fall in real wages, and this in her view is the crucial factor which marks Keynes from his latter-day followers, such as the Cambridge Economic Policy Group.

'The ironic truth', says Rosalind Levačić, 'is that Keynes' economic analysis has far more in common with monetarism than it does with the modern Keynesianism of his self-proclaimed disciples particularly its more radical versions.'

Keynes readily accepted the classical view:

> 'that with *a given organization, equipment and technique*, real wages and the volume of output are uniquely correlated, so that in general, an increase in employment can only occur to the accompaniment of a decline in the rate of real wages' [my emphasis].[4]

This clear but qualified statement becomes in Levačić's terms thoroughly unequivocal: 'Keynes agreed with the orthodox classical view of his day that real wages had to come down in order to reduce unemployment.'

This hardens Keynes' position and in the translation his qualification appears to have been omitted. Keynes' acceptance of the classical view hinges upon assumptions about the operation of the law of diminishing returns:

> industry is normally subject to decreasing returns in the short period during which equipment, etc., is assumed to be constant, so that the marginal product in the wage good industries (which governs real wages) necessarily diminishes as employment is increased.[5]

In sum, Keynes' view is anchored in the characteristic feature of the classical world – diminishing returns at the margin of production. This is, however, an empirical issue which may or may not hold true in practice: in any given period or over particular ranges of output we find that the law may be contradicted. There is considerable literature surrounding another proposition called the Verdoorn law (named after P.J. Verdoorn) which argues, with substantial evidence, that growth in output varies directly with growth in productivity particularly in manufacturing. Thus it does not necessarily follow that declining marginal productivity accompanies growth in output or employment.

Thus contemporary Keynesians are squarely within the tradition of

Keynes when they question the universal assumption of the classical school. And Keynes, or anyone else, would accept that real wages need not fall if the law of diminishing returns does not apply.

To argue that Keynes was a monetarist simply on the basis of his views about the real wage is simultaneously tenuous and superficial. It might be helpful therefore to attempt a definition of monetarist. This is no easy task because the product, much like Keynesianism, is so highly variegated that leading authorities do not entirely agree about its key features.

It would appear that the term monetarism was first used by Professor Karl Brunner in 1968[6] and was taken to mean three major propositions:

1. Monetary impulses are the major factors accounting for variations in output, employment and prices.
2. Movements in the stock of money are the most reliable measure of the thrust of monetary impulses.
3. The behaviour of the monetary authorities dominates movements in the stock of money over the business cycle.

There is no mention of the behaviour of real wages here and it would be difficult to find much agreement with the three propositions in *The General Theory*. If we take number one as a single example, it is abundantly clear that Keynes did not view monetary impulses working in this fashion:

> There is ... no ground for the belief that a flexible wage policy is capable of maintaining a state of continuous full employment any more than for the belief that open-market monetary policy is capable unaided of achieving this result.[7]

Moreover, if monetary policy worked at all, it worked via the capital market by influencing the structure of interest rates, which is hardly the monetarist view.

It might, of course, be possible to reclassify Keynes in the light of the latest variants of the monetarist thesis. In particular the new classical macro-economics, with its emphasis on the natural rate of unemployment and the formation of inflationary expectations, may contain similarities with Keynes' view of the required behaviour of real wages.

In this variant of monetarism, rational expectations eliminate the possibility of a money illusion so that, at the limit, monetary policy is unable to effect even transitory changes in real magnitudes such as output or employment. This obviously contradicts Brunner's monetarism, because in this latest version employment cannot be improved by monetary policy, only by falling real wages. This is the key conclusion which apparently justifies calling Keynes a monetarist!

There are several comments I would make at this junction.

1. Identifying a single, even if important, point of agreement between

economists is hardly ground for asserting identity in political economy. With this procedure Marx could just as easily be called a monetarist because he believed inflation was essentially a problem in the supply of credit money.

2   Keynes might have agreed that a fall in real wages is required to reduce unemployment below the natural rate. But if unemployment is already considerably in excess of the natural rate, are falling real wages required? The answer can only be a qualified 'perhaps' – to the extent that we can show that real wages are excessive, some reduction may be necessary to generate more jobs. But if a large number are still unable to find employment despite a willingness to take a lower wage than the going rate, we have a simple case of deficient demand.

3   Rosalind Levačić's position is very difficult to square with Friedman's documented views[8] that there is:

> a great deal of empirical work on the behaviour of real wages during the business cycle which has failed to confirm his (Keynes') hypothesis. *There is no clear negative relation between real wages and the level of employment over the course of the cycle of the kind that Keynes postulates.*

Does this make Friedman a crypto-Social-Democrat or a left-Keynesian?

Notes

Can Keynesianism be falsified?

1   *Canadian Journal of Economics*, 1981.
2   *The Conditions for Economic Recovery*, Martin Robertson, Oxford, 1983.
3   *Economic Journal*, March 1983, 11–12.

Keynes' legacy of half-truths

1   *The General Theory of Employment, Interest and Money*, Macmillan, London, 1936, 14.
2   Joan Robinson quotes Gerald Shove, a Cambridge contemporary of Keynes, as saying that 'Maynard had never spent the twenty minutes necessary to understand the theory of value' (Joan Robinson, *Economic Philosophy*, Watts & Co., London, 1962, 79). The comment is a reflection not only on Keynes but also on the attitude of some other Cambridge economists of the time to the theory of value.
3   Ibid., 383.

Futures finally refute Keynes

1 'Speculation and Economic Stability', *Review of Economic Studies*, 1939–40, 2.
2 Desmond Fitzgerald, *Financial Futures*, Euromoney Publications, 1983, 180.
3 *Trading in Financial Futures*, US Treasury and Federal Reserve System, April 1979, 54.
4 'Uncertainty and Liquidity Preference', *Economica*, August 1937.
5 A forward market is the same in principle as a futures market except that the latter has an organized trading floor and standardized contracts and requires margin to assure completion of the contracts.
6 Ibid., 301.
7 *Man, Economy and State*, republished by Nash Publishing House, 1970, 693.
8 'Hedging' is the use of markets with deferred settlement to 'insure' against anticipated untoward price movements. A trader can use futures or forwards to profit from the untoward price change – cancelling out his expected loss.
9 For example, Mark Powers, 'Does Futures Trading Reduce Price Fluctuations in the Cash Markets', *American Economic Review*, June 1970; Holbrook Working, *Price Effects of Futures Trading*, Food Research Institute Studies 1, 1960; Kenneth Froewiss, 'GNMA Futures: Stabilizing or Destabilizing', *Federal Reserve Bank of San Francisco Economic Review*, Spring 1973.
10 'Innovation by an Exchange: A Case Study of the Development of the Plywood Futures Contract', *Journal of Law and Economics*, April 1973.

Have the Keynesians been vanquished?

1 'Unemployment, Is Government Macro-economic Policy Impotent'? *Journal of Economic Affairs*, January 1983.
2 'Comments on the Relations of Science and Art' in *The Essential Tension*, University of Chicago Press, 1977.
3 'Falsification and the Methodology of Scientific Research Programmes' in *The Methodology of Scientific Research Programmes*, Volume I, ed. J. Woral and G. Currie.
4 'Keynes' Policies in Theory and Practice', *Challenge*, November-December 1983.
5 *On Liberty*, Penguin, 1982.
6 'Robertson, Money and Monetarism', *Journal of Economic Literature*, December 1980.
7 'Economic Growth and the Problem of Inflation', *Economica*, November 1959.
8 'Planning Full Employment' reprinted in *Collective Economic Papers*, Volume I, Basil Blackwell, Oxford, 1966.
9 'Price Inertia and Policy Ineffectiveness in The United States, 1890–1980', *Journal of Political Economy*, Volume 90, Number 6, 1982.
10 *Money and Inflation*, Basil Blackwell, 1982.
11 'The Understanding and Control of Inflation', *Canadian Journal of Economics*, November 1981.
12 B. Snowdon, *Inflation, Government and the Role of Incomes Policy*, Anforme Ltd, Newcastle, August 1983.
13 'A Theoretical Framework for Monetary Analysis', *Journal of Political Economy*, March–April 1970.

Was Keynes a monetarist?

1. Paul Samuelson, 'The Keynes Centenary', *The Economist*, 25 June 1983.
2. 'Keynes was a Monetarist', *Economic Affairs*, Vol. 4, No. 3, April/June 1984.
3. Macmillan, London, 1936.
4. Ibid., 17.
5. Ibid., 17–18.
6. 'The Role of Money and Monetary Policy', *Federal Reserve Bank of St Louis Review*, July 1968, 9–124.
7. *Op. cit.*, 267.
8. *Milton Friedman's Monetary Theory – A Debate with his Critics*, ed. Robert J. Gordon, University of Chicago Press, Chicago, 1974.

2 Labour economics

Trade unions in a free society

G.R. Steele
Source: Economic Affairs, February/March 1989, 9, 3, p. 34.

The trade union is a paradoxical, ambiguous and contradictory institution. It can only exist in a free society; but there it poses a threat to freedom itself. Its aims are both narrow (furthering the interests and particular groups) and broad (in the espousal of socialist doctrine). Its creed is that of cooperation, but the measure of its success is the ability to gain from situations of conflict. The trade union sits uneasily within the market economy; but it is only in the market economy that it can survive as an independent body.

Unions lay claim to the power to intervene in the labour market to improve members' terms and conditions of employment. To gauge whether the outcome is successful requires a reasoned case to be made for what might have been; a theory is required to describe the circumstances which would exist in the absence of the union. In one respect, the evidence is fairly clear. A multitude of statistical comparisons, based upon many different theoretical models, have established the fact that a unionized workforce enjoys higher wages then could be the case otherwise. What is less conclusive is the impact of the union on the allocation of resources and economic welfare.

From the writings of Adam Smith, economists have taught that a free market, and the allocation of resources by the interplay of impersonal forces, provide a criterion for economic efficiency. The union, like any other corporate body with any degree of influence over the market, represents a violation of this ideal.

It is always in the union's interest to attempt to increase its own power over the market, which it does either by increasing the number of imperfections, or by taking advantage of those arising from independent circumstances. Market imperfections allow unions to promote the sectional interests of groups of workers in three basic conflicts: between producers and consumers; between employers and workers; and between workers and workers.

Producers (both employers and workers) have an interest in limiting consumers' access to products other than their own. Here, the interests of employers and workers are more likely to coincide at a moment of time – when there is the potential for both to gain from monopolistic barriers to market entry – than they are through time. By their very nature, entrepreneurs are more able to adapt to changing consumer tastes (through diversification) and to new technology (through the choice of new investments) than is a group of workers committed to defending traditional skills and work practices.

Generally speaking, workers and consumers are the same set of individuals, so it is a paradox to suggest that their interests will always be diametrically opposed. This opposition manifests itself where the trade union attempts to impair the impact of changing tastes, new technology, new suppliers, and so on, upon the earnings and job security of its members. The role of the union is to protect workers against the threat of changes in the terms and conditions of their working lives – an objective which must be in conflict with advance through economic growth which both comes through and causes change.

Resolution of disputes between employer and workers (over the division of value added between pay and profits) may be achieved by bargaining. Where an individual worker bargains alone with his employer, there is usually a clear difference in the degree of damage to himself and to his employer, as a result of a failure to agree. Even so, this argument can be overstated, since workers' response to high-handed and dictatorial action by the employer would be likely to damage morale, production efficiency and recruitment. These wider considerations must constrain an employer's freedom of action.

The effect of trade union wage bargaining on efficiency in the allocation of resources will be different when an employer dominates a labour market (monopsony) than when there is competition in hiring labour. In a position of idealized competition unions are impotent. Any attempt to raise the rate of pay above market levels will force the employer into bankruptcy. Given this constraint upon the demands of trade unions, it is easy to understand why union leaders would wish to portray the world as emphatically uncompetitive. They will argue the legitimacy of demanding higher wages from employers making monopoly profits. They will certainly claim success in achieving higher wages from employers allegedly enjoying monopoly profits.

Where success is claimed, it may be fictitious or real. If fictitious, then no great harm will have been done. If real, then it is as well to understand that many monopolies are short-term phenomena, the symptom of success and a beacon to new entrants into the market. Wage claims based on ephemeral monopoly profits are an implicit denial that the pursuit of entrepreneurial gain is the key to economic growth. High wages conceded upon the basis of short-term entrepreneurial success will not only reduce the incentive to innovate, but will also divert the ultimate gain from consumers generally (where competition is effective in reducing product prices) to union members.

With monopsony, the outcome of bargaining is uncertain, but is unlikely to be consistent with efficiency. It is rather the division of the spoils of monopoly power between unions and employers. Although intervention is justified to limit monopoly profits where there is great and persistent divergence between actual markets and the competitive ideal, this is a role for governments rather than trade unions. Successful intervention by unions would have the effect of transferring the benefit of monopoly profits from employers to workers, without making any progress towards the competitive ideal.

The impact of a trade union entering a competitive labour market is to raise the wages of unskilled workers at the cost of unemployment for others, or to increase the wages of skilled workers by denying access to those who are forced to remain in less remunerative employment. More generally, the full impact of such an incursion is to create havoc with the allocative role of an efficiently operating labour market producing greater uniformity and rigidity in relative wages, and higher levels of unemployment.

Where such effects are recognized, it may be argued that they are secondary in importance to the idea of a minimum standard wage (whether explicit, legal or imaginary) below which no-one should be expected (or allowed) to work. State support, by whatever means, provides for this last category. (Needless to say, even the crudest attempt to calculate the consequential tax burden produces sums quite disproportionate to the level of national income.)

Even where the case regarding disruption of efficiency in allocating resources is conceded, it may be argued that union practices ought not to be judged solely in those terms. Union bargaining establishes rules acceptable to both managers and employees for deciding and enforcing regulations governing workplace behaviour. Moreover, the requirement of trade unions to be able to act with well-disciplined members may be beneficial to management efficiency. There is a greater certainty in decisions when these are taken within the context of well-ordered and accepted procedures. Although it would be preferable for management to be able to exercise its own direct control, union control may be a desirable second best.

Even where there arises disagreement between management and union, it may still be the case that the former would lose less from having to continue to deal with a strong union, than for it to attempt to undermine that leadership by encouraging disloyalty or dissension among union members. Although management may be left in an immediately stronger position to exercise its own discipline, the longer term implications would be uncertain. The factions which may be created within the union could leave industrial relations in an undisciplined state for some time.

The task of finding the best compromise, between social order and individual freedom, falls to government. Political action involves compulsion, creating a legal framework to limit the action of individuals. Within that ordered framework, a liberal government leaves individuals free – albeit constrained by the resources at their disposal – to strive for their chosen goals.

Since choice is limited by scarcity of resources, freedom cannot imply the power to act. Where there are wide inequalities in the distribution of resources, there are wider differences in the power to act, and social policy may be designed to set limits upon that degree of inequality. These are matters for political debate, but the ideal of liberal Western democracy is that laws should be known, universally applicable, and evenly applied.

Union attempts to secure compulsory membership – as a condition of earning a livelihood within its jurisdiction – may be represented as being part of an orderly framework of industrial relations. Trade unions demand of their members the same as the elected government demands of its citizens. Yet, there is an important difference. Government of a trade union cannot be democratic, for it lacks the institutions which are vital to a healthy democratic system. It has no organized opposition, no independent judiciary and no free press.

Despite these considerations, trade unions have made widespread progress in establishing the compulsory closed shop as a legitimate objective. Much of this is attributable to the fact that many employers willingly cooperated in order to avoid the potential fragmentation associated with multiunion plants. Here again, the conflict between order and freedom presents itself.

In applying to fill a vacancy, every worker is faced with a job, the conditions of which he has not negotiated. In that the union is regarded as a body whose functions are limited to those of particular employment, it is difficult to maintain that the obligation to join a trade union (in the case of a post-entry closed shop) constitutes any great imposition upon prospective workers. But wider considerations of conscience and the unqualified right to seek work become relevant when (as is often the case) the union attempts to extend its influence beyond those bounds. Although the right of an individual member not to pay an overt political levy has been recognized and accepted by unions, trade union activities retain a quasi-political character to which an individual member might reasonably take exception.

Conflict between individual liberty and union discipline requires practical solutions. It may become a matter for independent arbitration; but only the full authority of the law, supported by a parliamentary democracy, could deliver a judgment worthy of the widest respect.

Notwithstanding the existence of a universal franchise, a suspected class-bias within the judicial systems of Western democracies may explain unions' unwillingness to countenance a legal framework for industrial relations procedures and decisions. Furthermore, the tradition of voluntarism – the recognition that it is in no one's interests for there to be continual disruption of the production process, either by direct action, or as a consequence of persistent rancour – has brought at least tacit recognition from many employers that recourse to law should occur only in the last resort.

Many of the issues causing conflict within industrial relations are attributable to the failure of trade unions to keep pace with economic and technological advance. International markets, free trade, innovation and consumerism have brought changes to which trade unions generally have failed to respond. New patterns of welfare provision and changed standards of civilized behaviour have reduced the traditional paternalistic approach of many unions to irrelevant anachronisms. This is most strongly so in Britain, where leadership of the trade union movement is split between three categories: those who see unions as a vehicle to promote radical change in the political order; pragmatists who believe simply in the greater efficiency of a planned economy or the mixed economy of the Keynesian dream; and those who seek to preserve the status and remuneration of those in work in the old defensive manner of local activists: '... as trade unionists we do not attempt to solve the problem of unemployment. We are selfish and the most bigoted of protectionists.' (Letter to Sidney Webb from the Secretary of Mansfield and District Trades and Labour Council).[1]

The first two of these categories may continue to hold the public stage of the trade union movement, the third remains the strongest force in the branch. It is against this element which the current vogue of the right to manage is ultimately pitched.

Breaking into unemployment: the black economy and workfare

Graham Dawson
Source: Economic Affairs, April/May 1988, 8, 4, p. 22.

The number of claimants signing on at unemployment benefit offices in the UK in October 1986 was 3,106,519. This is the official unemployment figure, so it must be right. It is published every month by the Department of Employment and reported by the BBC, ITN and the national press, so it is widely accepted as right. It is used by economists seeking to explain why unemployment is so high and what can be done to reduce it, so for their sakes it had better be right. But the only thing that we know about it as a measure of unemployment is that it is wrong.

The number of people registering for employment at jobcentres in the UK in October 1986 was 381,163. This figure is not published every month by the Department of Employment, although the information is readily available. The October 1986 figure was contained in a written answer to a parliamentary question asked by Mr Ralph Howell.[1] As a measure of unemployment it, too, is wrong.

Being unemployed is more than being idle; it is being involuntarily idle.[2] Evidence of involuntary idleness consists of genuine efforts to find a job, including willingness to accept lower wages, move house or change occupation. The significance of the small number of people registering at jobcentres is that it reveals the enormous margin of error in the official unemployment statistics. These are a count of claimants and there are obvious reasons why the number of people claiming unemployment benefit may be very different from the number actively seeking work. For some people unemployment is not a problem; it is a solution, a way of securing a livelihood without having to work. The question is how many people are in this category. All we know is that the number of people in the UK who really were involuntarily idle in October 1986 is somewhere between 3,106,519 and 381,163. But where?

It is no use asking the econometric model-makers. They tend to dismiss the distinction between voluntary and involuntary idleness as 'fundamentally unhelpful'.[3] The technicalities of model-making are found to be more interesting. They are bound to be when empirical testing is unable to distinguish between rival hypotheses, and models are judged in terms of simplicity and generality.[4] In 1985 I attended a conference on hysteresis (or the tendency for the current value of a variable to reflect past values) and unemployment at the University of St Andrews. Remote from anywhere resembling the real world and surrounded by shops selling golf clubs and tourist trivia, it seemed natural that scarce research talent should be devoted to questions such as whether the world is 'log-linear'. I left convinced that econometrics should be redefined as 'economics as if people did not exist'.

How else can you find out how many unemployment benefit claimants really want a job? You can ask them.

So in October 1986 I went to Liverpool to conduct a pilot study for a series of surveys of unemployment benefit claimants in different parts of

Table 2.1 Average wages, 1986

Average last wage pw	Average current income pw	Average target wage pw
£77	£46	£90

the country. The advantage of surveys is that they give the researcher a chance to meet the people whose actions he wants to understand. By the end of the Liverpool survey I had lost some of my enthusiasm for such direct contact. Perhaps I should have guessed something would go wrong as I left the new Mersey tunnel and saw, not the expected sign 'Welcome to Liverpool', but 'Accident Black Spot'.

Arrangements were made for 150 unemployed people to complete a questionnaire in Liverpool University. Only eight-four turned up, despite the offer of a £7 fee. Nevertheless, the data from the completed questionnaires yielded some interesting results which make a strong case for further research. It was the unsolicited comments that first drew my attention. 'I received ten minutes notice in being made redundant.' 'Yes, whenever I get a sufficient amount or come into money I spend it fast, mostly on drink; I seem to panic when I have money to spend.' These are my data, I thought, but they are not very well behaved; they will not sit still while they wait for a nice computer to come along and crunch them up.

At the outset unemployment can feel like liberation. 'I felt better – money in bank – less tired – plenty of fresh air – an opportunity to do other things with my life without the frustrations and claustrophobia of factory life'. A couple of years after this man lost his job it was a different story: 'depressed and insecure; no success in finding even part-time work to supplement savings'. There is desperation and despair among other long-term unemployed men. 'To survive this unwanted gap in one's life one has to be either half-drunk or half-crazy most of the time it seems'. 'I feel like an autistic child in relation to other, working folk'.

There is something for everyone here. You want scroungers? I get you scroungers. They are mostly young. 'Yes, going on to social security from school meant a rise in money so I could drink more regularly though in no greater quantity.' One young man's health was adversely affected: 'A slight limp in left leg cause unknown'. 'Pull the other one' seems the appropriate response. Another had left his last job because it was 'restricting his creativity'. At this point I reached for my pocket calculator.

The questions on income in and out of work elicited the most useful data, for willingness to work implies a reasonably flexible attitude to wages. In Table 2.1 the Average last wage column averages answers to the question 'What was your weekly wage after tax, your "take home" pay?', which referred to the respondent's last job before unemployment. The Average current income column averages answers to the question 'What is your weekly income now from unemployment and/or supplementary benefits (remember to include any rent or rates paid for you, free school meals and so on, as well as money received)?' The Average target wage column averages answers to the question 'Leaving aside fares and other work expenses, how much would your weekly wage after tax (your take-home pay) have to be for it to be worthwhile taking a job?'

It is possible that the large mark-up of target wage over current income

Table 2.2 Average wages, adjusted for wage inflation

Average last wage pw	Average current income pw	Average target wage pw
£87	£46	£90

is explained by the availability of work in the black or underground economy. If officially unemployed people can obtain about 40 hours of unrecorded work a week and it is remunerated at about £1 an hour, the differential between current income and target wage begins to make sense.

Yet I do not find this interpretation of the data entirely convincing. There is no doubt that a substantial black economy exists in Liverpool, but it is unlikely that many of our respondents are currently active in it. The poor turn-out – only 56 per cent of those invited – probably reflects participation in the black economy. In other words, only those unemployed people who are unable or unwilling to find work in the black economy are available for completing questionnaires. If this is true, there must be another explanation for the mark-up of target wage over current income.

An alternative interpretation of the data arises from the fact that the Average target wage is closer to the average last wage than to the Average current income. It is possible that unemployed people, in arriving at their target wage, are anxious to ensure that they are at least as well remunerated for working as they were when they last had a job. Those who have been out of work for more than a year may be assumed to take inflation into account. So the Average last wage must be adjusted for wage inflation over the last five years. The result of a very approximate inflation adjustment (increasing the Average last wage figure by 7 per cent for each year out of work) is shown in Table 2.2.

The inflation-adjusted Average last wage is remarkably close to the Average target wage and might be taken as evidence, however flimsy at this stage, that unemployed people aim for the 'going rate' for the sort of work they are prepared to do.

If this hypothesis is true, it would help to explain the failure of real wages to respond to the fall in labour demand in the early 1980s. The emergence of a pool of long-term unemployed was expected to exert downward pressure on wages as they tried to price themselves back into work. This has clearly not happened, because, as one economist has put it, the long-term unemployed 'might as well be in Australia'. They give up looking for a job and gradually lose their skills and work discipline until they are virtually unemployable. While there is probably a lot of truth in this conjecture, the figures in Table 2.2 indicate that it might also be true that unemployed people exert no downward pressure on wages because they adjust their own wage demands in line with inflation.

From the outside, this looks like an unreasonable and stubborn refusal to face economic reality. To unemployed people, it might seem to be no more than an attempt to hang on to their dignity as human beings. They became unemployed through being in the wrong place at the wrong time, through living in an accident black spot, through bad luck. After that I think they want more than anything else to avoid being exploited because they are desperate for a job. A defiant refusal to accept the further penalty of a wage cut after the perceived victimization of redundancy overrules the calculations of the rational economic man. The problem is how to persuade unemployed people to stop thinking in this way and adopt a more flexible attitude to wages. It is likely that they are encouraged in their playing hard-to-get approach by the indefinite availability of welfare benefits.

The implication of the survey for policy is therefore to underline the urgency of devising a feasible workfare scheme or at least of extending the community programme. Those officially unemployed people who are too busy in the black economy to answer questionnaires would then have every reason to legalize their activities. The rest, since they would be doing a workfare job in order to qualify for benefit, would be likely to set their target wage for a labour market job as a mark-up over benefit. The Average target wage would fall until it was closer to the Average current income than to the Average inflation-adjusted last wage.

All this reasoning is based on one small sample survey and intended as no more than a prelude to further research. The most immediate task is to discover whether surveys using the same questionnaire in different areas confirm the Liverpool results. In order to try to find out more about the black economy, it might be useful to arrange interviews with five or six people active in it. Talking to a handful of participants at length appears to be more likely to yield useful information about the black economy than issuing a written questionnaire to a larger number of unemployed people. Finally, a round of surveys could be undertaken to investigate in more detail the ways in which unemployed people not active in the black economy calculate their target wage.

As I collected the last questionnaires, a university security officer told me that some of the people I had brought on to the premises had broken into a vehicle in the car park, taking the radio. Yes, mine.

Real wages and employment: four great economists: Pigou, Simons, Keynes and Hansen

Eli Schwartz
Source: Economic Affairs, April/May 1988, 8, 4, p. 25.

The discussion of the relationship between real wages and the amount of employment may seem highly contemporary. But the problem surfaced in the early part of this century and much of the writings of the four selected economists listed above still seem on the mark today. A discussion of the problem of wage-related unemployment should begin with the neo-classical view of the labour market first elaborated by Marshall and completed by Pigou.

The neo-classical schools' picture of the labour market combined elements drawn from the classical economists and the utilitarians. The demand for workers was the marginal productivity of labour and the supply was set by the disutility of work relative to the utility of the wage offer. Between them, these forces established the market wage. If because of improved productivity or an increase in product demand, the demand for labour increased, wages would rise. The workers would increase their hours of work or more workers would enter the market until at the increased wages and the increased amount of labour offered, the wage rate equalled the marginal product. If, on the other hand, there should be a backward shift in the value of the marginal product of labour, employers would lower their wages. At lower wages, some workers would find that the disutility of labour exceeded the utility of income. They would withdraw from the labour market; they would go home, add to the household economy, or wait for better times. (They would be voluntarily unemployed.) At a lower quantity of labour supplied and a lower wage, the supply of labour would once more equal the demand for labour.

The picture is admittedly simple; nevertheless, under conditions of full or nearly full employment, it yields some useful insights and should not be abandoned too readily. When there is mass unemployment resulting from a shortage of aggregate demand (whether triggered by a Friedman monetary collapse, or by a Keynesian mismatch between savings and investment), the micro-economic labour market model is not applicable. In the micro-model, an oversupply of the quantity of labour is cured by a fall in the wage rate, with the value of the marginal product remaining more or less constant. In the Keynesian macro-model, the shortfall in aggregate demand results in a fall in product prices, the wage level and the value of the product are not independent, and although the price of labour drops, the number of jobs offered may not necessarily rise.

The problem of mass unemployment in the Keynesian system cannot be cured in the labour market. Suppose that the whole labour force were for a moment put back to work. The economy would return to full employment incomes, but at this level, intended savings exceed investment and the system would spiral downward once again.

In a depression, in contrast to its presumed normal behaviour at near full employment, the supply of labour is likely to behave perversely. Thus, when the economy is operating near full employment and demand increases, an increase in the quantity of labour supplied can be obtained (up to a point) with higher wages. Again conforming to the neo-classical model, as wages fall at the initial start of a downturn, peripheral workers may leave the market. However, in a recession after a while, the quantity of labour available on the market becomes fixed and exceeds the number employed. A cut in wages will not decrease the numbers seeking work and an increase in demand can be accommodated by increasing employment and output without raising real wages. In short, the supply of labour is inelastic to a wage cut (will not shrink) and very elastic to any increase in demand even though wages do not rise.

It follows that we have two definitions of involuntary unemployment. It exists when a fall in the real wage will not cause workers to leave the labour market. This is Keynes' definition. The current macro-economic textbook definition is more likely to read: unemployment exists when there is a surplus of qualified workers ready and willing to work at the current wage. The difference is slight, but Keynes needed his own definition to complete his system – more of this later.

According to current economic doctrine, the remedy for mass unemployment is not in the labour market; it is to be found in financial or fiscal policy. An effective cure must close the gap between aggregate demand and potential output. For the monetarists, it involves a rise in the real money supply, either through a fall in prices with the nominal money supply constant or by a rise in the nominal money supply with prices constant. For the Keynesians, the remedy centres on an increase in the real government deficit financed by an increase in the velocity of circulation of money or by an increase in the money supply if the debt is monetized.

Here Keynes' definition of unemployment is useful. In the course of the depression, the more costly operating units are closed down first. As the expansion proceeds in a recovery, the less efficient capital stock is activated and prices rise at least slightly. If the money wage remains unchanged, there is some fall in real wages. Because of the way Keynes has defined the behaviour of the labour supply, the money wage stays constant and the increase in aggregate demand brings about an increase in output and employment.

Critics have pointed at, and apologists have tried to explain away, Keynes' so-called money wage illusion. Why should workers accept a lower real wage? perhaps Keynes has the better of the argument. The bargain is an exchange of more employment for a lower real wage and is not irrational in a depression. There are still many people waiting to be employed in all industries, so that the workers' market power is not so strong in any case. Moreover, in contrast to the case of a cut in money wages, the first movement is an increase in aggregate demand so that the offer of more work precedes or parallels the rise in prices. Thus although the value of the wage unit falls, the work week may lengthen and the total real weekly wage rise. Relatives are called back to work, and the total available household income may increase. Security of employment improves as friends and fellow workers find employment. Finally, even though the real wage unit falls somewhat, assuming elasticity in the demand for labour, the total real wage bill of society is higher.[1]

It is interesting that something parallel to the Keynesian view appears in the writings of Henry Simons, one of the founders of the Chicago School. In his 1934 essay, 'A Positive Program for Laissez Faire', Simons presents the view that the basic cause of the depression was monopoly and the essential weakness of the banking system.[2] But for an immediate cure for the depression of the thirties, Professor Simons was willing to tolerate some degree of inflationary fiscal policy: '... For the moment, however, attention must be focused on the task of escaping from the present affliction of extreme unemployment and underproduction. Unless the immediate crisis can be dealt with, there is no sense in talking about long-run policy'.

The depression is essentially a problem first of relative inflexibility in those prices which largely determine costs and second of contraction in the volume and velocity of effective money. The crucial characteristic of the situation is maladjustment between product prices and operating costs; and, given this condition, there is no necessary limit to the possible deflation and decline of employment. Sound policy will look, first, toward pulling the more sticky prices down and, second, toward pulling the flexible prices up, in order to create favourable prospects with respect to business earnings. Little can be accomplished quickly in the first direction; consequently, main reliance must be placed on reflationary government spending. Inflationary fiscal policy is dangerous, to be sure – but not so dangerous as the alternatives.

The key word in the quoted passage is reflation. Under the existing conditions, it might be easier to raise depressed prices than to lower those costs and prices that had proven sticky. In a later paragraph, Simons warns that if those prices and wages which had been inflexible downward should prove to be highly flexible upward, then the result of the monetary fiscal expansion would be wasted in a continuing inflation.

The aggregate supply curve of Alvin H. Hansen's world (as set out in two companion books, *Monetary Theory and Fiscal Policy*, 1949, and *A Guide to Keynes*, 1953) is only slightly different from Simons'. Hansen's supply curve rises only slightly, and is almost flat until it begins to approach close to full employment. At this point the aggregate supply curve begins to resemble that of the Henry Simons' model. The potential full, full-employment gross national product (GNP) cannot be reached without a recognizable increase in the price level needed to push past the bottlenecks and rigidities which have begun to appear. The fruits of a continued expansionary policy depend on the behaviour of labour and the bottleneck sectors. The degree of quiescence in wage demands determines how much of the final push results in increased output and employment and how much is dissipated in inflationary price level increases. Thus Hansen is wary of Cost Of Living Adjustments (COLA) and price escalator clauses. These devices make it more difficult to reach full full-employment.

Hansen is a realist, and nowhere does he make the post-Keynesian suggestion that the problem could be solved by price and wage controls.[3] For the difficulty is not the rise in the general price level but the mismatch between prices and costs in different sectors. Some prices and costs must rise; and other costs, prices and wages remain relatively stable if the economy is to reach a full employment equilibrium.

Neither Simons nor Hansen was dealing with the problem in terms of the Phillips curve trade-off. They were not thinking of some continuous rate of inflation which would coincide with an acceptable low rate of unemployment. The key concept is reflation – a one-shot rise in the price level to readjust relative prices and wages to achieve full employment. Presumably after this price plateau was reached, the economy could now churn along at a reasonably stable price level.

Moreover, once the economy begins operating at or close to full employment (whether it is maintained there by a stable monetary policy or by countercyclical fiscal policy is not germane at this point), any persisting unemployment is structural or frictional. It is not likely to be reduced by macro-economic measures. We are back in the Pigovian world, where unemployment – always an undesirable phenomenon – is caused by frictions and malfunctions in particular labour markets and not by a shortage of aggregate demand.

The typical textbook accolade gives Keynes the glory of slaying Say's law, but in fact, a weak form of Say's law remains in the Keynesian model. Keynes is kind towards but critical of such quasi-economists as Major Douglas, who ascribed the depression to the systematic failure of the capitalist system to distribute sufficient income to the workers and other recipients to buy back the total output.[4] The weak version of Say's law holds that the income generated in production necessarily equals the cost of production; it is sufficient to buy total output. But the economy will fall off from full employment if the amount actually spent by all the sectors fails to equal the initial level of full employment GNP.

It is clear that the diagnosis of a Keynesian depression (a shortage of aggregate demand) is inappropriate in the UK; where, although unemployment is uncomfortably high (9.8 per cent), nominal income is rising (at 5.9 per cent per annum), the money stock is increasing (at 23 per cent per year), and the price level still shows signs of bubbling up (at 3.7–4 per cent per annum).

Western economies currently do not conform to either the Keynesian or monetarist deflationary crisis, where prices, incomes and employment all fall simultaneously. The problem of unemployment is essentially Pigovian or micro-economic and stems from structural distortions or maladjustments in the system. The costs and prices of certain industries are too high relative to the rest of the economy and it is from these industries that the deleterious effects of concentrated unemployment spread.

The case of the inelastic aggregate supply curve where any additional stimulation is dissipated in a rise of the price level was foreshadowed by Simons and Hansen. It has been encapsulated in Friedman's 'natural rate of unemployment'; the source of this phrase is a parallel to Wicksell's 'natural rate of interest', but it may have been an unfortunate choice.[5] The 'natural rate of unemployment' is not really a purely theoretical concept. It is not natural in the sense that it could not be changed. Given adequate aggregate demand, it is the rate of unemployment at which the economy will settle under the existing economic and political institutions. Presumably, a more flexible and mobile labour market, a reduction in the minimum wage, and a more rational administration of unemployment benefit could reduce the natural rate of unemployment.

Pigou pointed out that if wages in a specific industry are stuck at an unrealistic level, there would be a concentration of unemployment in that sector of the economy. Nevertheless the unions may still constrain productivity increases by insisting on standardized work practices and continue to push for high wages. It may be that workers will tend to stay in this labour market even though unemployment is high. Jobs are rationed so that the workers queue for occasional employment, supplementing their income with unemployment benefit. Investments in housing and in intangible capital consisting of friends made and experience in the area make it difficult to seek work elsewhere. Those that remain employed may consider that as long as the industry survives over their working life, it is to their interest to maintain current wages rather than accept any reduction that might expand employment opportunities for others.[6]

Of course not all relatively high wages are a cause of unemployment. Wages in different industries can vary significantly, and these differences may be justified by objective economic factors. An industry may pay higher wages because of differences in skills or because of higher occupational risks. Also higher wages may be paid by industries which have advantages in location or benefit from abundant inexpensive supplies of natural resources, or possess superior technology. Unfortunately, early economic advantages based on a superior location or a jump in technology may not last forever. A relatively high-wage cost structure may be built on a historic advantage which has now receded. If the wage costs in such an industry are obdurately rigid, the industry will find it difficult to compete, it will not be able to maintain its labour force, and its long-term survival may come into question. Since the profit rate in an industry with obsolete costs will now fall below what can be earned elsewhere, the hope that new capital can be enticed in to restore productivity is an illusion. An industry which does not pay its investors a normal return is eventually doomed to extinction. It may survive for a time by drawing down past capital – but using up existing funds and wearing out existing plant and equipment. It may survive for a while by reason of a government subsidy. However, such a subsidy is not likely to be forthcoming indefinitely if the industry is large and the labour income in the industry is above that of the groups paying the taxes.

Though the hardships of a depression are almost unbearable, the preventive measures or cures are relatively straightforward. The problems posed by labour market imperfections in a reasonably employed economy are not life threatening, although they are uncomfortable and very persistent. Unfortunately the economic policy that might be brought to bear on these problems brings forth no consensus. Policies that could increase the flexibility of the capital and labour markets could be useful. But the industrial policies proposed by economic reformers seem very contrived, ineffective if not likely to exacerbate the problem, and not easily applicable in a democratic free-market society.

Institutional reform to tame union power

Charles K. Rowley
Source: Economic Affairs, October/November, 1986, 7, 1, p. 8.

Trade unions are labour cartels, the principal purpose of which is to extract 'rent' from the customers of their employers and to transfer it to their members. 'Rent' is defined here not in the familiar sense of a payment for leasing property but in the economic sense of a receipt in excess of opportunity cost (the highest valued of all the opportunities foregone by committing labour to a specific activity). Thus, if the value of labour committed by a union to a specific activity is £100 million in its next best use, and £110 million is extracted by unionization, the 'rent' is £10 million. It is an unnecessary payment to attract labour to the activity in question; it does not directly influence the allocation of resources.

Rent in this sense is a widespread phenomenon in any economy, and sometimes serves a socially useful purpose. For example, in the guise of profit in an economy undistorted by restrictive practices, rent serves to stimulate the animal spirits of entrepreneurship in what the Austrian economist Joseph Schumpeter called the process of 'creative destruction'. As such it is a major impulse of economic growth in a capitalist economy. But rent, as the concept is employed in the economic literature on rent-seeking is socially harmful, describing behaviour which diverts productive resources into unproductive activities designed merely to transfer surpluses from one recipient to another without adding to the surplus at all.

Where such rents are believed to be durable, self-seeking individuals will rationally invest resources in seeking them out, if necessary to the point where rent-seeking outlays earn only a competitive expected return. Where competition for durable rents is keen, the total present value of the available rent may be dissipated as it is earned, in the form of socially wasteful outlays. Since the durability of rent typically depends on some government protection, the more heavily regulated an economy, the larger and more monopolistic its government sector, the larger will be the loss of wealth because of rent-seeking dissipation. How can this analysis be applied to trade unions?

Trade unions are non-proprietary organizations. Neither the members nor their union officials hold alienable property rights in the institution, other than in office buildings and the like. Inalienability implies the inability to sell or otherwise to transfer the rights to other people. Pension funds, though often of substantial value, are inalienable and tightly regulated. The members, who hold the residual status in the organization, placing them in a position equivalent to the equity shareholders in corporate enterprises, can capitalize on that status only by participating in wage settlements (including fringe benefits) in excess of opportunity cost; that is, what they might have earned elsewhere. Members can leave the organization only by abandoning their residual status without remuneration and, even then, in closed shops, only by sacrificing employment prospects in occupations encompassed by the restrictive agreement. Members who have accumulated highly specific human capital, therefore, must experience significant alienation from their union officers before they exercise the option of exit.

Union officials depend for their success upon an ability to attract a membership which is willing to commit investments to the organization they serve. Investments take the form of initiation fees, dues assessments, and expected income foregone when called upon to strike and to picket. In addition, by joining a union, members sacrifice their individual contracting rights, often to a fairly remote central bargaining bureaucracy. Members require a union wage differential which is sufficiently high to offer at least a normal return on this investment. It is precisely in this sense that they are residual claimants within the trade union enterprise.

But in a large union these residual claims are distributed over many individuals in proportions essentially unrelated to their specific contributions to union activities, so that some benefit more than, or at the expense of, other members. The free-riding implications of such an arrangement would predicably erode union effectiveness in the absence of systematic coercion of the members by agents appointed for that purpose. Individual members would otherwise prefer to continue working themselves, thus avoiding any interim loss of pay, while others carried the costs of collective action. Union officials, by penalizing blacklegging of this kind, limit the undermining of union effectiveness by the ability of non-strikers to benefit from most union wage bargains. The power of union officials to expel, to fine or otherwise to handicap non-cooperative members thus may be viewed as consensually granted by members anxious to reduce their temptation to free ride.

This allocation of authority may initially have been consensual, but it rarely stays so. Instead, the voice prerogative of the union membership, in which some exert more influence than others by activisim in the unions, tends to be weakened by a principal-agent problem endemic in the non-proprietorial status of the unions (that is, nobody owns them), while members who wish to leave have their options severely circumscribed by adverse regulatory restrictions. In these important respects, unions differ sharply from corporate enterprises, where the principal-agent problem is far less evident. Shareholders in corporate enterprise (the principals) monitor management (their agents) both by the threat of selling stock in the event of unacceptable performance and by the reality of selling stock to a more aggressive organization. Voice and exit in such an environment offer powerful opportunities for monitoring.

The union members (the principals) do not possess such weapons to channel the behaviour of their hired agents, the officials, into conformity with their preferences. The union members cannot sell their shares or threaten to do so in response to undesirable behaviour by their officials. They cannot easily concentrate vote power in the hands of a few members by proxy arrangements to vote them out. Indeed, the officials sometimes have life-tenure and are not subject to vote pressures at all. Even where elections are required periodically, the membership may be apathetic, rationally influenced by the free-rider disadvantage which weakens the vote motive, physically separated from one another as a consequence of plant location, and so on. In such circumstances, determined union officials may manipulate information as ideology to galvanize their own support and to secure re-election even against a predominantly alienated membership.

Where principals fail to monitor their agents effectively, as with the principal-agent problem, the agents may be monitored by pressures from within their own labour market. In private enterprise such labour-market monitoring offers a powerful impetus to promote efficient performance even where pressures from the capital market are inadequate. Where the agents' individual marginal products are clearly identifiable, their opportunity-cost wage in the labour market outside (what they could earn in other jobs) is influenced by their performance. Where individual marginal products are not separable, as with team production, agents will tend to monitor one another, both above and below, each with an eye on their jointly-determined opportunity-cost wage in the labour market outside.

In trade unions such pressures from the labour market outside are much attenuated, at least in Britain, where there is little or no tradition of union officials moving between unions or between the union and the corporate or government sectors. There may be movement between union and political markets, but the nature of the opportunity-cost wage which governs such movements, as I shall indicate, is far removed from that which governs the ordinary labour market. In consequence, the implications of interaction in the labour market for monitoring are also very different, and are unrelated to efficiency in the usual sense of the term. Upward and downward monitoring, for purely internal objectives, surely exist. But in the hierarchical, time-serving environments inculcated by most union bureaucracies its impact is much less marked than in corporate enterprises.

Two important predictions follow from these environmental conditions peculiar to non-proprietary organizations. First, the tenure of union officials will be longer and the frequency of contested elections (in the absence of mandatory legislation) will be less than in proprietary private-sector organizations. Second, the discretionary power of union officials as agents will be markedly stronger than that of their counterparts in corporate enterprise. Both implications are important in analysing rent-seeking behaviour by trade unions.

The British trade union movement was uniquely privileged between 1906 and 1980 as a consequence of legal immunities first established by the Trade Disputes Act 1906. This Act was passed to nullify the effect of a House of Lords judgment adverse to trade unions in the 1901 case of Taff Vale Railway Co. v. Amalgamated Society of Railway Servants. The Act provided immunity from liability in tort for acts done by a person or by a trade union (or its officials) in contemplation of or furtherance of a trade dispute. It established a framework of legal immunities for trade unions which, with brief interruptions, was to influence behaviour in the British labour market for three-quarters of a century. No other country offered protection through immunity from the law, although most provided limited legal rights, such as the right to strike and to picket.

The legal immunities granted in 1906 provided only limited power to back union officials before the Second World War, as a consequence partly of high unemployment and partly of the constraints on rent-seeking imposed by free trade and a private enterprise economy. These constraints became relaxed after 1945, with the emergence of high employment, with the rapid relative growth of the government sector and the eventual advent of protectionism in international trade. In 1965 trade union immunities were further consolidated by legislation which made void any legal action against the threat to breach or to induce breach in any contract of employment. British trade unions were then poised to seek rent in the labour market from a privileged position of legislative protection.

Nor was 1965 the zenith of British trade union protection. Following a brief reversal in 1971, when the Conservative Government of Edward Heath attempted fundamental trade union reform, legislation in 1974 and 1976 reestablished all pre-existing immunities, and further extended immunity to all trade union actions, whether in breach of the law of contract or of tort, and however distant from the employment contract itself. Additional legislation to protect employment and, decisively, the closed shop, created a leviathan which, by the late 1970s, was to threaten democracy in Britain and, eventually, in 1979, was to topple the Labour Government which had nurtured it.

The legal immunities and positive rights thus extended to British trade unions aggravated the principal-agent problem already inherent in their non-proprietorial status. By immunizing trade union members against adverse legal consequences if their agents (officials) should transgress the laws of contract and/or tort, the incentives for members to monitor their officials, either through exit or through voice, were significantly diminished. By providing the same immunities to officials their discretionary power was further widened, since they could ignore the threat of legal redress, except for crimes, while pursuing their personal trade-union goals.

The positive rights of the closed shop and employment protection further exacerbated the breach between principal and agent. The closed shop effectively shut off the exit option for alienated members, unless they were prepared to sacrifice the rents on their specific human capital. Employment protection further immunized the membership against the adverse market consequences of otherwise job-destructive union behaviour, silencing any reactions that otherwise would have become apparent.

In combination, legal immunities and positive rights encouraged British trade union officials to engage in rent-seeking activities of an especially wasteful kind.

From 1964 onwards those trade unions blessed with the powers of collective action consolidated their associations with the British Parliamentary Labour Party with the intention of seeking rent in the British economy. They did so irrespective of the consequences of their behaviour for the destruction of wealth. Between 1964 and 1979, the British trade unions financed more than 75 per cent of the Labour Party's general expenditures and some 95 per cent of its election expenses. Throughout that period the total union vote amounted to less than 50 per cent of the electorate and, in the 1979 and 1983 elections, only a minority of the union vote supported the Labour Party. Political levies were deducted from members' wages at the discretion of the union officials unless members specifically opted out.

The trade unions sponsored 125 Labour MPs in the 1974–9 governments, influencing the behaviour of those governments – for example, via the so-called social contract. Using their block votes, the union leaders now control almost 90 per cent of all votes at the Labour Party Conference. They control 40 per cent of the votes selecting the Leader and the Deputy Leader of the Labour Party. Inevitably, such a concentration of voting power, consolidated during the 1970s by the legal privileges accorded to the union movement, culminated in the stifling of the ability of the Labour Party to reflect the preferences of increasingly disenchanted average voters and contributed to Labour's two major election defeats in 1979 and 1983. The arrogant rhetoric of certain trade union officials, together with the evident compliance with their demands by successively weaker Labour governments, severely tarnished the acceptable face of trade unions; in a free society they were seen as existing to protect their members against the waiting time advantage of capital in the process of collective bargaining.[1] Instead, trade unions were widely perceived as seeking rent through the political process to control governments and, essentially, to subvert the democratic process.

By the late 1970s, many trade union members perceived that such political rent-seeking ran counter to their prospects for employment. As governments began to recognize that they were increasingly impotent to influence the aggregate volume of employment and as both the private and the government sectors of the economy began to face market pressures, the power of some trade-union activities, notably wildcat strikes, secondary picketing and strike action designed to obstruct labour-saving innovations, became too apparent to be ignored by far-sighted union members. In 1979 a sufficient number of them deserted the Labour Party to usher in a radical Conservative government on a mandate for significant trade-union reform.

Following the catastrophic failure of the attempt by the Heath Government at root-and-branch reform of British trade unions between 1971 and 1974, the two Thatcher administrations have pursued a step-by-step, piecemeal approach to reform designed to restrict the legal immunities enjoyed by trade unions, and thereby to weaken the political power of the unions. They have been unexpectedly successful in this strategy.

The Employment Act of 1980 restricted the immunities conferred upon trade unions by the 1974 and 1976 Acts in three ways. Section 16 provided that immunities do not apply to picketing unless the picketing is conducted at the picket's own place of work. Section 17 provided that immunities do not apply to secondary industrial actions unless such action is undertaken by employees of firms which purchase from or supply to the employer in dispute. The principal purpose of such secondary action must be to interfere with those relationships in buying and selling and the action must have a reasonable likelihood of achieving such a purpose. Section 18 provided that immunities do not apply where a person induces an employee of one employer to break a contract in order to compel employees of another employer to join a particular union. In essence, the 1980 Act reduced the scope of union activity that is immune from tort liability. It did not weaken union immunities where they applied to trade disputes narrowly defined.

The Employment Act of 1982 dealt with trade union immunities directly. Section 15 removed the tort immunity granted to trade unions and employees' associations by the 1974 Act, setting maximum damages limits based on union size. Section 18 significantly narrowed the scope of trade disputes to issues arising wholly or mainly between workers and their employers. It also restricted immunity to disputes arising within the UK.

The Trade Union Act of 1984 sought to render trade union officials more responsive to their respective memberships; that is, to reduce the magnitude of the breach between principal and agent. The Act required ballots before strikes were ordered and periodic leadership elections. These requirements are not expected to weaken trade unions as such, but rather to apply the democratic process within a union movement which has not always or universally upheld it in the past.

The combined effect of this sequence of legislation has been to restore some balance in collective bargaining lost, to the advantage of the unions, between 1964 and 1979. The relatively high rate of unemployment in the UK also assisted that outcome although presumably it will not obtain indefinitely. In two path-setting disputes, the first between the Messenger Newspapers Group and the National Graphical Association and the second between the Coal Board and the National Union of Mineworkers, the new legislation was decisive in resolving extremely bitter disputes.

The rate of growth of the British economy since 1984 has improved, undoubtedly in part as a consequence of a more efficient and flexible labour market. Whether these changes would withstand a significant rise in aggregate employment remains to be seen. Certainly, there is now little political enthusiasm for the repeal of Mrs Thatcher's trade-union legislation.

Trade unions and society: some lessons of the British experience

Brian Chiplin
Source: Economic Affairs, 5, 2, p. 53.

Amid scenes of violence on the miners' picket lines, a monograph on trade unions and society is well-timed. The two authors take individual credit for specific chapters rather than seeking to provide a common approach. Although this decision leads to some overlap, particularly on inflation and the Harvard school, it does offer the advantage of a slightly different perspective on the main issues and avoids the pitfalls of compromise. Nevertheless the authors' views are generally consistent, if with some points of disagreement, and the framework adopted is essentially the same.

The main thesis of the book is to stress the public choice aspects of union behaviour which, in the view of the authors, allows trade unions to secure advantages for their members through the political market place. This conclusion seems to be reached on the basis of dissatisfaction with alternative views of the role of unions. In particular, for example, the implications of monopoly power in the labour market for the British disease are played down considerably. Thus, both authors see little scope for the unions to raise wages at the expense of profits – in marked contrast, for example, to the Liverpool view expressed by Patrick Minford. On inflation, the authors deny the impact of unions as a proximate cause of inflation but stress their role as a fundamental cause of the expansion of money supply. Again, the source of their power in this direction lies in their ability to exercise political muscle as a well-organized and large group in the economy.

The growth of sectional interests, of which the unions are only one, is seen as the major problem facing the democracies of the West. Addison is dismissive of corporatism as a possible solution and Burton is equally scathing on the contribution of market syndicalism. But in the final chapter he takes issue with gloomy prognoses of the demise of capitalism based on the ideas of Henry Simons. He stresses the escape routes from union monopoly power, which have revealed themselves predominantly in the US through, for example, foreign competition and substitution of workers with lower propensity to unionize. On the other hand, the success of the unions in the political market place is seen in their ability to dam up these escape routes. As Burton observes, 'if trade unions are successful in the political arena, in obtaining measures in the future that impede or suspend the market escape process, then the outlook is much more bleak'. In a sense, this statement encapsulates the fundamental issues at stake in the miners' dispute.

In sum, the book is a stimulating and well-written treatise which can be read with profit by anyone interested in the effects of trade unions on Western democracies.

The above is a review of Trade Unions and Society: Some Lessons of the British Experience *by John Burton and John Addison, The Fraser Institute.*

Notes

Trade unions in a free society

1   Bienefeld, M.A., *Working Hours in British Industry: an Economic History*, Weidenfeld and Nicolson, London, 1972.
    Hayek, F.A. *The Constitution of Liberty*, Routledge and Kegan Paul, London, 1960.
    Phelps Brown, H. *The Origins of Trade Union Power*, Clarendon Press, Oxford, 1983.
    Taylor, R. *The Fifth Estate*, Routledge and Kegan Paul, London, 1978.

Breaking into unemployment: the black economy and workforce

1   *Hansard*, Volume 106, No. 10, Column 55, HMSO, Tuesday 25 November 1986.
2   For example, W.H. Hutt, *The Theory of Idle Resources*, Jonathan Cape, 1939.
3   For example, Richard Layard, *How to Beat Unemployment*, Oxford University Press, 1986, 20.
4   For example, K.G.P. Matthews, *The Inter-War Economy*, Gower, 1986, 1–2 and 202–3.

Real wages and employment: four great economists: Pigou, Simons, Keynes and Hansen

1 In the US, the recovery from the depression did not coincide with a fall in real wages. But the depression covered a number of years when there was considerable growth in capital-embodied technical knowledge. This could offset what would otherwise be an increase in cost as output rose.
2 H.C. Simons, 'A positive program for laissez faire: some proposals for a liberal economic policy', Public Policy Pamphlet No. 15, University of Chicago Press, 1934, reprinted in H.C. Simons, *Economic Policy for a Free Society*, University of Chicago, 1948.
3 The problems of a policy of wage and/or price controls are twofold. It is not clear how accommodations to the movements in relative prices can be administered, and on a pragmatic basis it is very difficult to find any example outside of a police state where successive breaches of the controls did not vitiate the whole system within six months to two years.
4 Chapter 23, *The General Theory*, 370. See also A.H. Hansen, *Full Recovery or Stagnation*, New York, 1938, Chapter IV.
5 British economists have proposed the acronym, the NAIRU (Non-Accelerating Inflation Rate of Unemployment), instead of Friedman's natural rate of unemployment.
6 See Henry Simons' 'Some Reflections on Syndicalism', in *Economic Policy for a Free Society, op. cit.*, 131–132.

Institutional reform to tame union power

1 It has been supposed since Adam Smith that capital has an inherent bargaining advantage over labour because of its ability to 'wait out' labour. This idea has been examined at some length in W.H. Hutt, *The Theory of Collective Bargaining, 1930–1975*, Hobart Paperback 8, IEA, 1975.

3 Money and banking

Monetary policy since 1971

Tim Congdon
Source: *Economic Affairs*, October 1983, 4, 1, p. 60.

The government's economic programme over the last four years has been to watch and regulate financial variables (the money supply and the PSBR) in the hope that, over the medium term, their course would be consistent with a decline in inflation. This programme has been successful. The inflation rate has been reduced from over 20 per cent in the second quarter of 1980 to under 5 per cent today, a bigger fall than in any other industrial country. Whether or not official policy has amounted to monetarism in some precise technical sense can be debated, but an emphasis on monetary policy seems to have been vindicated.

But in *Monetary policy since 1971* Maximilian Hall, Lecturer in Economics at Loughborough University, concludes that it is now 'appropriate to downgrade monetary policy's contribution to economic management'. Instead of being organized with the aim of controlling inflation, monetary policy should 'play a more humble role, such as the maximization of sales of public sector debt to non-bank investors'. Can this remark, written in a book with a preface dated November 1982, be seriously intended? Mr Hall seems to have reached his view because of the many complications and disappointments accompanying the pursuit of responsible financial policies in recent years. But it would be a strange philosophy which said that, because a piece of work is difficult, it should not be done.

The tendency to reach large and perhaps rather tendentious conclusions spoils Mr Hall's book. In some respects it is quite useful. There are detailed descriptions of the institutional arcana of monetary control and a good account of their evolution during the 1970s. Unfortunately, the reader is never told how monetary control operates in Britain. The section (pp. 8–10) is too short and nowhere else is there a clear explanation of the main features of the system. These are that the growth of bank deposits is determined by the amount of new bank credit and the demand depends on interest rates, which are regulated by the Bank of England. The traditional textbook approach, in which deposits are a multiple of certain safe assets held by the banks, is seriously misleading. But at a number of points Mr Hall pays much attention to the reserve asset ratio, implying that the multiplier approach has some validity. This also is a serious mistake. No matter how accurate and thorough its sections on such esoterica as IBELs and banks' switching-out operations, Mr Hall's book is unsatisfactory in its treatment of much more important issues.

The above is a review of Monetary Policy since 1971 *by Maximilian Hall, Macmillan.*

Banking: why should the taxpayer bear the risk?

Forrest Capie
Source: Economic Affairs, June/July 1987, 7, 5, p. 26.

According to the Bank of England the central reason for attempting to control the banking system is to protect depositors from sharp practice or carelessness on the part of bankers. In the words of the recent White Paper, 'Banking Supervision': 'The primary role of the banking supervisor [the Bank of England] is to reduce the risk of capital loss to depositors as a result of the banks with which they place their funds being run imprudently'.[1] At the same time the authorities insist that the supervisor cannot, and should not, guarantee that banks can never fail.

Most modern developed economies have central banks which regulate their domestic banking systems. Regulations vary in the degree to which they rely on statutory rules; and traditionally the UK has relied less on statutory rules than have other countries. Until 1979 there was no deposit insurance in Britain, doubtless in part because of the heavily concentrated nature of British banking, and the reduced likelihood of a bank failure. The secondary banking problems of 1974, and associated difficulties for a major London clearing bank, together with the first European Community directive on the coordination of banking law, were responsible for the 1979 Banking Act, which introduced a deposit insurance scheme and made the Bank of England responsible for authorizing new banks and implicitly placed responsibility on the Bank for supervising the behaviour of all banks.

The environment in which financial institutions operate has been subject to rapid changes in recent years (there are now around 600 recognized banks and licensed deposit-takers in the UK). Some deficiencies were perceived in the original Act; and the failure of Johnson Matthey highlighted weaknesses in the supervisory process. The congruence of the three has made the new legislation politically attractive.

The main proposals are directed at making the Bank of England explicitly responsible for the supervision of banks. A new Bank of England

Board of Banking Supervision would be created, bringing expertise from independent commercial banks to bear on decisions on a range of lending practices. The distinction between banks and licensed deposit-takers would be removed and all institutions previously classified as banks (confined to institutions with not less than £5 million paid-up equality capital) subject to the same rules. It would be a criminal offence under the new regime to provide false or misleading information, and a faster and fuller flow of information from the supervisee would be required.

Individual large exposures have featured in recent bank difficulties both here and abroad. It is therefore proposed not to impose specific limits on such exposure but to require institutions to declare their policy, with all exposures above 10 per cent to be reported to the supervisors. An exposure in excess of 25 per cent of the capital base would require early notification to the supervisors. The central questions are:

1 Should the authorities be taking any such action, and if so is this the right form?
2 Do bankers have to be protected from themselves, which is the implication of the requirement to notify to, and agree with, the supervisor certain kinds of lending?
3 Do depositors require protection from unscrupulous or reckless bankers?

The view that appears to have developed in the twentieth century is that banks are less imprudent than prudent in their behaviour and that the failure of one bank is likely to lead to a failure of others. They therefore have to be protected from themselves; and as a consequence they have been restricted in some way. But banks are no more or less than imprudent than other firms. From time to time there is mismanagement or fraudulent dealing, but there is nothing to suggest that these failings are more prevalent in banking than in other activities. Banks in Britain have failed at fairly frequent intervals. There have been some striking examples ranging from the failure of the City of Glasgow Bank in 1878 (through extremely bad management) to the Johnson Matthey affair in 1985. There was no panic after the City of Glasgow failure. Indeed, in the late nineteenth century banks closed their doors at the rate of about two per year, but there were no runs. The same is true in large part for many other countries, including the US.

Another fear is that, unless guided, banks will lend too much to one customer. The proposed legislation carries the requirement that a bank should notify the supervisor (the Bank of England) of any large overlending. This requirement suggests that banks are incapable of organizing their affairs and are liable to lend too much to one customer. In other words, it perpetuates the notion of imprudence or incompetence. And it also implies that the central bank knows how to conduct commercial banking.

Do depositors require protection from incompetent or crooked bankers?

The answer is no more than they organize voluntarily for themselves. The 1979 Act introduced a deposit insurance scheme organized by the banks. The current bill envisages a continuation of this scheme but with the net cast wider over a larger population of banks. Why could such a scheme not be privately administered? Either the banks will wish to persuade customers of their prudence and offer the guarantee of protection, or an opening in the market will be exploited by another bank. The sole justification for the central bank to organize the insurance rests on its being the ultimate source of cash. That argument takes us to the role of the lender of last resort.

The authorities have the responsibility of maintaining the payment mechanism – the role of lender of last resort, which should not be confused with bailing out insolvent institutions. Even if there were a danger of runs, the existing techniques of the lender of last resort are sufficient to prevent any financial crisis. This assertion is true even where depositors are apprehensive and begin to shift out of deposits and into currency.

The function of lender of last resort is to provide the market with liquidity in times of pressure. It is not to come to the rescue of an institution that has got itself into difficulties. Providing liquidity is achieved by discounting all good 'paper' – bills and similar securities – presented to it. Obviously, the more that is required, the more expensive it will become – the higher will be the rate of interest charged. But if the central bank adopts this procedure, it can remain ignorant of any single institution. There is no reason that it should know the details of any balance sheet. It simply satisfies a demand for funds, at a price. A badly-run institution will be carrying poor-quality paper and in the extreme case will be unable to obtain a high enough price to see it through its difficulties – of its own making. Following this line, the central bank does not have to bother about the much-quoted problem of distinguishing between insolvency and illiquidity. For it is the market that requires funds in a liquidity crisis, and it is to this market that the central bank should address itself.

The principal objection that can be raised against this behaviour is that the public does not have sufficiently good information. Therefore when a badly-run bank fails, depositors may suspect that their own bank will be under pressure and withdraw their funds. But at some point they will redeposit their funds either with the original bank or another. The system will have experienced a liquidity crisis. The central bank will have calmed the market by providing the necessary funds, if it judges by price, as described above. In any event, the objection is better answered by insisting that there be a better flow of information throughout the market.

The best way of achieving financial stability is to encourage market efficiency. The only safeguards required – those on capital requirements – could be easily imposed. The aim of any new legislation should be to shift the risks of banking to shareholders and away from the taxpayer.

Will inflation follow rapid monetary growth?

Gordon Pepper
Source: *Economic Affairs*, June/July 1988, 8, 5, p. 6.

At the time of writing this article in April, the economy appears to be growing at well over 4 per cent per annum which is very rapid by past UK standards. The fall in the stockmarket in October has not dampened it down as expected. A good part of the growth is probably due to the government's supply-side measures. Such growth is, by definition, not an overheating. Neither is the phenomenon of prices rising in one part of the country and falling in another part; this is a sign rather of desirable flexibility in the economy.

It is nevertheless clear that there is some overheating, especially rising house prices but also increased wage settlements, certainly in London and the South East, and the area affected has probably now extended to include at least East Anglia, the East Midlands and as far west as Bristol.

The cause of the overheating is clearly not a relaxation of fiscal policy; the budget deficit has not risen but has fallen sharply. Even on a constant employment basis the budget deficit cannot explain the acceleration in the economy. Neither can last winter's acceleration of the economy be attributed to a reduction in interest rates, in either nominal or real terms, because until recently they remained high. Base rates at the beginning of March were 9 per cent, the same as at the start of August.

In Keynesian language, the overheating is caused by too sharp a fall in personal savings; the savings ratio has fallen to 4.3 compared with 6.6 a year ago. In monetarist language, it is caused by excessive monetary growth and the main reason for this is very buoyant bank-lending to individuals as distinct from that to companies.

The two explanations are in fact the same. Data for savings in the National Income Accounts are for gross savings less dis-saving. Borrowing to finance consumption is a most important form of dis-saving. The main reason why net savings have fallen is the increase in borrowing. This is a typical pattern; changes in net savings often occur because of an alteration in borrowing patterns rather than in gross savings.

It is interesting to note that the monetarist approach to economic forecasting predicted the overheating. The Midland Montagu *Monetary Bulletin* last August was entitled 'Alarm Bells' and asserted: 'for the first time since Mrs Thatcher became Prime Minister the behaviour of the money supply is beginning to give serious cause for concern'. Particular attention was drawn to the relationship between non-interest bearing M1 in real terms and unfilled job vacancies; the behaviour of the former suggested a sharp rise in the latter. This should be compared with the average of independent forecasts published by the Treasury. In August the consensus was that there would be 3.2 per cent growth of GDP in 1987

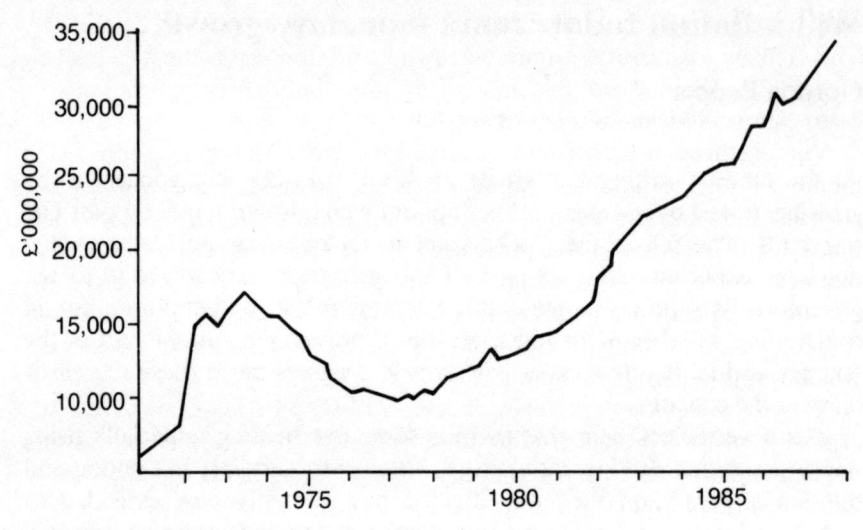

Figure 3.1 Bank lending to the personal sector, 1980 prices
Source: Datastream

and 2.5 per cent in 1988. In the February/March survey this had increased to 4.1 per cent in 1987 and 2.7 per cent in 1988. A *Financial Times* survey in April suggested a further rise in 1988 to 3.1 per cent.

This assertion about the success of a monetarist prediction will come as a surprise to those people who consider that the technique has been discredited by experience in the early 1980s. Monetarism has certainly become unfashionable. The mechanistic technique of focusing attention on merely one measure of money has indeed been discredited, and rightly so. I have always argued that regard should be paid to all the monetary indicators and, if any are behaving in a peculiar way, the cause should be investigated.

In the early 1980s the broader aggregates were heavily influenced by an increase in the demand for money for savings purposes, whilst the narrower aggregates, which are dominated by transactions demand, were distorted by the introduction of high interest cheque book accounts. There is growing evidence that the period of unusual distortion has come to an end. For example, the various monetary indicators are tending to point in the same direction and the rates of interest on bank deposits are no longer extremely attractive relative to those on competing homes for savings. The behaviour of the various definitions of the money supply is once again providing an important clue as to the performance of the economy.

The most recently published monetary indicators for the UK suggest that the economy was probably decelerating slightly on the eve of the budget. The six-month rate of growth of M0 fell from 8.5 per cent per annum at the end of December to 4.5 per cent per annum at the end of February. That for M4, which is now the Government's preferred definition of broad money, fell from 17 per cent per annum to just over 13 per cent per annum. The budget has, however, given a boost to confidence. This is likely to encourage more borrowing and, therefore, the deceleration may cease. There is no evidence giving one confidence that the current overheating will wane of its own accord.

Viewed through Keynesian eyes, the problem with the economy at the moment is an age-old one. During a business upswing, capacity utilization rises and industrialists respond by increasing investment. Room needs to be made for it. At least in the present cycle the Government is not making matters worse by competing for additional resources. Nevertheless, consumer expenditure needs to be reined back. The trouble is that this is difficult to do without discouraging the additional industrial investment which was the original intention.

Viewed with monetarist eyes, measures should be taken to curtail the excessive growth of bank lending to individuals. The difficulty here is that the demand for such loans is relatively insensitive to price, i.e. a modest rise in interest rates would have little effect, certainly in the short term. Such a rise would have a greater impact on industry, both because the cost of funds would increase and because sterling would rise as a result of the higher interest rates. A tightening of monetary policy in this way would help to damp down the economy but the effect would not be focused on consumer expenditure where it is needed.

I argue that the origin of the bank lending problem is on the supply rather than the demand side. Far too many financial institutions are competing aggressively to sell personal loans; some are using high pressure sales techniques. A way should be found to discourage them. I am also concerned about the amount of additional capital resources being committed to this business. One example is the move by building societies into the field and the additional capital they will raise if they become public companies and issue shares. Another is Barclay's £920 million rights issue. The additional capital employed in the industry means that loans may grow even faster in the future.

This brings me to a final and general point which is giving me increasing cause for concern. It is the way in which the Government appears to be uninterested in the control of the private sector. If a problem is not caused by the public sector, the authorities appear to wash their hands of it. If it is a problem within the private sector, the attitude of some officials is that it would be almost immoral to interfere.

One example of this is the official attitude to the deterioration which is occurring in the current account of the balance of payments. If it was a mirror image of a budget deficit (as it is in the US), the authorities would be concerned. As the private sector is the cause they profess not to be. They do not seem to distinguish between a deficit which is the counterpart of excessive consumer spending and one which is due to a boom in industrial investment. The latter can be beneficial but surely the former is usually undesirable?

Another example is the way the authorities are currently ignoring excessive monetary growth which is not caused by the public sector. They used to take countervailing action if M3 was growing too rapidly because of buoyant bank lending; they increased their sales of gilt-edged stock. In October 1985 the Chancellor announced the suspension of this policy of overfunding. The suspension was right in the circumstances but these have now changed.

Central banks existed and had an important role to play long before the invention of fiscal policy by Keynes and the growth in the role of governments. At the very least officials should reread some of the history of central banking, particularly those periods when there was a speculative financial bubble followed by a collapse in asset prices. But perhaps this last remark is better addressed to the US rather than the UK authorities.

Why Britain needs a monetary anchor

Peter Warburton
Source: Economic Affairs, June/July 1988, 8, 5, p. 14.

This article seeks to examine the anti-inflationary credentials of a policy of linking the pound to the deutschmark (DM) within the exchange rate mechanism of the European Monetary System (EMS). As it is contended by some that a low and stable inflation rate is the principal benefit of membership, this claim must be verified at the outset. The central proposition of this article is that a fixed DM-sterling link would exert, not a disinflationary but a progressively deflationary impact on the UK economy. While UK interest rates may fall closer into line with their German counterparts, strict lending controls would become necessary to restrain private sector credit demand. The trend towards the deregulation of UK markets would be reversed abruptly, leading to the re-emergence of mortgage queues and a probable curtailment of the campaign for wider share ownership. As long as fundamental differences in the organization and tax treatment of the housing and labour markets exist, realignments between the various EMS currencies are inevitable. It is argued that, without an effective system of domestic monetary control, the time will never be ripe for the UK to join the exchange rate mechanism.

After the re-election of the Conservatives to government last June, a tightening of monetary policy was widely expected. Indeed, Mr Lawson obviously saw merit in the idea when he signalled a 1 per cent rise in UK interest rates to 10 per cent in early August. Since then, the policy of repelling inflationary pressure through a strong exchange rate has erased the remaining traces of monetary prudence, and base lending rates have been ushered to 8 per cent, a ten year low. Of all the appeals for a formal-

Table 3.1 UK inflation rate during periods of DM/£ stability, 1976–88

		DM/£ rate		Average inflation rate (retail price index)
Period	Period average	Quarterly high	Quarterly low	
1976 Q4 — 1978 Q1	4.03	4.11	3.98	14.7
1978 Q2 — 1979 Q1	3.79	3.88	3.72	8.3
1981 Q4 — 1982 Q3	4.27	4.33	4.23	10.1
1983 Q2 — 1984 Q1	3.92	3.99	3.87	4.7
1984 Q2 — 1985 Q1	3.73	3.79	3.63	5.1
1987 (Mar) — 1988 (Feb)	2.97	2.99	2.92	4.0

Sources: *Economic Trends Annual Supplement*, 1988 edition, and *Financial Statistics*, March 1988.

ization of exchange rate policy, the voice of Samuel Brittan in the *Financial Times* has, perhaps, been the loudest. He wrote on 17 March:

> Once the DM standard has become credible, inflationary expectations decline, and the present (9 per cent) level of base rates would represent a much higher real rate than they do at present and a more effective brake on demand.
>
> The more important point, however, is that low inflation is guaranteed by membership of a common currency zone with Germany.

In order to shed some light on the latter claim, it is necessary to examine a variety of economic indicators relating to the floating rate era, which began in late 1971. During the following five years, it is difficult to find any example of lasting DM-sterling stability. Sterling depreciated almost

Table 3.2 UK exchange rate and visible trade performance, 1977–87

	Visible trade balance (£bn)		UK effective exchange rate (1975 = 100)	
	EEC*	Total	EMS currencies	All currencies
1977 — 1979 (av.)	−2.3	−2.4	85.5	83.3
1980 — 1982 (av.)	−0.1	2.4	102.1	93.8
1983 — 1985 (av.)	−2.5	−2.5	100.2	80.0
1986	−8.4	−8.5	86.4	72.8
1987	−8.9	−9.6	82.2	72.7

*Figures for all years relate to the eleven countries.
Sources: *UK Balance of Payments Pink Book* (1987 edition), trade figures press notice dated 25 March 1988, and *Financial Statistics*, various issues.

64   *Recent controversies in political economy*

Table 3.3   Foreign exchange market comparisons, 1987

	£billion
Visible trade	
UK exports of goods	79.6
(of which, to EEC countries	39.4)
UK imports of goods	89.2
(of which, from EEC countries	47.5)
Invisible trade	
UK credits	80.2
UK debits	72.3
Current account	
Credits	159.8
Debits	161.5
Increase in UK official reserves	12.0
Estimated annual volume of currency transactions in London during 1986	19,600
(of which, involving sterling	6,400)

Sources: UK balance of payments press notice, dated 11 March 1988, and *Bank of England Quarterly Bulletin*, September 1986.

continuously against the DM in this period. Table 3.1 catalogues six later instances of temporary stability, each of a minimum length of twelve months. Alongside each episode, the average UK inflation rate is shown. The elementary, but necessary, observation which follows is that the correlation between the DM rate and UK inflation rates between periods is clearly perverse. Broadly speaking, high UK inflation rates have coincided with sterling strength, *vis-à-vis* the DM, rather than sterling weakness. Advocates of EMS entry in 1984, at DM3.70 or above, have a great deal of explaining to do. If DM-sterling stability brings counter-inflationary benefits, then the currency instability of 1985 and 1986 implies an ominous resurgence of inflation. At this point, the clamour for EMS entry has more than a tinge of desperation to it. Which, if any, of the DM parities in Table 3.1 is the appropriate one for sterling in 1988?

Given the preoccupation with the US trade deficit in recent months, it is also pertinent to ask whether sterling's value compared to the EMS currencies has been consistent with approximate current account balance with the European Economic Community. Unfortunately, a regional decomposition of invisible transactions (services, interest, profit and dividend payments, etc.) is unavailable. However, Table 3.2 details the visible trade position of the UK with the other eleven EEC nations. It emerges that, apart from a period of exceptional sterling strength in 1980–81, British trade with the EEC has been in deficit for the past ten years. More worrying still, the regional imbalance was especially severe in 1986 and 1987, accounting for virtually all of the British visible deficit in these years. Against this back-

Table 3.4 Relative money supply growth in UK and Germany, 1971–87

Period averages	UK broad money growth (% pa) M3†	UK broad money growth (% pa) M4†	German broad money growth (% pa)	Relative UK broad money growth (% pa) Unadjusted	Relative UK broad money growth (% pa) Adjusted*	DM appreciation against sterling (% pa)
1971–75	17.4	16.7	10.3	6.4	6.3	12.0
1975–79	12.0	14.0	8.3	3.4	4.5	8.3
1979–83	13.2	14.0	5.2	7.6	7.9	−0.6
1983–87	16.1	14.6	6.7	7.9	7.0	7.5
1971–79	14.6	15.4	9.3	4.8	5.3	10.1
1971–83	14.2	14.9	7.9	5.8	6.4	6.4
1971–87	14.7	14.8	7.6	6.6	6.7	6.7

†Provision has been made in these calculations for the discontinuity in the official data during 1981.
*Adjusted for relative rates of GNP growth.
Source: IMF *International Financial Statistics*, CSO *Financial Statistics* and direct from the Bank of England.

ground, the strength of sterling last year is absurd. If trade balances are a valid criterion for establishing appropriate currency values, the pound was uncomfortably overvalued against the EMS currencies during 1987 and has become even more overvalued since March 1988.

It is generally accepted that the upward pressure on sterling throughout most of the past year stems from its role as an investment currency. Table 3.3 gives a flavour of the importance of trade flows in relation to capital market transactions in London. Using the rough estimate provided by a Bank of England survey of the London foreign exchange market in 1986, it appears that over £6 trillion of sterling was bought and sold in London that year. Annual current account flows of £160 billion and the size of official intervention pale into insignificance in comparison. Although the deterioration in the UK external position is serious indeed, the sheer volume of capital transactions is decisive. Only when the implications of the trade imbalance begin to undermine investors' confidence in sterling, will a major depreciation occur.

The neglected factor in recent policy discussions of sterling's relationship with the DM bloc is the role of domestic monetary expansion. The frugality of the Bundesbank's monetary policy is legendary. Curiously, though some deregulation of financial markets is taking place in Germany, few commentators dismiss the German monetary indicators as distorted and meaningless. As far as the UK is concerned, over a long time-scale (my choice is four-year averages) it is painfully obvious from the data in Table 3.4 that M4, the Treasury's new favourite, has scarcely behaved differently from the much-maligned M3. Both UK broad money measures have outstripped the comparable German money variable, in growth terms, throughout the floating rate period. Two calculations of relative, or excess, broad money growth are presented. Both use M3, which has increased slightly less than its new cousin, but the second column is adjusted for the relative movement of GNP growth between the two countries. It is fascinating to compare the annual rate of excess UK money expansion with year-to-year currency movements. For the whole 16-year experience, the two variables show an identical 6.7 per cent annual average change. International monetarism may not be ready for a revival quite yet, but it is far from dead.

The foregoing exhibits expose the difficulties of deciding on a correct DM or EMS parity for sterling. The consequences of labouring for years on end under the burden of an inappropriately high exchange rate are well known. If the Bundesbank has, inadvertently or otherwise, been pursuing too stringent a monetary policy during the past eight years then the whole of the EMS bloc has suffered unnecessarily slow growth and high unemployment. Had the UK government acceded to the CBI's request for EMS entry in 1984, it is difficult to imagine that the UK would have enjoyed the high growth rates of the past three years, or the sharp fall in unemployment. This is not to condone the manner in which monetary policy has been executed in the UK, but merely to contrast British experience with the deflationary consequences of EMS entry at DM3.70.

The acceleration in the pace of broad money growth during 1985, and its effects, were documented in a recent article by Tim Congdon and need not be repeated here.[1] Suffice it to say that in the past three years, UK monetary policy has become more expansionary relative to German policy, not less. Hence, the feasibility of a sustainable fixed DM-sterling link in 1988 has diminished, as compared to 1985, and not the reverse. Rather than the alternative to membership of the EMS exchange rate mechanism, a counter-inflationary monetary policy is the *sine qua non* of membership.

The notion that the UK can find monetary discipline only outside its own shores, if true, is a sad indictment of domestic policy. It is rather like suggesting to a rakish young man that he should join the Foreign Legion for some personal discipline. In both cases, the exercise of self-control would appear a better option. However, the reassertion of monetary control in the UK may threaten other priorities such as the extension of home and share ownership. The deregulation of the housing finance market has imparted perhaps the largest single impetus to rapid UK broad money growth. It is difficult to see how mortgage lending could escape the consequences of a tighter monetary regime. Similarly, the outlook for UK share prices and future privatization issues would be clouded for a time by the prospect of much higher short-term interest rates. Also, the reassertion of monetary control will probably entail a period of exchange rate volatility. As higher interest rates become necessary sterling may experience a sharp upward blip to the fury of the CBI, Samuel Brittan and others.

To regain monetary control, whether as an end in itself or as a means to full EMS membership, it is argued that these sacrifices must be made.

If the Treasury has serious intentions regarding M4, then an appropriate target range should be announced without delay. M4 has completed its trial run, its velocity of circulation recording a similar degree of stability over the past four years to that of the narrow money measure, MO. For the 1988-89 financial year, an 11 per cent to 15 per cent target for M4 would imply 6 per cent to 10 per cent expenditure growth. If, as we expect, economic growth will reach 4 per cent again this year, this leaves scope of 2 per cent to 6 per cent for inflation. Until this range is reduced to, say, 9 per cent to 13 per cent, it is futile to speak of lasting exchange rate stability for sterling against the DM, or of further progress in reducing inflation. It is not the political decision to enter the EMS exchange rate arrangements which matters but the re-establishment of monetary control. But, without the latter, the former cannot succeed.

Deregulating the Securities and Investments Board

Joanna Gray and Cento Veljanovski
Source: Economic Affairs, June/July 1988, 8, 5, p. 31.

There is increasing public concern about the nature and growth of financial regulation in the UK. Paradoxically, the deregulation of Britain's financial markets has been accompanied by an increasingly legalistic framework of regulation designed ostensibly to protect the investor. The government's decision not to re-appoint Sir Kenneth Berrill as Chairman of the main regulatory authority, the Securities and Investments Board (SIB), indicates some retreat from the approach which he adopted. It has been frequently claimed that the SIB was only doing what was legally required of it under the Financial Services Act of 1986. This article casts doubts on that contention and argues that there is ample scope for a more pragmatic, lighter and, above all, more cost-effective approach to the protection of investors.

The Financial Services Act of 1986, which came into force at the end of April 1988, provides the legal framework for investor protection. It has created a self-regulatory system within a statutory framework which is officially, but somewhat misleadingly, described as 'practitioner-based, statute-backed'. The SIB is the designated agency under the Act and stands at the apex of the new regulatory structure. Under it are a number of self-regulatory organizations (SROs) which must draw up rulebooks governing the conduct of their members' business (Figure 3.2).

The SIB is responsible for implementing the Act. While it has been claimed that the SIB's approach was pre-ordained by statute, a reading of the Act clearly establishes that, at least in law, it was given a relatively free rein. The Act specified a set of general principles governing the formulation of rules which are capable of a vast variety of interpretations. A minimalist regime of regulation would have been perfectly consistent with those general principles. Yet the SIB went far beyond this, so that the rules have become comprehensive and many orders of magnitude more numerous, complex and detailed than would have been permissible under the Act. Latest sightings of the rulebook place its weight at over 4.5lbs, yet the principles governing the SIB's rulemaking occupy little more than one page of the Act.

The SIB's approach has been to write a very detailed set of rules governing all investment businesses in the UK.

Was this necessary? It is necessary first to stress the Herculean task the SIB set itself. The financial sector is a vast and diverse industry, undergoing a period of rapid change and expansion. It offers a large variety of products to a wide range of individuals, from life assurance, where we are concerned with ordinary investors – the Aunt Agathas, widows and orphans – through to futures contracts, which are dominated by professionals. Logically this diversity and range of consumer sophistication would call for very different approaches to regulation.

The mistake in drafting the Act was to define investment businesses. This gave the SIB wide latitude and the ability to regulate the financial industry across the board. The requirement that investors in all markets be given equivalent protection has guaranteed that the comprehensiveness and detail of the SIB's approach infects all investment businesses.

In 'The SIB Rulebook: An Overview',[1] the SIB attempts to justify this approach to regulation. While the SIB was aware of the appeal of simple relatively general rules, it felt bound to give weight to three important considerations:

1 Certainty: firms need to know what they must do, can do, or cannot do and investors need to know what to expect and to what they are entitled. Certainty aids compliance and enforcement.
2 Consistency: general rules will be interpreted differently by each firm in a huge, competitive and diverse industry. This will penalize those firms which take a strict interpretation and the customers of other firms.
3 Standards: unless standards are laid down all firms will not operate to those of the best in a highly competitive environment.
4 It concludes that, given the breadth of subject matter the rulebook must cover and the consideration listed above, 'a substantial and ... complex rulebook [is] unavoidable'.

Take the SIB's considerations in turn. The quest for certainty ignores human and commercial diversity, not to mention the vagaries of language. This emphasis given to certainty was evidently the product of a lawyer's

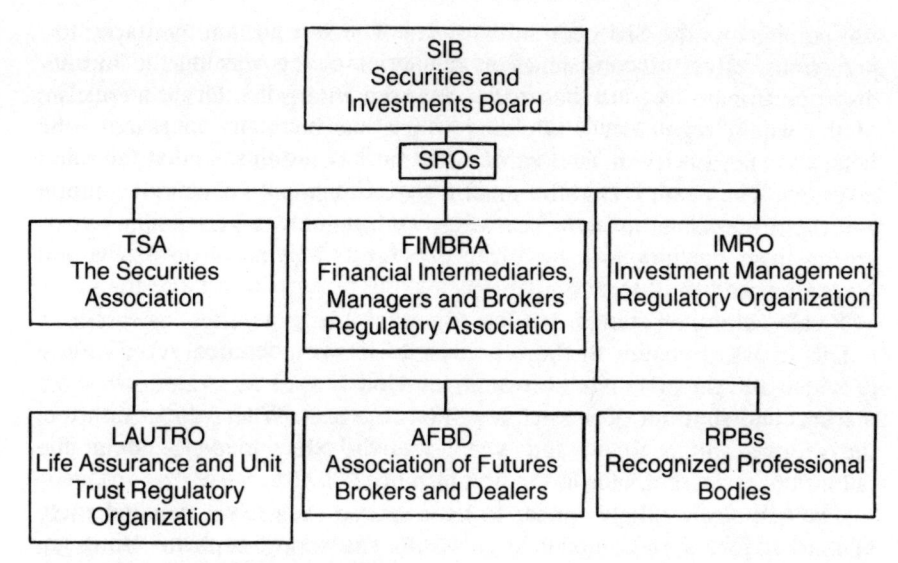

```
                    ┌─────────────────────┐
                    │         SIB         │
                    │   Securities and    │
                    │  Investments Board  │
                    └─────────────────────┘
                            │ SROs │
      ┌─────────────────────┼─────────────────────┐
┌─────────────┐   ┌───────────────────────┐   ┌──────────────────────┐
│    TSA      │   │        FIMBRA         │   │        IMRO          │
│The Securities│  │Financial Intermediaries,│ │Investment Management │
│ Association │   │ Managers and Brokers  │   │Regulatory Organization│
│             │   │ Regulatory Association│   │                      │
└─────────────┘   └───────────────────────┘   └──────────────────────┘
┌──────────────────┐  ┌──────────────────────┐  ┌──────────────────────┐
│     LAUTRO       │  │         AFBD         │  │        RPBs          │
│Life Assurance and Unit│ │Association of Futures│ │Recognized Professional│
│Trust Regulatory  │  │  Brokers and Dealers │  │       Bodies         │
│   Organization   │  │                      │  │                      │
└──────────────────┘  └──────────────────────┘  └──────────────────────┘
```

Figure 3.2 Structure of city regulation

lawyer who believes legalisms are certain. The common law of England is based on general standards, yet English lawyers find it fully understandable and workable. Laws which give people the right to sue for damages, such as the Financial Services Act, are often framed in general terms. The duty of employers to take reasonably practicable measures to protect workers from accidents is such an example, but it is only rarely suggested, that it has failed either to deter wrongdoing or provide a real remedy to those harmed. The mistake is the failure to distinguish between lawyers' and laymen's certainty.

Next is consistency. This principle betrays the SIB's total failure to appreciate the value of diversity and, indeed, its necessity in the marketplace. Practising lawyers daily cope and thrive on things being different. This is the hallmark of the common law. Lawyer and judge constantly distinguish one case from another, and emphasize idiosyncracies in order to establish that a law does or does not apply. That Department of Trade and Industry (DTI) and SIB lawyers should seek consistency in the face of an industry that has such patent diversity is an unexplained aberration. Perhaps the bureaucratic mind cannot cope with the idea of things being a little different from one another, and does not appreciate that diversity is essential for efficiency in competitive markets.

Consistency costs money and creates unnecessary barriers to entry, thus affecting adversely the efficiency of investment businesses, and which ultimately will harm investors. This happens in two ways. First, it stifles innovation. A new financial instrument is hardly likely to be consistent with past practices, and its introduction is likely to be inhibited by regulations. It has been said that a Warburg or Rothschild could not have created a financial empire had the SIB been in existence. The second, and perhaps most pernicious, effect of consistency in regulation is the way that it imposes disproportionate costs on the smaller financial enterprise. This is a criticism of the whole regulatory scaffolding which has been put in place – the failure to take sufficient account of differences between financial firms and investors. The result is that the small firm, the regional financial institution and the professional investor bear disproportionately the compliance costs arising from the new investor protection laws. This again acts to inhibit innovation and to distort competition.

Finally, common standards. This has much the same effect as certainty. It fails to take account of the relationship between the quality of service provided and the price paid. It would, if seriously applied, close down some markets and shut out of the market all but the best. Where does that leave the widows and orphans, and where was the SIB's evidence about the failure of the marketplace in the first instance?

The SIB's rulemakers appear to have spared themselves detailed study of market forces or compliance costs. As the contributors to the IEA's 'Financial Regulation – or Over-regulation?'[2] emphasize, the rules were framed without regard to the costs that they imposed on business and investors, or their impact on Britain's competitive advantage as a financial centre. The SIB was exempt from undertaking any assessment of compliance costs (which the Office of Fair Trading eventually did for some regulations) – now a routine procedure for all proposed government regulations affecting business. While it and the SROs were required to submit their rules to the Office of Fair Trading (OFT) for scrutiny to detect any anti-competitive effects, the advice of the OFT was ignored. The OFT formed the view that some of the SIB's major rules would reduce competition and harm small investors, but the politicians rejected this advice.

It could be argued that these criticisms pale in comparison to the benefits which the SIB's rules will yield in terms of protecting investors. But again this conclusion is by no means clear. No evidence has been adduced, either in the Gower Report which made recommendations on investor protection,[3] independent research or the experience in this country or elsewhere, that investor protection laws protect investors. This is a crucial point. Some draw attention to the scandals at Lloyd's and a series of recent revelations and prosecutions over insider trading and illegal share dealings. But these two areas, ironically, are not covered by the SIB's rules except tangentially. Lloyd's operates its own regulatory system and the prosecution of insider traders is the responsibility of the DTI under the Companies Securities (insider dealing) Act 1985. An appeal to this evidence, therefore, hardly sustains the case for the comprehensive regulation of financial markets.

The uniform character of many of the SIB's rules (not all, since most people speak favourably about the design of capital adequacy rules) is disturbing. There was no attempt to link the rules to benefits to investors.

The SIB's strategy appears to have been: if the rule is well intentioned, sounds as if it would protect investors and places a legal obligation on investment businesses to give certain information to prospective investors, then it can be assumed that it will protect the investing public. The rulebook abounds with such (implicit) speculations on its untested effects. In fact the way the SIB went about its business does not even approximate the high and exacting standards that it requires of those it regulates. In an SIB publication which formed their submission to the Secretary of State to obtain formal regulatory powers, it is claimed that its 'paramount responsibility is to see that regulation is effective in protecting investors' and that these regulations will support the growth of the British economy and the 'development of London as the world's major international financial centre'. Its rulebook requires an investment business to comply with the following:

> No matter shall be included in a relevant publication in relation to any recommendation included in it which states or implies that recommendation is based on the evidence of research or analysis unless such research or analysis has been carried out and the firm is in possession of that evidence and it is adequate to support the recommendation.

The SIB would not, if it were an investment business, scrape through its own rulebook.

The regulatory framework evinces a peculiar and awkward assortment of over- and underregulation.

There is no reason, for example, to regulate wholesale markets. These markets are well-informed and populated by professional investors. Here information is good, market forces strong, the parties able and willing to bear losses and the sanction of repetitive dealing sufficient to police and deter wrongdoing.

Yet in the areas where one can see benefits to small unprofessional investors from regulation, the new framework has failed. If there is one thing the prototype beneficiaries of investor protection – the oft-referred Aunt Agathas and widows and orphans – need above all others (apart from elimination of original sin in the investment markets), it is access to independent advice. The Office of Fair Trading (OFT) studies of SIB, LAUTRO (Life Assurance and Unit Trust Regulatory Organization) and (Financial Intermediaries Managers and Brokers Regulatory Association) FIMBRA's rules governing insurance and unit trust intermediaries point clearly to a significant decrease in the sources of independent advice.[4] The SIB has adopted the principle of polarisation in the sale of insurance and unit trusts. This requires anyone who sells these products to act either as an agent of one company or as an agent of the customer, giving best advice to the customer on the full range of products. The Director General of the OFT has argued that this will raise costs, decrease the number of people offering independent advice and, rather dramatically, their complete removal from small towns and rural areas. This, the Director General argued, would be acceptable if he could see benefits from the rule. But customers would continue to be ill-informed and the rules would make it more likely that they would be captured by the first salesman who came along. In short, the rule would distort competition, raise costs, reduce the available independent advice and not lead to an appreciable increase in protection for small investors. Moreover, the initial new draft LAUTRO regulations retreat from one area where there is a body of opinion that there should be more information – commission rates paid to insurance intermediaries. In addition, the Director General has argued that the setting of maximum commissions will create a cartel which will harm investors.[5] As we write, LAUTRO has made concessions, insurance brokers and other outlets will soon have to tell their customers how much they are being paid by insurance companies to recommend their policies.

There is little doubt that the SIB rulebook could be substantially rewritten to achieve the requirements of investor protection laid down by the Financial Services Act to operate a regulatory system with a lighter, less costly touch.

The principles stated in the Act that decide what the SIB must do occupy little more than one page. If one reads them they are unexceptional and reflect what most would accept are sound business practices. The ironic feature of these rules is that most are already the law of the land. Schedule 8 of the Act asks the SIB to take into account the general standards of the common law of agency plus what the SIB has called the know-your-customer principle. The law of agency defines the duties and responsibilities of those acting, either expressly or impliedly, on behalf of others. It was a mistake to codify this area of law and in haste graft onto it specific legal requirements (which incidentally would give investors the right to sue). In the light of the SIB's justification for this approach, it is by no means clear that the courts will find the rules as certain and clear as it believes they are. Indeed, it is doubtful whether the SIB needed to write its own rulebook – a set of guidance notes would have been sufficient to outline the common law rights of investors and the responsibilities and duties of those giving investment advice. The SIB's mistake was to devise detailed comprehensive rules rather than one phrased in general terms. This point is reinforced by the fact that the SIB discourages investment businesses from seeking direct authorization (which is required if a business is legally to give investment advice) from it, rather than an SRO.

It is perfectly possible, both legally and practically, to redraft the rules to achieve the standard established in the Act (insofar as they are achievable in any market) with the minimum effect on competition, volume of business, and the ability of investors to transact business efficiently. There is no reason why the rules cannot be framed to be comprehensible to the investment industry and investors (whose interests do actually coincide to a large extent: a point the SIB seems to have missed). It is impossible here to go through the SIB rulebook editing out costly bits and holding each provision up to the standards of cost-effective investor protection and competition. Specific examples would be revocation of the rules governing polarization and the detailed requirements concerning record-keeping which place a heavy paperwork burden on investment businesses. The City needs a rulebook embracing little more than the existing law of agency combined with enforcement.

Notes

Banking: why should the taxpayer bear the risk?

1   Cmnd. 9695 (3.1), HMSO, London.

Why Britain needs a monetary anchor

1   Tim Congdon, 'The Lawson Boom in the Light of the Crash'. *Economic Affairs*, February/March 1988, Vol. 8, No. 3, 14ff.

Deregulating the Securities and Investments Board

1   The Securities and Investments Board Limited, London.
2   Cento Veljanovski *et al.*, Readings 27, IEA, 1988.
3   *Review of Investor Protection*, Cmnd. 9125, 1985.
4   J. Gray, 'Insurance Intermediaries and the Financial Services Act', in *Foundations of Insurance Law*, Sweet & Maxwell, 1987.
5   *LAUTRO – A Report of the Director General of Fair Trading to the Secretary of State for Trade and Industry*, 1988.

4 Taxation

More state welfare or lower taxes?

Arthur Seldon
Source: *Economic Affairs*, February/March 1987, 7, 3, p. 4.

> The polls show that there is a large majority in the nation in favour of increased spending in preference to tax cuts.
> *The Guardian*, 19 January 1987

This uncritical sentiment, with a variation in language, could have been quoted from other influential British newspapers in recent months. The topical peg has invariably been the impending general election and the reaction of the politicians to public opinion.

Political and church leaders are also, and uncritically, accepting the apparent finding of the polls. Mr David Steel, in his foreword to the book on Alliance policies, *The Time Has Come*,[1] has asserted rhetorically: 'Does the taxpayer not require that more should be spent on reviving our sagging health and education services?' And the Archbishop of Canterbury has entered the argument: 'we have substantial evidence from opinion polls that many people would be prepared to pay more taxes and forgo tax cuts in order to help divert resources to the poor.'[2]

Observers might have wondered why the third alternative was omitted. The alternatives are not only higher taxation and more meagre government expenditure on welfare (or anything else). The third, but neglected, alternative, of course, is to raise finance for health and education and other welfare services by pricing them instead of levying taxes. The way to more expenditure on welfare is not necessarily through higher taxation. The British could have more welfare as well as unchanged or even lower taxation. They would willingly spend more on welfare, but they are largely limited to spending through the tax system.

Reflection might therefore have given newspaper editors, politicians and prelates cause for caution. They might ask themselves why the British should want to yield even more of their earnings to be spent by politicians and officials in Whitehall and town halls on services in which they have no direct influence, little say, and almost no choice. Is it because they think they will gain more in benefits for themselves than they lose in taxes? Is it because they wish to see more public expenditure directed to others – the deserving and the poor? Or is it because the pollsters' questions do not clarify the alternatives between which their samples are asked to choose?

The Economist Intelligence Unit published in December 1986 an assembly of essays, *The World in 1987* to tell the British (and the world) what to expect in economic and political affairs this year. One prognostication, by Professor Anthony King, the political scientist at the University of Essex, discussed the probable outcome of a general election. It claimed evidence that pointed to 'a nasty shock for Mrs Thatcher'.

The evidence was the Gallup Poll Political Index which has apparently found a remarkable increase in the willingness to pay higher taxes for more state health, education and welfare services from 37 per cent in May 1979 to 67 per cent in June 1986.

This mood has evidently been a general finding of other opinion polling. *British Social Attitudes: the 1986 Report*, by Roger Jowell, Sharon Witherspoon and Lindsay Brook of Social and Community Planning Research (SCPR), found a comparable upward trend in the willingness to pay higher taxes. The proportion of its sample that favoured higher taxes rose from 32 per cent in 1983 to 45 per cent in 1985. Such figures led one of their contributors, Nick Bosanquet, an economist at the Centre for Health Economics at the University of York, to conclude that

> The tide of sympathy said to have existed ... for tax cuts accompanied by cuts in government expenditure and public services seems to have receded.
>
> There is ... an increasing 'collectivist' or 'welfarist' majority, drawing recruits from all parts of the political spectrum, who appear to have lost faith in the message of the Government that it should govern less [...].

This is the view now accepted and reflected in the British press, politics and the established church.

Are the political scientist at Essex University and the economist at York University sure of their inference? What did their polls ask? Were their questions appropriately designed to elicit real preferences between tax and state services/benefits and the ways of paying for welfare?

The Gallup Poll asked for views on the statement that 'Government services such as health, education and welfare should be extended, even if it means some increase in taxes. The terms extended (services) and some increases (in taxes) are vague'. 'Extended' how far? How much is 'some' increase? The SCPR poll asked its sample whether it thought government should 'Increase taxes and spend *more* [italics in original] on health, education and social benefits'. Again, increase (in taxes) and more (welfare) are vague. 'Increase' by how much? Spend how much 'more'?

In neither of the two samples was the individual told, nor could he calculate, how much additional tax he would have to pay for extended services, nor what more or better benefits he could expect for his family by paying more in taxes.

No man or woman in a shop decides to spend more or less until he or she knows the price of each item and therefore the amount of each purchase that more spending will bring. The shopper asks 'How much does it cost?' If told simply 'more' (which is what the polls say), the reaction would be 'What does that mean? How much more?'. The higher the price, the fewer units the shopper will tend to buy (because more of alternative purchases are foregone). The number of units bought thus cannot be separated from the price of each unit. The same in principle is true of an employer buying labour, an employee deciding on a holiday, government buying materials in the market. Supply and demand are linked to the price of units of purchase: man-hours of work, weeks in Spain, stationery or red tape.

That is what economists mean when they say there is no such thing as demand without a price. And that is perhaps the most fundamental relationship established in economics. To discuss demand (or supply) without reference to a price leads to far-reaching error. There is no such thing as a shortage or a surfeit except linked to a price. At high enough prices a queue of would-be customers outside a store vanishes like summer snow. At a low enough price to farmers, a glut in the supply of their crop turns into a shortage and then into a famine. This is what happens when prices are stopped from signalling to suppliers how much consumers want to buy.

Can the citizen say he will pay more in taxes for government to spend more on state welfare services unless he knows how much more (or better) benefits he will receive? Would his answer be the same if he had to pay £100 a year more in taxes as if he had to pay £500 or £1,000? Would it be the same if his promised improvement in state benefits were 1 per cent, 10 per cent or 20 per cent?

These surveys and polls do not tell us, so they convey little or nothing as a guide to policy. If they had included such figures of individual tax costs and service benefits, they would have discovered a wide range of very different answers. It may be that the British are prepared to increase their payment to government from 46 per cent of their incomes (on some definitions) to 56 per cent or 66 per cent (the percentage it has reached in Sweden). But it is likely that they would part with 56 per cent or 66 per cent of their income only if the improvement in state services was nearer 20 per cent than 10 per cent and not at all if it were only 1 per cent. Such polls do not tell us what the taxpayer/voters would do, or want to do, because they did not tell their samples the figures from which individuals could know the costs or benefits to themselves and their families.

But it would have been possible to tell the samples interviewed, or at least to go some way to tell them. In four surveys in 1963, 1965, 1970 and 1978 (by Mass Observation and then by England, Grosse[3]) for the Institute of Economic Affairs (IEA) they were told the cost of alternative state and private services and then asked whether they would pay school fees and health premia if the state returned a proportion of the costs in tax rebates. There was not much less than a doubling in the readiness to pay more for welfare provided it was chosen by the individual rather than supplied by the state.

The proportion that would add a third of the cost rose from 30 per cent to 51 per cent for school fees, and from 30 per cent to 57 per cent for health insurance. By now the proportions might have risen further. And, of course, if nothing had to be added, they would have been higher still.

These results did not suggest a ready willingness to pay more in taxes for state education or medical care in the 1960s or 1970s. On the contrary, they indicate a growing inclination to retreat from, or go beyond, state welfare in favour of private education and medicine, even at the expense of paying for part of their costs as well as losing part of the taxes paid for state education and medical services.

It may be that opinion since 1978 (the year of the last IEA survey) has fundamentally changed in favour of higher taxes for state provision. That could be true insofar as there is a public apprehension, true or untrue, that the expenditure cuts have been mostly at the expense of the poor, the defenceless, and the most deserving. But it has yet to be understood by the British that it is the old, the poor, and the ill-housed with little influence who are least able to escape from bad schools, inattentive doctors or insensitive hospitals. If the taxpayers has tears, let him shed them for the underdogs in the welfare state. Much, if not most, of additional taxes and government expenditure would go in higher salaries for organized officials and wages for unionized workers rather than to the uninfluential, the excluded and the non-joiners.

But concern for the underdog, which in Britain long pre-dated the welfare state, does not exhaust the mixture of public attitudes to taxation and government expenditure. A sense of guilt about the poor does not exclude concern for those nearer the taxpayer – himself, his family, his friends, and his favoured good causes, including the very people – the old, and the poor, and the sick – who may fare worst in the welfare state. The taxpayer cannot be regarded as callous if he is concerned about the quality of the schooling supplied by the state for his children, or the medical care provided for his family. But here the record has been of deterioration that derives from the centralized political control, the bureaucratizaton, and the trade union influence that are inherent in state welfare. The deterioration did not start with the cuts, which began in 1975, and increased expenditure would not remove it.

Nor are the longer-term economic trends likely to make for a public opinion more in favour of a taxation and state welfare, as the opinion polls claim to have found. Rising living standards, even if limited to the 87 per cent in regular official employment, encourage more people with smaller incomes to want, and enable them to pay for, better education and medicine than the state claims (and fails) to supply equally out of taxation that is grudgingly paid and increasingly avoided and evaded. And technological change is facilitating newer forms of education and medical care, from which children and the sick could benefit, that the state has suppressed.

It would therefore not have been surprising if the trends in the 1960s and 1970s had been continued into the 1980s, and if they are now to be expected in the 1990s. The recent polls cannot therefore be accepted as unfailing indicators of trends in public opinion and preferences between taxation and government expenditure.

No politician, political party or government should act on the Gallup-type or SCPR-type polls on unspecified total expenditure and benefits unless checked by more refined priced surveys based on specified individual spending (in taxes) and individual benefits (in services).

For decades since the war price-less opinion polls had found that 80 per cent or more of national samples said they approved of the NHS or the welfare state. The IEA surveys found otherwise. This was the effort of a small research institute to discover the truth behind the opinion polls. The government, and the opposition parties, could check these results, first, by larger samples, second, by more refined surveys, or third, and best of all, by returning (some) taxes and seeing, in the real world, how the people spend them.

Political taxes: abolition, not reform

Barry Bracewell-Milnes
Source: Economic Affairs, October/November 1986, 7, 1, p. 19.

Political taxes are intended not to raise revenue but to discomfit political opponents or to serve other purposes of ideology rather than government finance. The contemporary sense of the phrase in Britain dates from the second half of the 1970s; it achieved a badge of recognition when it was used in a newspaper article by Sir Geoffrey Howe, later Chancellor of the Exchequer.[1]

The political taxes are inheritance tax (capital transfer tax, estate duty, succession duty); capital gains tax; the higher rates of income tax (formerly surtax); the investment income surcharge (now abolished); and wealth tax (often threatened but not so far introduced in Britain).

These taxes yield little despite their high rates. Inheritance tax is forecast to yield £910 million in 1986-7 or 0.77 per cent of total taxes and royalties (excluding national insurance contributions). Capital gains tax on individuals and trusts is forecast to yield £1,050 million (0.89 per cent). The investment income surcharge was bringing in only a few hundred million at its abolition in 1984. By contrast, the yield of a penny point on the basic rate of income tax is about £1,200 million. The yield of the higher rates of income tax is not published except in answer to parliamentary questions; but it is broadly of the order of a penny on the basic rate of income tax.

Thus inheritance tax, capital gains tax on individuals and trusts and the higher rates of income tax could be abolished at a revenue cost of only some three points on the basic rate of income tax – the amount by which Sir Geoffrey Howe reduced the basic rate in 1979. Capital gains tax on companies brings in the equivalent of about half a penny on the basic rate. Thus all these taxes could be abolished for about £4 billion.

Four billion pounds is about 5 per cent of the increase in taxation since 1978–9, the last year before the present Government came to power. If taxation had increased by 177 per cent instead of 187 per cent between 1978–9 and 1986–7,[2] this small reduction in the growth of taxation would have provided the resources to abolish the political taxes. Although chancellors are generally short of money from year to year, in a longer-term perspective the political taxes are not required for their revenue unlike serous revenue-raisers such as income tax and value-added tax.

With the exception of higher rates of tax on earnings, all the political taxes bear on saving. Because of its time dimension, saving is or can be subject to a wide range of taxes, to which there are no equivalents in the taxation of earning and spending. Saving may be taxed at the outset through stamp duty; on the income it generates through the basic and higher rates of income tax and the investment income surcharge; annually on its value through a wealth tax; on the increase in its value through a capital gains tax; on transfers of assets at death or during life, levied either on the transferor or on the recipient or even on both (as in Italy); and through various once-for-all levies on income or capital which may be more recurrent than the name implies: *wieder die Einmaligen* in the sardonic German phrase – 'once again the once-for-all' – and British experience confirms the aptness of this comment.

Why so many taxes on saving? Not all of them are currently levied in Britain; but every one either is levied or has been levied or has been the subject of a government white paper; and in countries like Sweden saving is subject to the full treatment.

Part of the answer is the instinct of tax officials and their political masters or fellow-travellers to tax both whatever moves and whatever does not: a tax on walking, on running, on sitting, on kneeling, on lying and on standing still. It is also easier to part the taxpayer from his money through a series of imposts even if the tax base is essentially the same. For example, some 80 per cent or more of the tax base of income tax, national insurance employees' contributions, national insurance employers' contributions and value-added tax is employees' spending out of earnings. And if it were more generally understood that, through the combination of these various imposts the state takes over half of the typical employee's earnings, even at well below the average income, the pressure for tax reduction would be much stronger than it is: a single tax at over 50 per cent would assure more resistance than the use of four separate levies in essentially the same function.

In *La Terre* Emile Zola gives a vivid description of the taxation of the peasantry under the feudal system. The following excerpt gives the flavour:

> The common man [...] paid in order to channel the rainwater from the moat into his land, he paid for the cloud of dust raised by the feet of his sheep along the paths in the summer, during the droughts. Anyone who failed to pay in cash paid with his body and his time, talliable and liable to forced labour at his lord's pleasure, forced to plough and harvest and reap and prune the vine and clean out the moat of his castle, to build and maintain the roads. And then there were payments in kind; and the rights of banality, the mill, the oven, the winepress, which cost him a quarter of his crops; and then watch and guard duty, which, when dungeons were abolished, were commuted into money payments.[3]

This tax regime may have been inspired both by the instinct to shoot at whatever moves and by the idea that more can be raised from a given tax base by a combination of levies than could be raised if they were aggregated into a single whole. This instinct and this idea seem to be important influences on the present British fiscal scene. Absolutely, the principal losers are employees spending out of earnings, because this is the larger part of the total tax base; but in proportion to the money at stake, the principal losers are savers.

The multiplicity of taxes on saving also owes something to the belief that capital is a tax base separate from income, or alternatively that there are three independent tax bases (or taxable objects) – income, spending and capital – each of which ought to contribute to the revenue in accordance with some concept of fairness or taxable capacity. This idea underlay, for example, the White Paper on Capital Transfer Tax and the Green Paper on Wealth Tax in 1974.[4] But it is not so. Ultimately, there are only two tax bases, spending and saving, of which the former is much the larger. Income is either spent or saved, and capital is past saving; neither income nor capital provides a tax base additional to saving and spending. There is no call for more than one general tax on saving; and the tax on saving that yields the most revenue and is the most deeply embedded in the tax system is the tax on investment income.[5]

In his 1986 Budget speech, the Chancellor said: 'My two previous Budgets abolished three unnecessary taxes: the National Insurance Surcharge, the Investment Income Surcharge and Development Land Tax. The abolition of the tax on lifetime gifts adds a fourth.

Mr Lawson omitted to add that the 1984 Budget introduced two new taxes (on controlled foreign companies and on offshore funds), both of which fall principally on saving. Nevertheless, the aim of abolishing unnecessary taxes rather than merely reforming them is admirable; and the political taxes are the first candidates for abolition.

The first effect of political taxes is to reduce output. Indeed, if output is not reduced, some of their advocates infer that the political taxes are not heavy enough. Thus according to Henry Simons:[6] The optimum degree of progression (in taxation) must involve a distinctly adverse effect upon the size of the national income.... It is only an inadequate degree of progression which has no effect upon production and economic progress.

Second, the poor pay most. Rich people's living standards are the least affected by the political taxes of which they are the target. The rich have both the opportunity and the incentive to draw on reserves, since additional taxes on saving make it economically cheaper to do so. For poorer taxpayers, by contrast, who are spending most or all of their income, a fall in income means a corresponding fall in living standards.

Third, the redistributive effects of political taxes are often perverse because a reduction in the inequality of income or wealth may be accompanied by an increase in the inequality of spending. In particular, it has been argued that all taxes on saving are regressive in terms of spending (in other words, they increase the rich people's proportion of total spending and reduce the proportion of the poor).[7]

There is no popular clamour for the retention of the political taxes in Britain (nor, indeed, for their abolition), as is shown by several recent examples. There was no outcry of disapproval when Sir Geoffrey Howe reduced the top rate of income tax from 98 per cent to 75 per cent in 1979, nor when Nigel Lawson abolished the investment income surcharge and reduced the top rate of capital transfer tax from 75 per cent to 60 per cent in 1984, nor when he abolished the tax on lifetime gifts in 1986. Similarly for the abolition of estate duty in Australia and Canada in recent years. In each of these cases, and others that could be cited, the taxpayers concerned welcomed the tax reduction, an economic distortion was removed and the majority of the population remained more interested in the taxes that affected them more closely.

Support for the political taxes is confined to a small but influential group consisting mainly of politicians and political activitists, government officials, journalists and academics. But the emotional and intellectual commitment to the political taxes sometimes met with in these quarters finds little echo outside. The committed supporters of these taxes constitute no real obstacle to their abolition.

In a paper published in June 1986 entitled 'The direction of tax reform: controlling the urge to change the system', the Institute of Directors set out a quantified programme of tax reform through tax reduction over the next ten years. At the end of this period, the top rate of income tax and of value-added tax would be 10 per cent and all the political taxes would be abolished; the taxes on capital would be abolished within the first two years. As we have noted, the abolition of the political taxes is not a costly exercise; the considerations are political rather than economic.

Capital transfer tax/inheritance tax is perhaps the most damaging of all taxes in relation to its yield, because it strikes at the heart of a capitalist economy – people owning their own firms and taking their own decisions with their own money. The 1985 Annual Report of the International Bureau of Fiscal Documentation notes: 'More and more countries in Asia and the Pacific are abolishing their gift and/or estate duty systems (Sri Lanka, India, Bangladesh, Fiji, Pakistan) or have simplified the rate schedule (Singapore, Malaysia). The revenue from these taxes is very small and often does not justify the cost of collection'.[8]

These are all former British territories whose estate duty systems have proved an unwanted element of their inheritance from Britain.

Most of the yield of capital gains tax still comes from inflationary gains because of price rises, despite the introduction in 1982 of indexation for subsequent price rises. Indexation has made an already complex tax virtually unintelligible. This illustrates the principle that ending the political taxes is better than mending them. There is no form of capital gains tax that is at once simple, fair and a serous revenue raiser. The only radical solution to the imbroglio of capital gains tax is its abolition.

With $19/20$ or more of the yield of income tax coming from the basic rate, the tax is already substantially proportional. The higher rates yield little revenue; but they bear disproportionately on entrepreneurs and others with a high potential for wealth creation and are thus disproportionately damaging to the economy. The British basic rate of income tax, at 29 per cent is now higher than the new top United States rate of 28 per cent. It is not enough to reduce the higher rates of income tax, still less to extend the slices of income on which they are charged. The only real solution is to abolish the higher rates and levy income tax in equal proportions.

Inheritance tax, capital gains tax and the higher rate of income tax may be regarded as the only general political taxes at present levied in Britain. But a programme of long-term tax reduction on the lines proposed by the Institute of Directors would have the welcome by-product of facilitating the abolition of a number of sectoral and discriminatory political taxes, of which two have been mentioned (the taxes on controlled foreign companies and on offshore funds).

A programme for streamlining the tax system by abolishing unnecessary taxes could with advantage take in the abolition of the remaining tax on capital (stamp duties) and discriminatory levies such as the minor excise duties (the forecast yield in 1986–7 is £20 million). But the heart of any programme for streamlining the system is inevitably the abolition of the political taxes.

Welfare taxation: opting out to shrink the state

Colin Clark
Source: Economic Affairs, February/March 1987, 7, 3, p. 38.

To restate the obvious, taxation, in all its forms, is now far too high. Likewise government spending, government borrowing and government employment, which all go on inexorably rising.

Politicians, journalists and academics sometimes criticize the burden and extent of taxation, but when they are asked, quite reasonably, where they would cut government expenditure, they give evasive or trivial answers.

In 1976, when she was Leader of the Opposition, I had a discussion with Mrs Thatcher. I told her that she would not get things straight until people paid for their own health and education. 'That', she said, 'is for the election after next'. The election after next has come and gone, and another is looming; and there is no sign of such change. Indeed, government expenditure goes on rising. Health and education, together with pensions, which rise with the price index number, are the really substantial items in government expenditure. They are the 'tax eaters', to use the luminous phrase coined by William Cobbett, the early nineteenth-century writer.

But, it will be said, the average family cannot afford to pay for its own health and education, still less to make provision for a pension in the case of old age or infirmity. Such a statement is, when more closely examined, nonsensical. The average family does pay for all it receives in the way of these services, but it pays through taxation, not directly. It pays in addition for a large and unnecessarily cumbrous bureaucracy, to redistribute its money for it. How else, might one ask, are these services paid for? Politicians have succeeded in creating the impression that there are a few rich taxpayers somewhere who cover the main burden of the costs of social services. This notion is far from the truth. Taxation of the wealthy only contributes a very small proportion of government expenditure. The services received by the average family have to be paid for by taxation on the average family.

If people could provide these services for themselves there would be large reductions in taxation. But how could this advance be brought about? People have arranged their lives on the assumed availability of pensions, free medicine, free education, and so on. It is governments which have created these expectations, and to fail to meet them, even in part, would be contrary not only to political expediency, but also to natural justice. The ensuing reductions in taxation would not always go to those who had lost social service and pension benefits.

The only possible solution – it may sound odd, but it has been privately endorsed by a leading taxation expert as practicable – is to introduce the new order progressively by creation of two classes of taxpayers. One class would receive social services and pay taxation as now, while the other class would be largely or completely exempted from personal income tax, but would have to make their own provision for all social services. The young and other new entrants to the labour market, and immigrants, would all be put into the non-taxpaying class, and would have to make their own provisions for social services and pensions. Voluntary transfers from the taxpaying to the non-taxpaying class would be permitted, within certain income limits.

But would there not be people who would happily accept non-taxpaying status, and still expect the state to do something for them when they became old or destitute? There would have to be a certain measure of compulsory saving, in order that such cases should be covered. Everyone should be required to purchase a minimum quantity of lifetime annuities, protected against price increases. This asset should be inalienable. The young should be subject to a larger requirement of compulsory saving, to be refunded to them when they wanted to buy a house or otherwise on reaching mature age.

Annuities are clearly the most economical form of provision, because nobody knows how long he or she is going to live. But how can they be protected against price rises? Some people are convinced that by the implementation of fiscal and monetary policies, or a combination thereof, prices can be stabilized. So much the better, if it happens. But if future governments cannot be trusted to maintain stable prices, the annuities scheme will have to be government-operated. Insurance companies cannot predict prices, or make financial provision for price increases. A better method would be to have the scheme administered by insurance companies, with the government making a block grant to them to cover price increases annuities provided by them.

Men and women would hold annuities separately, with or without marriage. We already have too many taxes or social service provisions which, in effect, discourage marriage. For instance, an unemployed man or woman, whose spouse is working, will lose unemployment benefit. The tax on two-earner families, at higher rates, can be considerably higher than if they were taxed separately unmarried. Single parents supporting children may lose much by marrying. And so on. The scheme should not apply to children below working age.

All children and adults should be covered by adequate medical insurance, some measure of which should be compulsory. It should be sufficient to cover foreseeable medical requirements, but exceptional cases of chronic illness or injury would have to be treated at government expense. Insurance should be offered by competing insurance companies, or under variants of the Kaiser scheme used in America, where hospitals set themselves up as public corporations, providing both hospital care, where required, and also (at a subsidized rate) general practitioner service. The hospitals under such a scheme would have a strong incentive to avoid unnecessary expense.

The annuities – bearing in mind that each adult member of a family would have some – should provide for a minimum amount of consumption.

We may put this minimum (bearing in mind that any dependants will have their own annuities) at £2,500 per year. A sixty-five-year-old (man or woman) has an average expectation of life of 15.2 years. To provide an annuity of £2,500 per year over this period will require £26,175 at an assumed real interest rate of 5 per cent or £30,150 at an assumed rate of 3 per cent. To accumulate such funds over the ages 25–65 would require annual savings of £217–£400, according to the above assumptions about the rate of interest.

This income, from a source which could not be alienated, is intended to cover the minimum requirements not only of age, but also of illness and unemployment, for which no state provision would be made other than in exceptional cases. Evidence is building up – British, Australian and American – that after disentangling other statistical variables, generous state provision for unemployment increases the amount of unemployment. We should indeed be impressed by the number of cases in which low-wage fathers of families go on working when they know their income is hardly above what they could get by claiming unemployment benefit.

Everyone should be encouraged to take out more than the legal minimum. Non-taxpayers would have to make their own provision for health, education, pensions and a variety of minor social services.

Under this scheme, the levying of personal income tax would eventually disappear, except for incomes above a high amount, which was the original idea of Pitt in 1798 and Peel in 1843 when they introduced income tax. To an ever-increasing degree, income tax is now a tax on wages and salaries, applicable even below the poverty line. With taxation at anything like its present rate, evasion on incomes other than wages and salaries is increasingly prevalent.

All political parties are committed to a monstrous welfare state demanding perpetually increasing taxation. Yet people have been led to expect the continuation of government welfare services on this enormous scale, and have a real sense of injustice if deprived of them. Some such device as proposed above seems to be the only way out of these difficulties.

What about policy to help the rich? A prime example is provided by subsidies to farmers. People are taxed so that the countryside is destroyed by the production of crops that no one wants to buy. Abolish these subsidies and let farmers compete in world markets. That will cut spending and, again, another benefit will follow. British farmers will compete to produce what Britain's soils and climate conspire to produce most efficiently. Britain will no longer be competing with underdeveloped countries. At the moment, the UK gives these producers aid to help them develop and compete in world markets, then subsidizes farms at home, so that the people who have been aided cannot compete. And the British government behaves this way not only in agriculture, but in industry as well – cloth and clothing manufacture, for example. The illogic seems obvious to everyone except government.

And finally to interest groups. Politicians used to buy votes, and laws were passed in an attempt to prevent this abuse. An example I recently discovered is that no alcoholic liquor can be supplied in a public place in Missouri on an election day – politicians formerly could buy a vote for the price of a cocktail. They still buy votes today, but by other means, and now with the taxpayers' money, not their own. They instead make lavish provisions for some interest group at the expense of taxpayers in general. None of these expenditures is a public good; indeed, to favour the interest group, they are often explicitly private – clubs, for example. Cut it out.

There is ample scope for cuts on government spending if one recollects the basic principles of public finance. The government should recollect these principles and carry out these cuts.

The ethics of tax and expenditure decisions

T. Nicolaus Tideman
Source: *Economic Affairs*, August/September 1986, 6, 6, p. 26.

David Stockman has provided a remarkably candid account of the processes by which tax and expenditure decisions were made when he was the Director of the US Office of Management and Budget. His reports of how concessions with principle were made to accommodate whichever politicians were required to form a successful coalition are startling and yet consistent with what has long been said about political practice. A few examples will illustrate the consistency. As a result of a 1980 campaign commitment that had been made to Jesse Helms (Senator from the tobacco-growing state of North Carolina), Stockman reveals, no effort was made by the Reagan Administration to abolish the tobacco acreage allotment programme, despite its bald inconsistency with the Reagan Administration's free-market philosophy.[1] Stockman saw the Clinch River Breeder Reactor as inconsistent with free-market philosophy, but he declined to oppose it because it was important to Howard Baker, the Senate Majority Leader.[2] Later it became necessary to placate 'The Gypsy Moths' – the moderate to liberal northeastern Republicans:

> I had done my best not to 'overlook' the Gypsy Moths. They had a list a mile long of cuts they wanted restored, and I had accommodated them where I could. My notes from a meeting with about thirty of them the week before shows just how expensive the session had been.
> Conrail – work out to the satisfaction of Lee, Lent and Madigan.
> Amtrak – add back $112 million.
> Low-income energy – add back $400 million.
> Elementary and special education – add back $300 million.

CETA youth and training – add back $200 million.
DOE weatherization – add back $200 million.
Medicaid cap – increase to six per cent in FY 1982.
Guaranteed student loans – $100 million add back, plus rewrite formula for families above $25,000 income.
For victory on the House floor the magic number was 218. We needed that many votes and not one less. With none to spare, each vote became all the more precious – and all the more expensive.[3]

British experience, with its strong parties and single-party governments, does not offer the same evidence of such readily detectable wheeling and dealing to secure the passage of legislation. Nevertheless, the holders of marginal seats can be seen to have disproportionate influence on legislation. And it would be rash to assert that American-style political trading would not occur in the event of a hung Parliament.

It is interesting to ask what, if anything, is wrong with political trading. Is this anything other than a spirit of compromise and democracy at work? A difficulty arises from a tension between two conceptions of the legislative function. On the one hand, legislators are expected to pass laws that promote the general good. On the other hand, legislators are expected to promote the particular interests of their supporters. If legislation is supposed to promote the general good, political trading amounts to wilful dereliction of duty by legislators. They pass laws that they know not to be good to secure the support of other legislators who have the bad judgment not to recognize the good in other proposals. But if legislation is supposed to serve the supporters of the legislators, political trading is simply a matter of securing the best deal that is possible under the prevailing circumstances. No opprobrium should be attached to it. Some means of dealing with the conflict between these two perspectives is required.

One way of dealing with the conflict is to deny that there can be any inconsistency. In this way of thinking, whatever benefits for one's supporters can be secured by legislative action, the very fact of approval proves that they are consistent with the general good. The difficulty with this approach is that it makes it impossible to argue that legislation ought to be passed because it is good. If legislative enactment is the test of whether a proposal is good, legislative rejection proves that a proposal was not good, and no assertion about the merit of a proposal is valid before its passage or rejection. To take this approach, we would have to deny ourselves the use of moral language in deciding whether proposals will receive legislative approval.

It is almost impossible to imagine a society abiding by a convention that moral language would not be used in discussing legislative proposals. Moral ideas are firmly embedded in our ways of thinking about legislation. But even if it could be done, there would be reasons not to do it. People like to be morally consistent, and so the idea that only moral legislation may be passed provides a restraining influence on legislative behaviour. For example, even if they could get away with it, legislators would almost certainly refrain from passing legislation that transferred money from one completely arbitrary group to another. Tax and expenditure proposals are limited to those that can be advocated with moral language. Another example of moral ideas constraining the behaviour of legislators is provided by the British practice of deferring to the European Court of Human Rights when it is politically unpopular and there is no legal obligation to do so.

There is a general benefit from the restraints that morality places upon the behaviour of legislators: potential losses to individuals from legislative enactments are thereby limited. While potential gains are also limited, there is nevertheless a net benefit from the restraint: the limitation on gains and losses reduces expenditures on influencing legislation, what economists call rent-seeking expenditures. As rent-seeking expenditures are a net drain on the economy as a whole, their reduction provides a general benefit.

How then are the roles of legislators as implementors of good laws and as advocates of their supporters' interests to be reconciled? The judiciary deals with the problem of conflict between advocacy and judgment by employing a code of conduct which specifies that no one should participate in decisions where he or she has a special interest. In defending the idea of judicial review of legislation, James Madison gives an articulate statement of the common-sense reason for not having issues decided by interested parties:[4]

> No man is allowed to be a judge in his own cause, because his interest would certainly bias his judgment, and, not improbably, corrupt his integrity. With equal, nay, with greater reason, a body of men are unfit to be both judges and parties at the same time; yet what are many of the most important acts of legislation but so many judicial determinations, not indeed concerning the rights of single persons, but concerning the rights of large bodies of citizens? And what are the different classes of legislators but advocates and parties to the cause which they determine?

While he did not say so, the logic of Madison's argument leads to the idea that legislators should not vote on issues where they or their constituents have a special interest. Here is an idea that is so radical that it may be almost unthinkable, but suspend judgment briefly and consider the possibility.

Present institutions already offer hints of recognition of the validity of this principle. The US Constitution specifies that a Congress may raise the pay of a future Congress, but may not raise its own pay. The US requires its legislators to report their financial interests, and the British Parliament has adopted a similar (voluntary) practice. Local councillors are required to disclose any financial interests they have in pending issues and to refrain from speaking or voting on the matter.

The judgment of legislators can be corrupted not only by their own financial interests but by that of constituents who might decline to re-elect them if they did not support their constituents' special interests at the expense of the general good. Thus the rationale for excluding a legislator with a financial interest from participating in a decision extends to the exclusion of a legislator whose constituents have a special interest in an issue. But here I would propose a distinction between a personal interest and an interest of one's constituents. While a personal interest reasonably excludes participation in debate as well as voting, there is an important role for legislators as advocates of their constituents' special interests. While disinterested judgment is required to determine whether any particular special interest can be accommodated consistently with the general good, someone must present the case for every special interest, and legislators are the logical ones to do it. Because financial interest is not the only source of clouded judgment, it would be reasonable to specify that anyone who felt strongly enough about an issue to want to speak on it would be regarded as unable to provide a disinterested judgment.

How could a principle of separation of advocacy and judgment for legislators be implemented in the UK? The register of financial interests would be replaced with a separate register for each issue before Parliament. An MP would list himself in the register if he had a financial interest in the matter, if his constituents had a special interest in the matter, or if he felt so strongly about it that he wanted to speak on it. The MPs on the register (except those with personal financial interests) would argue the issue, in terms of the general good, and the MPs not on the register would vote.

Such a system could not guarantee to prevent all forms of legislative chicanery, but it would remove an important barrier to the belief by sensible people that that which emerges from the legislative process represents a reasonable approximation to the general good. Such an institution in the USA would have kept David Stockman and the Reagan administration from promoting the inconsistent bundle of measures that the Reagan tax and expenditure programme became in the hands of Congress.

Notes

More state welfare or lower taxes?

1   David Owen and David Steel, Weidenfeld, 1987.
2   *Hansard,* House of Lords (column 37), 2 February 1987.
3   Analysed in Ralph Harris and Arthur Seldon, *Overruled on Welfare.* Institute of Economic Affairs, 1979.

Political taxes: abolition, not reform

1 'The Slow, Sure Path to Prosperity', *Daily Telegraph*, 30 April 1979.
2 From £40,942 million (*Financial Statement and Budget Report*, 1978–9, 20) to £117.6 billion (*Financial Statement and Budget Report*, 1986–7, 7).
3 Penguin Books, Harmondsworth, 1980, 87–8.
4 Cmnd. 5705 and Cmnd. 5704. HMSO, London.
5 This argument is discussed more fully in my *Is Capital Taxation Fair? The Tradition and the Truth.* Institute of Directors, London, 1974, especially Chapter 4.
6 *Personal Income Taxation.* University of Chicago Press, 1938, 19.
7 *cf.* my *The Taxation of Industry: Fiscal Barriers to the Creation of Wealth.* Panopticum Press. Upminster, 1981. Appendix III. The three effects discussed here are the theme of this book.
8 p. 24 Ibid.

The ethics of tax and expenditure decisions

1 *The Triumph of Politics*, 154.
2 Ibid., 155.
3 Ibid., 223–4.
4 *The Federalist*, 10, 26 November 1987.

5 Education

Parent power to privatize schools

Michael McCrum
Source: Economic Affairs, April/May 1987, 7, 4, p. 32.

Gas, telephones and British Airways have been privatized; London Transport is next in line. State ('maintained') schools should follow soon. With so much dissatisfaction among parents with the state system, the time has come for the consumer to be allowed a direct say.

As a start, the suggestion recently made by the Hillgate group, the authors of *Whose Schools?*, deserves serious consideration:

> parents should be offered a choice between a place at a state school, funded by a direct capital grant at the local per capita level, and receiving a credit at the national per capital level, which they could then use to buy a place at a private school.... This credit could be taxed for all who pay tax at the standard rate.

Such a scheme would at last implement Clause 76 of the 1944 Education Act which states that children 'are to be educated in accordance with the wishes of their parents'. It would mark the end of the near-monopolistic system in which most of the nation's parents, unless they move house, have no effective choice of school for their children and are bound to accept what their local authority allocates.

Chief Education Officers and others working in Local Education Authorities, and the National Union of Teachers, are passionately opposed to such a suggestion. They claim that proper educational provision is far too complex to be left to the whim of parents. Parents could not possibly be trusted to choose wisely. Only the middle-class parent would make good use of the education credit (a certificate issued by the government, equivalent to, and earmarked for, the school fee). As one Chief Education Officer of a large northern local education authority expressed it,

> I have to cope with many parents whose own education, and indeed IQ, are such that they cannot possibly know enough to be able to make a

meaningful choice for their children. We have parents who force their children to leave school at the earliest possible moment; we have parents who rely on our colleagues of the Social Service field even to run their own homes; we have parents who are illiterate; parents who are educationally subnormal, but their children should not suffer because of this....

Essentially, this is the 'Big Brother knows best' approach; it is the opposite of democratic. It assumes that someone other than the parent is both more competent to choose and should have the right to decide, whether the child's parents agree with the decision or not. But there is no reason that parents should not take expert advice (indeed, LEAs would have a useful role in providing a back-up advisory service for the small number of illiterate or otherwise disadvantaged parents), as most of us do in choosing our doctor, dentist, or insurance policy, or in buying a house, a car, or a washing machine, or deciding which package-tour holiday is best. It is precisely because a credit system would restore to all parents the responsibility of choosing, and enable them to learn how to choose, that it is democratic and desirable as such. Prospectuses of all schools would be available; parents would soon learn what to look for and would take the trouble to visit them before deciding to which to offer their patronage.

No doubt Citizens' Educational Advice Bureaux, or their equivalent, would have to be set up, but they are required now. Education credits would give all parents, the large majority of whom care a good deal about their children's school opportunities, a right of choice which at present only a very small minority have the money to exert. It is the poorer, not the well-to-do, parent (and child) who would benefit most.

Evidence that this suggestion is not impracticable idealism can be found in Assistant Commissioner Coode's evidence to the Royal Commission on Popular Education of 1861 (known as the Newcastle Commission). It has long been forgotten that before W.E. Forster's 1870 Education Act, which introduced state education, there were two-and-a-half million pupils aged between five and thirteen (of a total population of nineteen-and-a-half million) in private schools, of which only a tiny percentage were in so-called public schools. Coode said:

> It is a subject of wonder how people so destitute of education as labouring parents commonly are, can be such just judges as they also commonly are of the effective qualifications of a teacher. Good school buildings and the apparatus of education are found for years to be practically useless and deserted, when, if a master [by which he means what we today would call a Headmaster] chances to be appointed who understands his work, a few weeks suffice to make the fact known, and his school is soon filled, and perhaps found inadequate to demand of the neighbourhood, and a separate girls' school or infants' school is soon found to be necessary.[1]

In one school, cited by Coode in the Newcastle Commission Report, the number of pupils had been raised by an effective Headmaster from three to 180 in fifteen months in a school in a coal-mining area. Even when a strike occurred and the colliers' capacity to pay the fees was much reduced, they somehow managed to keep most of their children at this school, 'such had now become the desire of the children to remain at school, and of their parents to keep them there'.[2]

There is no doubt that, before the establishment in 1870 of state schools, many working-class and other parents made satisfactory choices of schools for their children. In any event, until parents have the right to choose and the money to make that right effective, they live in what economists call 'rational ignorance', since they cannot be expected to take the trouble to find out what is involved. Almost all parents are likely to be better judges of their own family circumstances and desires than local government politicians and officials. And those who are not now would learn in time.

As soon as parents have a real choice of school (that is, by having the power to withdraw custom and send their children elsewhere if they so choose), they will feel that they have a real say in their children's education. Having worked in independent schools for twenty years, I am well aware of how over a whole range of issues (exam results, curriculum, behaviour, dress, games and other out-of-school activities) a school reacts to parental pressure, and is critically sensitive to their demands and suggestions. The knowledge that, in the last resort, dissatisfied parents will remove their child provides the school authorities with a healthy incentive to take the consumer's wishes seriously. In such circumstances a school feels clearly accountable to its pupils and their parents, for the economic necessity of keeping a school full gives an edge to accountability that the state system lacks. Even the introduction of parent-governors is nothing like as effective.

There are at least four more advantages in a credit system, which will in the long run benefit the poorer parents most: first, parental responsibility for their children's schooling will be substantially increased. Truancy, for example, would be likely to be much less of a problem because parents would cooperate more readily with the teachers. Once they became aware that their views really counted with the teachers, most parents, not merely some, would take a much closer interest in what went on at school and in how their children were doing.

Secondly, schools would respond far more quickly and willingly to the educational requirements and demands of each generation of parents and children. An independent school feels accountable to its pupils (and their parents) and thus does all it can to give them the education they want. Pupils' happiness can, of course, be overrated as a criterion of a school's success, for it is possible for a school to seem happy and yet achieve little. But since the young, especially adolescents, are demanding and critical, happiness is usually a reliable measurement of effectiveness. If pupils come to believe that their teachers do not listen to them, if they think they are missing out compared with their peers in other schools, they will express their frustration to their parents and urge them to transfer them to another school. Some competition between schools tends to raise standards all round. The worse the school, the sooner it would have to change its head or close. Schools dependent on parental choice for pupil admissions find that their strengths and weaknesses are soon known. Those that fail to satisfy parents would no longer, as at present, remain in existence, for they would be unable to recruit pupils.

Thirdly, it is probable that more private money will be spent on education. Some parents will wish to add to their state credit from their taxed income in order to afford the fees of an above-average, and more expensive, school. That more financial resources should be available for education must be desirable.

Fourthly, once former state schools were financed directly through parents armed with purchasing power rather than indirectly by state subvention, the sharp distinction between the state and private sectors of education would tend to disappear, for some independent schools cost no more than their maintained counterpart. Few would deny that this development, too, is eminently desirable. British society, which at present seems to be ever more polarized, would thus suffer less from class antagonism and would gain in unity.

There is no reason that such a radical scheme for parental education credits should be introduced all at once. It could be developed gradually as parental wishes dictated and as the necessary administrative changes were put into effect. The present financial arrangements which depend on a combination of rates and taxes are complex and cannot be changed in the twinkling of an eye. But it is high time that at least those local authorities which already wish to introduce some such scheme, if only on an experimental basis, were enabled by government legislation to make a start.

In a fully developed and genuine democracy there should be a wide variety of educational opportunities, and the most effective way to ensure this spreads at the primary and secondary stages is to give all parents the necessary financial power to exercise their right to choose the educational programme that they think best suited to their children.

Per capita funding: the next step to better schools

John Marks
Source: Economic Affairs, April/May 1987, 7, 4, p. 34.

Britain requires better schools. Most people, including many in education, now agree with this statement but feel powerless to do anything about it.

This is especially true in the state sector where powerful producer groups – local education authorities, teacher unions, civil servants, inspectors and advisors – have long held sway.

What then can be done? First, it must be recognized that, in education, small is often beautiful. The natural units of education are the school, the teacher and the individual pupil or student. So power must be given to the people who are most important in education – to the headteachers and to effective classroom teachers who run the schools and, above all, to the pupils and their parents.

How can this be done? For headteachers and teachers, the solution is to give them as much control as possible over their schools – always provided that they run their schools so as to attract enough pupils and maintain adequate standards. For pupils and parents, the answer is to give them much more effective choice of school and to enable them to move their children elsewhere if they are not satisfied.

The key to this transfer of power is money – both in ensuring professional competence in teachers and true accountability to parents and pupils. But money on its own is not enough, despite the claims of the National Union of Teachers and their acolytes. Much more important is how the money is spent, and how to ensure that it is used in ways which give the ultimate power to pupils and their parents.

These are the principles which lie behind the suggestion in *Whose Schools?*[1] that schools be funded by direct per capita grants from central government. Schools which continued to attract pupils would flourish. But those whose numbers fell would have less money to spend and so would have to change their ways or shrink or, in the last resort, close. And for every parent who decided to move their child from one school to another, there would be a net financial loss to the neglected school and also a comparable gain to the chosen school.

Each school would be an independent trust, operating under the law of charities, and its operation would be controlled, within national guidelines on curriculum and inspection, by its headteacher and trustees or governors. They would have control over the school budget, the appointment of teachers, teachers' salaries and conditions, admissions policy, capital spending and fund raising. Given all these extra responsibilities, it is necessary that the per capita grant should not be solely based on the annual recurrent expenditure per pupil but should also include the capital expenditure, debt charges, school meal costs and expenditure on administration, both local and national. Together these factors add 25 per cent or more to the true costs per pupil and make such costs comparable to the average fees charged by independent day schools.[2] So such per capita grants would be large enough to make the establishment of new schools a real and practical proposition.

Such autonomy would give heads and teachers the professional and financial independence they now lack and enable them to run their schools without interference from local politicians or advisors. If teachers and schools genuinely wished for advice or for in-service training, they could seek it, and pay for it, where they chose rather than having it thrust upon them as often happens at present.

Are there precedents for such wide-ranging changes involving a mixture of public finance and private initiative in individual schools? There are many, both in the UK and abroad. The principle of funding by direct per capita grants was central to the operation of the direct grant schools, abolished in 1976. It is also implicit in the assisted places scheme, in operation since 1980, and is an essential part of the new scheme for city technological colleges proposed by the Secretary of State for Education and Science in October 1986. The voluntary-aided schools, established by the 1944 Education Act, have long had considerable control over teacher appointments, admissions policies, curriculum decisions and capital expenditure. The arrangements for funding secondary schools in the Netherlands has, since 1971, had many of the features suggested,[3] as does the system of funding adopted more recently in Japan.[4] And many lessons could be learnt from the magnet schools in the United States, both about funding and about creative initiatives to revive educational opportunities for socially deprived areas of the inner cities.[5]

The time for such reforms is now. The urgency is shown by the low standards achieved in many schools across the country,[6] and in the incessant politicization of education in increasingly more local authorities.[7] The desire for change is shown by the example of the John Loughborough School, a new independent school established in Tottenham in 1981 by the Seventh Day Adventist Church. It caters largely for local West Indian children whose parents wish them to have the sort of traditional education, based on sound moral and spiritual values, which they are unable to obtain in the local state schools. The parents are mainly working-class and pay fees of £600 a year (the balance is provided by the church). The school could fill its 300 or so places three times over. Yet, given the present educational system in the UK, there is no way in which such highly desirable initiatives can be encouraged.

A major new education act is required, to encourage, and not to stifle, the sort of changes outlined above. They would benefit good schools, good heads and good teachers. And they would even help politicians in the major task of reorganizing British schools which is being forced by the dramatic drop in the birth-rate – equivalent, according to the independent Audit Commission,[8] to the closure of a fifth of the country's schools over the next five years. These proposals would transfer the onus for these difficult decisions from the few to the many – from hard-pressed local politicians to the informed choices of millions of parents.

But above all, the proposals would benefit the pupils and especially those now trapped in inadequate schools in inner cities. Twenty-five years ago the British populace was told that the system of grammar, technical and secondary modern schools then existing was wasting the talents of millions of schoolchildren, especially from working-class backgrounds. What was required was the abolition of these different types of school, and independent schools as well, in order to create a new system of comprehensive schools to cater for the whole population. Now it is claimed that the low standards reached by pupils from many comprehensive schools is due to the class background of their pupils.

The time has come to encourage good schools, of whatever kind, to flourish and to enhance the educational opportunities available to all children. This can best be done by giving to all parents a right which the rich have always enjoyed – the right, together with the financial power to back it, to choose and to obtain the most suitable education for their children.

School grants: a bar to consumer sovereignty

Marjorie Seldon
Source: Economic Affairs, April/May 1987, 7, 4, p. 39.

State education is a Pandora's box. When all manner of ills had escaped from it, hope was all that was left within. Every Secretary of State for Education hopes that his or her reforms and changes within the system, will bang the lid on the box, its undesirable inmates will not be heard of again, and a new era in schooling will begin.

Alas, the ills are creatures of the system. It is the system itself that must be changed, and that is unacceptable to most politicians who believe, despite all evidence to the contrary, that spending more money and devising new laws will be wholly or largely beneficial.

Whose Schools? proposes radical reform. The key and crucial recommendation of the authors is that local authorities should no longer administer schools, which would become charitable trusts financed by direct grants from central funds. The size of the grant would depend on the number of children enrolled, schools would control their pupil admissions, and use their income as the governors and the head wished.

These proposals are valuable as a basis for constructive debate. They tackle bravely the system itself, seeking with rational argument to persuade politicians that this is what has to be done.

Implementation would move a long way towards the goal of unrestricted entry to and exit from a school in accordance with a parent's wishes. No longer bending to the whims of some councillors' vested interest in anarchy, homosexuality and racism, the schools would function better; parents, teachers and taxpayers would be happy.

The authors believe that this gradual approach to a market in education would more certainly achieve it. First, accustom parents, politicians and the public to the devolution of financing from the local authority to the schools themselves; then, in several years, make another change: give education grants or vouchers directly to parents. It is a persuasive argument, but the doubts and objections remain.

First, the plan is only a foot in the door of full parental responsibility, which is grounded in the payment of fees by individual parents. This is the essential principle. The good (as seen in *Whose Schools?*) could become the enemy of the best if satisfaction with improvement left the foot permanently wedged in the door with the bureaucrats leaning on it from the inside. For political and bureaucratic interference are possible when the income of a school depends on a block grant from central government. Even if the size of the grant is calculated on the number of pupils, it is still a grant from government. Would politicians and bureaucrats not look for opportunities to increase their power? Conditions of pupil entry might be imposed; there might be restrictions on the hiring and firing of teachers; and what would be the attitude of a future government obsessed with social justice?

The answers to these and many more questions are unknown. But it is known that if money came directly from the consumers to the school, attempts to interfere with consumer sovereignty would be resisted by the consumers.

Second, noone can suppose that proposals to alter a system of schooling which has developed an enormous bureaucracy, union militancy and political power will not bring together the vested interests opposed to any change, including many Conservative councillors. The government would calculate whether uncertain support from parents for the direct grant would be sufficient to stifle the noisy organized opposition from producers (politicians like Frances Morrell, officials, trade union leaders like Fred Jarvis) given prime time and space in the media. It is arguable that the decibels of opposition would be no less for the halfway house of the direct grant proposals than for the goal of tax refunds or vouchers, and that this objection weakens the rationale of a step-by-step approach to the market.

Moreover, a government with the political will to change the system will want the prospect of clear, widespread and sustained popular support. Consumer sovereignty must not appear to be a matter of central government possibly saving money by distributing grants to thousands of schools rather than purchasing power to millions of parents. Neither must it appear to be a matter of administrative convenience in transferring money from schools that lose pupils to schools that receive them. Consumer sovereignty must not only be created for the middling-income and poorer parents who have never enjoyed parent power: it must be seem to be created as a new power welded into their everyday lives. Money which bypasses parents and goes direct to the schools will not be seen as a personal family benefit. Parents are concerned primarily for their own children. And a piece of paper with a cash value inscribed on it makes them customers shopping for the best school they can find. The cultural and political appeal of such a system would be enormous in all social classes, because it moves with the grain of human nature; it offers tangible proof that parents can be expected to protect their children from the unhappiness of a bad or unsuitable school. This is the power that free state schooling has denied them (and their parents before them) since 1870, and that the parents of Tower Hamlets, Brent, and many other 'deprived' areas must urgently require to be created – or, rather, recreated, since, as Professor E.G. West showed in *Education and the State*,[1] it was developing well before 1870.

Third, if a government implemented the proposals in *Whose Schools?*, the unanswered question is whether either it or its political successors would be willing to enter the maelstrom yet again after a few years to introduce the further stage of parent power? The per capita funding scheme, which is essentially bureaucratic, would have settled down; and middle-class parents, who may have gained some benefit, would be disinclined to press for, or indeed tolerate, change that would benefit the less well-off.

Fourth, although the authors have built the principle of individual freedom into their plan, it would be understood and applied least by the less articulate parents and those whose grievances about their children's schooling have been exploited by the politically astute. The less politically sophisticated parents would not be given the personal property of a grant or voucher to take where they will and use as they like.

Fifth, such parents may suspect that the new scheme will perpetuate the 'two nations' of parents with well-educated children and parents with poorly-educated children, children in the best of the state schools and children in the worst. Not for them the hypocrisy of the affluent parents who on principle would not pay fees for a school but who are eager to buy the higher-priced houses near a prestigious free state school. But lower income parents also do not want to be supplicants; they want to be customers. Paying fees with a credit or voucher would lower the barrier between the 'two nations' and supply the dignity which the supplicant lacks. Despite the care and thought which the *Whose Schools?* authors have given to this dilemma, I think many parents will feel they remain supplicants under a direct per capita grant system with the Orwellian suspicion that some supplicants will be more equal than others.

Sixth, and not least, an upsurge in the private supply of new schools to meet the new demand for parents with purchasing power is more certain with a voucher or credit system than with per capita school funding. Schools, both state and private, riding high with finance direct from government, would not welcome the start-up of competitors; they would have a strong inducement to lobby politicians for restrictions on the predictable grounds of protecting the ignorant parent and the innocent child. Per capita funding, for example, might then be confined to existing schools or to schools with a minimum number of pupils. *Whose Schools?* is far from envisaging such natural 'political' reactions.

In contrast to purchasing power for parents, direct grants to schools are likely to be a permanent tax burden. The authors deny this prospect, suggesting that schools would be encouraged to seek finance from outside sources, businesses and charities. The question is how strong such motivation would be if schools were already receiving adequate state grants and there is no provision for cutting them down if governing bodies are not active in the pursuit of alternative private finance.

Funding private schools per capita, although at a lower rate than state schools, is an idea closely linked with the voucher system but lacking its graphic appeal of personal property.

The voucher or tax credit to individual parents is a more flexible instrument than the direct grant when the objective is to reduce taxation. Education and health consume about half of government expenditure. An endless merry-go-round ensures that most parents pay more in taxes than they receive in the benefit of free education and health care. (And many parents do not consider their children's schools are a benefit.) The value of the personal tax credit or voucher could be reduced gradually as incomes rose, enabling taxation to be reduced, and making possible full consumer sovereignty.

Two obstacles to the reconstruction of schooling are the 1918 Fisher Act, which provided for free elementary schools, and the 1944 Education Act, which prohibited the payment of fees for secondary schools. Succeeding governments have not dared to question the wisdom of allowing these rules to remain on the statute book. Noone could have foreseen in 1918 or even in 1944 that three-quarters of all families with school children would own cars, that holidays abroad would be commonplace, that young couples would prefer to buy their homes than rent council houses, that shopping would become a recreational activity for all classes.

Shopping ... but when for schools? And how? *Whose Schools?* asks the right questions. It has seized the nettle of radical change. But the debate on how best to achieve it will continue.

Schools as self-seeking syndicates

Dennis O'Keeffe
Source: Economic Affairs, April/May 1987, 7, 4, p. 36.

One of the most curious developments of the last twenty years in Britain is the way in which the education system has become unpopular. Schools and colleges are now seen as not producing the kind of education which will enable British industry to compete in the fierce world of international competition.¹ Too many ill-disciplined young people seem to be emerging from school. Too many schools seem to be transmitting questionable doctrines about history, race, culture and sexual morality.²

There is no doubt about the popular appetite for reform. The political party which manages best to articulate the educational anxieties of the public may indeed gain an electoral edge in the battle, conceivably even a decisive one. But merely to know what is amiss in education is not to be provided with the tools to rectify it. In order to change education in a desirable direction, the underlying causes of the débâcle must be understood. Only then will reformers be able to gauge the changes that have any chance of success.

Some thirty year ago, Professor Milton Friedman emphasized that the advanced capitalist societies have nationalized education systems.³ Today the terminology can go a little further. Insofar as socialism means the substitution of state economic activity for private, the advanced economies have mostly socialist or quasi-socialist education systems.

Nationalization will always tend to mean inefficient education, because the resources consumed are not continuously monitored by market processes. But it will not necessarily produce an inappropriate curriculum. That depends on the attitudes of the practitioners themselves. The concern here is the schools; but the argument extends equally to medicine, broadcasting and, indeed, to all socialist production within capitalist economies. The degree of congruence of values between the nationalized sectors and the wider capitalist societies of which they are a part depends on the values of the practitioners in those sectors. Their preferences become a crucial influence. Today it is sadly apparent in education that the competence and reliability of teachers can no longer be assumed. There is a chasm between popular expectation and what the suppliers of education appear to think is good for its consumers.

From the 1940s till the early 1970s the system seemed to cope both with the introduction of compulsory secondary education for all and with a far freer, more professional approach to teachers. (Before the Second World War, teachers were much more closely regulated than after it.) Awkward questions about costs, benefits and efficiency were not asked. But since the 1970s the school system has been increasingly subjected to a process of ideological entryism by people who do not share the values of the culture within which they live.⁴ The result is that the education system, far from occupying a central place in Britain's national and economic regeneration, now constitutes a veritable albatross around recovery's neck. Not only are British standards of literacy and numeracy abysmally low by international comparison; there is permanent distortion in the labour market which prevents it clearing. There is a shortage of engineers, technologists and mathematicians, and an oversupply of social scientists. There is at present no price mechanism for rectifying this imbalance. The malfunctioning of the curriculum has now become so bad that there is a real threat of some

British inner-city areas becoming ungovernable in the near future, if indeed some have not already sunk to that lamentable state.

These are the reasons for Mr Kenneth Baker's plans both to strengthen the central apparatus of educational decision-making and devolve power on the school as an administrative unit. This, too, is what the Hillgate Group proposes in *Whose Schools?*. It is the interventionist LEAs, with their politicized inspectorates and advisors and their ideologically engaged education committees, which are subverting the transmission of knowledge and culture. Cut them out and begin again – such seems to be the thinking of Mr Baker, Professor Roger Scruton, Baroness Cox, and Dr Marks and their Hillgate supporters.

A similar contestable logic informs the proposals for devolving finance away from local authorities and on to individual schools. Most headteachers have relatively little financial control. The salary bill of teachers and other staff, much the most important item of educational finance, is managed by the local authority, as are all major capital and many important current costs. There are local variations; but in general heads in the state sector have very little financial discretion. Good administration, moreover, is often effectively penalized. Unpopular sink schools are often very generously staffed, since their redundant teachers are not obliged to move. Nor is the administrative equivalent of financial liquidation – that indispensable spur to economic efficiency – often employed. Bad schools are very rarely closed. Instead, an appalling inequity is frequently forced on successful schools: they are often obliged to absorb, by amalgamation, unsuccessful schools – the equivalent of a successful branch of Marks and Spencer being required to amalgamate with an inefficient local Co-op.

In Cambridgeshire there has been a very limited experiment in financial devolution. Headteachers may, if they wish, manage a larger proportion of the budget than has been customary. (Participation is voluntary and the scope of the scheme limited. There is no direct grant per capita funding, for example.) More dramatic financial innovations are reported from Canada and Australia. In Edmonton, Alberta, the decentralization of budgeting to schools since 1980 is beginning to attract attention from all over North America. In Australia, the state of Victoria operates the most decentralized school system in the Western world. A school council in each case is responsible for approving the school budget and some aspects of curriculum. The impetus to reform in Victoria came from a veritable haemorrhage of pupils from state to private schools. The decentralization is in any event combined with a hefty dose of state-directed and all-too-familiar egalitarian social engineering.

In the USA limited administered reforms also constitute an attempt to enhance local educational discretion. The development of specialist magnet secondary schools concentrating on lines of excellence is seen as a way of promoting choice and control by citizens, urban renewal and administrative flexibility. The specialisation of such schools is praised, in aggregate, as able to arouse much more enthusiasm in the citizens.[5]

That anyone, anywhere and in any degree, is at last attempting to prize open some gaps in the defensive monopoly of state education is a belated reaction to years of neglect. Moreover, for at least one member of the Hillgate Group, Dr John Marks, the devolution of power away from the LEA and jointly to the political centre and a school funded now by direct grant, is to be regarded as a stage on the way to a consumer-oriented education system. Yet a certain unease is justified.

Any strengthening of the corporate state is to be regarded with suspicion, and that, at least in the short run, seems to be the Hillgate proposal.[6] Whether this is in reality a process of *reculer pour mieux sauter*, is not clear.

What is clear is that it is a high-risk strategy. An intolerant or hostile administration, Labour, Alliance or authoritarian Conservative, could employ it with disastrous curricular effects. Compulsory antiracism for all? In the case of Australian and Canadian advocacy centralism, even fanatical centralism is no tactic but clearly a vital strategy. Central goals set by a company whose output is disciplined continuously by market forces, by consumers' preferences, are quite distinct from central goals set by a state when the output is determined by suppliers, however decentralized. So the verdict has to be: once-and-for-all improvements will perhaps emerge, but the forces of syndicalism and special interest may regroup in the schools. Moreover, the Hillgate Group fails to consider that a good deal of the trouble may already be intractably dug in at the schools. The policy of redistributing power from education office to school and central government looks like too little, too late, and even a threat to the polity itself.

In the late 1980s one clear fact should be discerned about the economic history of schools in the advanced societies: they drifted willy-nilly into nationalization; indeed without anyone ever writing, so far as I know, an adequate explanation of why it happened. I am more impressed by Professor E.G. West's claim that education was developing satisfactorily on a non-governmental basis.[7] But nationalization is as much a recipe for inefficiency in education as elsewhere. And when things have gone as far wrong as they have in Brent, Haringey and the Inner London Education Authority (ILEA), controlling, or trying to control, what teachers do to children is a weak alternative to what really has to be done: removing the children from their unaccountable care.

The only kind of education system appropriate to a capitalist economy is a capitalist education system. Not only is the British nationalized education system inherently inefficient; it is also the source of many curricular and general socio-economic ills. The key phenomena of capitalism, the principles of which constitute in sum the indispensable code of voluntary exchange, are private property, money transactions, money wages, the specialised division of labour and the effective circulation of information. The code of voluntary exchange is the market code. All citizens under capitalism learn to use it. It is the basis of the historically unprecedented capitalist system of internalized social control. This cohesion may be contrasted with the cruel coercion to which collectivist societies resort.

All these phenomena of the market are absent or reduced in a nationalized education. There are no clear property rights, no money transactions, extremely inadequate circulation of information, a compressed system of money wages and a grossly inefficient and insufficient specialization of labour.

The idea that the local public in any meaningful sense own the schools is empty, as a visit to many an inner-city school will show. Often they are in disrepair precisely because they do not engender any loyalty or solidarity among parents, who would not subject their children to such squalor in their homes. Yet parents do not lift a finger to remove it. When everyone is the owner, nobody is.

Just as there are no clear property rights, so there are few money transactions. Teachers' salaries are inefficiently compressed; the salary structure does not reflect the pattern of relative scarcity. The ratio after tax between top and starting salaries is less than 3:1; and no account is taken of the shortage of mathematicians and physicists. Recent legislation requires schools to distribute at least some information but there is nothing like the advertising and market research on which capitalism thrives. The 1980 Education Act requires schools to publish examination results and the 1986 Act requires every head to produce an annual report – poor, skeletal proxies of market sensitivity. Any capitalist enterprise which behaved in this way would simply go bust.

It is now widely understood, even among former advocates, that nationalization has damaging effects on efficiency. It is much less commonly understood that nationalization also changes profoundly the composition of educational output, the curriculum. In a liberal society where there is no remorselessly centralizing state, the nationalized education system passed into the hands of the educational suppliers. Children get what the suppliers decide to give them.

As costs and benefits are buried, so the link between education and the occupational structure is weakened. This process is to some extent deliberate, and in primary schools more or less total. But some of the output of secondary education is virtually unemployable – and I have met ILEA advisors who rejoice in this calamity. In many British schools the investment aspects of the curriculum are largely suppressed. At the same time, for successful students, a free-riding consumerism, which gives no attention to real consumers who pay for their education, is encouraged. Hence the rise of the social science subjects of the modern curriculum and the retardation of the subjects crucial to the future of children and the society in which they will live: science, technology, and so on. For many children of lower ability, denied the practical, instrumental training they would demand if they could, and incapable of taking part in the discursive intellectual consumerism offered to successful children, primary and, even more, secondary education are now a dismal experience. The truancy rate rockets; scarce resources are devoted to what are often hardly more than police functions; and the only appeal the secondary school has is its youth-club character. Out in the shires the Conservative suppliers of state education may congratulate themselves; and in the inner cities an army of socialist ideologues is entrenched.

The 93 per cent of children who attend maintained schools are mostly trapped. They have usually no *de facto* right of exit. The ability of the citizen to seek what he wants elsewhere if his source of supply ceases to satisfy is at the very centre of the marvel of the market system, yet in an activity as important as education this crucial choice is excluded. The real way to constrain teachers who wish to misinform children about the realities of life in capitalist society is not to police them by the state but to rescue their pupils by setting up rival and superior sources of supply. This reform cannot be achieved by administrative means. Even the bureaucratic machinery required to root out indoctrinating teachers and advisors would be cripplingly expensive, hard to control, and probably impossible to implement.

The solution to the educational dilemma is to increase the number of children in private schools. The demand for private education is income-elastic. As society gets richer, that demand will grow anyway. There is every reason to believe that demand is also price-elastic: a fall in the price of private education will lead to an expansion in demand. That fall in price, whether achieved by vouchers, tax-relief, direct grant, or the assumption by the state of a part of the salary bill of private schools, would bring stronger relief to anxious parents and neglected and exploited children than any conceivable administrative change. The solution is not to switch power about within the education system. It must be where it was growing before the state ill-advisedly assumed an educational monopoly: in the hands of the consumer, the ordinary citizen.

Some of the misinformation widespread today would probably survive the total privatization of education. There are doubtless individuals who want their children to believe that this country has a shameful history, that men are typically exploiters of women, that white people are racist bigots, and that homosexuality is a natural form of sexual expression. If people believe that sort of thing, let them pay those who would teach it to their children. What must be stopped is their ability to force this unpleasant fare on the innocent and the unwilling. My conviction is that private money is commonsense money which will soon send nonsense packing. In any event, no other remedy will do.

The school curriculum has to be denationalized. Citizens and clients must choose what curriculum they want, deciding themselves how to balance their preferences between investment and consumption, between what philosophers call intrinsic and extrinsic considerations. The classic liberal assumption is that the consumer is rational: he knows his own interest and does not require a planner or supplier to decide for him. Nor does the possible incompetence of a minority justify an administered curriculum imposed on the majority. The market is the appropriate mechanism for determining what volume, and what mix, of resources are allocated to education. It is the appropriate mechanism also for establishing the mix of subjects, teaching styles, forms of streaming or setting, types of examination and kinds of educational research.

Nor is it enough to denationalize schools. Why should anyone believe that a sophisticated society requires a supply-led tertiary education system? It is in particular the armour-plated curriculum of teacher education which requires piercing with bolts of private money. Some of the institutionalized subject-matter of teacher-training – for example, the tendentious talk about multiculturalism and antiracism – would not last six months if it had to be paid for directly by the public.

The blame for current trends in education lies partly with the ghosts of Rousseau and Lenin and possibly with the early Dr Spock. Harmful views have been imposed on ordinary people, especially the uninfluential, by the suppliers of teaching. Only consumer power can bring education back under control. History gives compelling witness that the instrument extraordinary for the establishment of consensus, in education no less than in other forms of economic activity, is the market.

Dirigisme in higher education

J.R. Shackleton
Source: Economic Affairs, February/March 1986, 6, 3, p. 18.

The recent Green Paper *Higher Education into the 1990s* represents at best a missed opportunity, and at worst is likely to exacerbate the problems facing British universities, polytechnics and colleges. And its weaknesses can be traced largely to an uncharacteristic abandonment of the economic principles the Thatcher Government has made its own.

In approaching other activities in the public sector, the Government has made its watchwords privatization and deregulation. In market after market the cosy obfuscations of the post-War mixed economy have been dispelled, and Ministers have tried to wean the country away from the corrosive belief that Whitehall-knows-best. Even the Labour Party and the trade unions have begun to realize that things will not be the same again. We have witnessed a prodigious amount of backpedalling over commitments to renationalize privatized businesses, to stop council house sales, to restore British Telecom's monopoly and to repeal Thatcherite trade union legislation.

But in higher education the lessons of the Thatcher revolution have apparently not been taken to heart. Although the Department of Education and Science (DES) is headed by one of the Prime Minister's warmest supporters, it has produced a green paper which is both analytically weak and dangerously interventionist in its implications.

Of privatization there is no sign. We are told, without explanation, that 'no substantial part of established public-funding responsibilities can be shed'. There is no discussion of the fundamental arguments used (probably erroneously) to support state involvement in higher education. These are usually some compound of economists' ideas about public goods and income distribution; we are presumably supposed to take this for granted. One obvious possibility for some element of privatization is the development of a student loan system to replace, wholly or partially, the ever-more-troublesome grant system; but it is rejected. This is particularly to be deplored at a time when the advantages of a loan system, because it increases both equality and independence of central funding and control for universities and polytechnics, are being much more widely understood. It was interesting to see left-winger Andrew Gamble writing in *The Times* recently[1] in support of a system which a few years ago was abhorred by all but a handful of market economists.

It is said that a loan system is rejected because in its initial years it would involve an increase in public spending. A similar reason may lie behind the absence of any discussion of proposals such as that recently suggested for endowing a number of universities with a capital sum and then letting them seek future earnings as best they can.

At the very least, such questions should be thoroughly examined in a document of this kind. The absence of any such discussion – or an examination of the experiences of the private University of Buckingham – suggests that closed minds and vested interests dominated in the production of this Green Paper.

What of deregulation? Again, no sign of it. In spite of the proposals of the Lindop Committee,[2] the Government will not say whether or not it intends to liberalize unwieldy validation processes for polytechnics and colleges; indeed, the green paper hints at spreading such procedures to universities.

The Council for National Academic Awards (CNAA) and the Business and Technician Education Council (B/TEC) were originally conceived as quality-control devices. By a process familiar to students of regulatory bureaucracies of all kinds, these bodies now determine what can and cannot be taught in public-sector higher education. The CNAA in particular has also extended its remit to determine the managerial and organizational structures of polytechnics and colleges. Similarly, national priorities in the allocation of resources are increasingly determined by the University Grants Committee and the National Advisory Body, front organizations for the DES. It is ironic that a government professing market liberalism should be presiding over detailed planning of a significant sector of the economy on a scale unprecedented since the end of the Second World War.

My analogy is not meant lightly. The planning of higher education displays the familiar failings of central planners everywhere: a reliance on crude indicators of output (full-time equivalent students), demand forecasts based on simple projections of the past, an increasing emphasis on performance norms (staff-student ratios) irrespective of local conditions. And, of course, a profound belief that planners know better than the market – which in this context means the preferences of both students and employers.

Take as an example the claim, a central feature of the green paper, that this country produces insufficient scientists, technicians and other vocationally-oriented personnel. This belief is the basis for the attempt to direct resources away from subjects in the arts, humanities and social sciences. No real attempt is made to substantiate this belief. We are simply told that our (more successful) competitors produce more vocationally-oriented people than we do; it is assumed that the direction of causation is self-evident.

To economists this is an odd way of thinking. We are accustomed to arguing that, if there is a shortage of a commodity then, if markets are allowed to function normally, it will be reflected in a rise in its relative price. Thus if graduates possessing vocational qualifications are in short supply, their entry salaries will be bid up and they will find it easy to get jobs. In reality, the market has not generally responded in this way to the supply of vocationally-trained graduates. To an economist this suggests that perhaps there isn't such a shortage after all. But the green paper takes a different view. Employers are castigated for not providing clear signals of their requirements. Students, although less culpable, are said to be misinformed about real job prospects, or have been forced against their will to drop maths and science subjects after O-levels. Again, no evidence is adduced to support these claims. What studies suggest, on the contrary, is that school students are both reasonably well-informed and capable of making decisions for themselves.[3]

A more fundamental problem arises from the Government's conception of the role of higher education in the economy. Because in this country it is largely state-funded, it is seen as essentially a drain on the productive parts of the economy, a cost to society, and we are told we cannot afford to expand it until the economy recovers significantly.

In a more market-oriented perspective, this seems a dubious analysis – one more appropriate in the Soviet planning system, with its Marxist categories of productive and unproductive labour.

Higher education produces an output which people value and are prepared to pay for. This output is part of national income, not a drain on it. From one viewpoint we could look on education as a consumption good, part of the leisure industries – like going to the theatre or taking part in sports. In this context, it is likely to be increasingly demanded in the future. The true consumption demand for higher education has never been adequately gauged in Britain because the system is designed for (or, more accurately, has grown up to cater for) state-funded 18–21 year olds. My own view is that there is a considerable suppressed demand for higher education, although not necessarily of a traditional kind, which a more liberalized market could provide. What the Government should be doing is seeking mechanisms whereby the higher education system could tap this demand – to the benefit of the economy, rather than to its cost. In the US millions of students of all ages and backgrounds enrol in academic, general interest and hobby programmes in universities and colleges. Such programmes, mainly but not exclusively paid-for by students themselves, are structured to fit in with employment, family responsibilities and life-styles to an extent undreamt of here. Given a higher education system free to innovate and seek such markets, private funding and/or a loans-scheme, we could well be amazed at the consequences.

Education can, of course, be seen as an investment as well as a consumption good. This is largely how the Green Paper sees it. Because of this view resources are overwhelmingly concentrated on young people (with a longer pay-off period to this investment), who because of their dependent economic status are denied a real freedom of choice in methods of study, degrees of attainment and pace of progress.

The Green Paper is analytically weak in its view of the nature of investment in education. Implicit in the emphasis on science, technology and other purportedly relevant disciplines is a belief that higher education should inculcate formal skills which can be applied directly in work. This may be what employers say they want, but economists tend to be sceptical of what people say, and look rather at what they do. The evidence in American economic literature (and there is no reason to suppose that the UK would be any different) seems to suggest that what employers seek in practice are more general attitudes and aptitudes which can be demonstrated on a wide range of courses that do not have to be directly relevant.

Recent developments in the economics of education stress the role of formal education systems in helping to provide a screening mechanism, enabling employers to select candidates for on-the-job training which is what really creates productive employees. While we do not have to go to the extreme of suggesting that any form of higher education is equally valuable in preparing people for careers in industry and commerce, too narrow a focus, in these days of rapid technical and economic change, may be counterproductive. It may also tend to deter women from entering higher education and acquiring the qualifications which would enable them to play a fuller role in the economy.

One feature of the Green Paper is a formal departure from the principle laid down by the Robbins Report that higher education should be available for all who can benefit from it, irrespective of the cost to the taxpayer. The

Green Paper now argues that higher education entrants should not only be able to benefit, but that the benefits should exceed the cost. While this sounds a more realistic criterion, on examination this new principle raises more questions than it answers.

Since students are not forced to go to universities or polytechnics, we must assume that they anticipate that the private benefits of their education will exceed the private costs. What the Government seems to require, then, is some form of social cost-benefit calculus.

Two points: first, this approach fits oddly with the Government's virtual abandonment of (largely discredited) social cost-benefit analysis elsewhere in the economy (in, for example, defence and many other areas of state expenditure) and its substitution of market principles. Second, no criteria for such calculations are elaborated. It is only too likely that in practice yet more irrelevant political considerations will be dragged into play to determine who shall, and who shall not, gain access to our higher education system (among the more difficult to get into in the developed world). A little example of the kind of lunacies centrally-determined policies throw up: a friend with a degree in Performance Arts recently wished to obtain a teaching certificate so she could teach dance in Britain (for which, incidentally, there is a growing demand in the private sector). No chance – she hadn't got Maths O-level, and Sir Keith had laid down that all new entrants to teacher-training should have this qualification.

Those who see in the Green Paper more economic realism and a hope for a more efficient and responsive system of higher education are likely to be disappointed. It shies away from even discussing the possibility of making higher education really responsive to market forces. It substitutes instead an unprecedented system of centralized control and an ill-thought-out attempt at relevance. I hope it will be quickly forgotten and the position of the DES completely rethought.

Notes

Parent power to privatize schools

1   Quoted in E.G. West, *Education and the State*, IEA, 2nd edn. 1970, 164.
2   Ibid., 165

Per capita funding: the next step to better schools

1   Caroline Cox, Jessica Douglas-Home, John Marks, Lawrence Norcross and Roger Scruton, *Whose Schools? A Radical Manifesto*, The Hillgate Group, London, 1986.
2   John Marks and Caroline Cox, 'Education Allowances: Power to the People?', in *The Pied Pipers of Education*, Social Affairs Unit, London, 1981, 21.

3   Max Wilkinson, *Lessons from Europe*, Centre for Policy Studies, London, 1977, 20–22.
4   Richard Lynn, 'The Japanese Example of Indirect Vouchers', *Economic Affairs*, Vol. 6, No. 6, August/September 1986.
5   Caroline Cox, 'Specialist Comprehensives: One Answer to Curriculum Problems', in Dennis O'Keefe (ed.), *The Wayward Curriculum*, Social Affairs Unit, London, 1986; R. Blank, R. Dentler, C. Baltzell and K. Chabotar, *Survey of Magnet Schools*, US Department of Education, 1983.
6   John Marks and Maciej Pomian-Srzednicki, *Standards of English Schools: Second Report*, National Council for Educational Standards, London, 1985; John Marks, Caroline Cox and Maciej Pomian-Srzednicki, *Examination Performance of Secondary Schools in the Inner London Education Authority*, National Council for Educational Standards, 1986.
7   John Marks, *London's Schools: when even the Communist Party gives up!*, Aims of Industry, London, 1985.
8   *Towards Better Management of Secondary Education*, The Audit Commission, London, 1986.

School grants: a bar to consumer sovereignty

1   IEA, 2nd edn. 1970.

Schools as self-seeking syndicates

1   One index of what is wrong is illiteracy. Paul Johnson claims that seven million adults in Britain are illiterate ('Slanging the Spouse', *The Spectator*, 28 February 1987, 23).
2   Dennis O'Keeffe (ed.), *The Wayward Curriculum*, Social Affairs Unit, London, 1986.
3   *Capitalism and Freedom*, Chicago University Press, 1962.
4   O'Keeffe, *op. cit.*; and Frank Palmer, *Anti-Racism – An Assault on Education and Value*, Sherwood Press, London, 1986.
5   Caroline Cox, 'Magnet Schools', in O'Keeffe, *op. cit.*
6   *Whose Schools?*, 7.
7   *Education and the State*, IEA, 2nd edn. 1970.

Dirigisme in higher education

1   'University Finance: A Solution Spurned', *The Times*, 17 July 1985.
2   *Academic Validation in Public Sector Higher Education*, HMSO, Cmnd. 9501.
3   For example, G. Williams and A. Gordon, 'Perceived Earnings Functions and *ex ante* Rates of Return to Post-Compulsion Education in England', *Higher Education*, March 1981.

6 Housing

Removing housing subsidies

Tom Taylor
Source: Economic Affairs, December 1985/January 1986, 6, 2, p. 31.

The more the housing problem in Britain is examined, the more evident it becomes that there is an inexorable logic about the so-called 'Edinburgh diagnosis' and a force not much less so about the prescriptions – if one is capable of seeing beyond short-term sectional interests. It is clear from the two documents it has so far produced this year – 'The Evidence' (January 1985) and 'The Report' (July 1985) – that the Inquiry into British Housing, initiated by the National Federation of Housing Associations and chaired by the Duke of Edinburgh, has not had its eye on the response of the electorate.

The terms of reference were to inquire into the nature and extent of inadequacies in the availability or condition of housing in Britain and to make recommendations. Inevitably, the Committee found there was a housing shortage (in spite of a crude physical surplus) (the mortgage subsidy, for example, is wildly regressive – the bigger your mortgage, the larger your subsidy and the higher your income), in terms of type and geographical distribution, that the rate of house-building was declining, that access to housing of people with low incomes was difficult. Further, the condition of the housing stock was deteriorating; the depleted construction industry was in no state to respond quickly to an upturn; the effective choice of tenure was between owner-occupation and rented council housing. Perhaps the most severe difficulty concerned housing finance, more specifically capital investment in housing and the methods of providing subsidies. It is the causes of these difficulties and the proposals to remedy them that lie at the heart of the Report.

Many of the present-day difficulties are the result of *ad hoc* government interventions and controls extending over the past century. The consequence has been massive misallocation of resources, inequity not only between types of tenure but also within them and a change in tenure structure amounting almost to a revolution. It is almost inevitable that the Inquiry should advocate the phasing-out of housing subsidies, particularly mortgage interest tax relief, the introduction of a housing allowance related to individual requirements, the adoption of capital value rents, changes in the housing role of local authorities and methods for improving housing conditions. The Inquiry is right to insist on a movement away from the long-familiar notion of subsidising houses towards supporting households.

The initial reactions were on balance favourable, although predictably, in view of the large amount of owner-occupation stimulated by the existing legal and fiscal framework, more emphasis was placed on the abolition of the mortgage subsidy than the Inquiry does. Equally predictably, the Prime Minister rejected the proposal outright, with the main opposition parties a good second, limiting their rejection to the basic tax rate.

Unfortunately, the politicians seem to have failed to appreciate the integrity of the Edinburgh proposals, since without the phasing-out of mortgage relief the rest is unlikely to be effective, since the £4,000 million saved by the abolition of the subsidy can be used to pay the housing allowance. If electoral risk is the reason for the rejection, the politicians are guilty of following short-term self-interest, which the Inquiry is certainly not and which the electorate may well not be (it does not think in five-year spans) if the Report leads to a wider appreciation than hitherto of the housing situation.

The condition of the housing market gives cause for anxiety. A housing stock of 21 million represents a crude surplus of about one million over households, but when the necessary statistical adjustments are made, including an amount to make mobility a reality, there is a deficit of well over a million and rising. Further, the condition of this stock has been deteriorating for ten years, particularly for the past five.

Then there is the question of the change in the proportion of type of tenure. The revolution since 1913, when 90 per cent of tenures were rented, is by no means solely a response to freely expressed changes in tenure preference. No more than half the tenants in local authority and private rented homes are satisfied with their tenure and the 95 per cent figure for owner-occupiers must be interpreted with caution, since for many of them an alternative tenure is simply not available thanks to the distortions that state intervention has produced in the market.

Housing subsidies, in the wider sense of some £8 billion per annum, regressive and inequitable, cannot be sustained in their present form against the historical record. The inevitable conclusion must be the radical one – their removal and replacement by a market solution – that all accommodation must be traded in the market at cost – as far as possible with coincident means related assistance for poorer households, not houses. But it must be a package deal. The recent move away in council housing from subsidy to cash housing benefit may in principle seem right. In practice it is increasing inequity relatively to the subsidy to owner-occupiers and at the same time not alleviating hardship, since housing benefit works badly, if at all (it is an administrative shambles), and the eligibility and the rate of benefit have been cut since its introduction.

The future is gloomy. Insufficient is being spent both by government and by individuals and companies to arrest housing decline, let alone to sustain growth. According to the OECD (Organization for Economic Cooperation and Development), Britain in 1982 spent proportionately less on improving and increasing its housing stock – 2.1 per cent of GDP – compared with the average of 5 per cent for other developed countries. Again, the output of new houses – council and private – per 1,000 inhabitants in Britain was the lowest of the lot, which suggests that the housing stock per 1,000 inhabitants, at present about average, will very soon diminish.

All this is known by anyone who has studied the UK housing market. It is amply demonstrated by the submissions of various institutions to the Inquiry, and by some of their recent individual publications. The whole question of subsidies was raised in this journal not much more than a year ago ('Abolish the Mortgage Subsidy', *Economic Affairs*, July–September 1984). But my intention is not to criticize the Report. What the Inquiry has done is to obtain the evidence, follow the logic and give the result a purposeful thrust so that its impact may be felt by the whole community.

In the light of this consistency, it is unfortunate that John Parry Lewis should have raised at this time what he calls the myth of the mortgage subsidy (*Economic Affairs*, October/November 1985). The important question for the alleviation of housing problems and the reform of housing policy is not whether mortgage interest tax relief is a subsidy, but whether its existence affects the housing costs met by households.

There is wide agreement among those economists, officials and others who have studied housing problems that any reduction in costs met by households as a direct or indirect result of government intervention constitutes a subsidy. Mortgage interest tax relief is a major one of these interventions, which taken together have for a long time been important factors in the misallocation of resources in housing which lies at the root of the present distortions. It is precisely this problem that the Edinburgh Report has sought to tackle, recognizing that it has to be dealt with as a whole or not at all. Mortgage interest tax relief and the other interventions will have to be removed as an essential step to placing housing on a more rational footing. To assert, as does Professor Parry Lewis, that mortgage interest tax relief is not a subsidy is unhelpful and inaccurate.

Cutting the cost of housing: why more building land is the answer

Lord Vinson of Roddam Dene
Source: *Economic Affairs*, April/May 1989, 9, 4, p. 7.

In economics one thing we can be certain about is that if we subsidize the buyer and restrict the supply of a commodity the price will inexorably rise. That is precisely what we have done to housing by being over-restrictive in the granting of planning applications and being over-generous with the tax treatment of mortgages. In our economy today there is a direct causal relationship between planning and inflation. I believe that this action calls for more specific government intervention. Of course we want to preserve the environment and nobody wants a house built next door to him. But the fact remains that the demand for houses has reached the point where something has to give. The baby bulge is turning into the house-buying bulge. People are living longer, living singly and occupying houses longer. More people can afford a second home as prosperity rises. Raising interest rates suppresses but does not otherwise affect these pressures, which will surface again once interest rates come down.

No society can ossify in perpetuity its land settlement patterns. Our over-restrictive planning policies have forced up the price of land, and hence the price of houses, to the point where it is beggaring many of our young people, apart from underpinning inflation.

Over half the cost of a house in the south of England is represented by the price of the land. Yet if one were building in the prairies, the price of land would be negligible. I hope that it is not unreasonable to suggest that in a moderately advanced society land cost might represent up to 25 per cent of the cost of the house, as it does in a good many parts of the rest of Europe. That means that the other 25 per cent of the cost of a house in the south of England is pure scarcity cost. In other words, for a younger couple paying a mortgage of £100 a week, £25 a week is paid for the privilege of maintaining land scarcity. Not only does this represent a very substantial cost and reduction in the standard of living for those families but it has the perverse counter-effect of raising house prices overall, thus raising the collateral against which people can borrow.

Is this really the result that society wants? The best way to reduce this huge notional credit base is to release more land. Of course, we do not want to bankrupt existing householders by seeing a dramatic fall in the price of houses. Nor is this likely, because it would not be possible to build sufficient houses that quickly. Fortunately, as with most shortages, the problem is only marginal. But unless that problem is tackled and demand is met where it should be met, through the release of more land outside the green belt, we shall in the future have recurrent consumer spending booms based on recurrent inflationary rises in house prices. Raising interest rates will dampen the demand for houses, but it is a classic example of tackling symptoms, not causes.

Housing: anyone for rent control?

Robert Albon and Dr David C. Stafford
Source: *Economic Affairs*, June/July 1988, 8, 5, p. 40.

The much heralded Landlord and Tenant Act which implements the more important recommendations of the Nugee Report among its provisions, increases protection for leasehold tenants in England and Wales. It gives tenants the right of first refusal where a landlord wishes to sell a block of flats, and enables tenants to force the appointment of a manager in cases of neglect or, in extreme cases, to apply for a compulsory purchase order. There is also provision for a court to vary the terms of a lease if it fails to provide for proper management, and it gives residents' associations rights of consultation over the appointment of management agents. The Act applies to about 500,000 households. About two-thirds of those affected have long leases, the rest are Rent Act tenants. At the Second Reading, Mr John Patten, Minister for Housing, described the Bill as a consumer protection measure and stressed that there was nothing in the Bill 'which the good and the responsible landlord need fear'! So far, so good. But what exactly has the present government done to encourage good and responsible landlords or for that matter to provide a climate where consumer protection is tempered by choice and variety? The answer is precious little.

The Act is part of the Conservative Government's plans to liberalize the rented sector. If the government were prepared to spell out the means and the ends, we would be more confident of future progress. The fact that recent legislation received an unopposed second reading (an ominous sign in housing legislation) and the Minister continues to propound the virtues, so far rather unsuccessfully, of his assured tenancy scheme, suggests that liberalization is not going to advance much further after eight years of Conservative government. Indeed, Mr Patten actually drew comfort from the Labour and Alliance support for the assured tenancy scheme for what he sees to be 'a crucial breakthrough to establish an all-party consensus essential to reviving private renting'. For the moment, the assured tenancy scheme applies only to new building and refurbishment by developers and institutions, but Mr Patten has said that he is thinking of extending it to small landlords with existing tenancies. Thinking is one thing, the sting is that he has also given a pledge that no one with security of tenure under existing law need feel threatened by the proposed moves. Such is the kiss of death to reform!

After seventy years of rent control, the cumulative effects have been quite sufficient almost to eradicate the rented sector. Britain now has by far the lowest proportion of households in rented accommodation outside the public sector in Europe. Once renting was a normal and respectable choice[1] for householders. Sadly, this is no longer true in view of the suspicions, distrust and anxiety experienced by landlords and tenants in such a heavily regulated market. Yet surveys continue to attest to the unmet need for decent rented housing allocated by the open market, and not by favouritism, a public body or a black market.

Wherever rent control has been applied, the costs and consequences have been highlighted and condemned by academic and professional economists, such as Friedman and Stigler in the USA, de Jouvenel in France, Paish in Britain, Rydenfelt in Sweden, Cheung in Hong Kong, Cooper and Stafford in Britain, Albon in Australia.[2] Unanimously, these authors point to the inefficiencies and inequities of government controls in rented markets. Inefficiencies associated with rental market controls can be enormous including severe shortages of rented accommodation, a decline in housing quality, serious tenant immobility and houses kept empty rather than used. It is currently estimated that in Britain alone some 500,000 empty houses could be available for rent. Inequities are no less serious. Rent and eviction controls are unfair in any sense of the word. The redistribution from rent control is a haphazard one – almost like randomly selecting donors and recipients of a subsidy from the telephone directory. There is no evidence that either tenants are poor or landlords are rich in general. Some of each are rich and some are poor. It is unlikely that Robin Hood would find the pattern of enforced redistribution appealing.

Controls on rents and evictions also establish pressures for people to evade the law – they encourage illegal activity. Black markets replace, to some extent, legal ones. Rent control evidently encourages evasion and is bad law.

What is needed is a private rental market which is both efficient and equitable. Problems of low incomes should be viewed as being totally independent of the housing market and be dealt with separately. They are not, in any sense, the problem of the landlord.

Rental market controls inevitably have unintended adverse consequences irrespective of how well they are framed. Of course, the full set of controls is virtually never introduced in one action. More commonly, one control (e.g. on rents) is imposed, and this has consequences in the housing market. Legislators then react to these consequences by imposing further controls which, again, evoke reactions in the market. The interaction of controls and consequences results in a complex set of legislation which can prove a gold-mine for the lawyers who can understand it.

In Britain, the accumulation of controls is now largely incorporated in the 1977 Rent Act, modified by the 1980 Housing Act. Apart from academic criticism of control, professional bodies have recently been attesting to the unfavourable effects of control. For example, a recent report from The British Property Federation has said that too few homes were available for rent because the law did not permit private landlords to let on tolerable, let alone attractive, terms. The Royal Institution of Chartered Surveyors has argued the effect of statutory rent controls had been to reduce the capital value of rented property to about a half, even less in some areas, that of vacant possession property of similar quality.

While the precise impact of successive government policies on the decline of the rented sector cannot be measured, there is little doubt that the influences are most certainly adverse, individually and collectively conspiring against any reversal in the decline in privately rented housing.

The private rented housing sector has experienced a massive relative decline in its share of total housing from 90 per cent in 1914 to less than 10 per cent at the end of 1986. Rented houses have been sold for owner-occupation either to sitting tenants or on vacant possession. There has been practically no investment in private rented housing. The years of rent control and security of tenure have destroyed the sector and discouraged any new investment or initiatives. Britain is unique among the industrialized countries in financing homes for rent almost exclusively through the public sector.

According to the 1981 England and Wales Housing Condition survey, 60 per cent of privately rented dwellings were built before 1919 compared with less than 35 per cent of the owner-occupied and less than 4 per cent of the local authority housing stock. The majority of the remaining 40 per cent of privately rented houses were built in the inter-war period. Some 30 per cent of privately rented houses lacked one or more basic amenities, 30 per cent were in disrepair, and 20 per cent were statutorily unfit for habitation.

The geographical distribution of the privately rented sector is uneven and tends to be concentrated within the larger inner city areas. London alone accounts for over 25 per cent of privately rented dwellings and about 37 per cent of all households in furnished dwellings.

In the face of such adverse market characteristics, what hope exists for a reversal of the worsening trends in rented housing? For long embattled by the effects of the Rent Acts, what options may exist?

Under the Housing Act 1980, the shorthold tenancy was introduced to enable a landlord to gain repossession of rented property after a specified time. The minimum period was one year. Originally, it had been a requirement that a fair rent should be applied to shorthold tenancies but this was later waived, except in London. While tenants can appeal to a rent officer it is now no longer necessary to register a fair rent at the commencement of a shorthold tenancy.

Whilst these new shorthold tenancies have helped to ease two impediments to landlord letting, namely full security of tenure and potential capital loss, they have not induced landlords to return to the housing market. That a landlord no longer faces risks of considerable capital loss is a major attraction.

The Housing Act 1980 also introduced a new assured tenancy to allow landlords, 'approved' by the Government, to let at freely negotiated rents. Lettings were to be subject to the Landlord and Tenant Act, 1954, and not to the Rent Acts. The scheme has now been in operation for some years and about two hundred landlords have been approved – builders, insurance companies, building societies and housing associations – but they have had little impact on the rented sector as a whole.

The shorthold and assured tenancies provided some move towards deregulation, but their use has clearly not been widespread. They have done little to reverse the trend in the decline of the rented sector. In London, licences have been used proportionately far more than elsewhere, but the use of shorthold tenancies has been proportionately greater outside London.

Under the 1986 Housing Act, the Government lifted two restrictions on private landlords as part of the right-to-rent campaign. Landlords can now impose higher rents immediately as agreed by a rent officer, instead of having to phase them in over two years. Moreover, landlords in Greater London can let property on a yearly basis without needing to register a fair rent with a rent officer.

Another aspect of the 1986 Housing Act has been the extension of the approved landlord scheme. This could mean the refurbishment of empty dwellings to approved standards by approved landlords, let on assured tenancies and offering security of tenure, subject to five year rent reviews, just like most commercial leases. Such a move introduces the question of whether the government may soon abolish the right of secure tenants to hand on tenancies to their children. Evidently, such an initiative means that the pace of renewal of the rented sector would be set by the life-expectancy of existing tenants and the supply of approvable landlords. Maybe we are churlish to criticize these modest reforms as a step towards more radical reforms, but it has to be said that the 1986 Housing Act has not gone far enough to arrest the many criticisms of rent control.

Too often, there are those sympathetic to reform but who argue caution. Two major arguments are advanced. First, it is said that radical reform, e.g. complete abolition, is politically impossible. The reasoning is rarely articulated. The reasoning is rarely articulated. Those who propagate such a view should note that protected tenants enjoy their rights partly at the expense of the homeless and the job-seekers. Second, more radical reforms than those contained in the Housing Act of 1986 are cautioned on the grounds that a change of government would wipe out any benefits of reform attaching to landlords. Such a possibility leads gradualists, like Mr Patten, to propose that reforms should embrace cross-party support. Such a justification has not prevented the Conservative Government from privatizing several nationalized industries or abolishing the Price Commission! These initiatives have not only been popular among the electorate but the Government has gained even greater support for such revitalized industries in the face of Labour proposals to renationalize enterprises at original share issue prices. In short, a policy of piecemeal reforms justified on the basis of cross-party support to reduce the alleged risks of dramatic reversals of policy and impact on landlords is shabby shilly-shallying. It is worth noting that the Rent Acts of 1965 and 1974 were both imposed by Labour governments within a year of their respective elections! Did they ever seek cross-party support?

Britain stands out from most countries in the world in that it continues to retain a system of rigid rental market controls that have asphyxiated the private rental housing sector. Other countries removed their wartime controls, but Britain did not. Moves towards decontrol in the late 1950s were reversed in the mid-1960s. This continuation of controls has caused a dramatic decline in this once important sector of the housing market. Rental market controls must be abolished.

The only questions that remain include asking whether controls on rents and evictions should be removed gradually or in one fell swoop?

Various schemes have been devised over the years to lighten the impact of decontrol on tenants by either replacing subsidies from landlords with those from the state or by graduating decontrol over a period of time. Our own approach is to separate the issue of income maintenance from that of housing policy.

The most recent proposal for decontrol is that suggested by Martin Ricketts.[3] He suggests giving sitting tenants clearly defined property rights to the stream of subsidy from rent control for a period of, say, ten years. Tenants would have the right to remain in their property at a controlled rent for the nominated period or sell the right to whomever they chose (e.g. another tenant, the landlord or a housing association) for a lump sum. Under his proposals, all new tenancies would be decontrolled completely. His scheme is designed to enhance mobility, restore the incentive to invest in rental housing, partially protect the tenant's interest, and ultimately result in the complete ending of rent and eviction controls. Martin Ricketts believes that all this would be achieved and be politically palatable. We applaud his scheme as a serious attempt to ease the pain of the transition from a regime of rent control to one of a free market. Similar schemes have been proposed in the past. The late Sir Roy Harrod[4] proposed that sitting tenants be entitled to the difference between market and controlled rents for a period of ten years whether they remain in the property or not. Under his proposal, the landlord would be taxed the rent difference and the amount paid to the tenant for ten years. As in Ricketts' scheme, new tenancies would be decontrolled completely. The only difference is that all amounts are in flows per period rather than capitalized present values. Frank Paish proposed a variant of Harrod's plan whereby some of the tax on landlords would not go to sitting tenants but would be deployed elsewhere – 25 per cent in an allowance to landlords to maintain their properties and a proportion of the rest to fund an income maintenance programme.

The Paish variant of Harrod's scheme is preferable to that of Ricketts for a number of reasons. First, it has more chance of being welcomed by landlords who now get something out of it – the means to maintain better their properties. Second, it aids tenants as well because they will have the benefits of better maintained living conditions. In fact, the stimulus to better maintenance benefits everyone. Third, it creates some funds that could be used to help any real victims of higher free market rents. New tenants, renting at market rates, could be embittered by the generosity of Ricketts' scheme since there would be no provision for them at all.

These types of schemes are motivated by a desire to end rent control and to reap some immediate benefits while not losing too many votes for the sponsoring government. But the degree of generosity to tenants must be carefully judged. In one sense, sitting tenants are not really a worthy group at all, having already enjoyed a subsidy (sometimes of a large size for a long period of time) at the expense of their hapless landlords. Any enforced transfer has no clear moral justification, particularly when considered in the light of the circumstances of many of the tenants and landlords.

Other than in a political sense, the number of tenants deserving of compensation from landlords is nil. On the other hand, the number that society might wish to compensate – at the expense of taxpayers in general – could well be quite large. We do not suggest an approach which places the burden on landlords, even if they will be freed ultimately of the obligation to subsidise tenants.

If rent decontrol were to occur overnight, with no change to any of the existing subsidy arrangements, many tenants would be automatically compensated by both the current system of housing benefits (many tenants would become eligible when their rents rose) and by other elements of the welfare system. Only those tenants who were, in a sense, able to afford the market rent would be ineligible for compensation. We think that this would be an improvement in that the state would take over the responsibility for subsidies from landlords and subsidies would be far better directed. Aggregate increases in subsidy payments would be less than the transfer from tenants to landlords. Such a transfer of the burden of subsidy from landlords to government is justified. After all, the housing benefit system is supposed to be capable, technically and administratively, of providing support to lower income tenants. Those who argue, however, these costs to be too high for government to bear are merely offering a cynical defence of the status quo. Government does have the apparatus and duty to provide help to the lower income households at a level and degree it deems appropriate: it is not the duty or responsibility of the landlord.

We are arguing that if decontrol were to occur within the context of other housing subsidies remaining (and this is not our first-best solution), compensation for the most needy tenants would occur automatically. Other tenants have no moral or other basis to expect to be compensated and should not be considered in this regard. Certainly they should not be compensated at the expense of landlords. Martin Ricketts' scheme is too generous to tenants, indiscriminate in its compensation and involves an unwarranted continuation of the tax on landlords. We accept that not all landlords actually bear the tax. Some landlords will have purchased properties with a sitting tenant and will have paid a price reflecting its value under rental market control. They would be making a normal return from their investment and would, in effect, receive a windfall from decontrol.

A second question to ask is whether decontrol should occur alone or as part of a major change in policy involving the abolition of virtually all the subsidies and controls affecting the housing market?

Our preference is for the government to get out of the rented housing market completely, by abolishing rent control, reforming mortgage interest tax deductibility and removing council housing subsidies. Any welfare that remains should be directed at those on low incomes and be totally divorced from housing. Government interference, over many years, in the housing market must be branded as an abject failure by any criteria and each attempt at improvement seems to make things worse. The tendency has been to subsidize all sectors rather than none. If tenure-neutrality was ever the aim it has not been achieved. This is because the rates of subsidy differ markedly within and between tenure types.

An approach could be to go beyond the recently revised housing benefit scheme and aim for true tenure-neutrality where all segments of the market are subsidized at the same rate and at the expense of the taxpayer in general. This could involve, *inter alia*, the removal of rent control and its replacement by an across-the-board rent subsidy to tenants paid by the Exchequer. The subsidy would have to be proportionately the same as those for council housing, involving an adjustment of rents in that sector to conform with the general rate of subsidy. This would have to be combined with a properly targeted income-maintenance scheme available to all those meeting the criteria irrespective of housing tenure. Depending on the general rate of housing subsidy chosen and the generosity of income maintenance, such a scheme may or may not result in an increase in public outlays including tax expenditures. But the general subsidy approach to tenure-neutrality is less than ideal. Why not achieve tenure-neutrality by simply setting the across-the-board housing subsidy at precisely zero?

In this case, private rents would almost all rise by amounts ranging from very little in the case of fair rents where housing is not particularly scarce, to a lot in other cases. Most private tenants would pay more. Some could receive a double shock where rent subsidies were previously paid. Compensation would occur for those that were eligible for general income maintenance but many would definitely gain. In regard to the private rented sector, taxpayers in general would lose if income maintenance payments exceeded savings on rent subsidies.

Council house rents would also rise, again by varying amounts but probably more uniformly. Housing benefits would also be removed. Many would receive compensation under income maintenance and the effect on taxpayers would be ambiguous, but we think that it would be negative.

A reintroduction of taxation on the net imputed income from owner-occupation (i.e. mortgage interest deductibility would be allowed as a housing cost) could well raise the housing costs of many owner-occupiers buying their homes and might even have a downward effect on property values. But taxpayers would almost certainly gain in net terms as savings in tax expenditures would probably exceed any income maintenance payments to lower income groups in this sector.

Our guess is that society would gain from the removal of all housing subsidies. We have already shown the costs in economic efficiency associated with rent control. Efficiency gains would flow from the abolition of other subsidies which distort production and consumption decisions, impede mobility, and so on. Thousands of millions of pounds' worth of extra output could flow from the enhancement of labour mobility alone (see Minford et al).[6] Gainers could easily compensate losers from this set of changes with a social gain left over. Of course, society may not wish to compensate all the losers from the change. The income maintenance scheme would have the virtue that subsidies would be directed where they were most needed.

Any political repercussions of such a broad change may not be nearly as severe as from, say, individually tinkering with particular parts of the subsidy apparatus. Every tiny attempt to decontrol the rental housing market or reform the extent of mortgage interest deductibility is met with a howl of protest from those affected (including, of course, the bureaucrats who run the schemes). From the viewpoint of the recipients, their degree of acceptance of the loss of their subsidy could be enhanced by the knowledge that others are also losing. Threatening only one group can be and usually is seen as being horizontally inequitable.

A third question to ask is whether there is a role for the state after decontrol?

The short answer is no. We would consider some procedure that adjudicated in the event of a dispute between a landlord and a tenant over whether the rent was actually a market rent or not. This could be appealed to by either the tenant or a landlord. This procedure would draw on the rents on comparable premises, current property values and current cost levels. Even this type of adjudication or control causes us some worries as it creates machinery that could be applied to more damaging ends. Certainly, we reject the perpetuation of a fair rent (like that applied in Britain) that ignores the scarcity value of dwellings. It is a conceptual nonsense. The disallowance of scarcity as a factor in rent-setting robs the community of the important signal that leads to the elimination of that abnormal scarcity by the creation of new supply.

Obviously, security of tenure is another major concern of tenants. Interestingly, it usually becomes a concern when rents are regulated. Only then do landlords have an incentive to evict tenants for reasons other than their unsuitability (because of damage to house, failure to pay rent, annoyance to neighbours, and so on). That is, of course, why rent and eviction controls usually go hand-in-hand. If there is one there must be the other. We would like to see security of tenure become, as it once was, and is elsewhere, a matter of private contractual negotiation between landlord and tenant. Landlords would ensure a tenant's security of tenure for a specified period of time as long as the tenant observed certain conditions. The only role for the state in such circumstances, would be one of providing the machinery for the enforcement of voluntary private contracts.

Housing reform to 'create' jobs

Paul Ashton, Patrick Minford and Michael Peel
Source: *Economic Affairs*, February/March 1986, Supplement, 6, 3, p. 32.

The housing market in Britain is the object of massive government intervention. This involvement takes four main forms: the Rent Acts, the subsidizing of council-house rents, the subsidy to owner-occupiers through tax relief on mortgages and the system of planning restrictions on housing land. Some of the motives for this intervention appear to have been: the avoidance of tenant 'exploitation' (through Rent Acts); welfare support to poorer people but tied to housing to ensure no diversion into other expenditure (council rents); the building of a property-owning democracy (via mortgage relief); and the protection of the environment (through planning). All are regarded as politically sensitive, i.e., big potential vote-winners or -losers. This political sensitivity is clearly illustrated by the way even Mrs Thatcher's Government, although it has shown itself relatively brave in economic policy, has so far largely refused to tackle the central problems of the housing market.

Waste with current housing institutions

This article draws on work we have done in a book which is due to appear shortly from the Institute of Economic Affairs. In it we try to evaluate the economic inefficiency or waste (welfare costs in economists' jargon) which arises from government intervention; then, after reviewing the detailed mechanisms by which it is implemented, we suggest ways in which they could be modified to diminish this inefficiency without abandoning any cherished political aims.

There are two main sources of waste because of current institutional arrangements: (a) the direct waste caused in the housing market itself by inducing people to over- or under-use different sorts of accommodation;

and (b) the indirect waste caused in the labour market (i.e., unemployment) by the immobility which comes about from intervention in housing.

Direct waste, is probably quite considerable but not for the reasons analysts usually give. Of a total waste which we 'guesstimate', a large figure of 5 per cent of GDP, as much as 4.5 per cent of GDP is due to planning restrictions on housing. Yet this figure is certainly an overestimate, because we have been unable to put a price on what people would pay to protect the environment (for example, the Green Belt). If people had property rights in the environment, they would sell them to developers and a fair (that is, market) price would be set for such protection; and the market would also reveal the right amount of it, as decided by consumers. Although there are some problems in defining these rights, in creating a market for them, and in inducing people to reveal their preferences accurately for public goods like clean air and attractive countryside, the present bureaucratic planning system is so deplorably inefficient that the solutions should be studied and pursued. Nevertheless, this sort of work is still in its infancy and we are therefore stuck with the present system for some time at least until more research has been completed.

The other 0.5 per cent of GDP under (a) is the misallocation because of council house subsidies, mortgage tax relief and the Rent Acts. This distortion is not negligible, although it is dwarfed by the effect of planning restrictions. But it is the sort of loss that, both because it is largely concealed (in the form of invisible lost consumer-surplus) and because the solutions are politically difficult, may well not stimulate political action.

Not so the costs under (b). Clearly unemployment is such a serious political issue that, if it can be shown that housing reform can reduce unemployment, the issue will be seriously considered whatever its difficulties. It is well known (and fully documented by numerous statistical studies surveyed in our book) that the private rental sector is very important in enabling people to move jobs, and also that its size has been dramatically reduced by the cumulative operation of the Rent Acts, especially since they were extended to cover furnished accommodation in 1974, from 62 per cent of the housing stock in 1945 to about 10 per cent today. So it would not be surprising to find that by obstructing the movement of people from areas with high to those with low unemployment the Rent Acts have raised both regional and national unemployment. A statistical analysis of regional unemployment since 1963 confirms this assumption. We estimate from this analysis that national unemployment has been raised by around 2.25 per cent of the labour force by the Rent Acts. The formal value of this loss in economic resources to the nation is about 1 per cent of GDP – but of course most people will be concerned primarily about the unemployment effect itself.

What can be done, in practical political terms, to remove this major obstacle?

Reform of housing regulation

Immobility is created by the large gap between the protected or subsidized tenancy, which is linked to the worker's staying in his or her area, and the free-market tenancy which he must take if he moves to another area. This immobility in turn creates unemployment, because in the north of England wages are prevented from dropping sufficiently to create jobs for those who will not move.

Let us consider an idealized solution to this problem. Suppose all tenancies were at free-market rents under free-market conditions of tenure (i.e. some contractual basis agreed freely and solely between landlord and tenant). For the employed man in the north of England, housing will not then obstruct his decision to move: he will pay market rents wherever he is (minus whatever state rebate he may get in housing benefits).

But what about the unemployed man? Under our present system, his rent will be 100 per cent rebated if he stays in the north of England, whereas he will only get a partial rebate if he takes work in the south of England. His incentive to move is even less than at subsidized or otherwise protected rents. Furthermore, the comparison between his out-of-work income and his in-work income even if he takes work in the north will be now much more favourable to his remaining unemployed, because his rents have gone up, with 100 per cent subsidy if unemployed, but only a partial one if employed. Hence ironically, on its own, letting rents rise to free-market prices reduces mobility among the unemployed; it may well also increase unemployment in the north and will do so if the number of employed induced to leave (or not take) employment at low wages exceeds those induced to migrate to the south of England.

Since 1979 the Conservative Government has been following this policy on council-house rents and, to the small extent it has loosened Rent Act restrictions, also in protected private tenancies. It may indeed have worsened the problem.

Such are the complexities provoked by a system like Britain's where such heavy intervention has occurred. But there is an answer, which is perfectly reasonable and politically acceptable: this solution is to introduce a ceiling on benefits as a percentage of previous net income in work. We have suggested this elsewhere,[1] setting it at 70 per cent. Such a gap between income in and out of work is a form of pressure on people to take a new job at rather lower rates of pay than their last one if they cannot find one at the old rate. If they do so, the state will nevertheless, under our existing system (of which we would retain the principle but must improve the practice), support their in-work net income above a decent minimum living standard.

With this ceiling in place, the unemployed man will now find that his unemployment benefits do not go up. His incentive to find work in the north will be unchanged because he will still be 30 per cent worse off out of work. But his incentive to move to the south will now be considerably stronger because he now has to pay a larger proportion of the economic rent if he stays in the north.

A simple arithmetical example may be helpful here. Suppose in his previous job he was paid £100 (per week), with net pay of £80. His benefits under the ceiling are 70 per cent of £80 = £56 per week. Suppose he could earn in the south £120, net pay of £95; but his rent would be £15 higher, and so he is not interested in moving south (any more than in taking another job in the north at £100).

Now his northern rent goes up, because of deregulation, by £15. His out-of-work benefit will not change, remaining at 70 per cent of his work income if he stays north. But it will now be only 62.6 per cent of his work income if he goes south for a job (previously it was 70 per cent if you allowed for the rent factor). His incentive to move and take a job in the south will thus have increased significantly.

The ceiling we have proposed is not the only way to create pressures on the unemployed to take available jobs at lower wages than before. Others exist – from moral pressure, through 'workfare' schemes, all the way to straight compulsion via cutting off benefits for job-refusal (the work-test which legally ought to be applied to all unemployed under present rules). Let us assume that some such mechanism is functioning. Then we can pursue our main purpose which is to reduce the obstacles to mobility posed by housing regulations as such. Clearly, our argument implies that the rental sector should be freed from regulation entirely.

But in practice some timetable is necessary. And what respect should be given to the principle that retrospection should be avoided. The easiest course would be first to announce that over the next five years the ceiling on regulated rents would be raised to free-market prices in five equal percentage instalments – with all regulation of rents to cease in 1990. As for security of tenure provisions enjoined by the courts, a two-year transitional period could be announced in which existing security would prevail. At the end of this period landlords and tenants would be expected to have freely negotiated contracts and the courts would no longer be involved in enforcing statutory security.

Does this simple course – despite the precedent set by the 1957 Rent Act – involve unconstitutional retrospection? For regulated tenants, regulation is both recent (1965 is the earliest date) and subject to a system of fair rent adjudication, whereby rents are varied in accordance with a variety of statutory criteria which are subjectively assessed by rent officers. Rights, if any, in such regulatory benefits appear to be weak. A five-year phasing of rent increases and a two-year warning of security cessation appear adequate recognition of them.

For council tenants reform has only to follow existing policy to raise council rents to market prices, but over a similiar period to that for regulated tenancies, so that by 1990 these rents too are at market prices.

That this implicit policy does not violate council tenants' rights might be considered clear from its failure to be contested to date. Tenants who choose to buy their own houses are able to do so on most favourable terms, which might partially reflect their rights accumulated by years of tenure and partially the state's desire for them to become home-owners with a stake in society. But should those who choose not to buy have their rights to tenure reflected in some way? The problem for them appears to be the same as that for regulated tenants: 'what the state giveth [at least relatively recently – via the 1980 Housing Act], the state may take away'. Their rights are comparatively weak. The good fortune of those who can buy is undeniable.

What of security of tenure for council tenants? Here we have seen there are statutory grounds (non-payment of rent, etc.) under which councils may evict tenants; but in some cases, suitable alternative accommodation must be provided, and the power of a council to evict even for gross under-occupation is almost totally fettered. Council housing has developed a status of renter-of-last resort for the poor, the old, the handicapped and the unfortunate. There would seem to be every reason to move people out of this last-resort housing as soon as they are capable of renting normally. Many of these people will buy their own house within the next five years. Those that then remain will largely be the difficult cases, unlikely to move in any case. But we wish to ensure that those capable of moving are not deterred from doing so to their advantage by the existence of security of tenure (albeit at an economic rent) in their existing lodgings. This analysis points to an additional statutory ground for moving tenants who do not fall into the renter-of-last-resort category: namely, that they have the capacity to find alternative lodgings outside the council sector.

Step-by-step variants

Our proposals are step-by-step in one sense, in that they embody transitional periods and recognize existing legal rights. Even so, the announcement of such a programme for regulated tenants (not for council tenants, where we advocate merely an extension of existing policies) could create a storm of protest from housing lobbies and so on. The storm could be weathered – but it might be risky.

Are there other measures that would reach the same conclusion, if by a more roundabout route?

For regulated tenancies, one obvious variation would be to introduce a new criterion into the setting of fair rents – that of scarcity. This single amendment would allow tribunals to raise rents towards market prices. Scarcity could be made a binding criterion (i.e., rents must not be below market prices) by a certain time – for example, 1990. A second series of variants could build on the innovations in the 1980 Housing Act (the assured tenancy and the shorthold), as well as on the licence agreement which has always been outside full Rent Act protection. These categories should now be extended so as to deregulate all new tenancies and relets. This single measure should instil confidence into existing and potential landlords – who at present are trapped in a legal minefield involving licences (unprotected) and tenancies (fully protected) – and stimulate the supply of new (unrestricted) lets. (The efficacy of such a measure would, to a large extent, depend on how landlords – and investors – assess the probability of a future government being elected with an opposite policy.)

A third variant would allow the landlord to draw up these rent tenancies with a clause denying the tenant the right to go to the Rent Officer for an assessment of a 'fair rent'. Since no landlord would be willing to let without such a clause, this would effectively place all new tenancies outside the Rent Acts' rent provisions. This measure would still leave the problem of repossessing existing regulated tenancies. If rents were at market rates it would be easy (a mere matter of contacting market agencies) for landlords to offer tenants comparable accommodation at comparable prices where at present it is often impossible. A general mandatory ground for eviction, after the tenancy agreement has expired, could be made such an offer by the landlord. (At present a landlord may only – at the court's discretion – obtain possession by providing suitable alternative accommodation or a similar regulated residence – and the court must be satisfied that it is reasonable to order possession.) This provision would be our fourth variant.

By these four variants existing rents would be raised where there was scarcity (i.e., market rents exceeded regulated rents), existing tenants could be evicted after their contract is up once market rents were reached, and new tenancies would be unrestricted.

Other state distortions

These proposals are made to deal with mobility. They are all that is necessary to that end. Nevertheless, we noted earlier the other distortions in the housing market. These distortions arose not merely from the Rent Acts and council house rent subsidies but also from the subsidy to mortgage interest via tax relief. Strictly speaking, this tax relief is also a distortion within the financial markets, since much lending on mortgage in effect is done for general financial purposes.

There is a well-known solution to this tangle: make saving tax-free, and tax only consumption. The tax-free allowance on your income will then be not the mortgage interest on your borrowing but your total saving; if you borrow, it will not affect your tax position unless you add to your consumption.

There are by now so many distortions in financial markets, because of the complex incidence of a variety of taxes and tax relief on financial transactions, that it is a hopeless task to estimate the costs. They may be small because of the efficiency of financial markets in avoiding tax; but they are nevertheless worth clearing away, if only because of the urgency of making the City of London as competitive as possible and to allow individuals to own shares on their own account without a loss of tax efficiency.

Reforms of this magnitude in the tax system will take some years to put into place. Nevertheless, they will come as soon as the atmosphere of crisis that surround taxs revenues (because of their shortage) has subsided. Meanwhile, it is unlikely to be a high governmental priority to abolish mortgage tax relief. Its economic cost is small, and the political cost of abolition too high.

The proposals made in this article will reduce the living standards of those who use protected rental accommodation, whether council or private. These people are for the most part in lower-income groups. The distributional consequences of the proposals are therefore regressive.

As they stand, our proposals also have no revenue cost, because the higher rents will be paid by the renters themselves, under an assumption that out-of-work benefits are subject to a 70 per cent ceiling and that housing benefits are fixed (being related to income).

In principle it is possible for the distributive consequences to be offset by higher housing benefits (although the 70 per cent ceiling implies that only 70 per cent of this addition accrues to the unemployed). But this restriction must be seen against a background in which the highest priority is being given to raising tax thresholds over the next four years, in order to reduce the tax burden on the low-paid; and a second priority is being attached to relieving the low-paid of National Insurance contributions as far as possible.

How much will our proposals cost renters? Assuming that rents rise to market rates by 1990 on all regulated and council properties, the cost to the average person on these properties would be about £11 per week spread over five years. If this Government's plans for tax cuts go through in the next four years, that average person – if he is earning £120 per week – could gain up to £16 per week in tax cuts.

These proposals considered, seen in the wider context, can therefore be seen, potentially at least, to pose no distributional threat, without raising housing benefits, given the large tax cuts planned by the Chancellor.[2] The proposals can therefore be considered primarily in their efficiency aspect.

The British housing market is in a mess because it is overregulated, and this interference has serious effects on mobility, and so on unemployment. It is politically feasible to reform the regulatory system, particularly against the background of rising tax thresholds currently planned by the government. This intention offers a major opportunity to reform the housing market, since at times when taxes have been rising it would have created excessive hardship. We have suggested ways in which it could be done without sweeping aside existing institutions, by building on the 1980 Housing Act, the first step in the reform of housing law instituted by this Government. The step-by-step approach that has proved so successful in the reform of union law could be used here, too. It is time for the second step.

Mortgage subsidy – the myth

John Parry Lewis
Source: Economic Affairs, October/November 1985, 6, 5, p. 21.

Taxation relief on mortgage interest payments is not a subsidy. The myth that it is arose as a left-wing response to the criticism that subsidies of council-house building had become excessive; and many fell for it. I hope to show here why the relief is not a subsidy, and why it would be inadvisable, as well as inequitable, to remove it.[1]

Our national taxes fall on activities rather than on people or things – on the sale of petrol, of labour or of washing machines; and he who pays the tax (at its initial impact) is rarely the only person whose pocket is affected by it (in its ultimate incidence). Elementary texts abound in analyses of the effects on the parties to the transaction (or other activity), and their dependence on elasticities of supply and demand.

The essence of income tax is that, with certain exceptions, receipt of income generates a liability to be taxed. Exceptions include income received by charities and personal income below prescribed amounts. These are not subsidies. The tax is on the activity of providing labour, capital or rights for reward (in the occupation of property, or the use of an idea, for example), and both the payer and the payee are affected by its relative severity.

The treatment of interest is complicated. Payments of interest by businesses are clearly costs of production to be deducted from income before assessment for tax. Equally clearly, receipt of interest is income and is liable to tax. The consolidating Income Tax Act of 1952 sets out the then position quite clearly. Any person obliged to make annual interest payments and making them wholly out of profits or other taxable gains would be taxed as if he had made no such payment; but he would be empowered to deduct tax from the payment and to retain it. Thus, while (if the payer of interest used his power) the recipient of interest was taxed, the payer was effectively given relief, and the Exchequer derived no income from the financing of the loan. On the other hand, if the interest was 'not paid wholly out of taxable income', the borrower was obliged to deduct tax before payment and to remit it to the Inland Revenue.

Interest to banks and other institutions at intervals more frequent than annual was not covered by these provisions. In the words of Spicer and Pegler's *Income Tax*,[2] 'It is only right, therefore, that a taxpayer who has to use part of his income in paying such interest should be entitled to reduce his income by a like amount for income tax purposes'. Accordingly, virtually anybody with a bank overdraft could get taxation relief on his interest payments.

The principle was simple. Lending-and-borrowing was an untaxed activity, even though the receipt of income was taxed, provided that the interest was paid out of taxable income rather than out of capital.

In the mid-1960s the principle changed. As part of an attempt to reduce consumer expenditure, private borrowing was discouraged by a packet of measures that included the taxation of all lending for private purposes other than housing; and bank overdraft interest payments ceased to be an allowable deduction, with only housing loans excepted. It was considered that while economic policy warranted the taxation of private borrowing, social policy required that loans for private housing purposes should continue to be neither taxed nor subsidized.

Essentially that is still the position. To say that the tax relief constitutes a subsidy is like saying that owning a cat is a subsidized activity solely because owning a dog is a taxed activity.

But should this tax relief be continued? Any government that discontinues it can rightly be charged with taxing the financing of housing through loans in the private sector while continuing to subsidize housing in the public sector. It could get around this objection by also exempting recipients of building society interest from tax on their incomes. This unlikely measure would make building society investment so attractive that forces in the money market would soon drive down the interest rates offered and charged by societies until the rate offered (tax-free) equalled the post-tax rate available elsewhere. In the end both borrowers and lenders would be in the same position as they are now. So would the Exchequer, except for savings in its labour costs.

But if the government insisted on taxing borrowing for house purchase the consequences would be far less simple than the fall in house prices that some predict. The increased effective price of a loan would to some extent drive down demand, which would lead to a small reduction in the rates charged and paid by societies. This would have wider consequences in the money market.

The reduced demand would arise partly from a reduction in the average size of loan (because of the rise in effective costs of borrowing, that is, net of tax) and partly from a decline in the number of borrowers. The reduced loan would not produce a proportional fall in house prices because the requirement to repay existing mortgages and the desire to keep abreast with inflation create important resistances to declines in house prices. Instead, there would be more widespread resort to low-start mortgage schemes and other devices. Meanwhile people who would have postponed their borrowing should be swelling the demand for rented homes. Housebuilders would attempt to survive by building more low-cost houses, some of which might soon become a social liability.

If the abolition of relief were restricted to new mortgages there would be cries of unfairness from those about to enter the market, and the effects I have described above would arise more slowly and weakly than otherwise. On the other hand, if existing mortgages were affected there would be a widespread reduction in consumer spending as mortgage holders adjusted their patterns of expenditure. It would have far-reaching consequences, including a decline in the demand for labour. The Exchequer would have derived revenue, which conceivably would be spent in a way that would offset some of these consequences. But there are more efficient, and more easily defended, ways of raising taxes – even if it were the right thing to do, which is debatable.

Notes

Housing: anyone for rent control?

1 For example, the Grossmiths' hilarious book *The Diary of a Nobody* makes much of the Pooters' new-found status at 'The Laurels', Brickfield Terrace, Holloway.
2 These papers can be found in two books of edited readings offering a convincing indictment of rent control: IEA, *Verdict on Rent Control*, Readings No. 7, 1972, and R. Albon (1980), *Rent Control; Costs and Consequences*, The Centre for Independent Studies, Australia.
3 M. Ricketts, *Lets into Leases*, Centre for Policy Studies, London, 1986.
4 R. Harrod, *Are these Hardships Necessary?*, Occasional Papers on Social Administration, No. 16, Bell, 1947.
5 F.W. Paish, 'The Economics of Rent Restriction', *Lloyds Bank Review*, April 1952. Reprinted in IEA (1972), *op. cit.*
6 P. Minford, P. Ashton and M. Peel, 'Housing Reform to "Create" Jobs', *Economic Affairs*, Vol. 6, No. 3, February–March 1986.

Housing reform to 'create' jobs

1 A.P.L. Minford, P. Ashton, M. Peel, D. Davies and A. Sprague, *Unemployment – Cause and Cure*, Blackwell, Oxford, 2nd edn, 1985.
2 This conclusion is further strengthened if the suggestions we have made elsewhere for Negative Income Tax and public spending economies are followed up (ibid).

Mortgage subsidy – the myth

1 I have treated this subject more fully in *Urban Economics: a Set Approach*, Edward Arnold, London 1979, especially in Chapter 5.
2 25th edn, London, 1962, 495.

7 Health

The economics of training nurses in the NHS

Keith Hartley and Alan Shiell
Source: *Economic Affairs*, June/July 1989, 9, 5, p. 32.

Nurses play a major part in the delivery of health care. The National Health Service (NHS) devotes considerable resources to their recruitment, training and retention. Within nursing, a considerable proportion of manpower (15-25 per cent) is provided by trainees. Traditionally, the NHS has relied upon the substantial recruitment of young women to obtain enough qualified staff who also provide cheap labour during training.

Entry to general nursing is either as an enrolled or registered nurse. Enrolled nursing requires a good general education and a two-year training as a pupil nurse. Enrolled nurses cannot progress beyond their grade, nor can they automatically proceed to further specialization. Also, the EC only recognizes registration as a qualification leading to free movement between member states. Entry to registered nurse training requires a minimum of five 'O'-levels and three years' training as a student nurse.

Surprisingly little is known about the training of nurses and whether the substantial new investments are worthwhile. Yet the current arrangements have been heavily criticized. Dissatisfaction has been expressed about reliance upon unqualified student labour, the role of two- and three-year training programmes, the status of trainees and of the enrolled nurse, together with the costs of the high wastage rates during training and following qualification. Worries also exist that demographic changes in the 1990s will make it more difficult to recruit young people.

To solve these problems, the nursing profession has formulated Project 2000 which has now been accepted by the government (Figure 7.1). Project 2000 will be costly, especially during the transition phase. Once fully implemented it is claimed that the total costs of training nurses will fall due to the lower wastage rates of both trainees and qualified nurses. Any assessment of Project 2000 needs to consider not only its likely costs and benefits but also the economics of the current system of training.

Training is an investment in human beings, creating human capital. It involves current costs in return for expected future benefits, and is undertaken so long as it is expected to be worthwhile. Training costs can be borne by individuals, employers or the taxpayers. For individuals, training costs include tuition fees, plus any foregone earnings.

Training is distinctive since the property rights in the skills usually remain with the individual regardless of the source of finance. This affects the distribution of training costs between trainees, employers and the state. Training for transferable skills which have value to large numbers of employers is likely to be financed by trainees or the state. In contrast, the training costs for non-transferable skills which have value to only one firm are likely to be borne by the employer.

Applying this economic approach to nurse training raises three related issues:

1. Does the training of nurses create transferable or non-transferable skills? If the skills are non-transferable or if the NHS regards itself as the only employer for UK nurses, then it might be expected to bear the costs of training.
2. If the NHS regards nurse skills as non-transferable and hence specific to the state health services then it will tend to offer relatively high pay during training to attract recruits. Later, it will recover its training investments by paying wages lower than the productivity of the newly-skilled workers. However, if nurse training has substantial elements of transferability, such a policy is likely to attract trainees who, when qualified, will leave for alternative more highly-paid occupations where other employers have not borne the costs of training. Clearly, the expansion of the UK private health care sector will create, as well as employment opportunities abroad, a substantial market for skilled nurses outside both the NHS and the UK. Also, registered nurses whose qualifications are recognized internationally obviously have a marketable asset. In such cases, training costs might be redistributed from the NHS to the trainee whilst offering higher salaries to qualified nurses.
3. Project 2000 involves abolishing enrolled nurse training, moving to registered status and trainees being treated as students, none of which is costless. What are the extra training costs and is there any evidence of the likely benefits?

Estimates show that it costs the Exchequer, at 1985–6 prices, some £10,000 to train each registered general nurse (RGN) and under £4,400 to train each enrolled general nurse (EGN). Thus, a policy of substituting RGNs for EGNs is costly: are the additional training expenditures a worthwhile investment for the NHS? Interestingly, enrolled nurses spend a much longer proportion of their training making a productive contribution to health care, so enabling the NHS to recover more of its costs during

Figure 7.1 Project 2,000 proposals

- A new single level of nurse, registered with the UK Central Council, requiring three years training, and replacing the present registered and enrolled nurses.
- A new grade of helper to undertake specific tasks in support of, and under the supervision of, qualified nurses.
- During training students should be supernumerary and receive non-means-tested grants. Because of the need for practical experience, students will provide some service contribution but the amount will be considerably reduced.
- Training for enrolled nurses will end but the grade will not be abolished. Enrolled nurses will be given opportunities to convert to registered status.

training and before qualification. On this basis, enrolled nurse training appears to be good value for money. However, registered nurses might remain in the NHS for longer periods than enrolled nurses and, whilst working, make a much greater contribution to benefits in the form of patient care. On the other hand, if registered nurses are provided with skills which are more transferable (such as international recognition), they are more likely to leave the NHS. Unfortunately, this is an area where evidence is conspicuous by its absence.

Project 2000 claims that there will be benefits in the quantity of nurse education and in patient care, and that these benefits are 'considerable but unquantifiable'. Doubts arise as to whether educational benefits are the proper concern of the NHS. Moreover, should Project 2000 be introduced without convincing evidence that the extra benefits to patient care will be at least equal to the extra costs of the new training system? The possibility arises that Project 2000 might benefit nurses rather than patients.

A policy for the NHS, parts I and II

Patrick Minford
Source: Economic Affairs, October/November 1988, 9, 1, p. 21. December/January 1989, 9, 2, p. 23.

The NHS is in crisis. Yet those who call for more resources for it without reform carry little credibility. In 1947 the NHS boldly attempted to sever the connection between access to health care and the ability to pay. But even some sympathetic academics (such as Grand and Titmuss) have documented its failure in this attempt. Unfortunately it has failed expensively and is prone to chronic problems which cannot be solved simply by more funding.

The problems were inherent in the removal of health care from the market-place. If a commodity is offered free at the point of consumption, there will be excess demand, some rationing device must be found. The NHS uses several; some patients are not treated, some join waiting lists or go private, and more urgent cases are treated according to informal and often arbitrary priority schemes. Not only does this cause inefficiency in the allocation of resources, but it is also a cause of constant political embarrassment; the government is blamed for waiting lists and for particular failures of treatment, as recently we have seen with children in intensive care and constant claims by doctors of the inadequacy of resources.

On the supply side, there is monopoly power and politicization of management, whose main object must be seen as coercing government and taxpayer to provide extra resources. Monitoring of costs by ministers is handicapped by lack of power over management, who have an interest in denying proper information for control and can engineer a headline-grabbing scandal of closed wards to frighten off too enthusiastic a search for economies.

Economic efficiency and political considerations both point to a greater role for the market, with government intervention reserved to ensure effective protection of the weak, the poor and the unfortunate. This article argues that this can best be achieved within a privately organized insurance system.

In 1984, I argued for privatization of supply, charging for health-care supplies, compulsory basic health insurance, and direct cash help for those unable to afford this insurance. Individuals would then choose freely to spend extra private resources either directly on health-care supplies or indirectly through more expensive insurance. This solution I believe still offers the best prospect.

The practical questions are how precisely to arrange this eventual solution in detail and what steps can be taken to make it easier for politicians to introduce.

Health expenditure falls into three main categories. There is spending to maintain or promote good health; this is a wide spectrum covering diet, exercise, constructive leisure activities, preventative medicine, and anything else that forms part of a healthy life. While much ink has been spilt on the government's duty to spend on preventative health measures, beyond obvious things like free inoculations and public information campaigns, there is no case for intervention. Nevertheless, in a reformed NHS public health, hygiene and information on health issues would remain an important area of government activity.

The second category is care for those who are old or disabled or in some other way unable to look after themselves, but who do not require active medical assistance. There is already a substantial private sector and there is no good reason why the rest should not be privatized subject to safeguards against fraud and exploitation.

The idea of giving vouchers or cash help to those in need is also natural

Figure 7.2 Traps in health reform

The free market arguments for privatization rest on the monopoly power and resulting inefficiency of public provision, the denial of free choice to the consumer with bureaucratic choice inefficiently second-guessing consumer needs and creating queues. The current system also has the added burden of inefficiency from the incentive-reducing taxation needed to pay the cost of publicly provided health services.

Against this line of argument are ranged two main sets of arguments, which are the traps outlined in this box.

First, it is argued that health care is a service that morally should be available equally. Waiting lists, with first-come first-served, not price, should be used to ration scarce resources. Political difficulties arise, reflecting these moral attitudes, if waiting times become excessively long for essential treatments.

These attitudes are inescapable. Any reform must not confront them or it will risk political destruction. They are subject to qualifications, and it is these qualifications that allow elements of a free market solution as sketched in the current article.

It advocates the design of a basic health-care insurance policy, to be affordable by all, if necessary with income support. Essential, high cost, and emergency services would be insured differently from low cost and inessential services. Acceptable waiting times will be defined in the light of necessity and cost. To ensure equality in essential health protection, the policy would be compulsory with the poor covered, paid for but unable to switch the money received into other forms of spending.

By definition any voluntary spending above this minimum will be politically acceptable, since the voters will decide – if necessary they could do so by some form of direct consultation – on the characteristics of the basic contract; more they would not wish to pay for. But of course no one would be prevented from paying for more on his or her own account.

The second set of arguments relate to the possible inefficiency of the free market in health. It is said that information is inadequate for consumers to exercise proper choice; doctors have the information and must be regulated to prevent them abusing their powerful position.

In private health insurance two main problems arise. First, people who are a poor risk conceal their true riskiness and to protect themselves against this insurance companies have to charge higher than normal premiums. In turn this discourages the people with normal risks so that a vicious circle develops, of excessive premiums being charged for the worst risks only. This 'adverse selection' problem can be solved by regulation, forcing a large population to insure so that premiums can be kept down.

Secondly, private insurance companies have trouble controlling the costs of claims, because doctors have an interest in inflating bills by, for example, over-prescribing or over-testing. The insured have no interest in limiting costs and may have an interest in inflating them in certain ways. This is 'moral hazard' in health insurance in its particularly dangerous form of 'third party effects'; insurance companies have difficulty in controlling doctors because of their information advantage.

These arguments have been deployed over the years by health economists eager to preserve the NHS. But they neglect the ability of free markets to produce market solutions. Doctors are hired by companies to check applicants; if doctors have better information they may well be able to deploy it effectively in this sort of screening, so limiting adverse selection. Consumers do not have professional information about the qualities of different doctors or hospitals but they can consult independent experts who make a living from such comparisons. Reputations for good treatment will become an important market force – just as for airline or drug safety. Third party moral hazard can be contained by insurance companies sending their customers to their own hospitals or by paying only according to their own competitively priced scale of charges.

Competition is a potential force in both the supply of health care and of insurance. Hospitals that are inadequate will eventually go out of business, as will insurance companies that do not ensure minimum cost in satisfying claims. Much has been made of the explosion of health-care costs in the USA; but this has come about largely because of the growth of Medicare and Medicaid, both state programmes where cost control by the state insurer has not been subject to the disciplines of competition. The private sector in the USA has produced a variety of competitive innovations, including the Health Maintenance Organizations designed to protect people against doctors' over-treatment in fee-for-service, and the vertical integration of insurance, doctors and hospitals in particular companies such as Humana. The power of the American Medical Association has been broken not by government but by these private developments. The US health system is no model but it does exhibit interesting features, that a free market here could certainly imitate. (The issue of malpractice suits is a US problem which is as potentially important here, NHS or no; its resolution requires the courts to take into account the full social costs of their settlements. Awards that are too high act as a tax on the whole health-care sector, because they induce doctors to over-test and over-prescribe to protect themselves, with the effect that the cost of malpractice insurance soars.)

These problems should by no means be dismissed. But for the most part they can be dealt with by the market. Regulation may also have a role to play as a last resort. We have seen in any case that compulsory basic insurance, put in our proposal for other reasons, compensates automatically any adverse selection for basic care. No doubt too the government will continue to exercise powers of consumer standard inspection in the medical as in other areas. A little regulation to allow markets to work is preferable to a totally controlled, centralized organization like the NHS.

To conclude, there are indeed traps for the unwary health reformer but they can be skirted with a little care.

---

here; the gain would be that clients can shop around, and that they will find the most appropriate solution for their needs. Their own families may be in some cases the best source of home and help; the cash or voucher would not discriminate against this solution.

The last category is the NHS core-curative medicine dispensed by GPs and hospitals, both in the NHS and the private sector. This part is the most difficult to reform.

I list the traps awaiting the unwary reformer. The most dangerous is the morally charged nature of curative medicine; many feel it is wrong that an ill person should be denied treatment because he or she cannot afford it.

There is misunderstanding and confusion about the nature of most sorts of medical care. Some is urgent and unpredictable – such as accident medicine. But much of NHS work is elective. Most therapies are a complex bundle of skilled medical treatment, care and hotel conditions. This allows considerable flexibility and choice. Many people, and not only the rich, may wish to exercise choice over qualities of treatment. This would not mean, as some opponents of reform have argued, variation in medical standards, with poorer people getting inferior treatment; rather the non-essential elements, including timing, would naturally be tailored to individual choice.

The moral charge does not extend to waiting for certain periods or to being denied non-essential treatment, such as much cosmetic surgery, or to hotel conditions in hospital. This limitation on the universality principle fortunately gives some flexibility.

Politically, a major problem is the length of waiting times and waiting lists. As we shall see, the efficient economic solution will dramatically reduce if not totally eliminate this problem.

140   Recent controversies in political economy

From a purely economic viewpoint, there are three main sets of problems. Efficient insurance and effective consumer choice require good information on claimant patients, on rival medical services, and control on the costs of satisfying insurance claims. Competition, efficient resource allocation and minimizing the burden of taxation on incentives point to privatization and charging. But finally, if direct help is given to those who cannot afford to pay directly or through insurance, it should not worsen the poverty trap.

To satisfy the universality principle as seen by the typical taxpayer, a basic insurance contract should be devised, which provides essential curative medicine. It should define clearly what is expected to be paid for in different contingencies; presumably, from nothing for routine doctor's visits to all of bills for serious operations, but this aspect, the degree of coinsurance, would need to be carefully thought out, especially in the

Figure 7.3 Summary of proposals for the NHS

- Health insurance contract to be drawn up and costed (the NHS premium) for a basic curative service. Maximum waiting times to be scheduled initially for different services, but expected to fall sharply as the market works.

- NHS costs in National Insurance to be earmarked; one part as the NHS premium, the other as the NHS tax supporting the poor and those not insurable at the normal premium.

- Basic contract to be compulsory. Contracting out permitted to wider contract (if so, NHS premium rebated but access to NHS services only at full cost.)

- Privatization of supply of medical care, possibly on a regional basis, with each regional company forced to divest one major hospital or district.

- Privatization of insurance, again possibly by region. NHS premiums rebated. Private companies quote directly to consumers.

- Income support (approximating to a voucher) implemented by existing family credit and income support system.

- Those not normally insurable to have premiums topped up by government to whatever necessary for basic contract.

- Government left in role of regulator (for contents of basic contract, for competitive process and for consumer standards); and provider of income support to poor and of topping-up premiums to those not normally insurable.

- Exchequer cost self-financing if no efficiency gains; but these are likely to be considerable because of competition in supply and insurance and free consumer choice.

- Waiting times likely to fall dramatically because the gap between the cost of NHS treatment and privately-insured treatment will fall to the true difference so that more people will opt for enhanced insurance.

- Increased resources will flow into health care, for the same reason that the extra cost of enhanced insurance will fall to its true cost.

transition period. The contract would also specify maximum waiting times in these contingencies; again from long to short depending on the urgency of the treatment. In fact, as argued below, I expect waiting times to disappear as the industry organized itself to meet demand efficiently; waiting is essentially a feature of a planned and rationed health-care industry. But including maximum times in the contract would be a reassuring feature in the transition period.

The contract should then be priced, on the assumption that it is compulsory for the whole population (some will add to it, as we shall see). Compulsion is necessary to enable a fair actuarial premium to be charged, which requires a large pool of insured persons. It also ensures proper personal cover; health insurance can be compared to having third party motor insurance, in that it is a public good that people should be obliged to purchase.

Payment of this insurance premium should replace one part of National Insurance contributions currently devoted to the NHS; the other part represents the implicit tax being paid to support the poor and those not insurable on normal terms. The precise way in which this support would be given, essentially as now, is dealt with later.

Some will wish to take out larger policies and will pay accordingly as they do now; only they will be able to contract out of, or convert, their basic policy and so pay only the extra cost of the policy enhancement, whereas at present they pay twice to some degree.

So far the proposal mirrors a number that are circulating. But more radical action is needed to make the new framework work much better than the old. Merely relabelling national insurance and allowing partial contracting-out of the NHS could mean that the NHS would be left with the poor and the less cheaply insured cases so raising the average cost per case in the public sector. There would be improvement of some aspects, notably waiting times, and resources would flow into medicine through the private sector; fewer resources would be needed in the NHS because of the lower number of cases.

But there could be difficulties politically in having the NHS seen as a lower class service. Also, the service would still be bureaucratic and politicized, without competition either in the insurance process or the supply of the medical service. These problems are renewed by the move to full private supply and insurance, to which we now turn. Besides competition, this will ensure that no one part of the insured population is concentrated with one company or in one part of the industry.

Accordingly, we now propose to hand over the operation of the basic insurance contracts to the private sector, as well as the bigger contracts which are already private. A competitive insurance industry would keep cost and premiums down by shopping around the medical sector and by competing on the premiums offered to the public. Premiums would be paid to these companies.

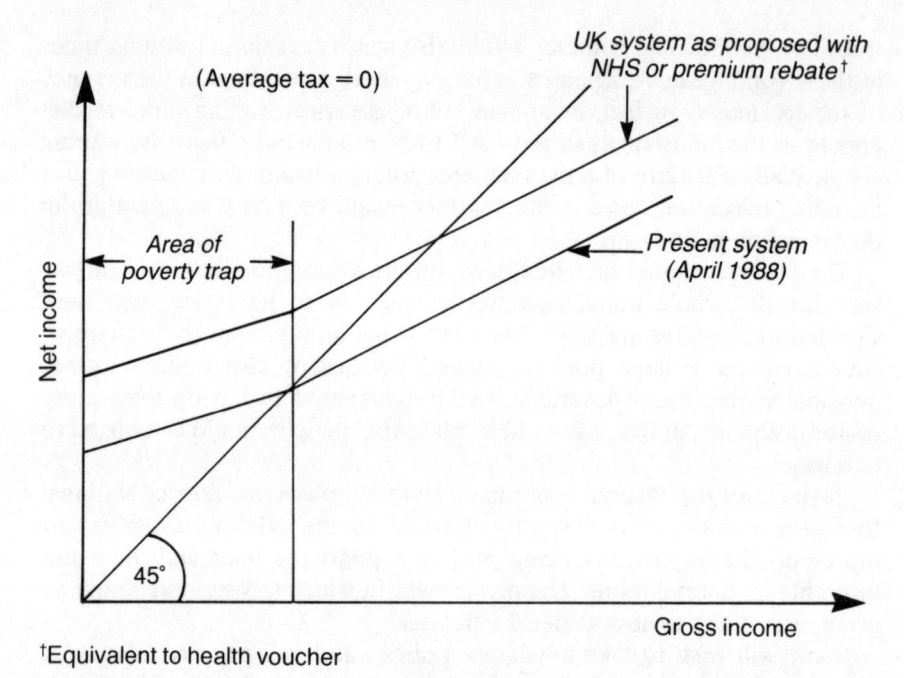

142 Recent controversies in political economy

Figure 7.4 Income support for health

†Equivalent to health voucher

The government's role would be limited to that of policing the compulsory insurance and vetting policies for compliance with the compulsory minimum contract; this would include regulating competition between companies to ensure no creaming off of good risks from a rival company's market. It could be argued that the state itself should remain as the provider of the basic insurance contract, since regulation would be complex in practice. But it should be possible to design rules of fair competition, much as is done in other areas raising complex issues; for example, takeovers and insider dealing, Lloyds underwriting, and the investment industry generally.

The precise details of contract design require careful attention and are not discussed in this paper. Essentially, the basic contract implies not a single normal premium but a lifetime premium structure rising with age, with designated renewal dates corresponding to these age points; companies would compete by offering a complete schedule of premiums for each age group, and would have to accept anyone who applied. Those falling outside normal risk categories must also be covered on the schedules with a relevant price; as discussed later, the government will top up their premiums (just as now it pays for them directly) according to politically agreed criteria of social support. Regulation would in this way ensure that companies competed across the whole population, offering a complete service.

We now turn to the structure of the medical industry itself. This has no need for public intervention, since the insurance contract has done all the necessary work. GP services are already private partnerships, but hospitals would need to be sold off to private organizations (including charities) in combinations that gave no group a monopoly in any region.

It is tempting to think of selling whole regions off as they stand. This would avoid breaking up current administrative units, with all their local expertise and information. The disadvantage would be the lack of competition within regions, which could be serious. Nevertheless, competition could be ensured by divesting each regional group of at least one major hospital (or possibly of one whole centrally placed district); the divested units would be sold separately to one or two major private firms operating across the country, no doubt already in the business of private sector medicine.

It is hard to predict what final structure would emerge from this sell-off. But probably, as in the US, links would be formed between GP practices, hospitals and insurance companies to minimize administrative and monitoring costs. These links need not be ownership, however, they could be merely contractual. Probably, too, health maintenance organizations would grow as in the US, offering the consumer the advantage of paying his or her GP a fee for health maintenance and not for treatment. In any case, subject to the control of regional monopoly, this restructuring is best left to the private sector to work out through market forces.

The break-up of the industry should ensure that firms negotiate with their own doctors, nurses and ancillaries as in a competitive labour market. Attempts might be made by some unions to exert monopoly labour power. But the existing and new labour laws should be sufficient to break any such attempts; there is an international market in doctors, ancillaries are easily recruited from the unemployed, and there is a large potential supply of trainee nurses among non-working women. Below, I argue for the opening up of the medical schools to competition, to ensure free entry into the medical profession – ultimately the only way to break its monopoly power. Firms will also have strong incentives in the competitive environment to resist labour power, as the alternative is to go out of business.

Very likely the new arrangements would benefit workers in the industry without the exercise of any monopoly power, as the health-care business will undoubtedly expand rapidly once privatized. This is, contrary to what is often implied, clearly a good thing provided that the labour market is not protected from competition by union laws or restricted entry. The health industry is a potentially dynamic part of the economy (as in the US) and it is not allowed currently to realize its potential for jobs and wealth.

The last element in this reform is the system of support for the poor upon whom the extra costs of the compulsory insurance contract would fall as an extra burden compared with their current NHS-related national insurance payments (including those made on their behalf by their employers). They would now also have to pay for those elements of health care not paid for by the insurance contract – for example, doctor's visits and medicines up to some modest level.

In my 1984 article, I argued that amounts should be added to supplementary benefit and to family credits to offset these extra payments; the extra costs in respect of children should be added to child benefit. This is still, I believe, the only practicable way. In that article I showed that it would not seriously worsen the poverty trap; the extra child benefit element involves no worsening at all, while the adult element does cause a modest worsening offset there by large rises in tax thresholds. Even this worsening can be avoided if the extra family credit and supplementary benefit payments and national insurance rebates are structured carefully to approximate to a voucher system. This involves subjecting the extra NHS-related supplement to the poor to withdrawal only when they qualify for the full NHS National Insurance rebate – see in Figure 7.4.

The reforms should yield a significant fiscal surplus which can be distributed in tax cuts or rising tax thresholds to achieve a positive improvement in incentives generally. While it is not possible to be precise about the arithmetic because there has not yet been a serious attempt to price the basic insurance contract or to assess the privatization revenue, one can make up a schedule of public finance gains and losses as follows:

1. Gains: Recurrent saving of NHS budget
   Privatization sale revenues implying a recurrent saving of debt interest resulting from liquidating government stocks.
2. Losses: Reduction of national insurance contributions by an amount equal to the cost of the basic insurance contract for the whole population (rebate of the NHS premium).

Cost of income support for the poor (defined as those currently receiving supplementary benefit and family credit) equals the difference between the cost of the basic insurance contract and the reduction in their National Insurance contributions.

Funding of those not covered by the new basic insurance contract – because already ill or too old to be normally insurable – can be thought of as paying an extra premium on top of the basic premium cost above. Much of this is transitional so the recurrent cost is mainly the extra interest on the public debt needed to fund these transitional costs, plus an amount for topping-up. This continuing payment will cover those who, even when insured privately from birth, begin with or develop above-normal risks. At each renewal date the state will top up premiums for those who move out of the normal risk category, with topping-up being regulated by agreed criteria (much along the lines of current sickness and disability benefits). The proposed system comprehensively covers the whole population as now.

The transition would be self-financing if the new system makes no efficiency gains; this is because one is simply giving people back the money they are currently paying so that they can pay for the same service privately and ensuring that the poor still get the service they are now getting at the same cost. The only change that costs extra money is the rebate to those already with private insurance, in so far as this insurance duplicates what is offered by the NHS. This element of duplication is likely to be quite small as existing private insurance tends to provide a supplementary service for the most part, leaving the acute and the expensive treatments to the NHS.

But the point of the change is to establish a system of incentives to achieve greater efficiency. By introducing competition in supply and insurance, by allowing consumer choice, and not least by depoliticizing management (so that it can take decisions free from media pressure on politicians to intervene), the efficiency gains could be large. This has been the experience so far in the privatization programme. There are good reasons for believing the NHS to be the inefficient supplier and its obvious failure to satisfy consumers is unlikely to be entirely due to the fact that it is free at the point of delivery. There are obvious parallels on the supply side with the large de-nationalized industries like British Airways, British Steel, and Austin Rover. On the demand side, the less close parallels are with education and local authority services (increasingly being charged for, especially with the introduction of the community charge). The essence of the market case is that we do not really know until the market has done its work in a way that no central planner can guess. In short, there are likely to be significant savings, available to raise tax thresholds and improve the poverty trap, or increase incentives generally through tax cuts.

The ideas outlined above have been designed for maximum flexibility in introduction; it is a privatization-cum-insurance-voucher scheme. By using the national insurance and income support system, greater flexibility is possible than with explicit vouchers (though these can still be used if politically their simplicity and transparency seem desirable). In such a sensitive area, a step-by-step approach seems inevitable.

From the public finance viewpoint, the privatization revenue and the phasing of national insurance rebates both create a source of financing to meet the largely transitional costs of those who will not be normally insurable.

Privatization of hospitals can occur independently of the switch to private in place of state insurance. Privatization could take place by region, starting perhaps with the prosperous Southern regions with large Conservative majorities.

Preparations for privatization could begin at once with internal markets whereby hospitals within the NHS become profit-centres competing with one another for the custom of regional health authorities (RHAs) and they can spend their resources in hospitals outside their region. Restrictions on competition between GPs should be lifted.

Preparation would include proper accounting procedures in hospitals so that costs can be allocated across activities and patients. All patients should be charged according to their actual cost, making it possible then to charge other RHAs on a real basis.

Turning next to insurance, the estimated total costs of the NHS should be charged explicitly against the national insurance fund; a part of national insurance contributions should be earmarked as an NHS charge. This charge is to be thought of in two parts, the NHS premium and the NHS tax, and it would be helpful to make this clear so that people should not expect eventual rebates of the whole amount.

It would then be possible to proceed region by region. An RHA which had prepared full accounts and costings would be in a position to make actuarial calculations of insurance premiums for normal and high-risk categories of patient in its region. It would invite quotations from competing private insurance companies for its entire population in the first instance. It would then hand over its population to the successful company. People in that region would then be rebated their earmarked NHS premium; for those in high-risk categories the government would also credit them with the extra premium over normal. Those in the region on family credit and supplementary benefit would be topped up as described earlier.

One could imagine this as a second stage after the region had successfully privatized its supply side. The RHA would then be left as a private hospital-service company, with whatever commercial links it desired to GP partnerships.

The ultimate scheme leaves no room for tax relief, because there does not seem to be a case for subsidizing health-care expenditure relative to other goods and services. Indeed, if anything the opposite is the case; we want people to remain healthy, so they should spend their money on prevention including healthy living, and the curing process should reflect its true expense to discourage careless illness.

Nor does tax relief play even a transitional role, for the same reason. It might seem attractive to give tax relief to private medical care in order to encourage people to increase their insurance and relieve the NHS of caring for them. But this would not in practice relieve the NHS of its role in caring for such people; the private sector is unable to cope in acute operative surgery or expensive treatments. Private insurance currently provides fast service for elective treatments, relying on the NHS for the rest. It is an add-on symbiotic service. People already are using this service precisely to speed up operations for which there are long NHS waiting times.

Giving tax relief would reduce waiting times for such operations. But it is a blunt instrument, not designed to mirror accurately the relative cost of private set against NHS care. It could develop into an unnecessarily large charge on the exchequer, and would prove difficult ever to remove. Besides, there is a basic economic inefficiency in subsidizing curative as against preventative medicine.

An alternative proposal is to allow contracting-out of the NHS premium in return for joining a full private scheme. This is quite different, because it assumes that the private scheme would offer a complete service outside the NHS; the contracted-out insuree would forfeit entirely rights to NHS treatment, except at full cost. Since in our scheme here it is envisaged that the basic insurance contract would be competitively priced, the person who pays privately will get no advantage. There is no objection to allowing this sort of contracting-out early on. The contract will not undermine the capacity of an RHA to offer a large viable population to insurers, since they will already have people who have contracted-out on their policies, and can put them into the insurable pool.

The transitional movement towards the final pattern of provision can be expected to take a number of different routes. As the ideas and experience spread, the pace of change is naturally likely to speed up. The programme enables constructive action to be taken without political storms and yet goes in an appropriate direction for long-term change.

Once the new system is in place, government will have two main residual roles. It will regulate the content of the basic insurance contract (not its price which will be determined by competition) and will ensure that information from medical research flows freely and effectively through the population. Other information – about the effectiveness of individual doctors and hospitals, for example – is best left to the market, though the government as regulator of consumer standards generally will obviously take an interest in professional incompetence and fraud.

The role of medical education will need to be considered in the context of university reforms. It would make sense for the medial schools to be privatized and to charge fees, with the government acting solely as a provider of scholarships to worthy students. These schools would negotiate contracts with private hospitals to collaborate, much as now occurs in the NHS. By introducing competition in the schools the restriction of entry into the medical profession, giving it its monopoly power, would be frustrated.

The basic insurance contract was to specify all aspects of medical services to be made available and their refund structure. One aspect of great political significance is waiting times. Maximum waiting times are to be specified in the contract for different categories of illness. The NHS currently operates a policy of urgency ratings to regulate waiting times and practices vary widely around the regions and even within them. These disparities cause political embarrassment; indeed there is the suspicion that waiting times are manipulated to cause enough embarrassment to get additional resources.

The private sector gets its business currently from treatments that are not too expensive where patients would rather pay than wait the specified NHS period. For such treatments NHS waiting time is determined by the marginal cost to patients of waiting relative to the cost of the private operation. For example, if a treatment costs £500 and the cost of waiting an

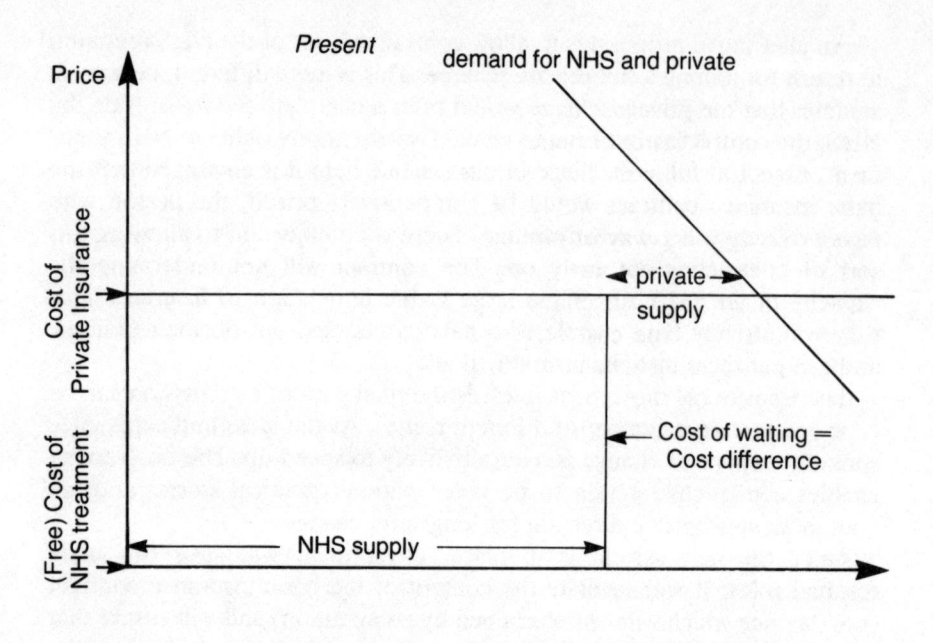

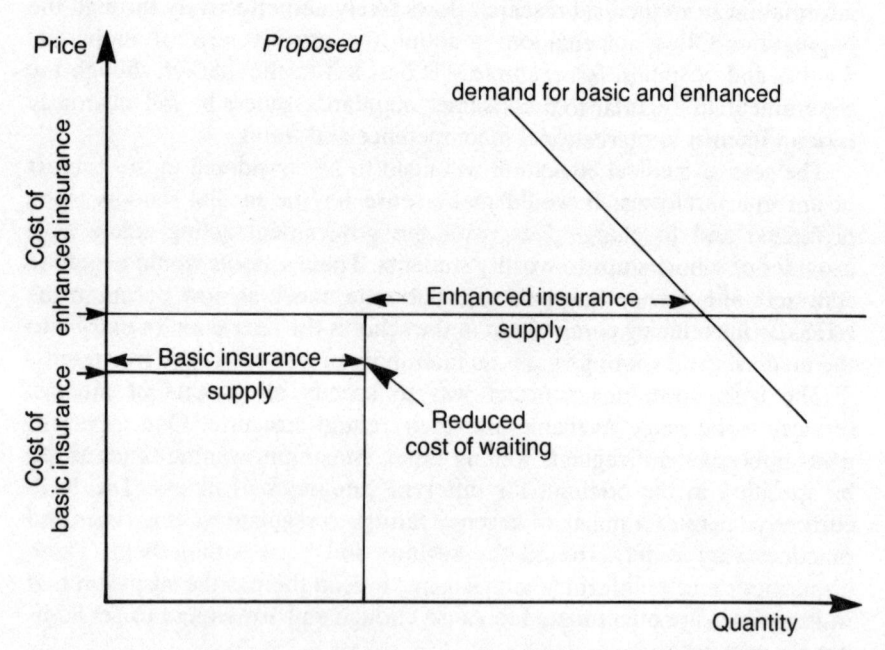

148 *Recent controversies in political economy*

Figure 7.5 The demand for enhanced insurance under present and proposed systems

extra week is £100 then the average waiting time will be five weeks.

Under the proposed new system, people will opt for extra insurance on a much larger scale because its extra cost will reflect only the extra resources needed to give a faster or better service. In the previous example, it might cost only £100 more to have the operation in one week rather than five; then the extra insurance will reflect that, so that waiting time will drop to one week. Another way of putting this is that, if you go private now, you pay up to twice; in the new system you will not pay the basic premium if you opt out of the basic contract. In other words, the cost of waiting will fall to equal the true cost of reducing waiting, with a gain in consumer welfare and a probably sharp reduction in waiting time. Figure 7.5 illustrates this point.

It is likely that waiting lists as we know them will be entirely eliminated and they are virtually unknown in the USA. The extra cost of providing a service essentially on demand subject to normal operational delays is probably quite small and waiting time would correspondingly be small too; the NHS operates with large queues not because it saves much money but because it is a necessary rationing device.

In setting the terms of the basic contract, waiting times will be set initially as a reassuring safeguard to reflect the average voter's trade-off between waiting for specified treatments and the cost to be paid, in the form of the minimum insurance fee plus the NHS support tax. Presumably the result will be similar to the average in the NHS today; non-urgent treatment will also be largely covered by more expensive policies that buy speed, leaving the basic policy to provide such treatment to those who prefer to wait. The political gain is that the maximum waiting times would be known and contracted for, so that any delinquent hospital would be disciplined. Furthermore, politicians would no longer be involved in policing delinquents; they would merely reflect popular feelings about the basic contract, pointing out the cost to those who want it expanded. Finally, the average voter would – as shown above – take out more enhanced insurance than now, have a much lower waiting time, and be better satisfied.

A private system might not entirely abolish waiting time but it would efficiently price and regulate it. Average waiting times would fall sharply as a result of efficient pricing; while all including the poor would be guaranteed maximum waiting times by the explicit terms of the basic contract. Waiting would cease to be an issue or politicians.

A major aim of reform is to ensure that resources move into health care in response to people's demands. Again, just as with waiting time, the new system will, by bringing down the extra cost of buying improved service to the true extra cost, increase the demand for enhanced insurance for this purpose too – for example, to pay for more nursing care or better hotel services. At present the buyer of these extra services pays up to twice for them, a considerable disincentive. Here too we would see a closer correspondence between consumers' demands and health supplies.

Part II

In my first article (*Economic Affairs*, Volume 9, **1**, October/November) I sketched out a market solution to the problems of the National Health Service. It consisted of privatizing the supply side, the consumer to pay for private insurance, with a basic insurance policy to be universally compulsory, and the government's role to be limited to helping the poor and chronically sick directly through income support. I recognize that moving towards this solution would take time and also discussed possible steps along the road. By now, the debate over the NHS is well advanced and we even have some hints of the conclusion on which the Whitehall review process is converging, under the new Minister for Health, Mr Kenneth Clarke. This article is devoted to the short-term issue of what should be done now, as a result of the review.

The NHS already has had one review, that of Mr (now Sir) Roy Griffiths in 1983.[1] It will be recalled, that he recommended that the NHS needed more management, but that the basic structure was sound. The government took Sir Roy's advice, and applied it, appointing managers to all health authorities. Yet today the problems are as bad as ever. The approach, of shoring up the existing structure, has manifestly failed.

The reason that it failed is obvious. First, there was no competition to spur producers to better efforts; instead, the existing vested interests – doctors, nurses, administrators, and ancillaries – continued to share power and resources. They and their unions had an understanding, and the new managers, lacking powers to break this consensus, could at best go along; in most cases, they were recruited from the existing ranks of doctors and administrators.

Secondly, the consumer was given no say in the allocation of resources. In particular, GPs at the gateway to the NHS held a monopoly of access to NHS resources, apart from the desperate measure increasingly tried by consumers, of going direct to hospital casualty departments, with long waits and no guarantee of any better service. The result has been an increasing remoteness of the NHS from patients' demands, poor quality service and excessive waiting times.

The consumer's impotence also ensured that the cosy consensus among producers was under no threat from outside, except from their political masters; but they, of course, were easily dealt with by the producers, who resisted attempts to discipline them by cutting services most likely to cause indignation among politicians and newspapers.

Waiting lists are the issue that causes most controversy in the NHS. They have been used with great effect by the producer lobbies to demand more money. Yet the irony is, as we shall discuss below, that these lists are the result of the NHS's monolithic planning structure and insensitivity to consumer demands; and that they cannot be removed without changing the system itself, any more than Soviet queues for groceries can be removed without allowing market forces to operate.

The current review must recommend genuine change in the system, if it is not to fail like its predecessor. And the signs are that Mr Clarke, the Treasury and Number 10 have seen this point, for all the bland reassurance in Clarke's speech at the Conservative Party conference.

The most obvious means of achieving competition and choice are privatization and allowing the consumer to opt out. But equivalent alternatives with a less radical appearance are also possible and under active consideration.

The current front runner in the NHS review is an internal market (that is, NHS units should compete among themselves for patients) with GPs holding the budget for their patients. This means that GPs would choose and pay the hospitals and consultants on their patients' behalf. The government would then refund GPs like an insurance company, monitoring their bills against best-practice costs elsewhere.

True competition within the NHS would be ensured by letting GPs use private hospitals, homes, consultants and other services. This is equivalent to opting-out but it is being done by GPs, rather than the consumer personally. The effect is the same, to enable NHS waiting lists to be reduced by transferring patients to the private sector with an NHS credit. (To produce exactly the same effect, GPs must be cash-limited on each patient according to some NHS-entitlement formula; anything over that, whether spent in the NHS or the private sector, must be paid for by the patient, unless on income support.)

So far so good. But there is a major problem. GPs operate a closed shop, are notoriously uncompetitive and are protected by their trade union, the British Medical Association. Resources have been thrown at them (doubled since the war, up 50 per cent since 1978), yet standards have dropped by all available measures. Home visiting has halved in the last twenty years, use of locums has risen by a third in the last ten, and hospital emergency cases which bypass the GP have risen by two-thirds since 1965.

The variations in referral rates (the worst fifth 400 per cent higher than the best fifth) and in prescribing (with an 80 per cent differential between best and worst region) tell the same story of huge deviations from best practice across the country. Another symptom is that a quarter of GPs spend less than 30 hours a week on the job. But if, like Yvonne Gibson, patients try to get their rights, they are refused by NHS GPs as problem patients.[2]

It will not be much use having GPs doing the shopping around if they themselves are under no competitive pressure; they will simply go for good incomes and a quiet life.

Under full opting-out, the consumer could switch from his NHS GP to a private GP, so ensuring true competition between as well as with NHS GPs. Something equivalent should be included in the new proposals. A simple device would be to allow patients to switch to a private GP and transfer to him their NHS drugs and hospital budget with them; patients could also transfer to him the current NHS charge for GP services (or capitation fee). To make sure this produces genuine competition, the capitation fee should be set as low as possible (to cover no more than the most efficient no-frills service available); and NHS GPs should be allowed to charge for extra services, just like their private counterparts.

Though the BMA would object to this effective new system, hard-working individual doctors have much to gain and there are obvious attractions to the consumer. The proposals would be both a giant step forward and attractive to politicians.

There are many other variants of this scheme one could pursue to introduce competition and consumer choice. Indeed, many of the suggestions for reform published in the past months have been much of this type.[3]

Other economists have supported the particular GP model that is now central to the review.[4]

All these proposals have been influenced by the highly successful experience of the health maintenance organizations (HMOs) in the USA, reflected in Professor Alain Enthoven's proposals to introduce them in an internal market within the NHS, *Reflections on the management of the National Health Service*[5]. The fact remains that we are dealing here with not so much an internal market as a total market to include the private sector, since in practice only the use of the private sector with its freedom of entry can ensure sufficient competition.

These proposals mainly differ on the extent of consumer choice. The first two studies envisage the consumer opting-out of his NHS GP service into private practice, whereas the last two do not. As I have argued above, the GP sector requires the competition that only genuine consumer choice between them can ensure.

Two other sets of proposals, David Green's *Everyone a Private Patient*[6] and Ray Whitney's *National Health Crisis*,[7] are more radical than these, in that like my blueprint in the last article in *Economic Affairs* they envisage private insurance and government income support. However, they too strongly endorse the HMO model as the likely market development under competition.

So the current of opinion is running strongly in favour of changes that will produce real competition across the health sector, with the government footing the bill for any opting-into the private sector that GPs decide to do. Assuming that the review accepts the consumer's right to opt for an alternative to his NHS GP, we have here a viable model of competition and consumer choice, but one that avoids the trappings of 'radicalism'.

In what follows, I want to deal with some of the arguments advanced by those hostile to such a release of market forces upon the NHS.

Health care is a special product the market cannot handle

Health economists who support the NHS make a lot of play with the special nature of health care as a product; they argue that because it involves insurance and because doctors know more than patients normal market mechanisms cannot work. But other products have the same characteristics and we would not dream of more than lightly regulating them; house rebuilding, for example, where we take out house insurance and builders know far more than we do, yet the market rules. Markets find ways of dealing with insurance and information problems.

This is shown not least by the world's biggest health-care market, that of the United States[8]. This market was finally freed of doctor monopoly power by a 1982 Supreme Court decision against the American Medical Association, declaring that AMA boycotts of the new health maintenance organizations were illegal. These HMOs and similar companies offer the services of doctors and hospitals to consumers in novel ways that compete with the traditional visit to the doctor for a fee followed by possible referral and covered by separate insurance.

For example, the HMO company will offer to insure you for your health problems for a fixed subscription, provided you go to their doctors and hospitals. But putting the insurance company and the doctors together they cut out the padding of costs in insurance claims. By shopping around for doctors and hospitals, they cut the basic costs as well. Finally, like house builders they advertise their own strengths and their competitors' weaknesses, so that the consumer has sufficient information about comparative performance to make a reasonable choice on quality and price.

Such failures in the American market system as there were, can now be seen to be due to overregulation which encouraged the monopoly power of the doctors; it had the effect of preventing the growth of a true market, such as has now grown up with remarkable rapidity since the monopoly was broken. So a market solution for the NHS – with its curbing of inefficiency and waiting lists and its provision of consumer choice – would work.

The NHS reduces waste in health spending

According to some economists, the NHS is an excellent instrument for curbing wasteful health expenditure[9]. They argue cynically that curative medicine is largely ineffective and preventive medicine little better, so that the problem of health care is that of stopping people spending on it as far as possible, while satisfying their need for '(an often illusory) reassurance'. The authentic voice of the planner!

But this view is not without flaws. First there is its contempt for the consumer's preferences; yet who is to judge a person's need to spend money on health care and reassurance, including even the taking of unnecessary tests, other than that person himself or herself? It is right to be concerned about waste by doctors whose spending and prescribing patterns are out of control; but the competition of the HMOs just discussed takes care of this.

Second the manifest variation in hospital and GP performance across the country (cited above) and the evidence of surveys of consumer dissatisfaction belie these authors' claims of efficiency.

But, third, the Achilles' heel of the NHS efficiency-claim is waiting time. We do not know exactly what the 0.75 million people waiting for NHS operations are suffering by way of loss in earning power or enjoyment of life; let alone what the millions of them lose waiting in NHS surgeries or outpatient clinics and so on. But a figure of £2 billion per year of pure loss or about 0.5 per cent of GDP, can be estimated.

Time will be spent in waiting for an NHS operation until its cost is just equal to the cost of going private. The average waiting time for NHS operations is just over four months and the average acute operation costs about £700: hence the cost of waiting four months is £700, or £40 per week. It can be thought of as the extra income, or welfare, obtained if the operation is brought forward by the waiting period of four months. Notice that £40 per week is about one-fifth of the average weekly wage, suggesting that people when pre-operative and waiting are on average about 20 per cent less productive or happy than they are after the operation.

If this cost is multiplied by the 750,000 people waiting for NHS operations, the total annual cost rises to £11.5 billion, plus whatever is due to other NHS queues, perhaps £2 billion in all.

Waiting lists can be dealt with by spending more on the NHS

This is the cry of the NHS administrator, and indeed it is also a trap into which politicians too easily fall – as witnessed by last year's Conservative Party conference, when promises were made to cut waiting lists by concentrating resources on them; needless to say, the promises cannot be kept, in spite of heroic efforts by the NHS and ministers.

Waiting lists are equal to average waiting time (set by the cost of going private as above) multiplied by the rate at which people are operated on. If the NHS can only handle a few people at a time then there will only be a few people in the queue; the rest will go private. But if the NHS becomes bigger and quicker, the waiting lists will grow, as more people join them from the private sector.

It is rather as if on a crowded beach on a hot summer day, an ice cream man appears and a queue forms. It soon reaches ten minutes in length, and many on the beach decide to do without. But now a second and a third ice cream man comes. Of course there are now three ten-minute queues formed along the beach. Waiting lists have risen in proportion to supply.

Thus we obtain the NHS waiting-list paradox. More spending equals longer lists, not to speak of more political ammunition for the critics.

Figure 7.6 Waiting time

Waiting time statistics do not go back very far, but the data since 1972 reveal a statistically significant relationship with both the cost gap (NHS/private) and real disposable income:

Log of waiting time = −7.0 (5.35) + 0.34 (2.87) log of previous year's cost gap + 1.05 (6.01) log of real disposable income

t-values in parenthesis. $R^2 = 0.85$. Durbin-Watson = 2.05. Sample period 1972–1985.

This regression suggests that a 1 per cent rise in the cost gap raises waiting time by 0.34 per cent while a 1 per cent rise in incomes raises it by 1.05 per cent. The effect of income must reflect the increasing desire of people to have operations which involve a loss of earning power and other expenses (even if the operation itself is free), as they get richer; this effect is on average more powerful than the rising price of their time spent waiting. Presumably, more and more ordinary people are drawn into waiting, while those at the top end of the income distribution increasingly go private.

The key point is that waiting time can be explained as a rational private decision, and quite independently of the supply of NHS services. It follows that more NHS provision will not alter waiting time, only waiting lists (= waiting time × rate of removal from the lists) – upwards in proportion!

Opting-out as under these proposals, however concealed, will be expensive to the Treasury

Waiting lists are the core of the failure of the NHS. But the bureaucrats say that they will eliminate waiting lists by greater efficiency and that there is no need to change the system in any radical way. How wrong they are!

The main enemy of opting-out has been the Treasury's expenditure division, which begrudges the £0.4 billion direct cost of opting-out (as those with existing private insurance get their NHS money back). Yet a rise in the tax base of £2 billion will yield the Treasury around £0.8 billion in extra taxes at current rates. To this can be added NHS cost reductions from introducing competition, which cannot be estimated but could well, judging by the gains from contracting out by health and local authorities, be of the order of 20 per cent. By contrast, existing policies promise a continuous drain on revenues, as the inexorable demands for NHS supplementation proceed. Mr Lawson should overrule the mandarins.

A related concern of the Treasury is with the timing of private sector expansion. That the private sector would expand rapidly under opting-out is in little doubt.

Regression analysis of data since 1962 suggests that the long-run response of private hospital demand to a 1 per cent fall in the cost gap versus the NHS would be a rise of 3.8 per cent, with a 0.94 per cent rise in the first year. Suppose that opting-out reduced the cost gap by 50 per cent on average, this would imply a 50 per cent expansion in the private sector

Figure 7.7 Tax relief versus opting-out

Tax relief has been floated as an alternative to opting-out. However, it is inferior (if better than nothing on the demand side). Opting-out works by reducing the price differential between the NHS cost and the private cost. Strictly speaking, if the NHS service is valued properly, it eliminates the differential by giving the consumer exactly what he gets by value from the NHS as spending power in the private sector. Tax relief goes in the same direction. But it is not so exactly targeted on the differential and so it is less efficient – that is, it achieves less economic benefit per pound of tax revenue. First, it is worth more to a taxpayer than to a non- or low-taxpayer; and more to a high-rate taxpayer than a standard-rate taxpayer. Secondly, it is related to the amount spent privately, regardless of the value of what is provided by the NHS; yet opting-out would rightly give nothing if the NHS did not provide the service at all, and little if it provided it in small degree and with very long delays. Whereas if the NHS provided it routinely but with some delay, opting-out would give nearly the whole cost of the service. Tax relief subsidizes cosmetic surgery as much as hernia operations; opting-out gives spending power for hernias but none for the cosmetic surgery. Finally, tax relief suffers from a longer-term problem which does not affect opting-out. If in time the NHS becomes more market-orientated and charges more fully for its services, giving rebates or assistance to the poor and chronically sick, then opting-out payments will decline as the differential of NHS v. private cost declines; but tax relief will be seen as for health expenditure, and it will be hard to withdraw. We risk then ending up with tax relief for health-care spending in general, when logic dictates if anything a tax advantage for preventive spending and preferably no tax subsidies at all.

These arguments reveal incidentally that tax relief would be less popular than opting-out because the latter's benefits are more widely spread and also bring non-essential operations for painful conditions within the reach of many ordinary people.

---

in the year opting-out began with a 200 per cent expansion in the long run and about 150 per cent in five years. The equivalent contraction in the NHS would be about one-tenth of these percentages; about 5 per cent immediately rising eventually to 20 per cent.

The Treasury's concern is that the NHS could not in practice contract at this speed, so that there would not be the appropriate saving of public resources, and that total medical spending would rise, putting upward pressure on costs. Yet with the long leads involved in NHS reform, this concern looks misplaced; one need only look at the way electricity privatization is being prepared for now, eighteen months ahead of enactment, with the public sector generators cutting back plans and the new private boards already commissioning new private generating capacity. If the NHS is privatized at least partially on the supply side, then unneeded NHS resources could be sold or transferred to the private sector. Finally, it is not likely that there would be much if any expansion in total demand for medical services; eliminating queues does not alter demand in a steady state, it merely clears a backlog. The Treasury is quite mistaken.

These proposals will provoke a political hornets' nest

On the contrary, they will allow many ordinary people locked into waiting lists to get private treatment; as much of a master-stroke as was the sale of council houses to their grateful tenants. A political running sore would, as then, be transformed into a political running mate.

To understand the political and economic significance of waiting lists, it helps to think about the queues for basic groceries in the heyday of Stalinist Russia. (Those who would appreciate a really vivid picture should read *Galina*, the autobiography of the famous Russian soprano, Galina Vishnevskaya.)[10] For the ordinary Russian, the only way to acquire these groceries was to join a separate queue for each; he or she would spend most of each day queueing, just to get together the raw material for the evening meal. Exhausted by this process, they would have little energy left for constructive activity. But equally, this system rendered them helpless in the face of the party bureaucracy who controlled even the ration books.

Yet the politician who can offer citizens control of their medical services stands to reap an enormous reward. They will turn round and say 'Thank you; nobody before you told me this was possible. I will never vote again for the party that kept me in bondage'.

These proposals will create a two-tier health system

Since there is already a flourishing private sector, we already have two tiers (or more) of health-care provision. Allowing people to opt out of state provision at cost would extend private medicine to the majority of the population and create a genuine health-care market for millions of ordinary people.

The market can be made to work in health care without sacrificing the interests of the poor and the chronically sick. The NHS gives them spurious equality by sacrificing the interests of the mass of ordinary people. It is an illogical waste.

Few lessons for the NHS

Ray Robinson
Source: Economic Affairs, February/March 1987,7, 3, p. 41.

Over the years the IEA has supported a succession of writers who have espoused the virtues of private medicine. With the appearance of yet another work, this time by the latest standard bearer, David G. Green – *Challenge to the NHS* – one is entitled to ask 'What has he to say that is new on the subject?' Moreover, with the title he has chosen, and a subtitle

158 Recent controversies in political economy

Table 7.1 Percentage increase in price of health care, 1980–3

	UK	USA
Hospital Care Price Indices	21	31
Pharmaceutical Prices	26	34
Doctors' Earnings	25	31

which refers to the lessons for Britain, one is also entitled to search for the relevance of developments in the US for the NHS.

On the first question, Dr Green argues that there has, in recent years, been an emergence of various competitive pressures in the USA which have resulted in the breakdown of supply-side monopoly and a far more marked degree of cost containment. But let us look at the context of this claim. It is well known that, whatever its merits, the US health-care system has, in the 1960s and 1970s, been plagued by rampant cost-inflation. In contrast, the NHS, whatever its faults, has proved a strong countervailing monopsony and, as a result, has been far more effective in achieving cost-containment. Recent figures show that per capita expenditure on health care in the US is still nearly three times the British figure (although, of course, some of this difference reflects higher standards of service as well as higher prices). This is the massive cost-differential benchwork from which discussions of relative performance must start. So, even if the claim that recent developments in the USA have reduced the rate of cost inflation is correct, it simply suggests that its comparative failure in relation to Britain has been reduced marginally.

But there is reason to doubt whether the cost gap has actually been reduced in the way that Dr Green suggests. He cites a good deal of partial evidence about innovations in, *inter alia*, insurance and supply arrangements and their alleged effects on costs. But he produces very little systematic empirical evidence. Some such evidence is produced in the recent OECD report,[1] which contained the following information on relative price trends over the period from 1980 to 1983.

Far from suggesting that the cost differential has been reduced, these figures indicate that the cost gap between the UK and the US has actually been increasing.

In short, it is possible to argue that there have been a range of innovations introduced into the NHS which derive from a recognition of the desirability of certain features of a competitive market model. Various value-for-money initiatives and more recognition of the necessity of being responsive to user requirements are two such examples. But it is doubtful whether these lessons owe much to US experiences, now or in the past.

How to pay for the NHS

Norman McKenna
Source: *Economic Affairs*, June/July 1987, 7, 5, p. 13.

The NHS has become a political sacred cow which both government and opposition claim to be 'safe with us'.

As at present constituted and financed, it cannot be safe with any political party forming the government. Yet a simple system of payment for treatment according to ability to pay would secure the viability of the NHS while ensuring that there was no bar to effective treatment because of inability to pay.

Official NHS accounting seriously underestimates its true costs. It excludes any estimate of capital resources and, in hospital costs, also any charges for land, local rates, and so on, which have to be borne by independent, commercially-operated health care suppliers. No reliable figures are available on NHS assets. The DHSS report *Under-used and Surplus Property in the NHS* (1983) identifies some 50,000 acres of land and a vast range of buildings, including some 2,000 hospitals and large numbers of health centres, clinics, residential accommodation, laundries and offices held by the NHS. Virtually no figures are available for other assets or equipment which would normally be treated as capital but which the NHS provides from its receipts of government revenue and regards as acquired out of free income. Additionally, until very recently, NHS hospitals have enjoyed Crown Immunity which has distorted – and, for some time to come, will continue to distort – their costs to the economy. The costs of specific operations and/or treatments in private hospitals cannot therefore be compared with the official NHS figures.

With the consequent proviso that the figures are certainly too low, the planned expenditure for 1985-6 on the NHS was £17.3 billion, which included £2.8 billion for local authority personal social services (PPS); expenditure was finally nearer £18 billion. The target expenditure for 1986-7 has recently been raised from £18.7 to about £20 billion. NHS spending will be absorbing about 7 per cent of total national resources and about 13.5 per cent of all government expenditure. The direct comparisons often made between this figure and those for other countries (such as 10.5 –11 per cent of GNP in the US and in the range of 8–10 per cent in several European countries) are meaningless since the figures for UK NHS expenditure are substantially below the costs to the economy. Even these artificially low figures are far higher than envisaged by the founding fathers of the NHS in the 1940s; they confidently anticipated that once a healthy population had been established, the demands on the NHS would decline sharply. In the event, between 1971 and 1985, expenditure on the NHS, adjusted for inflation, rose by more than half, by 57 per cent.[1] The pressure for more spending accelerates, with more visits, more prescriptions, more

Recent controversies in political economy

Table 7.2 NHS and local authority per-capita spending, England, 1980–1

Total population	Births	0–4	5–15	16–64	64–75	75 and over
£225	£995	£260	£275	£145	£455	£1,160

consultations and more operations every year (see below).[2] Because limits have had to be set on the money allocated to the NHS, the consequences have been all too evident in the unofficial rationing of treatment – mostly at the discretion of the medical profession (people over fifty-five, for example, are not normally put on kidney machines) – or in the ever-lengthening queues for urgent as well as non-urgent treatment. DHSS statistics show that, after falling by 2 per cent from 674,000 to 661,000 between October 1985 and April 1986, the waiting list for hospitalization in the country as a whole is again rising. At the Great Ormond Street Hospital for Sick Children alone there were in April 1986 sixty-four children waiting for an urgent operation of whom twenty-nine had been waiting more than a month, and 687 waiting for non-urgent operations, an increase of 29 per cent in six months. The position was similar or worse at other London hospitals.

Four major factors have contributed to this inexorable rise in expenditure.

1. The False Premises. A fundamental contradiction inherent in the NHS enshrines the notions that demand has only to be expressed for supply to be provided free of charge and all demands should be treated as potentially equal. Only a rich and exceedingly fast-growing economy could sustain a service based on these premises. Britain's is neither rich nor fast-growing by world standards. Moreover, a service which seeks to meet every demand made upon it free of charge encourages waste and abuse (below).
2. Demography. A progressively aging population has made, and will continue to make, rapidly accelerating demands on the resources of the NHS. In 1971 there were 6.5 million people over sixty-five, in 1980 7.2 million. The number over seventy-five rose from 40 per cent to 43 per cent and now stands at nearly 3.7 million. Although current projections suggest that the UK population will increase only very slowly over the next 15 years, the numbers over sixty-five will rise to about 7.5 million by 1991 with an even steeper rise in the proportion of the very elderly over seventy-five, and especially in those over eighty-five where the increase is expected to be sharpest.[3]

The public expenditure White Paper for 1984–5 to 1986–7 gives the costs of health care by age-group (Table 7.2).

The total spending taken by people over seventy-five had risen from 9 per cent in the mid-1950s to 26 per cent by 1981; and by people over 65 from about 20 per cent to about 43 per cent. Figures for later years are not yet available, but these trends will certainly have continued.

Clearly the rising proportion of very elderly (over seventy-five) in a population which is virtually static, coupled with the increasing demands they make on increasingly costly techniques, threatens to undermine the NHS.

3   Technology. Advances in medical technology (including new diagnostic techniques) and in pharmacology, which have come thick and fast in the past fifteen years, are imposing an accelerating financial burden on the NHS. Clinical tests alone have increased sevenfold and are still at only a quarter of the number per patient in the USA. Magnetic resonance imagers, which give exceptionally high definition pictures of internal organs without recourse to radiation, have become a very valuable diagnostic tool. They cost around £1 million each, plus the high costs of installing them in heavily screened areas. Digital angiography scanners, for investigating diseases of the vascular system, cost around £350,000 each. These sophisticated techniques, which must be fully utilized to be economic (but, in practice, rarely are), reveal more conditions awaiting treatment. Furthermore, there has been a major shift in the past 40 years in the relative importance of groups of diseases. With one well-publicized exception, infectious diseases have ceased to be significant (except among children under five), and their place as the dominant cause of deaths has been taken by cancer, stroke, heart diseases and, to a lesser (and currently declining) extent by chest diseases, which together now account for over 80 per cent of deaths among people over thirty-five, with the proportion broadly rising with age.

The techniques for dealing with these dominant conditions and others like chronic renal failure are often in the forefront of current advances in medical technology and therefore inherently costly. As they become fully established, they are more widely used. In recent years, innovations in treatment – all at high cost – have become widely established (Box A).

The total number of NHS patients on dialysis or with a functioning kidney transplant rose from 1,270 in 1971 to 11,235 in 1984 and is estimated to have totalled nearly 15,000 in 1986. The number of coronary by-pass grafts rose from about 250 in 1971 to 9,443 in 1983 and is estimated to have totalled between 15,000 and 20,000 in 1986. The NHS has given the average cost of dialysis for patients with chronic renal failure as £10,000 to £15,000 a year but, for the reasons indicated above, these figures are far below their costs to the national economy.

Technological advances are imposing high costs on the NHS drug bill. The cost of developing a major new drug to the point of clinical acceptability may now run to £100 million. The NHS drug bill rose from £0.77 billion in 1971 to £1.46 billion in 1985 (both in 1985 terms).

BUPA has recently estimated that medical costs in total are now rising by 18 per cent a year before adjustment for inflation.

4 Waste and Abuse: A service which seeks to meet every demand made upon it free of charge, and in which doctors, nurses and management are not personally faced with the financial consequence of their decisions, encourages waste and abuse. The *General Household Survey*, which reports serious complaints, and the corresponding consultations with GPs or attendances at clinics or hospitals as outpatients, together with that on GP consultations analysed by socio-economic groups, confirm that, except for emergencies and serious illnesses, the demands on the NHS do not reflect overriding need but are, to a substantial extent, discretionary.[4] That no patient visiting a GP or receiving clinic or hospital treatment has the remotest idea of the cost breeds the attitude 'It's free, so why not use it?', irrespective of necessity.[5] The result is an over stretched and therefore less efficient service. A fifth of GPs regard at least three-quarters of their work as trivial. A third of the advice offered in surgeries is not followed. Another third is followed incorrectly.[6]

Among family practitioners, where the costs of prescribed drugs rose from £0.943 billion in 1975 to £1,406 billion in 1983 (both at 1983 prices), there is evidence of widespread over-prescription and, perhaps more important, of prescribed drugs (sometimes very costly) being neither properly nor fully utilized.

Drs King, Pendleton and Tate claim that 'bossy, authoritarian doctors' are wasting about £500 million a year in drugs because their patients rarely understand their advice. The nominal prescription charge of £2.20, which in any event is paid by only a minority of patients, is today little more than the cost of a gallon of petrol or a glossy magazine; it is ineffective as a check on waste.

According to surveys conducted in the West Midlands,[7] hospital clinical tests often requested have no bearing on the medical condition. Tests are requested but their results ignored. Laboratories are too small and therefore inefficient, sometimes with appalling under-use of equipment.[8]

In the 'hotel services' provided by NHS hospitals there are well-documented samples of unnecessarily high-cost cleaning, porterage and laundry services and of the waste in catering. In addition, recent reports of poor hygiene and insect infestation in NHS hospital kitchens are serious enough to be alarming. The Institute of Environment Health Officers claimed in 1985 that 600 of the 1,002 hospital kitchens broke food health

Figure 7.8 High-cost high technology

Hip-joint replacement surgery, a highly effective technique for replacing diseased hip-joints, particularly prevalent among the elderly, by metal joints.

Haemodialysis and kidney transplantation to alleviate renal failure – transplantation of the failed kidney by a compatible kidney from a donor is the ideal method of treatment but when, as often, a suitable replacement kidney is not available, the patient is connected to a renal machine and remains under treatment for life or until a compatible kidney can be found.

Coronary artery by-pass, or 'open heart' surgery to by-pass diseased and blocked coronary arteries which serve the heart muscles.

Neo-natal intensive care in specialised units for young babies born prematurely or with diseases.

Haemophilia treatment for patients deficient in blood-clotting factor; treatment and monitoring must continue for life.

Bone-marrow transplant used in many cases of leukemia or cancer of the blood cells to replace the patient's bone-marrow with compatible bone-marrow from a donor.

---

regulations and that ninety-seven would have been liable for prosecution but for their Crown Immunity. These findings were supported by the National Association of Health Authorities, the Royal College of Nursing and the British Pest Control Association. In the salmonella epidemic at Stanley Royal Mental Health Hospital, Wakefield, nineteen people died.

The open-ended availability of the NHS and the lack of a realistic patient-oriented costing system encourage waste and abuse. Demography and technology are driving up the costs of treatment inexorably. The necessity, particularly with Britain's still relatively weak economy, of setting cash limits to NHS spending must lead to more unofficial (and therefore irrational) rationing of treatment, to lengthening waiting lists for non-essential (and even for essential) treatment, to a deterioration in pay and other more general conditions of service for NHS staff relative to those in the rest of the economy, and to a continuing decline in morale. On current prospects for economic growth, there is no way of maintaining even the present standards of NHS health care without a radical reordering of public expenditure priorities. (If AIDS reaches plague proportions during the next few years, as some virologists believe, and if, as seems all too likely, no effective prophylactic or clinical treatment is developed before then, a 'free-for-all' NHS will not remotely be able to cope.)

It is thus not surprising that the number of people covered by private health insurance in the UK has more than doubled from about 2.5 million in 1976 to more than 5 million in 1986.

A viable state system which seeks to provide effective standards of treatment while ensuring no bar to it because of inability to pay must meet three criteria:

164   *Recent controversies in political economy*

Figure 7.9 Example of payment for treatment related to income tax assessment. Scale of payment (example) 0.025 per cent of the total cost of treatment, etc., in financial year for every £1 of taxable income with the proviso that the total amount payable shall never exceed 10 per cent of the taxable income.

Total cost of treatment in one financial year	Adjusted taxable income[1]	Amount payable towards the total cost of medical treatment for the financial year
£300	£100	£7.50
	£500	£37.50
	£1,000	£75.00
	£2,500	£187.50
	£3,000	£225.00
	£4,000 and over	£300.00
£750	Up to £7,500	10% of taxable income
	Over £7,500	£750
£1,000	Up to £10,000	10% of taxable income
	Over £10,000	£1,000
£2,500	Up to £25,000	10% of taxable income
	Over £25,000	£2,500
£5,000	Up to £50,000	10% of taxable income
	Over £50,000	£5,000

[1] Special provisions would be necessary (for example, by incorporating a special scale of allowances) for people with dependents. A married man with two children could incur costs for medical treatment four times more than those incurred by an unmarried man (or a man with no dependents) in receipt of the same taxable income, since the former's personal allowances would not reflect his larger liability for medical costs. The term 'adjusted taxable income' has been used to allow for this difference without attempting to suggest the sort of 'medical allowances' which would be regarded as equitable.

It would be desirable to avoid the (possibly heavy) burden of payment for health care all at one time on an individual who (or whose dependents) had received treatment when he or she might have convalescence expenses or be otherwise financially or psychologically ill-equipped to pay. A mechanism for securing payment should therefore aim to spread the burden as far as practicable. One possible way of effecting this measure could be by requiring the individual responsible for the payment to submit his or her bills for treatment to the Medical Office within one month and recoding his or her assessed income to income tax, say, three months after the submission of all bills for the whole course of treatment. In order to equalise what could still be heavy burdens falling due towards the end of the tax year, provision could be made in such cases for charges due in excess of a certain amount to be recovered from the income assessed to income tax over a 12-month period instead of over the shorter period of the remainder of the year.

As an example, if an individual whose adjusted taxable income (as defined above) was £2,500, received treatment as follows, all within a period of two months:

Initial consultation with family practitioner	£25
Initial drug prescription provided by the FP	£15
Two subsequent check-up consultations with FP	£30
Two subsequent drug prescriptions	£30
Total cost of treatment	£100

The liability of that individual for payment towards the costs of the treatment would be 0.025 per cent of £100 × 2,500, i.e., £62.50. The six 'bills' (three for the consultations with the Family Practitioner and three for the prescriptions) would all have been presented to the 'Medical Office' within one month of their receipt and his or her liability for payment would have been advised (in this case, £15.63 + £9.37 for the first consultation and the prescription and £9.37 + £9.37 for each check-up consultation and further prescription). The total liability would then be recovered during the remainder of the tax year (or into the following tax year) by an appropriate change in the individual's tax coding.

If six months later, but still within the same tax year, the same individual incurred further medical costs, say as follows:

Initial consultation with the family practitioner	£25
Referral to specialist	£35
Hospitalization for one week	say £1,250
Post-hospitalization check-up by specialist	£35
Total cost of treatment including hospitalization	£1,345

his or her liability for this further treatment would be limited to 10 per cent of the 'adjusted taxable income' for that tax year, that is, £250, less the £62.50 already payable in respect of the earlier treatment, i.e., a further £87.50; this amount too would be recoverable by a further recoding of the income tax with the recoding applied over an appropriate period up to 12 months.

---

1   It must not be constrained financially from offering effective treatment to everyone genuinely in need of it.
2   It must incorporate a realistic accounting system using strictly commercial principles which will permit detailed internal monitoring and external comparison with costs undertaken in the private sector.
3   Its rates of pay and conditions of service must not be less attractive than in comparable work and responsibility in the economy generally. The brain drain from the medical services, which has continued for years, is not restricted to highly qualified doctors, as witness the growing discontent among nurses employed in the NHS and the alarming numbers of British nurses who have recently found jobs in Australia, New Zealand and the Middle East.

These criteria cannot be met while retaining a service which is free for all at the point of treatment and then tinkering with isolated elements in the cost structure, by farming out hospital support services like laundering, cleaning and catering to private contractors or by introducing nominal prescription charges. These peripheral measures have been tried and have, in many cases, resulted in real economies but they are, even at best, without significant effect on the total costs of the NHS. A radical solution is required to ensure:

a   that everyone who provides and everyone who receives advice, treatment or services from the NHS (GP, specialist, clinic, hospital and community health services or the centrally financed health services) and people providing and benefiting from the local authority personal social services should know the full commercial cost of each major element;[9]

b   that everyone contributes towards these costs (whether incurred on their own behalf or for dependents) according to ability to pay.

The first of these provisions, which would have to be prefaced by a realistic patient- and treatment-oriented accounting system such as operates in the private sector, could be achieved by billing every patient with the full commercial cost, broken down into its constituent major elements, of the advice or treatment received, whether in the GP's surgery, the specialist's consulting room, the health clinic or the hospital. The second, which would have to be prefaced by full computerization of the Inland Revenue system, could be achieved by the patient (or the person on whom the patient was dependent) presenting the bill to a medical office installed with a computer terminal linked to the Inland Revenue's central computer system for income tax, and paying towards the cost on a scale related to the current assessment for income tax. Patients, or people on whom patients were regarded as wholly dependent for taxation purposes, who paid no income tax – like those receiving only a state retirement pension or unemployment and/or supplementary benefit – would pay nothing. Patients, or those with dependents as patients, who were assessed at higher rates of income tax would normally pay the full cost, with qualification and similarly by gradations up and down the income tax scale.

The qualification concerns the burden of exceptionally prolonged and costly treatment (such as life-long renal dialysis or long-term care for the mentally diseased) which could still be financially crippling even to someone paying the highest rate of tax. This reservation could be met by providing an upper safety-net and graduating the payment scale for treatment and services to the patient's liability to income tax (or to that of people whose dependents were patients).

An example of an income-tax-related scale for the payment of health care, together with a practical illustration of how it could operate, is given in Figure 7.9. Anyone who tried to evade the liability for payment could be penalised in their next income tax demand.

A system of payment for health care according to ability to pay (with the necessary safety-nets) would very materially shift the centre of gravity of the sources of NHS revenue from what is now essentially exclusively government funding towards a vast multiplicity of individual users purchasing (wholly or in part) the services they receive. An element of consumer control of the market would have been introduced, which is now lacking.

The payment mechanism outlined here could be introduced without immediate basic structural changes in the NHS. The structural changes necessary to streamline it and to improve its efficiency to meet the imperatives of consumer-oriented market forces would follow by evolutionary processes.

Such a system would be flexible and by suitable changes in its design could be tailored to achieve primary savings (both in direct NHS costs and in the central government's financial support for PSS costs) of 40 per cent or, say, £8 billion in a year at current (1986-7) targetted expenditure with the possibility of higher retrievals as the costs of the service rise. An accurate estimate of the achievable savings could be arrived at only from a detailed analysis of the numbers and costs of all the main categories of treatment and services provided by the NHS and the income-tax pattern of the population but it is doubtful whether the necessary statistical data is available.

The figure of 40 per cent achievable savings is readily demonstrated. First, the Family Practitioner Service (planned expenditure in 1985-6, £3.472 billion including about £1.75 billion for prescribed drugs) provides, in general, a very large number of relatively low-cost treatments; it is assumed that two-thirds of the costs of these could be retrieved from payments and from a heavy curtailment in non-essential prescriptions and/or underuse of drugs.

Second, the cost of the centrally financed health services (planned expenditure in 1985-6, £0.614 billion) is assumed to be virtually non-recoverable.

Third, in the hospital and community health services (planned expenditure in 1985-6, £9.648 billion) it is assumed that 40 per cent of the costs could be retrieved. The local authorities' personal social services' spending (planned in 1985-6 at £2.733 billion) is heavily directed to long-term care of the elderly and mentally handicapped. Perhaps no more than a third would be retrievable.

Fourth, NHS and local authority PSS capital spending (planned in 1985-6 at £0.779 billion and £0.076 billion respectively) would, of course, be unaffected. Except in the cost of prescriptions in the FPS, this figuring takes no account of the savings that should be achieved from a more efficiently managed NHS (which a senior DHSS official recently estimated could total £1.75 billion).

Part of this saving should be applied to improve the remuneration and conditions of service, particularly of the NHS professional staff,[10] thereby raising morale and standards of service and making possible stricter discipline over waste. The less loyalty to and pride public service employees have in their jobs and the service the more difficult to eliminate unnecessary waste.

Every patient would be aware of the full commercial costs and know that, unless he or she were in the nil income tax bracket, a proportion (or the whole) of the cost would have to be paid. Therefore the discretionary element in the demands now being made, on the centrally-financed sectors of the NHS in particular (such as the unnecessary expenditure of GPs' time on trivial complaints which should never require a consultation) and the waste of drugs in the Family Practitioner Service, should be very substantially reduced. The pressures on the Family Practitioner Service would thereby be eased to the benefit of the quality it could offer.

This proposal does not overlook the objection that people in the zero income-tax bracket would know they would not be required to pay and could therefore still make medically unnecessary demands. Short of some complicated compensatory mechanism, moral pressures from the majority of the community contributing towards the costs of their sometimes unnecessary health care on those who were not contributing might go some way towards limiting this source of abuse.

Even after ploughing back a part of the proceeds, it should be possible to eliminate the health-care element in both employer and employee national insurance contributions (which now provide only about 8 per cent of the cost of the NHS) and, more important, should make way for a very substantial easing of income tax on the individual taxpayer. If out of total savings to central government of 40 per cent of its funding, say, £7.5 billion at current (1986–7) spending, the national insurance element of £1.6 billion were eliminated, a further £2 billion were applied to improving pay and conditions of service, including a 12.5 per cent average increase in salary and pay (say, £1.5 billion) and a doubling of capital spending (about £1 billion in 1986–7) inclusive of equipment not at present regarded as capital expenditure), a balance of £2.9 billion would be available to reduce the standard rate of income tax by almost three percentage points. Again, this calculation takes no account of the savings achievable from the more efficient and less wasteful service which would result from the proposed financial reforms.

People who would be paying most towards the cost of their (and their dependents') health care under the tax-related payment scheme outlined here would be those to benefit most personally in cash retained from a general reduction in the standard rate of income tax.

Both these forms of relief – in national insurance contributions, and in the standard rate of income tax – should contribute significantly to a reduction in unemployment. The first would reduce total labour costs. The second (supplemented by lower national insurance employee contributions) would increase take-home pay and thereby diminish the attractions of the black economy.

Other schemes for funding health care have attracted attention. Two such schemes, the health maintenance organizations (HMOs) and the preferred provider organizations (PPOs) originated in the USA and in recent years have spread rapidly there. The many different forms of HMOs – group, network and independent practice associations – integrate health care with insurance. Their economic significance lies in their competition to established suppliers, the increase in bargaining power they give to the consumer, and the discipline they impose on the monopoly power of organized medicine. But they have an incentive to underprovide medical services and, because subscribers have no insurance if they go to a doctor outside their HMO, they are 'locked in'.[11]

Although the proposal outlined here represents a radical change in political attitudes from the original and still current concept of access to all, virtually free of charge at the point of treatment, it should be politically defensible against criticism which sought to claim it was inequitable. Provided no one at either end of the income scale is denied equality in treatment because they cannot pay, it is wholly equitable that people who can pay should do so in proportion to their ability. There is indeed a precedent, for users of the local authority personal social services already pay according to ability for some services, particularly for residential care.

The existence of a private sector in health care is often urged as morally wrong because it draws off professional resources from the NHS and makes for a two-tier system. Neither argument holds. The supply of medical resources is not inelastic; stronger incentives (as in higher remuneration and improved working conditions) would attract more doctors and nurses into the NHS. And the glaring shortcomings of the NHS as now constituted have already led to a two-tier (or rather, multi-tier) system and it is becoming more entrenched every year. Payment in accordance with the user's ability to pay would put the NHS and the private health-care sector so much more on a common basis as to remove the issue of private medicine from the political arena. And it would introduce an element of competition between the two which would spur both to higher efficiency and better service.

If government is to cope with the financial disease of the NHS by the deep surgery required, it will call for a highly sophisticated campaign of presentation which is nowhere in sight.

Without a radical approach to stop in its track the manifestly Gadarene progress of the NHS, the claim that it is 'safe with us' will increasingly be perceived to be hollow and carry a heavy burden of political opprobrium.

Rejoinder: few lessons for the NHS

David G. Green
Source: Economic Affairs, February/March 1987, 7, 3, p. 42.

When the case for the supply of health services in a competitive market has been advocated previously, supporters of the *status quo* like Mr Bosanquet have demanded that free-marketeers should study real functioning markets because the free-market case was said to be too reliant on theory. This demand was perfectly reasonable, and as a result, in the last three or four years the IEA has had a hand in studying how markets have functioned in practice, both historically and today. *Mutual Aid or Welfare State*[1] describes how medical services were supplied in the market-place in Australia before federal governments began to subsidize private health insurance premiums in the early 1950s. A second study, *Working Class Patients and the Medical Establishment*,[2] considers how ordinary people obtained primary medical care in the market-place in Britain before the NHS. And *Challenge to the NHS* analyses the defects and advantages of US health care today. All told, this historical and contemporary evidence contradicts some of the claims made by Mr Bosanquet and his colleagues at York University. The evidence suggests that the market failure said necessarily to render markets incapable of supplying health services were either absent or capable of being overcome.

Mr Bosanquet was invited to respond to *Challenge to the NHS*, part of the new evidence. He has not done so. It is not clear whether he disputes the evidence, either in part or as a whole; or whether he accepts that any or some of his past opinions require modification in the light of recent US developments. Or does he believe he was right all along? Instead of responding to the findings, he demands that other work be done on the detailed record of the NHS. There is nothing wrong with this demand in principle, and indeed the IEA Health Unit has been established precisely to do such work. But it would be as well to pause for a moment to see how far the debate has progressed to date. It is, I suspect, just such an appraisal that Mr Bosanquet wishes to avoid.

Three principal claims have been made by Mr Bosanquet and his colleagues at the University of York.

1 Professional monopoly power is a universal feature of health service provision.
2 The consumer is too badly informed to be sovereign in the marketplace.
3 Third-party insurance suffers from 'moral hazard', leading inevitably to price escalation.

Drawing on Australian and British historical evidence and American contemporary evidence, I have suggested that doubts can be thrown on all three claims. The proper academic response would have been to reply point by point to my contentions. To demand more work on related, but analytically separate, matters evades the issues at stake. Moreover, Mr Bosanquet's demand for more work is part of a pattern. There is now in our universities and polytechnics a type of academic whose whole intellectual approach is based on never drawing any real conclusions about the faults of the welfare state. For them the life of the intellectual is rather like a never-ending royal commission of inquiry, established in the first place as a delaying tactic. When challenged, they respond with one or more of a ready string of accusations like 'using code words as a substitute for detailed analysis' or 'hangs uneasily between analysis and imagination' or 'leads through stereotypes to dogmatism and ideology', to name only three used by Mr Bosanquet in the small space at his disposal.

But this tactic is a double bluff. The demand for more empirical work could sound like no more than an excuse for doing little or nothing about the unsatisfactory NHS *status quo*, which Mr Bosanquet and like-minded academics support out of emotional attachment rather than rational judgment. And dismissal of the evidence from America and our own recent past as ideology is no more than a tactic for ignoring inconvenient findings. The result of these evasions is that the radical questions are not being asked. Let Mr Bosanquet respond point by point to the evidence I have presented. What, in his view, is the current state of the debate?

Ray Robinson's contribution is free from such prejudice. He cites OECD figures on health costs between 1980 and 1983 in support of this conclusion that US costs have not been falling. But most of the dramatic change has occurred since 1983, and it shows that in the 1984, 1985 and 1986 figures, not yet available in comparative form for the OECD. The downturn in costs started in 1983; using the range 1980–3 includes figures for 1980–2 when cost escalation was at its worst.

This is a difference of scholarly interpretation which can be settled rationally.

Notes

A policy for the NHS, part I

1   'State Expenditure: A Study in Waste', Supplement to *Economic Affairs*, April/June 1984.

A policy for the NHS, part II

1   (Sir) Roy Griffiths, *Report to the Secretary of State for Social Services*, NHS Management Inquiry, 6 October 1983.
2   *Daily Telegraph*, 11 October 1988, 17.
3   Examples include: Michael Goldsmith and David Willetts, *Managed Health Care: A New System for a Better Health Service*, Centre for Policy Studies, 1988; Madsen Pirie and Eamonn Butler, *Health Management Units: the Operation of an Internal Market Within the National Health Service*, Adam Smith Institute, 1988.
4   Nicholas Bosanquet, GPs as Firms, Creating an Internal Market for Primary Care, *Public Money*, March 1986, 65–68.
5   Alain Enthoven, *Reflections on the Management of the National Health Service*, Nuffield Provisional Hospital Trust, 1985.
6   David Green, *Everyone a Private Patient*, Institute of Economic Affairs, Hobart Paperback 77, 1988.
7   Ray Whitney, *National Health Crisis*, Shepheard-Walwyn, 1988.
8   See the accounts of the US market in chapter 3 of David Green, *op. cit.*, and of chapter 8 of Ray Whitney, *op. cit.*
9   Notably, Nicholas Barr, Howard Glennester and Julian Le Grand, *Reform and*

the National Health Service, Discussion Paper 32, The Welfare State Programme, Suntory-Toyota International Centre for Economics and Related Disciplines, CSE, May 1988.
10 Galina Vishnevskaya, *Galina*, Sceptre Books, Hodder & Stoughton, 1984.

Few lessons for the NHS

1 *Measuring Health Care*, OECD, 1985.

How to pay for the NHS

1 DHSS report, *Health Care and its Costs*, 1983, and *Sixth Report of the Social Sciences Committee of the House of Commons – Session 1984/5*.
2 The numbers of doctors working in the NHS rose from 30,000 in 1972 to 43,000 in 1984 (*Compendium of Health Statistics*, Office of Health Economics, 1984) and the total numbers of NHS employees rose by 27 per cent between 1975 and 1984.
3 The demands of the elderly on the NHS due to the demographic factor are exacerbated by the increasing drift of the very elderly out of the private sector into the NHS as the costs to them of private health insurance rise.
4 The evidence is summarised in *Health Care, UK – 1984*, edited by Anthony Harrison and John Gretton and published by the Chartered Institute of Public Finance and Accountancy (CIPFA).
5 A recent BBC TV programme highlighted the abuse of the hospitals' casualty departments, specifically in London, by drunks and drug cases.
6 Drs Jennifer King, David Pendleton and Peter Tate, *Making the Most of your Doctor*, Methuen, London, 1986.
7 By John Stilwell, Centre for Research in Industry, Business and Administration, Warwick University.
8 *Health Care, UK 1984*, CIPFA.
9 The local authority Personal Social Services are only partly financed by central government and then indirectly through the Rate Support system, and their users pay a larger part of the costs (an estimated 15 per cent in 1983–4) than of NHS costs (about 3 per cent in 1983–4). There is no reason that the same principle of payment for Personal Social Services according to the beneficiaries' ability to pay should not apply in the same way as for the centrally financed NHS costs. Indeed, some PSS users, particularly those in residential care, already pay according to ability to do so.
10 Staff most seriously affected by poor remuneration are junior doctors whose hours of work are often so long as seriously to prejudice their professional judgments, and nurses, both of whom have been prominent in the brain drain. In 1983, nearly one-third of hospital medical staff had to be recruited from abroad. That pattern persists, particularly with junior doctors.
11 A review of HMOs and PPOs in the USA is in David Green, *Challenge to the NHS*, Hobart Paperback No. 23, IEA, 1986, 68–73.

Rejoinder: few lessons for the NHS

1 George Allen & Unwin, Sydney, 1984.
2 Temple Smith/Gower, London, 1985.

8 Environment

Europe's congested airspace – time for market solutions

Sean D. Barrett
Source: *Economic Affairs*, June/July 1989, 9, 5, p. 29.

Delays at airports plagued European aviation in the summer of 1988. Passenger groups have established SCREAM, The Sufferers Campaign to Resolve the European Aviation Mess. They invite us to SCREAM for a liberal, expanding, uncongested air transport system; better use of airports and airways today, and expansion for tomorrow. They propose a more realistic balance of environmental and transport needs to ensure busy, quiet and passenger friendly airports; and a European Master Plan for airport and airspace development including Pan-continental airspace management using Eurocontrol and a trust fund for infrastructure expansion.[1]

The European Civil Aviation Conference (ECAC) forecasts a doubling of annual aircraft movements between 1987 and 2000. Europe's scheduled air fares are the highest in the world and its markets are the most tightly regulated. It is likely that deregulation will mean an even faster growth in passenger demand as new airlines replace high cost collusion with competitive fares. Air travel between Britain and Ireland, for example, doubled in 1988 compared to 1985, the last full year before liberalization. The route had declined over the period 1978–85.[2]

The gains from competition were obtained by allowing markets to operate. Three bulwarks against competition were removed. New market entrants were permitted. They were allowed to charge fares outside the set IATA rules, the international airlines' cartel. Their capacity was decided by the customer rather than agreed in advance by colluding airlines.

Competition between airlines has brought obvious benefits in the US and in the limited European markets, such as between Ireland and the UK, where it has been tried. What is now needed to secure further gains in efficiency, is to extend markets and competition from airlines to airports and the management of airspace. The barriers to market forces in European aviation must all be removed.

Table 8.1 Market forces in aviation

Barriers to market forces in European aviation	Market solutions to congested air space
• **Airline competition barriers** Bans on new entrants, price competition and market share competition Computer reservation system bias against new airlines. Policy failure to deal with anticompetitive behaviour such as collusion, anticompetitive mergers, and abuses of dominant position such as predatory pricing, geographical price discrimination. • **Airport competition barriers** 'Grandfather rights' allocation of airport capacity to established airlines only. Ground handling monopolies. Air Traffic Control monopolies. Lack of inter-airport competition. Monopoly provision and underinvestment. • **Airspace competition barriers** Public monopoly control. Underinvestment due to property rights defects.	• **Airline deregulation** with freedom of entry, pricing and capacity provision; neutral computer reservation systems and the full application of competition policy to control predation and anticompetitive mergers. • **Airport competition** Abolition of ground handling monopolies; competitive tendering for air traffic control; a market in airport slots; competition in the ownership of airports serving the same region; operation of airports as commercial enterprises rather than public services. • **Airspace competition** Creation of a market in airspace to replace the administrative division of airspace between military and civil aviation; privatization of national air traffic control. Creation of a market in noise property rights.

Removing the barriers to airline competition in Europe requires removal of the ban on new entrants, price competition and competition for market share. The European Community must also activate Articles 85 and 86 of the Rome Treaty to deal with collusion and abuse of a dominant position in aviation. Large high-cost airlines can use geographical price discrimination to drive low cost new market entrants out of business unless prevented. Computer reservation systems owned by established airlines must not be allowed to discriminate against new airlines or the airports which they serve. If bias cannot be eliminated airlines should be required to divest themselves of their computer reservation systems. Mergers which reduce competition should not be permitted.

Without these changes, established airlines in Europe will be able to prevent new entrants and markets will not be contestable.[3]

Airports in Europe are typically operated by public agencies rather than by commercial enterprises. This has resulted in their operation as local monopolies and in under-investment. In addition, airport managements engage in a wide range of anti-competitive practices.

The capacity of airports is divided into slots and these slots are allocated by committees of airline representatives. Seniority is a key criterion in these allocations which are therefore known as grandfather rights. The system contains a strong bias against new entrants to the market and promotes collusion between established airlines. The grandfather-rights system means that even if European governments adopted a pro-competition policy and licensed new carriers they would still be banned from most of Europe's main hub airports. The grandfather-rights system is also inefficient in that some grandfathers may operate small aircraft thus lowering the capacity of the airport. Grandfather rights represent an abdication of their responsibilities by airport managements. A market-led pricing system is obviously superior for attaining the optimum use of scarce airport capacity.

The extreme form of grandfather rights is the ban on new entrants at Heathrow since April 1977. Since then passenger numbers at Heathrow have grown from 24 to 38 million, and the entire increase in capacity has been allocated to the established airlines. This inefficient allocation of airport capacity was not required by capacity constraints. The Civil Aviation Authority stated that 'had the present rules not been introduced, the international scheduled services thus prevented could probably have been operated at Heathrow, although in some cases with great difficulty'.[4]

Grandfather rights also determine the supply of ground handling services. At Heathrow, British Midland, the second largest carrier in terms of aircraft movements, sought to do its own ground handling in 1984. It was compelled to use an airline with grandfather rights and at a price almost twice the cost of its own operation at Birmingham. The issue was examined by the Monopolies and Mergers Commission. It recommended, *inter alia*, that in deciding handling arrangements the British Airports Authority should not limit its consideration to airlines with existing self-handling rights and should take account of the charges made to other airlines and the cost savings available'.[5]

Control tower monopolies should be tackled by periodic tendering for the provision of these services. The Monopolies and Mergers Commission in 1983 stated that 'evidence from some non-NATS airports suggests that the private sector can provide airport ATS at lower cost than can the (Civil Aviation) Authority.'[6] Air traffic control has been privatized at airports such as Bournemouth, Liverpool, Exeter, and Perth. Competitive tendering operates at Manchester. Here the Civil Aviation Authority was successful in the competition by a programme of cost-reduction compared to its period of monopoly.

The precedents of successful privatization and competition in air traffic control at airports should be extended to the national air traffic control of airspace between airports in Europe. In Saudi Arabia the government contracts out the national air traffic control service for five year periods. In Switzerland the service is provided by Radio Suisse, a private corporation.

Currently the management and bureaucratic structure of air traffic control in Europe is unable to respond to the demands of traffic growth. The service is fragmented and uncoordinated. Under commercial operation the service would have access to the managerial and financial resources required to develop the service. The commercial pressures of competitive tendering will eliminate from the system inefficient operators and outmoded equipment. Eurocontrol estimates that air traffic control delays affected 49 per cent of flights within Europe in the summer of 1988.

Airports and air traffic control have traditionally been viewed as public utilities provided by governments. This had resulted in widespread anti-competitive conduct in the operation of airports and air traffic control. Competition and privatization would improve resource allocation in the system now, and secure the investment in management and plant required to cater for growth. Airports and traffic control should be treated as highly attractive commercial enterprises and market forces released to tackle the inefficiencies which cause congestion and delay. Since competition in the market for air traffic control is not possible, the Demsetz solution of competition for the market is appropriate.[7]

Large parts of European airspace are reserved for military use. The allocations were made when civil aviation was far smaller than today. For example in France it is estimated that military aircraft accounts for 10 per cent of total traffic but have reserved 40 per cent of national airspace.

The military exclusion areas cause heavy concentration of civil aviation in the remaining airspace. Diversions away from the exclusion zones are estimated to increase journey lengths by an average of 10 per cent compared to the direct route. In the case of Brussels–Zurich the average civil aircraft has to travel 45 per cent longer than the direct route.

A market in airspace should replace administrative allocation. The opportunity cost of the historic allocation of airspace between military and civil aviation should be made explicit in defence budgets. The creation of an airspace market would provide the cost data for more efficient allocation decisions. High-level satellites could take over the surveillance functions of military aircraft thus freeing airspace for civil use. Military training flights could be transferred to airspace areas with low civil aviation demand.

Demsetz points out that the appropriateness of recognizing a property right depends on the scarcity of the resource concerned relative to the cost of enforcing the property right. When land was abundant it was treated as common property. Airspace is now scarce and a system of property rights is appropriate.[8]

Heathrow and Frankfurt are already experiencing capacity problems at airport terminals. Runway capacity problems are predicted by the Association of European Airlines at 19 of 46 major European airports by 1995 assuming that the high growth of aviation in Europe continues.

Failure to expand airport capacity is both a function of the organization,

Table 8.2 Airport and airspace charges as a proportion of airline costs

	%
Aircraft and passenger handling	12.22
Aircraft passenger charges	5.15
Landing charges	4.07
En-route navigation	3.61
Airport navigation	0.85
TOTAL	25.90

Source: Civil Aviation Memorandum No. 2, 25.

management and finance of airports and the success of environmental groups in opposing expansion. In the London area such opposition has blocked a fifth terminal at Heathrow and second runways at Gatwick and Stansted. Night flying has also been successfully opposed.

Coase shows the superiority of negotiable property rights over a veto in terms of economic efficiency.[9] The Coase solution in relation to airport noise should include the following factors:

1. The measures of noise nuisance from airports have fallen:
   The White Paper on Airports Policy states that in London 'the area within the 35 NNI (Noise and Nuisance Index) fell from 826 sq km to 507 sq km between 1974 and 1983'.[10] ICAO Chapter 3 noise standards will further reduce noise levels at airports.
2. Some noise nuisance compensation has already been paid:
   Noise insulation grants have been approved for 41,000 dwellings near Heathrow and Gatwick.
3. Noise nuisance costs have been capitalized:
   Heathrow was first built in 1944. Properties purchased since then have had included in their price a value of aircraft noise nuisance and all the other factors associated with the presence of the airport in the neighbourhood. The evidence is that the economic activity generated by airports increases property values by more than the noise nuisance reduces them.

In the light of these factors planning permission for airport expansions might stipulate noise standards rather than allow a veto on development. Compensation should be paid only to those who suffer a drop in property values following the announcement of the airport investment project. Owners of noise blighted properties should have the right to sell to the airport company. The airport company is likely to gain on the transaction as property values rise subsequently.

The European Commission estimated in 1984 that airport and airspace use charges account for 25.9 per cent of airline costs within the European Community. The composition of the costs is shown in Table 2.

These revenues make private investment in airports and airspace attractive. Civil aviation in Europe is expected to double by the end of the century. Restraints on competition and defects in property rights have reduced investment. Competition and privatization, combined with the establishment of property rights, will attract to the sector the funds and management skills which the sector requires to eliminate congestion at Europe's airports.

Green for stop

Robert Whelan
Source: *Economic Affairs*, August/September 1989, 9, 6, p. 38.

It is difficult to turn on the television now without being confronted with the environmental enthusiasm of Mr Jonathon Porritt, the Director of Friends of the Earth. He and his organization have made environmentalism the rage – indeed the obsession – of the chattering classes. The edition of Sir Robin Day's 'Question Time', in which Mr Porritt featured, was so completely dominated by Green issues it should really have been called 'Gardeners' Question Time'.

Environmental issues are supposed to be more important than others because, if we go on 'raping the earth' as Mr Porritt puts it, the global ecosystem will collapse and the human race will die out. So widespread has this doomsday picture become that, in March this year, the Duke of Edinburgh made a Presidential Address to the Royal Society of Arts in which he envisaged the forthcoming extinction of humanity as a result of pollution of the environment. When the President of one of our most distinguished learned societies can make such a prognostication, then things have clearly gone very far indeed.

Jonathon Porritt has recently written a book entitled *The Coming of the Greens*,[1] in which he presents what he himself describes as a 'warts and all' picture of the Green Movement. He reveals that this movement has no formal structure, but rather consists of a loose grouping of individuals and organizations sharing some of the same aims. There are the eco-feminists, the Marxists, the anti-nuclear lobby and the animal rights activists. There are many different shades, from Dark Green (as in Greenpeace) to Light Green (as in National Trust), and it has to be said that relations between the factions are not always amiable. Indeed, the feelings of the Dark Greens for the Light Greens are similar to those entertained by Militant Tendency for Mr Roy Hattersley.

However, the most significant thing about *The Coming of the Greens* is not the revelation of what divides Green groups, but what unites them. Throughout the book Mr Porritt quotes different Green spokesmen to the effect that what is wrong with the world is our obsession with economic development measured in terms of GNP.

How, they ask, can GNP be taken as an indicator of welfare, when it fails to take into account the state of the rivers and the hedgerows? Why should we try to help developing countries to achieve something closer to our Western standard of living when it is this very industrial model of society which has led to the poisoning of the river, the pollution of the atmosphere and the breaking down of the ozone layer?

Mr Porritt, speaking in his own persona, and presumably on behalf of Friends of the Earth, is quite specific. After attacking 'GNP-determined, male-dominated, growth-fixated consumerist industrialism', he claims that: 'the hydra-headed monster of industrialism has, frankly, slipped its leash. We shall not tame it again. It is not so much decapitation we should be aiming at as the decommissioning of the entire monster.'[2]

So here we have it. Mr Porritt and his fellow Greens want to put out of action the engine of the industrial society which has given us, in the developed world, the highest standard of living ever known; and which is the only hope for millions struggling to emerge from poverty in the less-developed countries.

At a rally for the tropical rain forests on Hampstead Heath, organized by Friends of the Earth, the environmentalist Norman Myers told the crowd that we, with our consumerist lifestyles, all have our hands on the chainsaw which is cutting down the world's forests. This was greeted with rapturous applause from an almost entirely middle-class audience (the choice of Hampstead Heath as the venue was revealing) who all, no doubt, enjoyed the benefits of central heating, refrigeration, television and motor transport.

I wonder how many of them went home to unplug their refrigerators and decommission their video. No doubt they felt better for their day in the park agonizing over the rain forests.

Of course, it is easy to laugh at the inconsistency of the Greens. There is already evidence that environmentalists are managing to slow down the processes of growth and development in the West by throwing ecological spanners into the works of everything scientists and industrialists are trying to do. Even more objectionable is the attempt to put a brake on progress in the less-developed countries by imposing their concept of sustainable development.

Sustainable development is meant to be development which does not spoil the environment by over-exploiting natural resources in the interests of short-term profits. The Greens argue that we must take the long-term view and preserve resources for generations coming after us.

Of course this sounds entirely reasonable. It has only one major flaw, which is that it ignores all historical evidence to the effect that increasing demand actually makes resources more available, or less scarce, by stimulating exploration, leading to refinements in extraction processes, and reducing costs by economies of scale. The reason that the world is now full of extremely cheap coal is just because the Industrial Revolution made coal so valuable that people went looking for it. The best thing we can do for coming generations is to exploit resources, not conserve them. Market forces will always take care of shortages, if and when they do occur, by providing cheaper alternatives.

What sustainable development actually means is less development than would take place if the Greens didn't interfere or, in some cases, no development at all. It makes some Greens feel so good to think about the millions of acres of untouched rain forest in Amazonia that they cannot bear to contemplate the cutting down of trees at all, even to build roads which will link peasant communities with towns and ports, giving them the opportunity to participate in the money economy and derive the benefits of modern medicine, education and communications.

The Greens, who want to tie environmental strings to all Third World aid, are trying to get charitable and official aid agencies to subscribe to the theory of sustainable development. Not all of them want to play along. Oxfam says that 'No matter how important the threat to plants and animals ... Oxfam's prime concern must be to improve the living standard of poor people'. This is like a red rag to Mr Porritt who says that 'To imply that protecting 'birds and animals' might actually constitute a threat to poor people is real Dark Age stuff ... whoever wrote that simply hadn't read *Our Common Future*, which time after time hammers home the mutuality of interest between poor people and their environment.'[3]

Our Common Future also known as *The Brundtland Report*,[4] has become the Green Bible. It is the report of a United Nations Committee on Environment and Development which uses the phrase 'sustainable development' several thousand times, insisting from the first page to the last that economic growth cannot take place unless programmes of development are ecologically sound, and that investment in the environment is therefore the best way to ensure economic progress.

There is only one thing wrong with this theory, which is that it isn't true. Poor people want food for their children, a roof over their heads and clothes for their backs. They are not concerned about the state of the hedgerows or the hole in the ozone layer. To claim, as the *Brundtland Report* does, that the problem of increasing food production to meet demand 'requires a holistic approach focused on ecosystems' might meet with a few short expletives from a hungry man.[5]

The Brundtland Report ignores completely the real conflicts between environmentalism and development. For example, many African countries are currently ravaged by plagues of locusts which have been getting worse for the last four years. There is only one chemical product which is capable of dealing with these plagues: it is called Dieldrin and is manufactured by Shell. Unfortunately it has now gone out of production and will not be available again, since environmentalists in America designated Dieldrin one of the 'dirty dozen' chemicals which pollute the environment, and managed to persuade the World Bank and other aid agencies to ban its use.

Some locusts have been observed in Spain, and there are even reports that they may have crossed the Atlantic. It will be interesting to see if ecological objections to Dieldrin continue to hold up when the locusts are eating Western crops – not to mention our prize roses.

In fact, there is a connection between the economy and the environment, but it is the mirror image of the picture which is painted by *The Brundtland Report*, Jonathon Porritt et al. Environmental projects do not produce economic growth, but economic growth will pay for environmentalism. Prosperous societies like the Western economies are clean, healthy and pleasant to live in (as our long and increasing lifespans testify) because we generate enough wealth to pay for our basic needs, and then have enough left over for environmental projects which make life more pleasant.

Poor countries – like many of those in sub-Saharan Africa – are comparatively dirty, degraded and unhealthy (as people's shorter lifespans testify) because where people are scraping for a living they do not have time to worry about preserving the environment.

To put right environmental problems costs money – sometimes a great deal of money. The joint American and Canadian clean-up of the Great Lakes over the last fifteen years is reported to have cost $8.85 billion. Western countries, with their multibillion dollar economies, can afford this sort of work. African countries, with their devastated economies and institutionalized corruption, cannot.

If, as Jonathon Porritt believes, 'the whole continent of Africa is falling into an ecological collapse', then the way to stop the slide is obvious.[6] We need to share with the Africans the economic system which has made us rich.

Unfortunately this is not the agenda the Greens have in mind for the Third World. Jonathon Porritt believes that:

Capitalism itself continues to put Greens in a moral dilemma.[7]

The way most of us live in the Western world now poses a fundamental threat to the planet.[8]

Western style development in the Third World can wipe out the rainforests, create thousands of square miles of desert, reduce millions of Africans to famine and chronic poverty.[9]

If the Greens really believe that Western-style development is responsible for this list of disasters, then it is not surprising that they are so keen to prevent economic growth and progress along Western lines in the Third World.

At the recent World Bank conference in Berlin the group of twenty-four poorer nations warned the Bank and Western agencies against attaching environmental strings to loans and grant aid. Given the failure of the Third

World countries to fight off population control programmes which were tied to aid grants in the same way, it seems almost certain that this warning will be ignored. Indeed the World Bank is already allocating green dollars specifically for environmental projects. As we have hitherto regarded all dollars as green, including those used to stimulate mass-market, industrial economies, it makes one wonder just how much of the current Western ecological angst the recipient countries are going to have to embrace. Probably a lot. Whether or not they will have become more prosperous, or even have better environments, is a debatable point.

Roads and transport are private goods

Gabriel Roth
Source: *Economic Affairs*, April/May 1986, 6, 4, p. 11.

Traffic congestion is not a new phenomenon. The citizens of Rome were reported to have been kept awake at night by the noise of heavy goods vehicles (carts drawn by horses) that were prohibited from entering the city by day. Travel speeds tend to decline as cities grow, for two reasons. First, urban growth is associated with more and longer trips: the amount of travel increases more than in proportion to growth in population or urban areas. For travel speeds to remain the same, the capacity of transport infrastructure (like roads) has to be increased more than in proportion to urban growth, at a cost that, under present policies, soon becomes prohibitive. Moreover, increased motorization, encouraged by poor public transport, makes more acute the shortage of road space in urban areas. If present policies are continued, city centres as we know them today will stagnate and jobs and residences will move to outlying areas that can provide improved accessibility, as in Karachi, Lagos and Manila.

One way to reverse these trends might be to make more use of economic markets to allocate the scarce resources that are critical in urban transport: vehicles and road space. The use of markets implies that scarce resources have owners; that the owners can charge prices for the use of their resources or sell them to others. This article applies these concepts to vehicles and to road space.

The role of the private sector in the provision of public transport vehicles can range from zero, as with buses in Bombay, Moscow, Washington DC, and most Western cities, to the competitive extreme in Phoenix, Arizona, where there is not only open entry but taxi operators may charge whatever fares they wish, the fare-scales being displayed in large letters on the sides of the vehicles. In between, there are many possibilities for private-sector involvement; some are illustrated in Table 1. It provides a primary division of public transport systems by ownership.

Systems under state ownership can have state or private management but the commercial risk under state ownership is generally assumed by the public (that is, state) sector even if the management is private. There are some exceptions: to an increasing extent, even state-owned systems are contracting with private operators for the supply of some services.

The right-hand side of Table 1 covers the systems in which the ownership is private. The main subdivision here is between monopoly franchises (concessions) and competition. Franchises can be given to a single operator for a whole area (as in Singapore), or to operate one or more routes, as in Kingston, Jamaica. Routes can be operated either by single operators (the New York express bus service) or by route associations, as in New Jersey, Buenos Aires and Manila. The routes franchised often overlap in part; the franchised operators compete against one another to that extent. Where a company has a monopoly franchise (Singapore Bus Services), it usually bears the commercial risk but, in some cases (parts of Melbourne and Sydney), the private franchises receive a subsidy from the public sector to provide a specified standard of service.

Competition in urban transport, in the sense of travellers being able to choose between operators for similar journeys, is generally confined to taxi-cabs. In many cities these services operate under restricted entry, which means that the total number of licences is fixed by the authorities, and newcomers have to buy an existing licence which, in New York, can cost over $50,000. Hong Kong issues new taxi licences every three months and distributes them by sale at public auctions. Some cities (such as London and Washington DC) allow open entry to all vehicles and drivers that meet the specified requirements.

In most cities, tariffs are fixed by a government body. But there are exceptions: in Phoenix, Arizona, taxi operators can set their own fares; they are required to have the rate printed in large letters on the sides of the vehicles. Open tariffs are to be found in many other cities, either legally (Hong Kong's 'Public Light Buses' or Istanbul's 'Dolmus') or illegally (taxi-cabs in Bangkok, Lagos, Pittsburgh). The prices charged for taxi rides are negotiable in many cities, with tourists invariably charged more than locals.

Table 1 also indicates the responsibility for elements in the provision of public transport. Vehicle ownership can be government or private. Specification and enforcement of safety standards is invariably a government activity. Specification of routes and services, and of tariffs, is a government responsibility whenever vehicles are operated under state-ownership or under a franchise allocated by the state. Under competitive conditions the specification of routes and services is a private-sector responsibility, while the fixing of tariffs can be the responsibility of either government (fixed tariffs) or the private sector (open tariffs).

The private sector can work in a subordinate capacity even in cities where state ownership is the rule. One way of using the private sector is to employ it to manage state-owned systems. In the USA, the ATE Management and Service Company manages over fifty public transport systems, including such major ones as Baltimore, Cincinnati and New Orleans, while its smaller rival, ATC, manages about twenty, including Knoxville (Tennessee) and Austin (Texas).

The role of private-sector operators in cities where public transport systems are state-owned and managed is associated with the separation of the policy-making and the 'operating' functions of the providers of public transport. In discussing the position in US cities, Kenneth Orski[1] pointed out that:

> while public agencies were both the purchasers of service on behalf of the taxpayers and the suppliers of that service, ... increasingly local officials view transportation agencies as policy-making bodies that decide what services are needed, and ensure that those services are delivered *by others* [my emphasis] in the most cost-effective manner.

For example, in the County of Westchester, near New York City, the transportation department specifies services, sets tariffs and allocates routes, but the provision of buses, and the employment of the crews, is carried out by sixteen separate private bus companies. These companies operate at a profit; deficits, if any, are covered by government funds. Deficits tend to be lower when the buses are operated privately. Such arrangements are common in the USA; most involve government subsidy. But there are some cases, such as express bus routes in New York, where franchised private companies operate routes at a profit. In Thailand, the Bangkok Metropolitan Transport Authority, while running its own comprehensive system at a substantial deficit, allows some routes to be run by private operators who receive no subsidy.

While there are many cities in which public transport is provided by private operators without subsidy,[2] the most successful systems are generally those in which small vehicles are individually owned and operated but organized in route associations. The 'collectivos' of Buenos Aires and the 'Jeepneys' of Manila are probably the best-known examples. But there are also cities in which state-owned and privately-owned large buses operate side by side, the former at a loss, the latter at a profit, as in Calcutta.

There the state-owned buses are operated by the Calcutta State Transport Corporation (CSTC). The fleet comprises 1,200 buses, of which 700 are single-deckers, carrying up to 190 passengers each. Usually, fewer than 700 are put into daily operation, mainly because repairs and maintenance have not been carried out and sometimes because of a lack of drivers. Since the CSTC has a staff of about 11,000, the manning ratio per operational bus is sixteen. Given this exceptionally large staff, the insufficiency of drivers is perhaps hard to understand. The CSTC has also been plagued by slack fare collection, with fare evasion estimated at over 15 per cent of revenue. As a result of low productivity and fare evasion, the system requires a subsidy in the region of over £700,000 a month. Revenues cover only about half of the system's operating costs.

Private buses in Calcutta number about 1,800. These buses are operated mainly by small companies or individual owners grouped into route associations. Most of the private buses are similar in size to the single-deckers operated by the CSTC. Fares for private and state bus services are the same. Yet private operators have been able to survive financially without subsidy. Their success is attributed to very high productivity, which is reflected in low manning scales and high fleet availability. The drivers of private buses receive a percentage of revenue, which gives them a strong incentive to combat fare evasion. As a result, fare losses are extremely low. Private bus operations are estimated to cost roughly half those of the CSTC, and are more than covered by revenues.

Although by Western standards the quality of private and public bus services in Calcutta leaves much to be desired, the private operators can provide more reliable and frequent services. They are organized by route associations, which regulate services and apply fines when buses run behind schedule. The private companies, which hold almost two-thirds of the market, play a major role in meeting the demand for transport in Calcutta, and thus substantially reduce the financial burden on the government.

Recent work[3] has thrown new light on the role of taxis in the USA, where they carry as many passengers as mass transit systems. Many taxi firms have expanded from providing only exclusive rides to shared rides, services shaped by the customer, and even fixed routes. After a private taxi firm in 1973 successfully provided subsidized shared rides in the Californian city of El Cajon, there are now about 70 public transport services in California alone provided by taxi firms; they have become important suppliers of public transport also in Arizona, Minnesota, Michigan and Illinois. Phoenix uses taxis to provide Sunday dial-a-ride services and to operate regular dial-a-ride and fixed-route services in less heavily populated areas. Many other large cities have established subsidized taxi systems for elderly and handicapped persons. Small towns in Minnesota, Michigan, and California have contracted with taxi firms for all of their communally provided services, usually in the form that customers want. Regional public transit agencies in California, Michigan, and Virginia have contracted with taxi companies for customer-specified and fixed-route services.

Roger Teal illustrates[4] the development of taxi services by citing the example of Private Sector Systems:

> Seven years ago the company operated 25 taxis in one corner of Los Angeles. It did not operate a single public transportation service. As a result of astute management, substantial growth in transit contracting opportunities, and acquisitions of other companies, Private Sector Systems is now the provider for ten different transit services, representing $3.2m in contract revenues. These services include general

public and specialized transit services, dedicated vehicle and integrated fleet operations, and fixed-route transit as well as demand-responsive service. In addition, the company has expanded into airport service and social service transportation. The exclusive-ride business has also boomed due to acquisitions and new franchises, and the company now operates over 400 taxis in four different service areas. Public transportation contracts have been the key building block in the company's rapid rise to transportation prominence in Los Angeles County.

Teal ascribes the success of the taxi firms to their ability to switch their vehicles and staff between the different services they provide: vehicles (cabs or mini-buses) provide hospital transport in the mornings, 'normal' (exclusive ride service) in the afternoons, and serve fixed routes at night. This pattern is similar to those reported in other countries: the Istanbul 'Dolmus' and the Caracas 'Por Puesto' also switch from exclusive to shared rides following changes in passenger demand.

In addition to the legal taxi activities described above, there are many illegal taxis ('jitneys') serving US cities, including New York, Chicago and even Washington DC. They are tolerated because they provide low-income areas with services they require. Glenn Garvin recently suggested[5] that in Pittsburgh there might be twice as many jitneys as legal taxis. According to Garvin:

> Jitney drivers are friendlier, more helpful, and more willing to honour a request for unusual service. Jitney drivers will deliver a package, drop off the laundry, pick up a bottle of liquor and bring it to the house, escort a child, and occasionally even carry a customer in return for a promise of payment later in the week. And the jitneys are cheaper. Generally speaking, a $2.60 cab ride will cost $2.00 in a jitney. Moreover, the cab driver will expect a tip, which is unheard of in the jitney trade.

Some of the jitneys run along Pittsburgh's bus routes, charging the same fares as the buses; others work from supermarkets, helping customers get their shopping home. Yet others operate from jitney stands, of which there are at least forty-four in Pittsburgh. These stands, which might be petrol stations or small shops, are operated by 'dispatchers' paid $10–$20 a week by each operator to take phone calls, print and post business cards, and help seek customers.

The jitneys have several competitive advantages over the formal cabbies. They pay neither taxes nor licence fees and are not insured as taxis, which is manifestly unfair, but saves $2,000 a year per vehicle. They assemble groups of passengers going in the same direction, which is obviously desirable but which cabbies are not allowed to do. They do not have to install taxi-meters, but charge by a system of zone fare cards. They ignore government regulations but (like the private buses in Calcutta, and some of the professions and trade unions) are kept in order by their peers; passenger complaints are taken seriously and offenders are apt to be expelled from the jitney stands.

Thus it must not be assumed that unregulated transport is found only in developing countries. Indeed, economic realities and political pressures are forcing transport planners in both the UK and the US to relax many of the regulatory barriers that restrict the efficient use of urban transport facilities.

It may be concluded from experience the world over that private operators can provide public transport services at lower cost than government and that private services can be provided without subsidy when the public sector is often unable to do so. But can the private sector also deal with the second problem of urban transport, that is, can it provide transport infrastructure, the track on which vehicles, both state and private, can move speedily and safely?

Unlike the state sector, which relies on the purse of government to meet losses, the private sector cannot operate without profit. It has to be paid to provide infrastructure. There are a number of examples, historical and contemporary, showing how infrastructure providers respond to effective demand for their products.

First, there are the examples of private urban rail lines provided in numerous cities in the nineteenth century. The first such line is reported to have been established in New York in 1832, for horse-drawn omnibuses. By the middle of the nineteenth century, 'almost all American cities and towns of any size, or those of even a modest delusion of metropolitan grandeur, had horse- or mule-powered street railway companies'.[6] But horse transport was slow and fouled the streets, and so the private sector made many attempts to replace the horse by mechanical power. One solution was to use steam trains on separate rights of way; in 1863 underground steam trains were run in London and in 1868 similar equipment was used in New York, but above ground. In all these cases, the owners of the track controlled the vehicles that ran on them, and were remunerated from the fares paid by passengers. And when, in the 1880s, electric tramcars (in America, streetcars) were perfected, their installation spread all over the world.

In the 1960s a bus operator, Momin Motors, in Dacca provided a road about seven miles long for its buses, paid for out of fares. The company recovered its investment thanks to its private ownership of the franchise and the vehicles. This road has since been absorbed in the highway network of Bangladesh, but its construction provides a vivid illustration of the private provision of a public service even under the most difficult circumstances. There are also numerous examples of the private provision of local roads by property developers in both Western countries (the USA) and developing ones (the Philippines). In California, for example, a group of developers have agreed to finance the cost of intersection improvements in the cities of Costa Mesa, Irvine and Santa Ana to relieve traffic congestion

Table 8.3 Urban public transport: comparison of institutional alternatives

	State ownership		Private ownership					
	Public management	Private management	Area franchise	Monopoly franchise (concession) Route franchise by single operators	Route franchise by route association	Restricted entry by fixed tariffs	Restricted entry through open tariffs	Competition Open entry through fixed tariffs	Open entry through open tariffs
Responsibility for: Management & operations	Some totally state activities contracted to private operators							
Vehicle ownership	state	generally state	private	private	private	private	private	private	private
Safety standards Routes Tariffs Services	state state state state	state state state state	state	private	private	private private private	private private private	private private private	private private private
Examples	Bombay London Moscow Bangkok Toronto Tidewater Tunis Westchester Wash. DC (most western cities)	Baltimore Knoxville New Orleans (About 70 US cities)	Singapore Melbourne Sydney	Hereford Hong Kong New York (Steinway) Kingston (Jamaica) Kuala Lumpur	Buenos Aires Manila (jeepneys) New Jersey Calcutta	New York (taxis) (most taxi operators)	Hong Kong (PLBs) Istanbul (dolmus)	London (taxis) Wash. DC (taxis)	Phoenix (taxis) Pittsburgh (jitneys)

Source: Urban Transport Sector Policy Paper, World Bank, Washington DC, 1985.

generated by new development. The developers have paid US$1 million into a specially created fund. In Metropolitan Manila, 1,827 kilometres (37 per cent of the 4,912 kilometres road system) were built by private developers, who are remunerated from the sale of accessible property. Because of the shortage of government funds, over half of current road construction, and most of the maintenance, is privately financed (although this arrangement does lead to some problems, such as discontinuities in the road system).

But can the private sector provide trunk roads, for the use of the general public? With track for trains and buses, the road provider can control the vehicles using it and can ensure that they pay enough to cover costs. But can this be done with roads for public use? The answer lies in tolls, as is illustrated by the following examples.

Conventional toll collections are made on urban expressways in Bangkok, Caracas, and on many bridges and tunnels in the USA and some in the UK. These tolls involve substantial collection costs, both to the highway authorities and to the vehicle users who have to stop to pay the tolls. Tolls have also been criticized by economists because of their tendency to divert traffic from less- to more-congested roads.

Area tolls are another example. In 1975, in an attempt to combat city-centre traffic problems that were becoming progressively more acute, the Singapore Government introduced a scheme to restrain the use of private cars. In it a charge is applied to low-occupancy vehicles with less than four people in them entering the central business district during the morning rush period (7.30–10.15 a.m.); a cordon around the district demarcates the restricted area. Vehicles can enter only at clearly marked points, and low-occupancy private cars are required to display a special area licence disc for which a fee is charged (around £1.80 a day or £36 a month). Private cars with four or more occupants, goods vehicles, and buses are exempt from paying the fee. Area tolls have the advantage that they can be used to divert traffic from more-congested to less-congested areas, and the collection costs are reported to be low. But they cannot discriminate between points of high and low congestion, nor between brief and prolonged usage.

Electronic road pricing is also an example. In March 1983 Hong Kong's Transport Secretary announced his Government's decision to implement Electronic Road Pricing (ERP) in the Territory. A twenty-one-month pilot stage, costing about HK$33 million, was set in motion. Its objective was to test the proposed technology, which was described as follows in the Government's publication *A Fair Way To Go*.[7]

> The technology behind the Road Pricing system is quite simple and of proven reliability.
>
> A small, inexpensive and extremely tough solid state device called an 'Electronic Number Plate' (ENP) is attached in minutes to the underside of each vehicle.

190　*Recent controversies in political economy*

　　At carefully selected sites in the road system, sensing loops are buried in the road-surface, rather like those sometimes used at traffic lights. The loops are connected via a roadside computer and a special telephone line to a central accounting centre. A display at the side of the road reminds drivers of the current charge at the toll station (information on charges are sent to vehicle owners in a leaflet). The roadside computer receives from the loops the coded number of each vehicle's ENP passing through the toll station. This is then relayed to the accounting centre computer where the vehicle owner's account is charged the relevant toll. Once a month a statement, looking rather like a credit card account, is sent to the vehicle owner. When the amount reaches a certain level he gets a bill.

The pilot stage ended in mid-1985 and the technology was proven to be reliable and usable. But the introduction of ERP has been postponed (but for tunnels) because of objections of two kinds: motorists object to paying more taxes and also having their journeys monitored.

The second objection might be met by giving motorists the option of receiving unitemized bills. The first is more difficult, since the fiscal system of Hong Kong (like that of the UK) recognizes no formal connection between the amounts paid in road-user taxes and expenditures on roads.

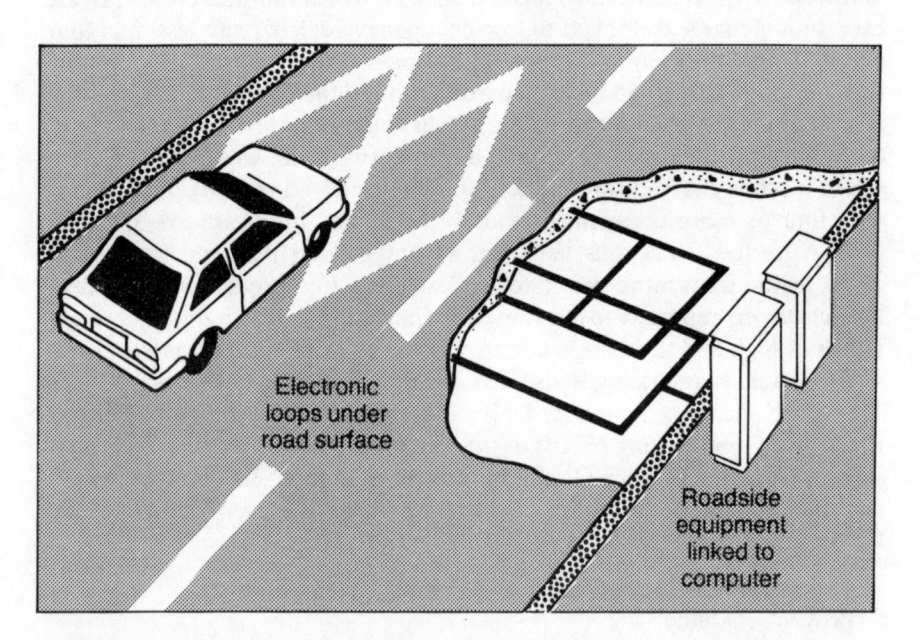

Figure 8.1 The electronic loop system

The simplicity of the electronic loop system as shown in the Hong Kong proposal 'A fair way to go'.

Although the Hong Kong Government proposed a reduction in vehicle licensing fees in its proposal for ERP, it did not satisfy the objectors, who feared that the fees could easily be raised subsequently.

The Hong Kong authorities might have been more successful if they had proposed a body to treat the scarce resources of roads exactly as, say, electricity or telephones.[8] A financially independent 'Hong Kong Road Authority' could, for example, be established to act like a private concern by charging market-clearing prices, paying all its costs (including rent of land, payable to the city) and expanding the road network as much as they could afford and as far as was financially viable. Furthermore, the ERP technology developed in Hong Kong could allow private suppliers, independent of government, to add road links (such as the Cross Harbour Tunnel), install their own pricing loops, and collect payment by means of monthly bills, as do the private long-distance telephone companies in the USA. The Hong Kong ERP proposals, proven to be technically workable, can be used not only to restrain traffic but also to privatize road space. ERP offers the possibility of the private sector providing not only vehicles but also roads on which to run them. And this possibility, if allowed, would give road users the strongest defence against the authorities collecting excessive revenues from a road network restricted in size: the power of the private sector to provide, at a profit, alternative road links would limit the power of the government to extract monopoly profits from its own network.

There would, of course, be obstacles to the private provision of roads. How would the land be acquired? Who would determine the standards of private roads? Would the owners of such roads be entitled to exclude certain types of vehicles (trucks and lorries) or drivers (with poor safety records)? But these questions may pale into insignificance when compared with the appalling prospects for congested city centres if radical new market-based urban transport policies are not applied.

Chopping and changing forestry policy

Linda Whetstone
Source: *Economic Affairs*, August/September 1988, 8, 6, p. 21.

Forestry policy has not only successfully escaped the Thatcher axe, it has managed to go in the opposite direction. The latest development, announced in the 1988 budget, is no exception.

Whilst other sectors (agriculture excluded) have seen government support removed *en masse*, forestry has enjoyed increasing government support despite the feeling of hostility engendered by an expansion of forestry. This has not come about because the rationale for supporting

Table 8.4 New planting by Forestry Commission and private woodlands in thousands of hectares

Year ending 31 March	England FC*	PW*	Wales FC	PW	Scotland FC	PW	Great Britain FC	PW	Total
1980	0.9	1.0	0.8	0.6	14.1	7.0	15.8	8.6	24.4
1981	0.5	1.1	0.7	0.6	10.4	7.0	11.6	8.7	20.3
1982	0.6	0.9	0.3	1.0	10.1	10.7	11.0	12.6	23.6
1983	0.5	1.6	0.5	0.9	8.0	10.2	9.0	12.7	21.7
1984	0.4	1.5	0.3	1.1	7.7	14.3	8.4	16.9	25.3
1985	0.2	1.1	0.2	0.9	4.8	14.6	5.2	16.6	21.8
1986	0.2	1.1	0.1	0.8	4.0	17.5	4.3	19.4	23.7
1987	0.1	1.4	0.1	0.8	5.1	17.3	5.3	19.4	24.7

Note: These figures should be treated with caution if used for purposes of comparison because the planting season lies either side of 31 March and in any one year planting can be advanced or delayed because of the weather. The private woodlands' figures are based upon the areas for which grants were paid during the year but also include an estimate of areas planted without grants (these amount to 1–5 % only of the total).
*FC (Forestry Commission) PW (private woodlands).
Source: Forestry Commission.

forestry is overwhelmingly persuasive but because the strength of the bureaucracy has prevented any reform.

Forestry policy was due for a change because of the ill-feeling caused when the pop stars and celebrities invest in conifers for the tax advantages. The media and electorate associate such activity with the expansion in the areas of boring conifers that seem to march inexorably over hill and mountainside previously grazed by sheep or covered in heather. The tax advantages were scrapped and the grants substantially increased, but a better scheme would have been to leave the tax advantages and scrap the grants. The grant for planting broadleaves (such trees as oaks and beeches) has gone up from £1,200–£1,575, from 0.25–0.9 hectares, while that for conifers has risen from £630–£1,005.

Forestry has been taken out of the tax structure altogether with expenditure for planting and management no longer being allowed as a tax deduction against other income. Furthermore, all proceeds from the sale of trees are no longer subject to tax. This latter change may seem sensible in view of the length of time trees take to mature – the generation that plants is rarely the one that harvests. The first provision means that forestry is now being treated unlike any other business and there is the possibility that planting will prove very unattractive if it has to be paid for out of taxed income.

Such 'Alice in Wonderland' policies could only have come about in the following way. The Prime Minister would have decreed that celebrities must no longer be encouraged to desecrate the countryside with the assistance of the taxpayer. The government's advisers on forestry would have been consulted on how this should be made effective and the government's advisers on forestry are the Forestry Commission. The Commission exists to encourage timber production; to provide jobs in rural areas; to enhance the landscape; increase recreational opportunities; and encourage conservation. It advises the government on forestry policy and applies that policy through its commercial operations and by administering grants to private forestry.

Traditionally, the private sector has quietly scorned the commercial side of the Commission but they have endeavoured to cooperate where possible because it is the Commission which both advises on levels of grants for planting and administers them. The Commission, which has been criticized by conservationists and others, needs the support of the private sector if it is to survive and it seems that it is such support throughout Parliament, and particularly in the House of Lords, that is keeping it in business. When faced with a decree to change forestry policy the Commission would have realized that some concessions would have to be made, so it set to work to persuade the Government that certain policies could be abandoned in return for the strengthening of others.

For economic efficiency they should have continued to allow the offset of establishment costs against tax, abandoned any form of tax on felling and ended grants completely. It would have also accorded with Government policy. After all, every other business is allowed to offset costs against tax, so why not forestry? Scrapping all taxation on felling would have provided a sufficient incentive (assuming that encouraging forestry is a 'good thing').

The Forestry Commission had to produce some suggestions that seemed radical, but they could not choose the obvious option outlined above because their hold over the private sector depends on their ability to distribute subsidies. They could only suggest that the tax incentives, which so held the imagination of the media, should be abolished and grants greatly increased. When grants go the Commission will disappear too, as the private sector will see no further use for it and there is little enthusiasm for it elsewhere.

Turning from the latest policy change, we must ask why it seems impossible for a determined radical government to change a policy that is generally very unpopular and is also far from their ideals. The existence of a department of state to manage an industry is almost inconceivable in Britain in the late 1980s, but it does exist.

The National Audit Office Report, *The Forestry Commission and its Objectives and Achievements*,[1] studied the Forestry Commission in detail and concluded that there are no important environmental, balance of payments or strategic reasons why forestry should be subsidized. It also looked at the job-creation benefits claimed by the industry and concluded that the cost of creating jobs in forestry, the number of years over which they become available and the increase in urban unemployment relative to rural unemployment made this policy suspect. No one, bar the Commission itself, disagrees with the National Audit Office, and the only reason that the Commission continues to exist is that it is the government's adviser on forestry. If the government obtained independent advisers, they would hear a different story.

Unbiased advisers would argue, like the National Audit Office, that there are no good reasons why forestry should be subsidized and they would agree with the Public Accounts Committee that rural jobs in tourism are cheaper to create than jobs in forestry.

They could argue that maintaining a viable economy in the outlying areas of Britain – the most plausible of the pro-forestry arguments – is desirable. But, given the cost of forestry subsidies and the strong environmental arguments against a further expansion of forestry, a more suitable policy could be to recreate the pyramids in the Highlands.

The pyramids prove a formidable tourist attraction in Egypt and they would surely encourage large numbers to visit the Highlands. Unlike forests, they would only impinge on a limited area of the 'flow country', they would leave the wildlife, flora and fauna largely unscathed and could not possibly pollute water supplies. Jobs would be created immediately in construction and the whole of the Scottish tourist industry would benefit within ten years of the start; in forestry there is a lag of up to fifty years before all potential new jobs are created.

If anyone doubts the sanity of this suggestion they should ask themselves whether it is any more stupid than taxpayers being asked to give around £50 million to subsidize investment in trees, which are cheaper to import, and the planting of which enrages most of those who see them.

If one group in the community wants to extract money from others they must either have exceptionally good reasons for doing so or they must expect endless criticism and a crazy policy as a result. The forestry industry has certainly got both.

Not in my backyard

Richard L. Stroup and Donald R. Leal
Source: *Economic Affairs*, August/September 1989, 9, 6, p. 34.

Two years ago, the British government stopped trying to find a shallow burial site for low-level nuclear waste after it ran into extremely strong opposition from the towns it was considering as waste sites. In the United States, the 'Not In My Backyard' (NIMBY) resistance to waste facilities has been just as formidable. Places as remote as Moab, Utah, have flatly rejected waste treatment facilities, while the federal government has been trying unsuccessfully since 1982 to find new disposal sites for radioactive waste. We all can learn from mistakes made in the United States.

The only way out of the NIMBY problem is to understand the reasons underlying the opposition and to deal with them effectively. Efforts to cope with the problem in the US (and apparently in Britain) have failed to do this. Nineteen state governments have passed laws delegating siting authority to powerful government bodies, but as happens so often in politics, actions did not follow the words. Few if any of these laws have actually resulted in new waste sites. Massachusetts' siting law, for example, created a council with the power to prevent local opposition and proposed compensation to the community that accepted a site. But in the eight years since its enactment the council hasn't selected a single waste dump.[1]

Similarly, the federal government has proposed compensation of hundreds of millions of dollars to the state that will accept a high-level nuclear repository. The governor of the state considered the prime target flatly rejected the offer, declaring that his state will not accept the stigma of being the 'country's nuclear wasteland'.[2] This, mind you, was in sparsely populated Nevada, with less than 1 per cent of the population density of England, and where nuclear testing has been accommodated for several decades near the proposed site of the nuclear repository.

Risks of living near a disposal site, whether nuclear or chemical, are surely far lower than the political resistance would indicate. Reported cases of health damage from hazardous waste of either type are rare.[3] A recent US Environmental Protection Agency report estimated that fewer than 100 annual cancer cases could conceivably be linked to all non-nuclear sources of hazardous waste risks – storage tanks, boilers, incineration and waste oil.[4] (Actually, despite many large studies over many years, there has yet to be clear epidemiological evidence linking any cancer deaths to such sources.) Managing hazardous wastes certainly requires care; but this care is accomplished by proper siting, construction and operations.[5] Regardless of political regulation, we can expect dumps in the future – at least private ones, where owners and operators are liable – to be even more carefully built and monitored as courts in the US impose increasingly large penalties where even a reasonable probability of damage from hazardous waste can be shown.[6]

Of course, there is a genuine risk to having a hazardous waste site in your backyard. There is a remote threat of health problems as a result of accidental releases. But perhaps the most consistent result of living near a site is the probability that residents will experience a drop in property values and aesthetic values.

For a number of reasons waste disposal sites have acquired a reputation that exceeds the actual hazard. Being forced to accept a hazardous waste dump elicits outrage, a term that Peter Sandman, Professor of Environmental Journalism at Rutgers University, uses to identify an emotional reaction that cannot be accounted for by the realistic dangers.[7] Like nuclear plant accidents, hazardous waste dumps are viewed, not as benefiting others, but inflicting dangers over which individuals have no personal control. If the dangers are seen as large, then outrage naturally follows. This reaction is encouraged by the news media since outrage gets reporters front-page headlines and journalism prizes. 'Without outrage the hazard story has little staying power; it is a Sunday health feature,' says Sandman.

Politicians often have a similar incentive to incite outrage. The ain't-it-awful aspect, and the us-against-them approaches are very saleable. Self-righteous statements about outsiders and giant corporations threatening to pollute the landscape bring much favourable attention to politicians seeking recognition and popularity. For environmental groups, important participants in the politics of NIMBY, outrage is important because it brings both attention to their general cause, which often has an anti-growth element to it, and additional funds. In America hundreds of millions of dollars are collected and spent each year by these groups, according to their annual reports, and most of their fund-raising letters feature environmental horror stories designed to shock and outrage potential donors.

Against this background, the narrow interests of politicians and the relative indifference of most voters (since most are at a distance from the site) complicate the issue. The US government's attempts to site a high-level nuclear dump show how these can operate.

Under an amendment to the Nuclear Waste Policy Act proposed in 1987,[9] the state that accepted a high-level nuclear dump would be eligible for benefits of $50 million a year during site investigation and licensing and $100 million a year once it began receiving waste. Nevada's Yucca Mountain is considered the most attractive site because it is technically suitable and remote from centres of population. But the governor of Nevada, Richard H. Bryan, flatly opposed the site and he was supported by most of the citizens of the state.

One reason for the opposition was the fact that the state legislature intervened to make sure that the state government would benefit from the compensation intended for local governments. Legislators created a county around Yucca Mountain with no inhabitants that would be administered from the state capital in Carson City, 270 miles away. This would permit the state to collect and distribute funds that otherwise would have gone principally to people closer to the Yucca Mountain site.[10]

The state legislature's action diffused the benefits of the compensation. This means that few citizens will benefit directly, so most citizens might as well succumb to outrage and reject the stigma of being the country's nuclear wasteland. It is virtually costless for them, under current policy, to dismiss the compensation as bribery. Calling it (in the words of Nevada's governor) 'nuclear blackmail', however, simply shows that outrage, which is fanned by such rhetoric, is itself a valuable political chip in the hands of the governor.[11] The dictionary (Webster's), after all, defines blackmail as the extortion, not the mere offering, of money in connection with a possible threat of danger. Blackmailers do not offer compensation.

While Britons might dismiss the politics of a cowboy state, the difficulties in Britain suggest that political pressures over waste are universal. In both countries there has been a gradual change in the identity of the holder of the property right to site a dump. Historically, this right belonged to the waste facility developer as landowner. The owner was of course held accountable for any damage through liability laws. Only if strong evidence of substantial, imminent, and irreversible danger were presented to a court, could injunctive relief be granted to halt waste site activity. But rising public concern, sometimes in the presence of fear and outrage, has in effect meant that local communities have now gained the right to veto almost any sort of waste site development.

Compensation packages, in effect, recognize that the community has a veto right that it may be willing to exchange for other benefits. State siting agencies represent state government attempts to pre-empt this right, but as always when a right is politicized, it will be reassigned to whoever has the most political power at the time.[12]

It seems unlikely that the political genie will be put back into its bottle soon, as in a return to common law with its rules of evidence and standing. So the challenge in forming a strategy to deal constructively with the NIMBY problem is to discover how, for a proposed site, to first minimize a community's genuine costs in safety and property values; second, arrange to compensate them for any that remain; third, publicize these facts to undercut the potential for outrage; and fourth, allow the people to decide in the least tainted political setting.

Since any damages which might occur from a hazardous waste site are almost certain to be very localized, it follows that any political right to approve or reject a proposed facility should devolve to the local community. A mechanism should be established by which the community residents can, if they choose, exchange that right in return for something of greater value. Ideally, the developer of a site would reach agreement with every member of the community on what compensation would satisfy him or her. But the transaction costs of such agreements would be extremely high,[13] and one holdout could block a well-designed, safety-conscious facility.

So, we are proposing that:

1. The developer be held accountable for any actual damage done to others, via a bonding or insurance scheme.
2. A compensation package be offered by the would-be site developer.
3. The compensation package be designed not only to enhance the overall welfare of the community but also to clearly improve the safety of its residents.
4. The local community (narrowly defined) be required to vote on it.

The community that accepts a waste site will end up being safer than when it started out. Ideally of course, the community would be able to decide how its compensation would be split between direct safety measures and other benefits. Our concern at this time is simply that the safety measures would have to be strong enough to overcome the claim of anti-siting activists and politicians that safety is being sold out for financial gain to the community.

Our suggested compensation would include a combination of financial and safety incentive payments to the community. Financially, for example, the developer could offer to pay property taxes (or rates in Britain). The size of the payments could be based on a sliding scale in which the highest payment would go to residents located in the immediate vicinity and become progressively lower the farther away residents are from the facility.

At least one effort has been made to use property tax payments to persuade a community to accept a site. In Lisbon, Connecticut, the local planning commission turned down a plan to build a new incinerator, even though it was expected to generate $1 million in tax revenue. So the developer proposed to pay the property taxes of every landowner in Lisbon at the 1986 rate for the next 25 years. This was equivalent to about $1 million a year, too, but this time the direct beneficiaries were the community residents. When this package was submitted to a vote, the residents supported the facility.[14]

The developer would be required to guarantee solvency by the posting of a bond or evidence of insurance against possible damages, so that anyone suffering damage caused by the site would be compensated at the developer's expense. The developer would also agree to submit the site to an independent inspection to receive certification, both before operation began and periodically, say, every six months afterwards.

Certification could be based on standards developed through independent testing by a reliable, knowledgeable, and respected agency, similar to Underwriter Laboratories, a non-government body that tests and certifies the safety of many American products. Of course, the purchase of insurance would itself probably bring on this sort of process. Premium payments would be based on the potential risk inherent in operating the dump. They would decline if the operator reduces potential risk through added safety features; they would go up if the operator is lax in maintaining safety features, and insurers would probably both inspect facilities and suggest or require cost-effective controls. Finally, the developer would post a bond that would assure continuation of control even if the developer goes bankrupt after the facility closes.

A compensation package could also pay for programmes that enhance safety – not just by reducing the risks from the waste site but also by improving safety throughout the community.

The developer should provide programmes tailored to local community concerns about safety. They might include providing smoke alarms, sprinkler systems, testing and mitigation of radon (a naturally occurring radioactive gas) in local homes, additional emergency medical care, and extra traffic lights in accident-prone areas.

The purpose of such a package is twofold; it would lead to a safer community, but the attending publicity would also force careful consideration of the actual risks posed by the dump. Opponents who challenge such waste dumps and the news media that report their claims would have to be more precise about the risks. Risks would actually have to be compared – the risks increased by the proposed waste dump compared with the risks reduced by the safety measures.

Government risk studies suggest that if actual safety is the concern, much could be done at low cost to make a community safer, and that such efforts would far outweigh any increase in safety from a well-built waste site. It cost the government $25 million to clean up an abandoned hazardous waste dump in Nashua, New Hampshire – a clean-up that is expected to reduce cancer incidence by just one case every twenty-five years![15] That same amount of money, says Paul Portney, an analyst at Resources for the Future, a Washington, DC environmental think tank, could reduce the incidence of lung cancer by more than 10,000 if it were spent on cutting down the amount of radon in 25,000 homes. Just making these comparisons would be useful for a community considering a waste dump.

Would our approach – a community vote on compensation that includes improvements in overall safety – actually work? The siting of North America's first fully integrated waste management dump in 1984 near Swan Hills, Alberta, suggests that a community vote on compensation can be successful. Along with financial benefits to the community, the Alberta Special Waste Management Corporation proposed a sophisticated monitoring system with groundwater wells surrounding the site and a data collection system that tracked the health of local wildlife. Referenda were held in five candidate communities. Two towns were prime contenders. In one, Swan Hills, 79 per cent of the voters accepted the plan; in the other, 77 per cent approved.[16]

And, as we saw before, the voters of Lisbon, Connecticut, too, accepted a proposed waste site when the developer offered to pay their property taxes. Unfortunately, the site was not developed. Connecticut does not allow such votes to be binding. The town's planning commission overrode the voters and opposed the facility! No matter how ingenious, any effort to counter the NIMBY problem means entering into politics, where the outcome always depends on the strength of interest groups.

Our proposal requires a voting mechanism that must be authorized by the government body. The vote would have to be binding, not, as in the state of Connecticut, easily overruled. Compensation should be flexible and the site developer, whether public or private, should tailor it to the particular site and community.

Notes

Europe's congested airspace – time for market solutions

1. *SCREAM (Sufferers Campaign to Resolve the European Aviation Mess)*, Joint Campaign of International Federation of Airline Passenger Associations and Air Transport Users Committee, Geneva and London, 1988.
2. For the benefits of Anglo-Irish airline deregulation see Barrett, S. and Purdy, M., *Economic Affairs*, December/January 1988, 27–30.
3. Bailey, Elizabeth, E., and Williams, Jeffrey R., Sources of Rent in the Deregulated Airline Industry, *Journal of Law and Economics*, Vol. XXXI, April 1988.
4. Civil Aviation Authority, in *Traffic Distribution in the London Area – Draft Advice to the Secretary of State*, CAP 517, March 1986.
5. Monopolies and Mergers Commission, *The British Airports Authority*, HMSO, Cmnd. 9644, 1985, 41.
6. Monopolies and Mergers Commission, *The Civil Aviation Authority*, HMSO, Cmnd. 9068, 1983, 203.
7. Demsetz, Harold, Why Regulate Utilities?, *Journal of Law and Economics*, Vol. II, April 1968.
8. Demsetz, Harold, Towards a Theory of Property Rights, *American Economic Review*, Vol. 57, May 1967.
9. Coase, R.H., The Problem of Social Cost, *Journal of Law and Economics*, Volume 3, April 1960.
10. Ibid., p. 38.

Green for stop

1. Jonathon Porritt, *The Coming of the Greens*, Fontana, 1988.
2. *op cit.*, p. 233.
3. *op cit.*, p. 38.
4. *Our Common Future: World Commission on Environment and Development* (The Brundtland Report), Oxford University Press, 1987.
5. *op cit.*, p. 144.
6. Jonathon Porritt, *op cit.*, p. 13.
7. *op cit.*, p. 193.
8. *op cit.*, p. 254.
9. *op cit.*, p. 40.

Roads and transport are private goods

1. C. Kenneth Orski, 'Redesigning Local Transportation Service', in Charles Lave (ed.), *Urban Transit: The Private Challenge to Public Transportation*, Pacific Institute, San Francisco, 1985.
2. Gabriel Roth and Anthony Shepherd, *Wheels within Cities*, Adam Smith Institute, London, 1984.
3. Roger F. Teal, 'Private Enterprise in Public Transportation: The Case of the Taxi Industry', *Transportation Quarterly*, Vol. XXXIX. No. 2, April 1985.
4. Ibid.
5. 'Flouting the Law, Serving the Poor', *Reason*, Vol. 17, No. 2, June–July 1985.
6. Kenneth Orski, 'The Private Challenge to Public Transportation', in Lave (ed.), *op cit.*

7   *A Fair Way to Go*, Government of Hong Kong, 1985.
8   *Cf.* my *A Self-Financing Road System*, Research Monograph 3, IEA, 1966, in which I sketch the economic and financial principles that could be applied to such an authority.

Chopping and changing forestry policy

1   National Audit Office, 1986.

Not in my backyard

1   Mark Crawford, 'Hazardous Waste: Where to Put it?' *Science*, Vol. 29, January 1987, 150.
2   T. Romaro, 'Nuke Dump Trade Irks Bryan, Pleases Nye Rep', *Reno Gazette Journal*, 6 February 1987.
3   Although a number of companies have reached out-of-court settlements with plaintiffs claiming their health was affected by hazardous waste, only one instance has been medically verified. Well contamination in Perham, Minnesota, led to a number of cases of chronic arsenic poisoning. See Edward J. Feinglass, 'Arsenic Intoxication From Well Water in the United States', *The New England Journal of Medicine*, Vol. 288, No. 16, 19 April 1973, 828–830. In addition, a US district court held the Velsicol Chemical Co. liable for health damages for Hardeman County, Tennessee, residents who could demonstrate that their health had suffered from contamination of groundwater from a Velsicol landfill.
4   US Environmental Protection Agency, *Unfinished Business: A Comparative Assessment of Environmental Problems*, (Overview Report), Vol. 1, February, 1987, 30.
5   See Jennifer McQuaid-Cook and Kenneth J. Simpson, 'Siting a Fully Integrated Waste Management Facility', *Journal of the Air Pollution Control Association*, September 1986, 1031–1035.
6   Sterling v. Velsicol Chemical Co., DC WTENN, no. 78–1100, 1 August 1986, from *Chemical Regulation Reporter*, 8 August 1986. (The court held the Velsicol Chemical Co. liable for damages in the amount of $12.7 million.)
7   Peter M. Sandman, 'Apathy versus Hysteria: Public Perception of Risk' in *Public Perceptions of Biotechnology*, (Bethesda, MD, Agricultural Research Institute: 1987), 226.
8   *Ibid.*, p. 226.
9   See Senate bill, S. 1481, sponsored by J. Bennett Johnston (D-La.), chairman of the Energy and Natural Resources Committee, and James A. McClure (R-Idaho), the committee's ranking Republican Minority member.
10 Luther J. Carter, 'Siting the Nuclear Waste Repository: Last Stand at Yucca Mountain', *Environment*, October 1987, 29.
11 T. Romaro, 'Nuke Dump Trade Irks Bryan, Pleases Nye Rep.' *Reno Gazette Journal*, 6 February 1987.
12 Rena Steinzor and Velma Smith, 'The Toxic Combat Zone', *Environment*, July/August 1988, 5–9.
13 James M. Buchanan and Gordon Tullock, *The Calculus of Consent*, (Ann Arbor, Michigan, University of Michigan Press: 1962), Ch. 6, for an analysis of the tradeoff, in group decisions, of high transactions costs when unanimity is required, versus the deprivation costs likely when a smaller group, such as a mere majority, can decide.

14 *New York Times*, 6 May 1986.
15 Paul R. Portney, 'Reforming Environmental Regulation: Three Modest Proposals', *Issues in Science and Technology*, Vol. IV, No. 2, 79–80; US Environmental Protection Agency, *Unfinished Business*, February 1980; and, Richard Wilson, 'Analysing the Daily Aids of Life', *Technology Review*, February 1929, pp. 41–46.
16 James McQuaid-Cook and Kenneth J. Simpson, 'Siting a Fully Integrated Waste Management Facility in Alberta', *Journal of the Air Pollution Control Association*, Vol. 36, No. 9, September 1986, 1031–1035.

9 Competition policy

Leveraged acquisitions and the market for corporate control

Ken Robbie, Steve Thompson and Mike Wright
Source: *Economic Affairs*, February/March 1990, 10, 3, p. 9.

In the mid-1980s the volume and particularly the value of takeover activity in the UK rose dramatically, with signs of a slow down appearing in 1989 (see Table 1). While there was a significant increase in the number of acquisitions of very large firms, the period has also been marked by an increase in the incidence and size of sales of large subsidiaries or divisions to other groups. In addition, the current merger wave in Britain has also witnessed new forms of ownership transfer. The acquisition of companies by either the management who run them (a management buy-out, MBO) or by a new management team (a management buy-in, MBI) has now become a significant part of the UK market for corporate control. MBOs and MBIs currently account for a little over one third of the number of transactions and over one quarter of transaction value. A key factor in the development of these newer forms of ownership, and indeed of a small number of notable takeover attempts, has been the use of various forms of debt to fund the purchase. It is now possible for transfers of ownership to take place which would have been unthinkable a decade ago. Hence, the market for corporate control, whereby management teams compete for the right to manage corporate assets ought to be enhanced. With these developments greater pressure is placed on managers to maximize shareholder wealth with a consequent reduction of the problems which stem from the divorce between ownership and control present in quoted companies owned by a large and diffuse set of shareholders.

The developments now occurring in the market for corporate control are closely linked to innovations in corporate financing techniques, which both permit larger acquisitions and new forms of organization such as buy-outs. The market for corporate control in the US has been characterized by complex financing structures in which high leverage (debt) has been a key element. The growth of both quoted and unquoted markets for subordinate (mezzanine) debt, which carries considerably lower levels of security than senior debt (hence the term junk bonds), has been an important addition to the various equity and senior debt instruments already available, especially in the funding of buy-outs. (In Britain, unlike the US, there is no quoted market for mezzanine debt.) The subsequent divestment of certain subsidiaries or bust-up of a bought-out company may be an important means by which high levels of debt can be brought down to manageable levels.

The current wave of takeover activity has been marked by a shift in methods of payment from share exchange to cash. In 1985, 52 per cent of acquisition prices were satisfied by the issue of ordinary shares, with a maximum of 62 per cent being achieved in 1987. Following the crash of October 1987, there was marked reversal in payment methods with some 70 per cent of the record value of £15.4 billion spent in 1988 on the acquisition of independent companies and sales of subsidiaries between company groups being in the form of cash. This proportion rose to 80 per cent in the first quarter of 1989. Correspondingly, although the amount of debt issued to finance acquisitions rose to record levels in 1986 (£2.5 billion) and 1988 (£1.8 billion), this was in the context of a very buoyant takeover market and the proportion of acquisition finance in the form of debt fell. However, the source of cash to pay for acquisitions is important. Improvements in corporate profitability in this period were undoubtedly a key factor in financing acquisitions. Although average capital gearing ratios have increased in the last year, this has been from historically low levels. Companies' borrowings have also risen sharply, but profit levels have generally been sufficient to cover the increased cost of servicing financial structures.

With respect to MBOs, the last four years have witnessed marked changes in financing methods. According to figures produced by CMBOR, the proportion of mezzanine debt in the financing of buy-outs for prices of at least £25 million has risen from 3.1 per cent of financing in 1985 to 13.1 per cent up to June 1989. Vendor loans or equity retentions accounted for 4 per cent of financings four years ago and 10.3 per cent this year. In the first six months of 1989, a total of £140 million of mezzanine debt was committed to buy-outs and buy-ins worth a total of £1054.6 million, a marked increase over the previous year on an annualized basis with substantial further increases taking place with the completion of the Isoceles, Magnet and Pembridge deals.

Two particular problems with the policing role of the capital market are that acquisitions may not be motivated by a desire to maximize profits and that size of a firm *per se* may pose a deterrent to takeover. Debt is a possible way of dealing with both of these points of criticism.

The availability of debt to fund various types of acquisition enhances the possibilities for transferring the ownership of assets to managers who will get better performance from them than is the case in their existing state, with consequent increases in shareholder wealth. The advantages of debt are derived from several sources. Debt may pre-commit or bind managers to certain levels of performance. These levels of performance enable debt servicing costs to be met, the consumption of managerial prerequisites to be reduced and surplus cash to be disgorged to the market place for subsequent reinvestment in profitable projects rather than being wasted on the pet projects of corporate managers. Together with the disclosure of greater information to institutions than would normally be the case, through the provision of regular financial reports and the board status of institutional investors, greater control may be exerted upon managers than is available through the diffuse set of shareholders of a stock market quoted firm. Typically undiversified financing institutions may have an enhanced incentive to ensure performance targets are met.

The use of greater debt to fund acquisitions, buy-outs or other forms of corporate restructuring is closely linked to executive remuneration. If remuneration is related directly to the performance of the company, which managers are able to influence, then executive objectives may be brought more closely into line with those of shareholders. The exercising of share options changes the ownership structure of the firm as executives become shareholders. The incentive for managers is the capital gain if they meet performance targets, together with the threat of being fired if they do not. Corporate restructuring involving buy-outs may give managers a significantly larger share of the equity than is possible with an executive share option scheme. In the UK buy-outs have generally meant that equity ownership has been concentrated in a small group of senior managers who, in smaller deals will usually have a majority of the equity.

In a corporation with a diffuse set of shareholders, managerial preferences for growth may mean that surplus or free cash[1] is spent on excessive diversifying acquisitions rather than being distributed to shareholders in the form of increased dividends. Such a policy may subsequently produce unsatisfactory performance and require corporate restructuring. Problems with past diversification may require either a reversion to core businesses or a shift to new ones. The problems of diversification may relate to the difficulties in controlling unrelated businesses and to an insufficient presence in markets where economies of scale and scope are important. In rapidly changing markets there may be problems in the capacity of head office management to plan the investment behaviour of diverse product divisions. There may be insurmountable problems in designing control systems which can convey appropriate and reliable information to head office, with the difficulties being exacerbated by insurmountable cultural differences between the different parts of a conglomerate firm.[2] As a result internal capital and labour markets may be ineffective. It may, therefore, be appropriate to break up (unbundle) conglomerate firms, either in part or completely, re-focus the spread of a firm's activities and return some investment decision-making to the external marketplace. The act of breaking up into individual units brings increased transparency of information for decision-making to external investors. Whilst complete breakup of a corporation and the return of funds to shareholders occurs in the US, it is absent from the UK market.

The need to restructure the spread of activities may be the result of changing market conditions or mistakes in earlier acquisitions. Merger activity may be regarded as a process of search to obtain the optimum combination of activities in a particular market. Any search process is bound to bring mistakes, either in terms of performance of the entity acquired or the extent to which it can successfully be integrated into the new parent. Restructuring through divestment is a means by which such mistakes may be corrected. The high level of Pan-European mergers seen in the late 1980s may provide the possibility for subsequent full or partial divestment as acquirers encounter major cultural barriers to the integration of new subsidiaries.

In the UK, the unbundling approach to acquisitions has generally been limited until quite recently, although some major firms like Hanson Trust have developed on the basis of continuous acquisition programmes followed by divestment of unwanted elements and a disproportionate recouping of the purchase price. In mid-1989, a consortium of investors using an acquisition vehicle company, Hoylake, attempted a hostile highly leveraged acquisition of BAT, citing the possibilities for unbundling the incoherent set of activities which comprised this conglomerate company. The move provoked a response from incumbent management which involved divestment proposals and share buy-backs. In 1986, the attempted acquisition of Allied Lyons by Elders IXL, which was highly leveraged, also proposed a subsequent sell-off programme to reduce debt to manageable levels.

The hostile buy-in bid by Isosceles for Gateway supermarkets in 1989, which followed an earlier failed takeover attempt, contained a pre-agreed sale of sixty superstores to Asda as part of a strategy to shift from a quantity to a quality market niche. The Isosceles bid prompted a white-knight defence by Newgateway, which included the senior management of Gateway not part of the Isosceles bid. Newgateway also proposed to restructure the firm, but institutional shareholders by supporting Isosceles took the view that the incumbent management had had their opportunity to restructure the business and had not acted.

Other large buy-outs and buy-ins in the UK such as the stock market cases of Virgin, Dwek, Invergordon, British Syphon and Lowndes Queensway have also engaged in significant restructuring after the transfer of ownership has taken place. The Cope Allman buy-in involved a large subsidiary of a group. The buy-in team clearly perceived the possibility for strategic repositioning which was not being achieved under the existing ownership structure and which required subsequent divestment of ill-fitting subsidiaries.

An increased threat of being taken over for failure to perform brings pressure on managers to introduce restructuring. Earlier studies of the takeover process have found that acquisitions of quoted companies are concentrated at the smaller end with acquisitions among the largest fifty firms being few and far between.[3] The availability of new forms of debt may now mean that increased pressure is placed upon very large firms who may hitherto have been protected from a hostile takeover bid because of their size. The threat of such a bid may put pressure on managers to maximize shareholder wealth in order to minimize the risks of being taken over. If such bids succeed they are likely to mean the removal of underperforming management. The existence of such a threat may provoke action to avert an unwanted takeover bid. Hence firms may sell-off or demerge unwanted subsidiaries, engage in share buy-backs, leverage cash-outs or other forms of capital restructuring or encourage friendly buy-outs/buy-ins. In all of these moves the introduction of greater amounts of debt has an important role to play.

Repurchasing of shares by quoted companies may be financed by distributing surplus cash or by greater borrowing. Such moves may boost a company's share price through increasing the underlying value of shares and thus inhibit hostile takeover bids. There may, however, be desirable reasons why ownership and management of a company ought to change; making a hostile bid more difficult may remove the possibility for such action to occur. There may also be scope for greenmail, whereby firms may be pressured into buying-back large blocks of shares acquired by outsiders who otherwise threaten to sell them to a hostile bidder.

The development of MBOs, LBOs and MBIs, which are largely financed by debt type instruments, may provide a means of defence against a hostile takeover bid. In the case of a buy-out of a stock market quoted company, a bid defence is provided against a hostile predator where a white-knight defence strategy is not feasible or desirable.

With buy-outs, an extra dimension of hostility may occur since managers may attempt to wrest control from an ineffective owner-manager, or subsidiary managers may seek to break away from a group structure which frustrates the efficient functioning of their part of the whole. Management buy-out teams in subsidiaries may thus provide a threat from within and may add an extra pressure on corporate managers to operate efficiently. Such a threat may also focus corporate management's attention on rewarding adequately those subsidiary managers whom it does not wish to see break away. However, the returns from buying out may be substantially greater than those offered by executive share option schemes.

MBIs and LBOs may occur as hostile takeover attempts. With the use of high levels of debt they offer the possibility of takeover bids for very large firms which may previously have felt immune from the acquisition. These deals remain relatively unusual in the US, despite the high level of publicity given to them. They have only recently appeared in the UK in the cases of

Table 9.1 The UK market for corporate control

Year	Independent acquisitions	Sell-off of subsidiaries	Buy-outs	Buy-ins	Total
		Value of Transactions (£m)			
1982	1,373	804	348	315	2,840
1983	1,783	436	364	8	2,591
1984	4,253	1,121	403	3	5,780
1985	6,281	793	1,141	39	8,254
1986	11,637	2,810	1,188	297	15,932
1987	11,277	4,086	3,220	307	18,890
1988	16,870	5,253	3,717	1,226	27,066
1989 Q2	4,004	2,401	1,838	390	8,633
		Number of Transactions			
1982	296	164	238	8	706
1983	302	142	234	8	686
1984	396	170	238	5	809
1985	339	134	261	29	763
1986	536	158	313	49	1,056
1987	905	220	344	89	1,558
1988	937	287	373	105	1,702
1989 Q2	339	138	182	63	722

Source: Business Monitor and CMBOR an independent Research Centre founded by Spicer & Oppenheim and Barclays Development Capital Ltd at the University of Nottingham.

Isosceles and Lowndes Queensway. The bid for BAT by Hoylake is perhaps more appropriately seen as a leveraged acquisition. However, where a divorce between ownership and control exists, the notion of hostility begs the question 'Hostile to whom?'. For where management has underperformed, a bid which is hostile to management which has underperformed may be only too welcome to other shareholders.

In many continental European countries, hostile bids have been difficult because of limitations on information, complex and interlocking shareholdings, closely held voting shares, and various statutory limitations. With the approach of 1992 and attempts by the EEC to harmonize company law and merger policies, these barriers to the operation of the market for corporate control are being gradually reduced. Together with a desire by firms to position themselves to take advantage of or protect themselves from the effects of the proposed European Single Market, there has been a substantial increase in merger activity across continental Europe accompanied by the appearance of hostile bids.

The use of greater amounts of debt to fund various types of acquisition raises the question of attitudes to debt and leverage on the part of managers, financing institutions and the regulatory authorities. In the UK, unlike the US, the corporate debt market is considerably underdeveloped in comparison to that for equities. Institutional investors in the public markets have in the UK traditionally had a preference for equity or gilts. For the mezzanine debt market to develop in the UK there would need to be growth of interest in this kind of instrument in the wider corporate sector beyond buy-outs and the introduction of a secondary market, which itself would require the relevant regulatory bodies to be satisfied, including compliance with the appropriate levels of information disclosure.

The Bank of England has expressed caution about increasing gearing levels, although their attitude to the buy-out market has been relatively relaxed. However, it has been recognized that the appropriate level of gearing depends upon individual firm characteristics, so that some firms may comfortably be able to service highly geared structures whilst others may not. Of course, as well as the several traditional ways of calculating gearing ratios such as income gearing (interest coverage) and capital gearing, other financial ratios such as a multiple of cash flow are especially relevant in the evaluation of a leveraged structure. Concern at the possibility of bankruptcy has been put forward as a further reason for caution in increasing levels of debt as part of corporate restructuring. However, there are devices to limit the effects of rising interest rates such as collars and swaps. Even if problems do occur, the possibility for sell-offs to reduce debt levels also exists. The use of debt may mean that corrective action is taken sooner than in a company financed with relatively low levels of debt and where bank covenants are not so strict. If managers fail to meet interest payments, financiers may be able to insist on particular corrective action. If dividends are waived in a company financed primarily by equity, shareholders may have little power to rectify the situation. As a result, corrective action may be delayed until matters are considerably worse. On a cautionary note, however, there is some institutional concern about entering into deals where it is necessary for disposals to be achieved at predetermined prices in order for debt levels to be manageable since in an uncertain market these may be difficult to achieve.

Leveraged acquisitions may take a variety of forms as we have seen. They raise important policy issues about the functioning of the market for corporate control, many of which are positive. In particular, debt financing places a greater discipline on management so as to minimize the risk of wasting resources on pet projects and managerial prerequisites. Debt financing also enables a greater threat to be placed on large companies which might otherwise have been immune from takeover. The reactions by BAT and Gateway managements to hostile leveraged bids demonstrates that this kind of pressure can force necessary action which was previously not being taken. There are concerns that amounts of debt may be excessive, but to reject the principle of greater use of leveraged acquisitions on these grounds risks throwing out the baby with the bath water.

The economic effects of anti-takeover gimmicks: an American view

Robert W. McGee
Source: *Economic Affairs*, February/March 1990, 10, 3, p. 14.

There is ample evidence to suggest that acquisitions and mergers are generally beneficial to society because they shift assets from less productive uses to higher; from less to more efficient managements. The old shareholders benefit because they receive a premium for their shares. New shareholders benefit because they are buying a company that is about to become more efficient and competitive. Non-tendering shareholders benefit because their stock increases in value as a result of the tender offer. Society benefits because a restructured, lean and efficient company provides higher quality goods and services at lower prices. Employees benefit because a healthy company provides more job security than a weak, non-competitive, inefficient company. Even an unsuccessful takeover attempt can benefit these groups because the threat of a takeover often causes management to improve. The only group that stands to lose as a result of an acquisition or merger is top management, which may be replaced if the takeover is successful. It follows that attempts to prevent takeovers reduce the welfare of all these groups, with the exception of management, who stand to gain by thwarting a takeover attempt.

Many of the ethical problems connected with takeovers relate to the directors' attempt to prevent their company from being taken over. Management has a fiduciary duty to act in the best interest of shareholders, yet a successful takeover will often result in some members of top management losing their jobs and perhaps forcing them into early retirement. Given this possibility there is tremendous pressure on directors to breach their fiduciary duty and try to either prevent a takeover attempt from being successful or make plans to cushion their fall in the event the takeover attempt is successful. In America, defensive tactics used by management often include hiding behind the antitrust laws or the Williams Act or some State anti-takeover law, or making the company less desirable as a takeover target by adopting a poison pill. Other defences include selling the company's most attractive assets, going into debt, giving a third party lock-up rights that allow it to repurchase in the event of a hostile takeover, repurchasing company stock at a premium, paying a large dividend to deplete cash, merging with a white knight or awarding golden parachute contracts to directors (and perhaps middle management).

The business judgment rule is often cited as justification for management to fight tender offers and there is some judicial support for this position. Yet it seems that attempts to prevent shareholders from considering offers that could increase their wealth is a breach of their fiduciary duty, is a conflict of interest as well, since shareholders, if given the opportunity to consider a takeover offer, might decide to accept the offer's terms, thus placing top management jobs in jeopardy.

Some commentators have suggested that laws should be passed to guarantee shareholders the right to receive and vote on tender offers without being subjected to obstacles placed in their path by the managements who are supposed to represent their interests. Yet new laws are not really needed if courts would recognize attempts by management to thwart takeovers as breaches of fiduciary duty. Some courts have recognized breaches of fiduciary duty where management attempts to thwart a takeover to protect itself. For example, the US Second Circuit Court of Appeals found that management breached its duty of loyalty when it issued new shares to fund a newly-created employee stock option plan when the reason for the moves was to prevent a takeover. Shareholders could remove many obstacles to takeover bids (and increase the price of their shares at the same time) by inserting provisions in the company's shares articles of association that include provisions to prevent resistance. The shares of companies that have such provisions would be more attractive to investors than those of companies that do not have any safeguards to prevent management from resisting takeover bids. Companies that have super-majority consent rules or similar blocks will be less attractive to potential raiders than companies having rules that allow raiders to make offers. Some managements use the excuse that they are fighting a tender offer so that other potential raiders can have the opportunity to make a higher bid. But quite often, the use of delaying tactics gives management time to thwart an offer by a raider. Even if the use of stalling tactics does result in a higher bid by another raider, the effect is a net loss to society. If there were no transaction costs, the increased price the target company shareholders receive would be offset by the increased resources the bidder would have to transfer to complete the deal, so there is no net gain. But since transaction costs would be increased, there is always a net loss to the general shareholding public as the result of delaying tacts. The only groups that benefit by blocking tactics are the entrenched management of the target company and the lawyers and accountants who help block the takeover bid.

Poison pills can be defined as financial schemes made by management to make the company a less attractive takeover target. Poison pills may take several forms, many of which involve debt restructuring, preferred stock or, discriminatory targeted repurchases. An important question to ask is who benefits and who loses by the introduction of a poison pill?

The obvious losers are the potential raiders. A raider may decide not to attempt a takeover because of the poison pill. If an attempt is made, it may be unsuccessful and costly. Even if it is successful, the cost of a success is higher.

The less obvious losers are the shareholders of the target company. Since the evidence suggests that target company shareholders tend to benefit by a takeover, thwarting a takeover by the use of a poison pill (or by any other means) prevents shareholders from earning a premium on their shares. Ironically, it is management, which is supposed to protect shareholder interests, that usually institutes the poison pill.

Another group that stands to lose by poison pills is consumers. Since the raider is prevented from making more efficient use of the assets than the current management, the company is unable to improve the quality of its products and reduce costs, with the result that consumers will have to pay higher prices to purchase goods or services of lower quality.

An even less obvious class of losers consists of the thousands of other industries that would get extra business if the target company was taken over and run more efficiently. If the target company's sales were £10 billion before the acquisition and the raider was able to cut costs to the point where the company could reduce prices by 10 per cent, an extra £1 billion would become available to purchase other goods and services even if the number of units sold did not increase. If prices were reduced by 10 per cent, it is likely that the number of units sold would increase, so sales would be something more than £900 million. Customer A might decide to use the £10,000 it saves to buy an additional machine for its factory. Customer B might use its £15,000 savings to buy another car for the corporate fleet. Customer C might use its £100,000 savings to invest in employee education or training. Customers A, B and C all benefit because they are able to buy something they could not have afforded in the absence of the takeover. The company that sold the machine to customer A, the car to customer B and the education and training to customer C also benefit because of the takeover, as do the customer C employees who receive the education and training. It is impossible to predict what the target company's customers would do with their savings in costs, but the fact that they would do something cannot be denied.

If all these groups stand to lose by the introduction of a poison pill, why are such pills introduced? Someone must gain by their introduction, otherwise, the poison pills would never be introduced. Management is clearly the foremost advocate of poison pills. It does not take long to see how management stands to benefit by the introduction of a poison pill. Poison pills decrease the chances of a successful takeover. If a takeover is successful, a high percentage of managers stand to lose their jobs and it is natural that the managers should take action to prevent job losses by introducing a poison pill.

It appears that by introducing a poison pill management is working against the interest of its shareholders. Yet some American courts have upheld the right of management to introduce poison pills. In one case, the Delaware Supreme Court upheld the right of management to restrict the right of its shareholders to sell their stock, an interesting result in light of the fact that the managers are supposed to be the agent of the stockholders. As a result of this case, American companies are adopting poison pills in record numbers. Three recent studies found that the mere announcement of such an adoption causes the company's stock price to fall, perhaps because of the decreased likelihood of a successful takeover, which would cause the stock price to rise.

But not all American courts have ruled that management may interfere with the voting rights of shareholders. New York and New Jersey have crushed some poison pills, and an Illinois court, while dissolving one poison pill, allowed the same company to adopt a different poison pill a few weeks later.

Greenmail is a payment by the directors of a company to a bidder to 'buy off' a bidder. It is often depicted in the popular press as a bribe that is paid to a raider to prevent a takeover attempt from proceeding. The raider is seen as being unjustly enriched at the expense of the target company and shareholders.

Greenmail payments do, indeed, stop takeover attempts dead in their tracks. But an analysis of greenmail payments raises questions as to their propriety. Since the evidence suggests that target company shareholders (as well as consumers and the economy in general) tend to benefit by takeovers, should management prevent a takeover by making greenmail payments? Rather than protecting shareholders, it appears that making greenmail payments harms shareholders, since it prevents them from obtaining the benefits that go with a takeover – primarily an increase in the price of their shares. Consumers are also harmed, since blocking a takeover prevents the new owners from using the acquired assets more efficiently, leading to better products or services at lower prices. Preventing takeovers tends to protect management, many of whom would lose their jobs if the takeover attempt were successful. It appears that management, unwittingly or not, make greenmail payments to protect themselves from losing their jobs, to the detriment of shareholders and consumers.

Some commentators have called for legislation to prevent or regulate the making of greenmail payments. But legislation in the United States is not necessary. All that is needed is a statement in the corporate bylaws that greenmail payments will not be made. If courts would start to recognize greenmail payments as a breach of the business judgment rule, such payments could be stopped.

Golden parachutes has become a controversial subject in recent years; a golden parachute is a severance contract to compensate high-level corporate officials when they lose their jobs if their company were taken over. As takeovers become more sophisticated and junk bond financing makes it possible to take over even the largest companies, directors are no longer protected by working for a very large firm. Furthermore the fact that, characteristically, about half the target company's top management are no longer with the company three years after the takeover, creates a tremendous amount of anxiety and gives them a strong incentive to seek ways to protect themselves in the event of a takeover.

Most commentators have seen golden parachutes as to the disadvantage of shareholders because senior managers benefit and the shareholders don't get anything. But this analysis is simplistic. There are circumstances under which shareholders can benefit by having the corporation enter into golden parachute contracts with top management employees.

One beneficial effect of golden parachute contracts is that they can help reduce the conflict of interest that would otherwise exist between the directors and shareholders. Management may resist a takeover attempt that would be in the shareholders' interest because they stand to lose their jobs if the takeover were successful. They are working against the shareholders' interests. Having a properly constructed golden parachute will eliminate or at least reduce this potential conflict of interest because management would be less likely to attempt to thwart a takeover attempt if their incomes were protected by golden parachutes. The evidence suggests that merely having golden parachute contracts raises the company's stock price by about 3 per cent when the existence of the golden parachute contracts is announced. This price rise might be due to the investing public thinking that a takeover attempt was more likely than before, but it might also be because the market sees that the potential conflict of interest between management and the corporation has been reduced, making the stock a better investment.

Since the evidence suggests that takeovers are good for the shareholders of the target company, as well as for the general public, it seems logical that company and government policy should be to encourage top management to negotiate takeovers that seem to be in the shareholders' interests. Yet present policies, such as the Deficit Reduction Act of 1984, penalize companies and managers who enter into golden parachute contracts, and state and federal officials are advocating placing further restrictions on golden parachutes. Since a well designed golden parachute contract reduces top management's conflict of interest with shareholders, legislation that restricts or prohibits such contracts usually works against the shareholders' interests, and the interests of the economy in general. Legislation that restricts companies from entering into golden parachute contracts with their top management should be repealed.

But not all golden parachute contracts resolve the conflict of interest problem. Depending on how the contract is designed, it may serve to make management more entrenched than before, which tends to work against the shareholders' interest. A well designed contract will reduce this conflict of interest whereas a badly designed contract will do the opposite. One way to make such contracts work for the benefit of the shareholders is to extend them to the managers who would be negotiating the takeover and restructuring the company afterwards. But extending golden parachute contracts to lower level managers who would not be involved in takeover negotiations would be more difficult to justify on the grounds of shareholder interest. Giving too many golden parachutes raises the cost of the acquisition, making it less attractive to potential raiders, while not gaining any corresponding benefits for the company. Beneficial Corp., for example, awarded golden parachute contracts to more than 200 of its executives, which had to make Beneficial stock less attractive to raiders. It is difficult to justify such actions if the premise is that top management should be serving the interests of shareholders.

Another good effect of golden parachute contracts is that they make it easier to attract top management. Golden parachute contracts are a form of compensation, a salary substitute, an insurance policy against job loss, and potentially an additional pension. Absence of a golden parachute makes a job offer less attractive to a manager, and since golden parachutes are a form of compensation, companies that do not have them would probably have to offer higher salaries to entice top managers to join the company.

While a properly constructed contract reduces the manager's conflict of interest, an improperly structured contract will do just the opposite. If the golden parachute is too golden top management might be too willing to sell the company, so they may tend to take the first offer that comes along rather than negotiate a higher price for their shareholders. Managers and board members who hold a great deal of stock in a company will have less incentive to take the first offer than those who own little or no stock, so the company might provide incentives that encourage top management and board members to own shares in the company. Yet present insider trading laws provide a disincentive, and some top managers and board members are selling their shares so that they will not be accused of insider trading. Offering stock options and restricted stock appreciation rights that are exercisable only if control changes is one possible solution.

The Williams Act was passed by Congress in 1968 to regulate takeover bids. The Act requires raiders to give advance warning that they are going to attack, and requires them to disclose other detailed information as well. Anyone who acquires, directly or indirectly, a 5 per cent beneficial interest in a certain security must disclose detailed information outlining his background, identity, source of funds, and acquisition plans. The number of shares owned and any agreements between the acquirer and other persons may also be disclosed. The party acquiring 5 per cent must disclose the information to the target company, the Securities and Exchange Commission (SEC) and the exchange where the stock is being traded. Once the offer is announced, the offerer may not make purchases other than through the tender offer. Open market purchases (at a lower price) are forbidden.

The Williams Act also gives the target company shareholders the right to withdraw their tendered shares within seven days after the tender offer is published or within sixty days from the date the original offer was made. This deadline has been extended by the SEC to fifteen business days from the start of the offer and ten business days from the start of any competing offer, provided the original raider knows about the competing offer and has not accepted the shares the shareholders seek to withdraw. If the offer is for less than all the shares of a particular class and the shareholders are willing to offer more shares than the bidder is willing to purchase, the bidder must purchase the shares on a pro rata basis rather than first-come, first-served. Originally, this Williams Act rule applied only to shares tendered within the first ten days of the offer, but the SEC later extended the allowable time to the entire offer period. If the raider increases his bid during the offer period, all tendering shareholders are entitled to receive the same – the highest price offered. The Williams Act also prohibits fake statements or material omission of facts, or any fraudulent, deceptive or manipulative acts or practices.

Since the acquisitions and mergers are good for the economy in general, and for target company shareholders in particular, government should not place hurdles in the way of consenting adults who want to enter into such activity. Yet it appears that the Williams Act is one of those hurdles. The Act is aimed at reducing the number of tender offers made, and increasing the cost of those that are made. Raiders must give advance warning of their intent, which gives entrenched management the opportunity to thwart the takeover bid. Once the declaration to acquire is made, the raider can no longer purchase shares on the open market, where they are cheaper. A premium must be paid on all shares subsequently acquired. If the shares are acquired at more than one price, the raider must later make up the price differential to those shareholders who willingly sold at a lower price before.

Once the decision is made to acquire the target company, it is in the raider's best interest to acquire as many shares as possible before the word hits the market that the acquisition is being made. The Williams Act limits the number of shares that the raider can acquire before making his intentions known, which both places a chilling effect on acquisition activity and drives up the cost of any acquisition attempt. Both the shareholders and the raider are harmed as a result. The shareholders are harmed because they stand to benefit if the acquisition attempt is successful. The raider loses because the disclosure rule drives up the cost of the acquisition and makes it less attractive. If successful, the raider will make the company operate more efficiently, which is good for the company, consumers and shareholders. Inefficient management that the shareholders cannot remove (because they are entrenched) can be replaced by a management team that does a better job. Preventing such events from happening hurts just about everyone except the target company's present management.

There is ample evidence to suggest that anti-takeover legislation tends to harm, rather than protect shareholders. Several studies confirm this thesis. Government protection of incumbent management in New Jersey caused the stock prices of eighty-seven affected companies to fall by 11.5 per cent. Stock prices for seventy-four companies incorporated in Ohio dropped by 3.2 per cent, or $1.5 billion, after the legislature passed restrictive legislation, according to a Securities and Exchange Commission study. New

York's statute cost stockholders $1.2 billion, or 1 per cent of stock value, according to a Federal Trade Commission estimate. Yet there is pressure for more legislation, both at the federal and state levels. Such legislation hurts shareholders and reduces the odds that a takeover attempt will be successful. By supporting such legislation, management harms the shareholders it is supposed to be working for.

Management often hides behind legislation to protect itself at the expense of shareholders. Fostering and supporting anti-takeover legislation is only one way that this can be accomplished. Management can also use the Williams Act and the antitrust laws to slow down or stop a potential raider. A threatened management need only point out some possible infraction by a raider to the appropriate government agency to stop a takeover attempt. By pointing out that a raider might have breached the Williams Act, the Securities and Exchange Commission will investigate, raising the raider's costs and slowing down the momentum of the takeover. Whether there is in fact an infraction is not as important to management as the fact that calling in the SEC can make a successful takeover attempt less likely. The management facing the bid is not penalized for using this ploy. In fact, it is often commended for doing so, under the guise of protecting shareholders from a hostile takeover. Yet shareholders benefit from a takeover, so this rationale for hiding behind some law is seen for what it is – using the force of government to protect management at the expense of the shareholders.

Another tactic, one that has been used not only to slow down a takeover bid but also to harass competitors, is to allege that some action by a competitor or raider violates the anti-trust laws. By pointing out a potential anti-trust violation, the target company lets the federal government slow down a raider at very little cost. The target company cannot successfully sue under the anti-trust laws, because only those who have been harmed can sue and takeover targets stand to gain rather than lose as a result of a successful takeover. Defending an anti-trust action, or even responding to an anti-trust inquiry, is time-consuming and costly. This tactic can be used very effectively to thwart a takeover attempt or at least to increase its cost and reduce the odds that the attempt will be successful. In the Mobil–Conoco merger attempt, for example, the Justice Department's request for information prohibited Mobil from acquiring Conoco stock and also prohibited Mobil from competing with other raiders for control of Conoco, even though Mobil's offer was about $1 billion more than that of the nearest competitor. It is difficult to see how shareholder interests are served by this kind of tactic.

Some companies, such as Marshall Field even went as far as to establish department stores where competitors already had stores so that any takeover attempt would raise anti-trust questions. There is evidence to suggest that most takeovers actually increase competition rather than reduce it and that the anti-trust laws actually reduce competition in many cases by setting up artificial barriers to market entry and by protecting established firms at the expense of newcomers. Attempts by target company management to use the anti-trust laws to thwart a takeover attempt seems ethically questionable, at best.

The evidence that acquisitions and mergers are good for shareholders, the economy, society, business and consumers is overwhelming. The only group that stands to lose from a successful takeover attempt are the managers, who stand a very good chance of becoming unemployed. A number of ethical issues arise because of the inherent conflict of interest that exists with top management in the event of a takeover attempt. On the one hand, the management is employed to act in the best interest of shareholders. But if management does act in the shareholder's interest, it stands to become unemployed.

Because of this built-in conflict of interest, a number of ploys have been used by management to protect itself at the expense of shareholders, whose interests they are hired to protect. One such ploy is the poison pill, which can take many forms, but which is always used to thwart a takeover attempt – often in the guise of protecting the shareholders. Greenmail, a form of bribery using shareholder money, is sometimes used as well. Management often uses the force of government to protect itself at the expense of shareholders by hiding behind laws that actually harm shareholder interests. Golden parachutes can reduce this conflict of interest if used judiciously but may exacerbate the problem if too many managers have them.

Rather than tightening the regulation of takeover activity, legislation that prevents shareholders from receiving tender offers and enforcing existing laws to prevent management from abusing their fiduciary duty to protect shareholder interests should be repealed.

Monopolies and mergers: an MMC perspective

Sydney Lipworth
Source: Economic Affairs, February/March 1990, 10, 3, p. 20.

The Monopolies and Mergers Commission is an independent body set up to investigate individual cases put to it. We are not part of Government, though we may be consulted during the course of competition policy review. Our perspective is in one sense narrow – to the extent that we look in depth only at the segments of the industry and commerce involved under the references put to us by the Secretary of State for Trade and Industry or by the Director General of Fair Trading. We have no broad and continuing remit to look at industry and commerce as a whole. In another sense our perspective is wide. The Commission comprises a range of experience from industry, commerce and the professions. We are well represented by economists and lawyers but we do not pretend to be a body of specialists. The argument for this broad representation, which has stood the test of our forty years' history, is that we are required by statute to take a view on the public interest, in itself a broad concept. Competition features high in our counsels, and we need to be well educated in practice and precedent, but it need not be the only aspect that we take into account.

In this article, I propose covering briefly the nature of the Commission's work and to look at changes in policy which may affect that work, the type of monopolies and mergers work which has come our way in the last two years, and how we are going about that work.

The essence of our work is inquiry in depth into the operation of the relevant companies, usually the principal companies, in particular markets. The Commission's task requires a thoroughness of approach, and our procedures are designed to achieve this. However we are not a court, our procedures are not adversarial in the legal sense, and we have freedom under the legislation to devise our own procedures. It is important that these should not become ritualistic but should be sufficiently flexible to get to the bottom of the matter. Similarly, in analysing the workings of markets the Commission does not apply rigid tests or methods. For example, in looking at whether a firm has a dominant position the Commission does not use rigid market share tests. It is more concerned with effect than form, so that high market shares may or may not imply market power. The Commission's assessment will depend on a careful consideration of many factors including the strength of existing competition, buyer power and supplier power, potential competition from both new entrants and imports, and the severity or otherwise of entry barriers, i.e. what impediments are there if any to new firms entering the industry or existing competitors expanding.

The finding the Commission is required to make is whether a monopoly or merger operates or may be expected to operate against the public interest. The relevant test is contained in section 84(1) of the Fair Trading Act 1973. This provides:

> In determining for any purposes to which this section applies whether any particular matter operates, or may be expected to operate, against the public interest, the Commission shall take into account all matters which appear to them in the particular circumstances to be relevant and, among other things, shall have regard to the desirability:
> 1 of maintaining and promoting effective competition between persons supplying goods and services in the United Kingdom;
> 2 of promoting the interests of consumers, purchasers and other users of goods and services in the United Kingdom in respect of the prices charged for them and in respect of their quality and the variety of goods and services supplied;

3   of promoting, through competition, the reduction of costs and the development and use of new techniques and new products, and of facilitating the entry of new competitors into existing markets;
4   of maintaining and promoting the balanced distribution of industry and employment in the United Kingdom; and
5   of maintaining and promoting competitive activity in markets outside the United Kingdom on the part of producers of goods, and of suppliers of goods and services, in the United Kingdom.

As can be seen, this provides a broad test, as well as five specific criteria, all but one of which can be said to relate to competition.

The Commission normally pays most attention to competition, but that does not preclude wider issues being brought to bear. Competition itself can be seen as both positive – the promotion of competition – and negative – the prevention of anti-competitive practices. The two are closely linked, but the Commission's duty is to find whether a merger or monopoly operates against the public interest, naturally taking into account all matters it thinks are relevant, including any countervailing benefit which the merger or monopoly might be expected to bring.

The essential question to be decided is whether a monopoly or merger works against the public interest; it need not be positively beneficial. If there is an adverse finding the Commission's role is not to recommend what it believes might be the perfect structure of a market, but to recommend such remedies which they believe will remove any adverse effects which they have found. In these circumstances the remedies might be radical if, for example, the market showed no sign of self-remedy, or minimal if some adverse effects were found but competition was generally thriving; and of course none at all if no adverse effects had been found.

I now turn to recent changes in policy; first, mergers. Merger policy was reviewed by an interdepartmental group under the chairmanship of Mr Hans Liesner, Deputy Secretary and Chief Economic Adviser in the DTI. After retirement from that post he became one of the three Deputy Chairmen of this Commission. The review was published early in 1988.[1] It left the existing institutional and legal structures virtually intact. The main changes proposed, and now incorporated into the Companies Act 1989, were a non-mandatory notification system and the opportunity for companies to give enforceable undertakings to the Director General of Fair Trading in place of an MMC reference. Both changes were designed to increase efficiency and flexibility of handling to those cases in which the objectives of merger control can be met without an MMC investigation, though the review confirmed that reference to the MMC remained the centre-piece of merger control procedures. It remains to be seen how many cases can be dealt with by the statutory undertakings route.

A second, roughly simultaneous, review concerned Restrictive Trade Practice policy. The detail is set out in a White Paper.[2] Reference to this major change in policy is made here for completeness: mergers and monopolies are two strands of competition policy, one aimed broadly at pre-empting potential anti-competitive behaviour following the creation of new market dominance, the other seeking to cope with such behaviour where market dominance has already been established. RTP is a different strand; it aims at remedying anti-competitive behaviour that is not necessarily the result of market dominance. It is interesting to speculate, as was speculated in the 1950s when the present RTP legislation was brought into being, what knock-on effects a change in one part of competition policy will have on another. Under the new RTP proposals the MMC will come into play again, since tribunals who examine new cases will be drawn from its membership.

On another aspect of competition policy, the European dimension, little can be said here because the draft Merger Regulation is under discussion at the time of writing. Should it go through, some merger cases which we would have investigated would be dealt with in Brussels. Irrespective of that development, we need to and do take account of Community law in the cases that we do investigate. We need to maintain the good communications between DGIV and ourselves, whilst preserving the independence of our own investigations.

The impact of the policy changes on the work of the MMC is difficult to predict. Under the statutory undertakings proposals, the Director General will be able to deal with some cases that might otherwise have come our way. If the Merger Regulation comes into effect, similarly some of the larger cases would be dealt with in Brussels. Although in a separate category, the new RTP tribunals would be faced with a substantial body of work in the event of new legislation in that area.

Whether or not the MMC is busy is of little consequence in itself to the outside world. What matters is that the regulation of monopolies and mergers is working. It is primarily a regime of deterrence. A year in which the MMC completes twelve to fifteen investigations in these two areas is an extremely busy one. But that is a tiny fraction of the number of total and qualifying mergers. In 1988 we completed four merger investigations: Mitek/Gang-Nail, Emap/Parrett & Neves, Government of Kuwait/BP, Thomson/Horizon; we completed six monopoly enquiries: three into advertising restrictions by doctors, osteopaths and civil engineering services, and inquiries into British Gas, artificial lower limbs and opium derivatives.

Because a number of inquiries were carried over from 1988, 1989 will mark the highest point in the Commission's history for investigations completed within a year. These will include monopoly inquiries into beer (a commodity accounting for some 3.3 per cent of consumer expenditure), credit cards (some 5 per cent of all consumer expenditure though this figure overlaps with measures of expenditure on goods and services) and petrol (2.7 per cent of consumer expenditure). In addition we completed a monopoly inquiry into Cross-Channel Ferries. As to merger inquiries we completed Minorco/Consgold, Emap/T.R. Beckett, Badgerline/Midland Red West Holdings, Elders/Scottish & Newcastle, Strong & Fisher/Pittard Garnar and Hillsdown/Pittard Garnar, Gec-Siemens/Plessy, Thomson Regional Newspapers/Century, Grand Metropolitan/William Hill, Glynwed/Lees, Monsanto/Rhône Poulenc, Coats Viyella/Tootal, Yale & Valor/Myson and Blue Circle/Myson, and Atlas Copco/Desoutter.

At the time of writing, there is no sign at all of our work drying up. In addition to our work on monopolies and mergers, there are other types of inquiry (privatization/regulation, anti-competitive practices and efficiency audits of nationalized industries) all connected with competition, of which the Commission completed five in 1988 and 1989 respectively.

The third development of monopolies and mergers control relates to procedure. During 1987 and 1988 the normal period for a merger investigation was reduced from six to three months, a significant reduction in the period of uncertainty for the companies concerned. This acceleration must be achieved without loss of quality, and must be subject to the overriding requirement that the Commission should be thorough and fair.

Apart from the general advantage of efficiency, acceleration is of benefit both to firms appearing before the Commission as well as to the market by reducing the period of uncertainty. It also concentrates the pressures of an inquiry on all concerned in meeting essential deadlines.

As the Monopolies and Mergers Commission enters its fifth decade, its workload may increase or reduce from time to time as policy changes occur. This has happened in the past. But the difficult decisions that are referred to it will not become easier. The challenge to the Commission will be to continue to maintain its high standards and thoroughness, while having the flexibility to cope with the evolving pattern work.

Can we privatize competition policy?

Graham Mather
Source: Economic Affairs, March 1990, 10, 3, p. 22.

At first sight it may seem strange to suggest that shareholders may need more scope to defend companies against hostile bids, to 'lock in' able managers and to adopt long-term investment strategies.

Yet there is an undoubted concern in British markets that there are companies in which shareholders and managers may legitimately seek to protect themselves from a takeover bid based on a short-term cash price. And, whilst doctrines of contestable markets seek to allow the widest scope for buying and selling equity investments, contract theory more generally permits owners – and shareholders – to choose to whom and on what terms they will part with assets, and even to 'lock themselves in' by setting terms and conditions on which they will not sell.

The framework which determines these possibilities in London's equity markets is not legislation, but rather the attitude of financial markets towards differential voting structures or other defensive techniques.

Too often it is assumed that the existing framework in which shares are bought and sold is necessarily the best, and that changes can be secured only by legislative intervention or government interference in the working of the market. But rather than looking to governments, is it not time to look at the position of shareholders themselves?

Is it not possible to find a way by which shareholders would determine themselves, to a greater degree, the level of protection they wished to accord to corporate managers?

Such a greater freedom would not necessarily lead to a rash of poison pill defences. But it would allow shareholders themselves to determine the level of bid proofing they wished to secure, against the background that a contestable market in corporate control is demonstrably good for shareholders, customers, business and the economy.

The need today is to open up a more sophisticated market in corporate control and force institutions to come off the fence in their attitudes to longer term corporate strategies. While the price of protecting inadequate managers would be a visible fall in a company's share price, the benefit would be an ability to adopt longer term business strategies. Current Stock Exchange attitudes, which restrict defensive voting structures, may deny shareholders the chance to balance these factors.

A truly free market would allow shareholders themselves to settle the degree of bid protection which they wish to confer upon managers, recognizing that the price of differential voting structures or other defensive measures may be ossification of boards, adverse market reaction and reduced competitiveness and share price.

Existing stock market attitudes, which tend to preclude changes in voting structures of this type, may no longer be desirable. Although they are claimed to be a protection for small shareholders, in practice they may allow large institutions off the hook. Institutional investors can talk long-term but behave short-term: they can claim to be supporting a management and its strategy, but deny those managers the continuity they may need to implement their plans.

The danger may be that, as a result, progressive managers will wish their companies to stay unlisted. Or, increasingly, they may seek, listings on the stock markets – including those in the United States – which have more flexible rules. Meanwhile, because shareholder choice of structure is limited but regulatory intervention is strong, major bids attract lobbying, litigation and regulatory manoeuvrings on a world scale with increasingly random outcomes.

The peculiarities of the current British approach are not the result of company law, which allows companies maximum freedom to establish an appropriate and convenient internal management and voting structure. They are, rather, the result of Stock Exchange listing approaches which deter companies from seeking to build in a long-term approach through these structures. Ironically, of course, their US or European counterparts are not so handicapped; and it is probably wishful thinking to imagine that European companies, in particular, will quickly change their ownership structures, which are the result of long-established business procedure rather than legislation which could be altered at the stroke of a legislative pen.

The object of the traditional British attitude is desirable: to maintain an open market and bring the threat of takeover and its consequences to bear on under-performing managers. But the stock market is a means to facilitate a market in ownership, not an end in itself.

The danger is that, because shareholders are confronted with an all-or-nothing choice, the British stock market fails to offer them some of the gradations of protection which are available in Europe or America. Taking advantage of these protections may have a high price: but that should be for shareholders themselves to weigh and decide.

It is insufficient to say that existing stock market restrictions are to protect small shareholders. They do not apply, of course, to some companies with historical differentiated voting structures. In practice, rather than protect small shareholders, they allow institutions to have it both ways. Were there to be an option to adopt defensive structures, institutions would have to choose.

The effect could be to depoliticize takeover, reduce frenetic and artificial lobbying and legal manoeuvres, and allow the market in corporate control to reflect more closely the wishes of managers and shareholders.

Notes

Leveraged acquisitions and the market for corporate control

1 M.C. Jensen, 'The Eclipse of the Corporation', *Harvard Business Review*, Sept/Oct 1989.
2 S. Thompson and M. Wright (eds), *International Organization, Efficiency and Profit*, Philip Allan, Oxford, 1988.
3 B. Chiplin and M. Wright, *The Logic of Mergers: The Competitive Market for Corporate Control in Theory and Practice*, IEA Hobart Paper 107, 1987.

Monopolies and mergers: an MMC perspective

1 *Mergers Policy: A Department of Trade and Industry Paper on the policy and*

procedure of merger control, HMSO, 1988.
2 *Opening Markets: New Policy on Restrictive Trade Practices*, HMSO, Cm 727, 1989.

10 Privatization

Privatization – by political process or consumer preference?

John Blundell
Source: *Economic Affairs*, October/November 1986, 7, 1, p. 59.

Over the past few years many articles, pamphlets, and books have been written on privatization by academics, politicians, political commentators – some with, some without vested interest. An unfortunately high percentage is woefully lacking in good micro-economic analysis.[1]

Typically, both opponents and proponents misrepresent the role and attributes of markets and entrepreneurs. To opponents, privatization automatically leads to redundancies, low wages, bad working conditions, and poor – if not life-threatening – service. To many proponents, it is the unleashing of the dynamic, creative entrepreneur, who is in all ways at all times an omniscient optimizer with the latest management techniques and most modern equipment ready at his finger-tips to supply maximum quality at minimum cost.[2]

For every published work on the subject there is a different definition of privatization. Ten years ago, if you wanted to sell a state-owned industry, you were in favour of denationalization.[3] If you wanted to contract out a local government service, you were in favour of privatization. And if you wanted, say, to sell council housing, you were in favour of selling council housing.

Today, privatization covers all these and many other policy options. Definitions range in length from Professor Murray Rothbard's one word, desocialization,[4] to Professor Alan Peacock's four pages.[5] Consequently headlines such as 'Thatcher to Privatize X' or 'Reagan to Privatize Y' tell us nothing of real importance. The answers to fundamental questions – who will provide the good or service?, who will pay for it?, will there be freedom of entry? – are by no means apparent.

From its original narrower meaning of contracting out, privatization has come to denote the process by which goods and services currently financed and provided by the state sector shift, either how they are paid for, or how they are provided, or both, to the private sector, with or without concomitant changes in the regulatory climate.

In box 2 of Figure 1, provision of the good or service remains in state hands but now the individual consumer has to pay a sum of money at the point of consumption. How such a sum is determined is another matter, but a charge, small or large, is now levied for something previously free.[6]

Vouchers, box 3 of Figure 1, straddles the middle. The basic idea of the voucher is that the state issues the individual with a coupon which can be exchanged for specified goods or services. One variation of the educational voucher concept envisages it being spent at either government or independent schools and incorporating topping-up with private funds, hence its position in the middle.

Contracting-out, box 4, is the newly fashionable term for tendering, a practice employed by most local, regional and national governments at all times. Under contracting-out, the state accepts bids or tenders from private companies to provide a service of good(s) for a stated price. With services, the winner receives an exclusive monopoly contract for a specific period. (With goods, the contract tends to be for one item or a bundle of items and not for continuing long-term supply.) The service is still financed from taxation; most aspects of the service are still set by political processes, and there is no freedom of entry.

Box 5 is split between load-shedding and franchising. Load-shedding occurs when the state moves out of the picture completely; it no longer provides or finances the good or service, and there is freedom of entry. In franchising, as with load-shedding, the state is not involved in provision or financing: both are accomplished privately. But, as with contracting-out, the state issues and enforces a monopoly for one supplier for a specific period. The most clear-cut modern example is the exclusive contracts granted to cable television companies. (An earlier example is Henry VIII's attitude toward printing presses, an interesting media coincidence.) This analysis helps in evaluating Dr Keith Hartley's case[7] for contracting-out.

Dr Hartley, and he is by no means alone, sets no limits to contracting-out. Anything currently performed by government can be the subject of a contract between a state agency and a private sector company. It is by no means clear how far he would apply this but, from his mention of mercenaries, one has to assume that he believes that the Ministry of Defence should put out tenders for airforce services, for example; and that such a privatized air force would provide better service at lower cost. Indeed, *The Washington Times*, tongue-in-cheek, recently imagined[8] the fighting of the Battle of Britain at a saving of 40 per cent by private airforces.

Secondly, Dr Hartley assumes that contracting-out is a one-way street – as in the Figure, always downward/rightward from the top left. No argument or evidence is provided for this one-way movement. As his case stands now, there is no reason in logic that the movement should not be the

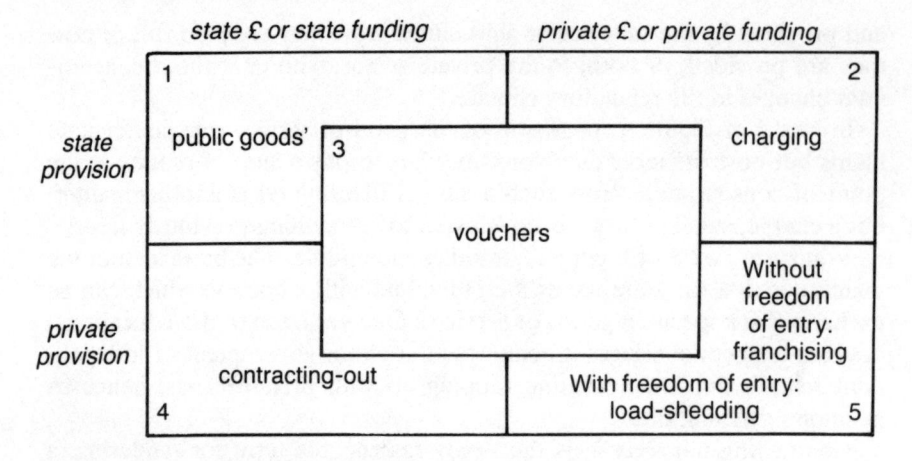

228 Recent controversies in political economy

```
             state £ or state funding      private £ or private funding
         ┌────────────────────────────┬────────────────────────────┐
         │ 1                          │                          2 │
 state   │  'public goods'  ┌─────────┼─────────┐      charging    │
provision│                  │ 3       │         │                  │
         │                  │         │         │                  │
         ├──────────────────┤  vouchers         ├──────────────────┤
         │                  │                   │        Without   │
         │                  │                   │        freedom   │
 private │                  │                   │        of entry: │
provision│                  └─────────┼─────────┘      franchising │
         │         contracting-out    │   With freedom of entry:   │
         │ 4                          │          load-shedding   5 │
         └────────────────────────────┴────────────────────────────┘
```

Figure 10.1 Main privatization forms
(It can mean any downward/rightward movement from the top left corner box 1)

other way, away from private provision, private financing and freedom of entry towards state financing and monopoly through increased use of contracting. Indeed, any government wishing to extend the scope of its activities could use contracting-out to do so.

Finally, the lack of discussion of the scope or role of government and any limits on contracting-out leads to the following paradox. One contracting-out expert, Robert Poole, has anticipated[9] Dr Hartley's dream world, a Californian city in the year 2000 which has contracted-out every single function. The council staff now consists of only three people: a manager, a lawyer, and a secretary who administer contracts. But the contracting-out literature tells us nothing about the nature of such a society, the overall size of the state sector, the burden of its taxes and so on. It could be a free society with minimal government based on open markets, private property and rule of law. Equally, it could be the most oppressive and vicious, arbitrary and capricious society known to man. And under contracting-out the oppression would be efficiently administered and cost so little our dictator could buy more of it! In short, the extent of contracting-out in a society is no guide either to whether it is a free society or to the direction in which it is moving.

'Competition leads to innovation and the introduction of new ideas, the latest management techniques and modern equipment', claims Dr Hartley; and in a general sense one can agree on the thrust of this argument. But for contracting-out it is not very appropriate.

One can envisage a situation in which a directly-employed refuse department is replaced by a monopoly contractor who is innovative and brimming with new ideas, whose management techniques are of the highest sophistication, and whose equipment is of the latest design. Indeed, some of the contracting-out literature[10] features photos of refuse vehicles operated by one man, white and dressed in white, sitting in a sealed air-conditioned/heated cab, who manipulates a robot-like arm to pick up the bins.

But where a directly-employed department has been replaced by a monopoly contractor via a political process, market information concerning the applicability of the latest and best technology and management has not been generated. Consequently, politicians, contractors and taxpayers can have absolutely no idea of whether or not it is appropriate. Indeed, the odds against it being anywhere approaching optimal are gigantic, and will almost certainly be entirely inappropriate.[11] If the monopoly were rescinded in favour of freedom of entry, the information so generated might indicate a solution involving old-fashioned equipment, managed and run by illiterates and innumerates.

I have visited areas in the USA where there is neither a state nor private monopoly on refuse collection. I have seen there a variety of companies competing for business. From current observations, I would venture that the firms involved tend to be small and family-owned. They tend to use very basic equipment and marginal labour. It seems to be very much a first step on the economic ladder, both for the entrepreneurs and the workers, who are nearly all black and very sweaty and dirty – a far cry from the air-conditioned whites of the literature. The entrepreneurs follow house sales and rentals very closely. As soon as you move in, they are on your doorstep soliciting your business.

The awarding of monopoly contracts, either state or private, removes such basic, first step jobs and the entrepreneurial chances they bring, and the lack of market information leads to inappropriate amounts of technology – but one aspect of the enormous knowledge problem which exists under contracting-out.[12]

The tendering process under contracting-out is a competition, but it is not the same as the continuing competitive or market process.

To win a competitive process in the open market, you have to serve the wants of the individual consumer. To win a tendering competition, you have to serve primarily the wants of elected politicians and bureaucrats and only remotely the wants of individual consumers. These are two different kinds of activity; the company that can win a political process is not necessarily the one that would win in a market process.

The clearest example of this difference is the lengths to which cable TV companies will go to secure a monopoly franchise – a very similar process to securing a monopoly contract. One analyst of the US cable industry, Lyla H. O'Driscoll, lists[13] the following examples of actions clearly motivated by the politics of the process and not by consumer preference:

(a) stock offerings to important local leaders whose benevolence may be decisive;

(b) tree plantings;
(c) studios and production training for city residents;
(d) channels set aside for use by city government, the schools, and community-service organizations active in the franchising process;
(e) services they knew to be unfeasible at rates they knew they couldn't maintain.

Such are the rewards of winning a tendering competition, either under contracting-out or under franchising, that my own 1983 prediction[14] that 'the sort of person attracted to the comparatively easy life of a monopoly contractor can be expected to change for the worse as more and more services are contracted out' now seems a serious understatement; 45 of the top 100 contractors to the US Pentagon, possibly the government agency most involved in contracting-out anywhere, are currently under criminal investigation for fraud involving their contracts.

The activities of the managers of firms involved in the tendering process have to be viewed as what economists call rent-seeking. Rent in this sense is not what is paid for the use of someone's house but the payment(s) to a person or group beyond what would be earned in a competitive market environment. The farmer who lobbies for agricultural price support schemes is a clear example of a rent-seeker. Under such schemes he can make, say, £20,000 a year, whereas without them he would have made perhaps £15,000 a year. He thus earns an annual rent of £5,000. Another example would be the doctor who supports a licensing scheme to restrict entry to his profession to drive up his income. A third would be a property owner in an inner-city area who presses for designation as an enterprise zone to increase the value of his holdings.

Entrepreneurs and managers adjust their actions to changes in the market – such as the spread of contracting-out – in a way that will tend to maximize profits and salaries. What can we expect of such rent-earners?

We can expect them to be alert to opportunities to increase the number of contracts they hold. The naïve view prevailing in literature is that they sit back, wait for contracts to be offered for tender, and then do their best to win them. Better service, lower costs, smaller government and lower taxes: what could be better?

I have four objections to this thesis. The first is that although contracting-out certainly seems to provide an appreciably better service at an appreciably lower cost, there is no guarantee that it will lead either to smaller government or lower taxes. If Lambeth Borough Council, say, puts a building out to tender tentatively budgeted at £14 million and accepts a bid of £12 million, what happens to the saving of £2 million? Would we expect it to be passed back to the ratepayer or to be spent on some further, new, extra activity of the borough? I would expect the saving to be used to expand the government.

Second, contractors would be more enterprising in generating new contracts than is generally supposed. They will find new activities for the local authority and put forward very persuasive arguments on the need for them and their abilities to satisfy the need. We cannot assume that savings will be passed on to the consumer. We should assume they will not, and will be used to buy more state activity. And we can expect pressure from alert contractors to increase the scope of the state. The net result is probably more and almost certainly not less government, restrained only by the amount of money available to the local authority.

Third, as we move to more and more contracting-out, we are creating new groups of rent-seekers. As these groups mature, they will begin to consider ways of protecting their rent-earnings. They will identify other such groups and note that one of the many easy ways to achieve their goal is to lobby for restrictions on entry. Their arguments will be couched in terms of the public interest, safety and so on. They will expect and receive grandfather rights; that is, only new potential entrants will have to surmount the newly-imposed hurdles. And we can expect them to be very good at achieving this restriction because they will have built up considerable political contacts and *savoir-faire* as a part of their daily contracting business with politicians.

My fourth objection is: first stage or last stage? In 1983 I welcomed contracting-out 'but only as a first step towards complete state withdrawal and a free and open market'.[15] This was a mistake now repeated by Dr Hartley where he writes of contracting-out as 'an intermediate stop *en route*' to open markets.

Four reasons now make me think that it will be a last stage. First, the contractors will be doing a reasonable job, and certainly a much better job than will have been done before. It will not be the best job that could be done but all the improvements that would arise from the knowledge generated by opening the market will remain unknown and unimaginable in the full to voters. Secondly, the costs of the rents earned by the contractors will spread over the whole population. The result of these two effects is that there will be no major interest group advocating a move from contracting-out to load-shedding.

Thirdly, turning to the other side of the equation, the benefits of the rents are concentrated in a few, very skilful, well-connected, highly articulate hands – those of the contractors. They will fight tooth and nail to keep their highly-protected, highly-profitable positions and avoid the rigours of open competition. Fourthly, there are the politicians. There is a sense in which contracting-out allows them both to 'have their cake and eat it'. Initially, the politicians are perceived as providing a better service at a lower cost and they gain immediate and possibly medium-run advantages. An important long-run advantage, though, has to be the increased distance contracting-out provides between the politician and the on-the-spot provider, the contractor. Voters who complain of a contractor's performance do not associate the poor service as closely with the politician as they did in the days of a directly employed labour force. Under contracting-out, the politician can easily take credit for savings and good service and almost as easily pass on blame if problems arise.

This escape-route, coupled with the diminution in status that load-shedding represents to the population, makes him a very unlikely proponent of such a second-stage move.

I have many other disagreements with Dr Hartley. The idea that contracting-out provides a 'unique opportunity' to compare private and state enterprise in some sort of test seems to be both unnecessary and methodologically suspect.

His claim of no 'open-ended' financial commitment under contracting-out is also suspicious. The closely analogous system of monopoly-franchising shows that unscrupulous contractors have hoodwinked their supposed political masters mercilessly and suggest caution about endorsing so sweeping a claim.

The absence of any substantive discussion of the costs to the authority of contracting, recontracting and monitoring, coupled with undue emphasis on acceptance of the lowest bid – not necessarily the best in either the short or long runs – are also worthy questions.

All that is clear is that contracting-out tends to give a better service at a lower cost than directly-employed labour. It is high time that advocates of contracting-out begin to address the kinds of questions raised above:

(a) How far should contracting-out be extended?
(b) Is contracting-out a one-way street?
(c) Does the extent of contracting-out tell us anything about the nature of the society in which it takes place?
(d) Is the latest and best technology and management always appropriate?
(e) Does contracting-out deny 'first-step' businesses and jobs a place in the market?
(f) Is tendering a political process or a competitive market process?
(g) Will contractors be led into criminal fraud?
(h) Do contractors earn rent?
(i) Will savings result in lower taxes and/or smaller government?
(j) Will contractors lobby for increased government activity?
(k) Will contractors lobby for barriers to entry to protect their rents?
(l) Is contracting-out the first or last step towards open markets?

The contracting-out element of the Thatcher Government's privatization programme has to be viewed in a much wider context than the important but narrow debate above.

For decades market ideas were not at all popular. As recently as ten to fifteen years ago, advocates of many now-successful pro-market reforms were considered out-and-out cranks. The long-term work of the IEA in the UK and others around the world has, through academia, to some extent rehabilitated the intellectual and hence public view of markets.

The result is a number of policies – such as contracting-out and, say, enterprise zones – have been given a market tag. Earlier this year, for example, I heard a leading political figure in America speak to President Reagan of how new ways 'to harness markets' (sic) are being discovered – not new ways to open up or reintroduce markets, but new ways to use markets for policy goals.

The debate on contracting-out highlights three crucial broader points. First, that market clothes are being stolen – incidentally, a clear sign of continuing success – for half-baked attempts at reform by people who do not as yet fully understand or trust the open competitive process.

Second, reforms which fall short of full, open, free markets will have detrimental unintended and unforeseen consequences. Third, that much remains to be accomplished both in the refinement and application of market analysis and the spread of its subtle insights.

If my analysis – that contracting-out will tend to be a last stage – is correct, what alternative solution to current poor service and high costs under direct labour exists? The answer is to move straight to load-shedding, that is, to privately financed private provision with no barriers to entry. Only under load-shedding can individual choice be catered for and an approximation to an efficient, optimal situation can be reached. Only under load-shedding do we have the open-market discovery process which generates the knowledge we require. Without such a process we are taking stabs in the dark at every single aspect of the provision of the service.

To return once more to the case of refuse collection, we do not know what will happen under load-shedding. All that we know is that under load-shedding the information to make decisions, the frequency and quality of service, price, technology and management, will become available to both entrepreneurs and consumers. Initially, possibly, a lot of small firms may emerge and then slowly be taken over to form a larger firm or firms. Once people start paying directly as consumers for the service, they may be encouraged by the pricing policies of the firms (which might be based on, say, volume) to install rubbish compactors. Firms might quote lower prices to householders who sort their refuse into, say, four categories: paper, glass, cans and other. Homeowners' associations might come to special arrangements with contractors for their members' road. But economists cannot predict the future – although they can do their best to prevent interest groups obstructing it.

British Telecom – has privatization delivered competition?

Peter Curwen
Source: *Economic Affairs*, August/September 1986, 6, 6, p. 35.

It is nearly two years since British Telecom (BT) was privatized – a privatization on a scale which dwarfed all those before it. With the gas industry scheduled to come to the market in early December amid much controversy about its regulatory framework, it is particularly important to ask whether the privatization of major industries is likely to have a positive effect upon competitiveness within the markets they serve.

It has long been recognized that privatization creates conflicting pressures which must be traded off, one against the other. The obvious example is conflict within government between the desire to introduce competitive forces into what was previously a monopoly, and the desire to maximize the receipts from a flotation. The Government has always professed to give priority to the stimulation of competition, but the failure to break BT up into smaller pieces before its flotation inclined most commentators to take the opposite view. That the company was more valuable when sold as a single entity is beyond dispute; but if the Government was to remain true to its own philosophy it had simultaneously to persuade the public that the safeguards against unfair competition were worth the paper they were written on. In the event, these safeguards proved unconvincing. The fledgling Mercury, now wholly owned by Cable and Wireless, was given the sole right to provide a telecommunications network in competition with BT until July 1989. Since Mercury had to develop a network from scratch, few commentators expected it to make more than minor inroads into BT's markets before that date. In the absence of any real pre-existing competition, the Government deemed it necessary also to set up a regulatory agency, the Office of Telecommunications (Oftel) under a Director General (DGT), currently Bryan Carsberg, and to issue a licence to BT which constrained its operations, in particular through a limit upon price rises in any year of 3 per cent less than the rise in the Retail Price Index.[1]

An examination of the most important developments during 1985 and early 1986 will help us assess whether the telecommunications market has in practice become more or less competitive, and whether the regulatory system is appropriate.

When BT was privatized concern was expressed whether a newly privatized company should be allowed to use its appreciable cash-flow to acquire other companies with the aim of enhancing its market power. This difficulty surfaced when, in June 1985, BT declared its intention of acquiring 51 per cent of the shares in Mitel Corporation, the Canadian manufacturer of telephone exchanges (PABXs) and other equipment.

Plessey and STC, Mitel's main British rivals for BT's custom, were not amused, and lobbied Leon Brittan, then Secretary of State for Trade and Industry, to prevent the take-over. He duly passed the case on to the Monopolies and Mergers Commission (MMC) with a six-month deadline for publication of its report.

The potential threat to competition arose because US experience (not to mention common sense) suggested that ownership of an equipment-producing subsidiary would distort purchasing patterns in favour of the subsidiary, especially when reductions in orders for equipment were to prove necessary. In its Report, published in December 1985,[2] the MMC concluded that the proposed take-over would seriously affect both the UK manufacturers of PABXs sold primarily to BT, and the independent distributors which, in many cases, sold a lot of Mitel PABXs. They recommended therefore that the acquisition was not in the public interest, but were willing to see it proceed subject to stringent conditions.

The MMC report was promptly overruled by the Secretary of State who argued that competition would be protected if, in addition to the provisos requiring BT to run Mitel at arm's length, BT and the Office of Fair Trading were to agree on a ceiling for Mitel's share of the PABXs that BT sells in the UK. He thus appeared to be favouring the national champion argument, to the effect that UK companies would have to be allowed to grow to a scale which would allow them to take on international giants in open confrontation, even if a price had to be paid in loss of competition in the domestic market. In March 1986 the acquisition was duly authorised and effected. The subsequent reduction in domestic competition is more likely to be noticed than its contribution to making a 'national champion' out of BT.

The second issue is concerned with the role of regulatory agencies. When Oftel was set up, many commentators were quick to point to the evidence that in the USA regulatory agencies were commonly 'captured' by the companies which they were set up to regulate. This argument provoked the somewhat cynical response that Oftel was not worth capturing, and that it would remain relatively toothless unless it were given the power to license new competitors.

An early opportunity to assess Oftel's teeth came in July 1985, when the future of the System-X switching system was cast into doubt. While it was in state ownership BT spent £350 million developing the System-X switching system in conjunction with GEC Telecommunications, Plessey and STC. System-X proved to be a technical rather than a commercial success. The newly privatized BT therefore sought an alternative system to market, and chose the System-Y developed by Thorn-EMI and L.M. Ericsson of Sweden. This decision posed a clear dilemma: should BT be allowed to shop around for the most efficient system available, or should the contributors to System-X be offered some protection in return for their investment?

The object of the exercise for BT was not to drive domestic suppliers to the wall, but rather to reduce their costs in the face of external competition. Bryan Carsberg of Oftel tried to steer a middle path by ruling that BT should order no less than 80 per cent of its switches from Plessey-GEC for the next three years. As BT was anticipating a similar pattern of purchasing in any case, this requirement hardly seemed to be a controversial ruling, although BT's head, Sir George Jefferson, expressed the view that commercial judgments were his province and not that of the DGT. But although the regulatory body may find it relatively easy to follow a path which it believes will demonstrate its impartiality, its attempts to be fair-minded may be simultaneously construed both as an unwarranted intrusion and as evidence of weakness by people who believe competition should be introduced irrespective of potential damage to domestic suppliers.

The issues raised by this dispute concern both the degree of flexibility required in a regulatory body and how to determine the degree of competitiveness in sectors of an industry not fully dealt with at the time of privatization. When BT was privatized, a distinction was drawn between basic conveyance – essentially voice and telex transmission – and Value Added Network Services (VANS), representing such services as mailbox systems for sending messages between personal computers, electronic reservation and credit-card verification services, and Prestel. Basic conveyance was restricted to BT and Mercury until July 1989, but the distinction between conveyance and a value-added service proved difficult to define, so the approach adopted was to define VANS and treat everything not covered by the definition as a basic conveyance.

Subsequently, BT and IBM jointly proposed a sophisticated computer communications system for large companies which they called a managed data network (MDN). The Government took the view that BT and IBM in tandem would stifle competition, and vetoed the link-up. This decision neatly side-stepped the question of how to classify MDNs, and so fears were soon expressed that, since no-one knew whether MDNs were basic conveyance or VANS they might be treated as the former, thereby giving BT a virtual monopoly of provision and allowing them to be cross-subsidized out of telephone revenues. To prevent such cross-subsidization the Government is introducing a special licence for MDNs which treats them as VANS. VANS suppliers currently lease private lines from BT and Mercury for a flat fee. It is now proposed that this lease will be resaleable for the transmission of computer data.

Initially, such a move would undercut the VANS offered by BT, and introduce some competition, but so long as BT's telephone lines are used for transmission, BT has something to gain as well as to lose. But in the longer term groups of heavy users of MDNs may club together to form mini-Mercuries operating independent networks, thus potentially causing BT a severe loss of revenue. A corollary of this development is that Oftel will also have to make sure that companies such as IBM do not themselves become dominant suppliers of circuits for MDNs.

It would seem that the Government and Oftel have shown both a considerable degree of flexibility and some determination to promote competition in resolving this dispute.

Because the Mercury network was intended only to link a number of major cities in a figure of eight fibre-optic loop running alongside railway lines, Mercury's prospects were fundamentally affected by the terms by which it could connect into the existing BT network. Mercury asked for unrestricted access, but BT refused to allow access to the loop for calls which originated from further than local distance away from the loop, although it agreed to connect up any calls originating from within the loop.

Mercury asked for Oftel to determine the exact rules of interconnection. In September 1985, Bryan Carsberg's determination was published; it essentially sided with Mercury, since its underlying rationale was that any person should be entitled to dial any other person, and that a customer should be free to choose which network should carry his call.

The document spelt out BT's charges to Mercury, and based them upon BT's costs rather than its prices, thereby effectively giving Mercury a bulk discount which would allow it to make a profit, not merely upon its own part of the call but upon BT's part as well. The prices in the document were index-linked, implying the possibility of reductions if technical economies more than offset rising labour costs.

The pricing structure was organized so as to provide incentives for Mercury to expand its network rapidly and to restrict the BT link-up only to the local element of a call. In case this arrangement proved overly prejudicial to BT a penalty would be imposed on long-distance interconnection if Mercury's revenues rose above 7 per cent of BT's.

The document specified that the two networks were to be physically linked at thirty-six trunk exchanges by March 1986. The costs of connection were to be borne by Mercury, but it has to pay only half of the costs of installing any new capacity required to handle the extra traffic which it generates.

These rulings were poorly received at BT since they inevitably implied increased competition in the most profitable parts of its network, namely trunk and international calls. Its initial response was to issue a barely disguised threat to raise small residential rentals by way of compensation.

In principle, the general rebalancing of tariffs to remove historic cross-subsidies between business and residential sectors of the network, with a view to bringing prices more into line with costs, could not be faulted. But this revision implied the switching of profitability away from the increasingly competitive business sector and towards the still-monopolized residential sector, a move hardly compatible with liberalization of the network, and very much at odds with the fact that BT's international rates were already lower than those in, for example, America and Germany while local call charges were already higher.

The purpose of the RPI-minus-3 per cent formula imposed by the Government was to force BT to increase its efficiency and cut its costs, in the expectation that if profitability was good BT would not have to avail itself of the maximum figure allowed by the formula. But BT has sought to raise its prices, on average, by the maximum permissible amount. Then is the formula too generous? BT's recent profit figures have been excellent, but the roughly 19 per cent return on capital they represent for the services governed by the formula is not so outrageous as to suggest that the formula itself is entirely at fault.

How has competition fared here? Although the pricing formula is broadly acceptable, and the principle of relating prices to costs certainly is, in practice the end-result has proven to be essentially unacceptable because BT has been able to side-step the full brunt of competition without breaking any rules.

The lessons to be learned from BT show that the passing of a near-monopoly from public into private hands creates a host of dilemmas which cannot readily be foreseen at the time of privatization. The issue is then whether these difficulties can be resolved to favour increased competition. The resolution of the various disputes suggests, first, that Mercury will shortly be providing significantly more competition for BT than was anticipated at the time of privatization and, secondly, that BT is clearly not going to be allowed to undertake mergers or to renege on its licence conditions.

The commitment to competition does seem to be there, but it is still not all it might be. BT and Mercury do have an exclusive right to operate public telephone networks until July 1989, and it will be several years beyond that date before other companies will be offering significant competition. It is clear that increased competition and the interests of BT shareholders are far from compatible.[3] It is too late to do much about it now because the overriding desire to have a successful flotation necessarily led to rather too many concessions being made to BT. Some of these concessions are being whittled away (for example, with respect to VANS), but progress is rather slow. And the apparently reasonable pricing formula has not worked entirely as expected.

Should British Gas, then, follow in the footsteps of BT? The past two-and-a-half years have demonstrated that releasing a large nationalized industry into the private sector, whether in whole or in parts, in practice simply does not secure the release of that industry from the heavy regulatory hand of government. Indeed, once a regulatory agency such as Oftel has the bit between its teeth, the industry concerned may end up being more heavily regulated than it was before privatization – in which case logic suggests that the industry be kept in state ownership but subjected to effective competition from private-sector companies. Such companies might need to be set up for the purpose, or an existing company such as Cable & Wireless might be invited to play such a role.

Ideally, all artificial restraints on the landing and export of natural gas should be lifted, and pipeline links with Europe should be encouraged. The avowed ultimate purpose of the exercise is to make the nationalized industry more efficient. The issue of ownership must therefore become secondary to that of competition, since if, for example, competition is sufficient to force down prices and promote efficiency, there is no longer any requirement for regulations designed with the same outcome in mind, and they will become redundant.

BR – privatization without tears

David Starkie
Source: *Economic Affairs*, October/December 1984, 5, 1, p. 16.

The public sector can be privatized in a number of ways but with British Railways (BR), attention has focused on the sale to the private sector of assets in non-rail subsidiaries. Hotels have been disposed of and other non-rail activities have been grouped under a holding company – British Rail Investments Ltd – with a view to selling equity in them to private sector share holders. Suggestions have recently been made for treating similarly the wholly-owned subsidiary, British Rail Engineering Ltd (BREL), which carries out extensive repair work for BR and builds much of its rolling stock.

On the operational side there have been proposals for the private sector to take over railway lines. The two most publicized schemes are from Victoria to Gatwick Airport, and Fenchurch Street to Southend. The Fenchurch Street line runs for about 40 miles through southern Essex and operates very much as a separate part of the rail network. A business consortium has expressed an interest in its purchase.

It is arguable whether such transfers would promote the objective most strongly canvassed by the privatizers – increased efficiency in the supply of services and therefore more benefits to consumers. Efficiency is associated with competition, but it is not necessarily true (even if it seems likely) that a simple transfer of assets to the private sector has the effect of sharpening competitive forces.

Professors Michael Beesley and Stephen Littlechild[1] have argued that privatization without increased competition will, nonetheless, procure benefits. Private firms are able to respond more easily to demand by having better access to capital, and they will have a stronger incentive to produce goods and services in the quantity and variety that consumers prefer, especially where monopoly power is limited by the existence (even when only potential) of close substitutes. But privatization which enhances competition is more likely to secure a wider range of benefits. The issue thus is what form of privatization will increase competitive forces within the railway industry.

A major barrier to competition in the railway industry is its large, unavoidable fixed costs of production, which arise because many inputs into the industry are 'lumpy'. To run one train service between two cities, for example, requires a minimum outlay on track, formation, motive power, rolling stock and administration. As these inputs are used more intensively, i.e., as more services are run, their cost is spread over more units of output so that average costs fall until the point when the railway is used so intensively that the track becomes congested and management over-stretched. But railways normally operate on the falling segment of their cost curves. Either market demand will have decreased, leaving spare capacity in the system, or new technologies such as centralized traffic control (CTC) will have enabled higher capacities to be achieved from existing plant. Railways therefore are referred to as 'natural' monopolies in the sense that a single, vertically-integrated firm can fulfil market demand more cheaply than two.

Although railways are natural monopolies in this sense, their true monopoly power as means of transport has now been all but eliminated by competition from aviation and road transport. But despite this competition BR is not as efficient as it might be. A cost analysis by Stewart Joy[2] (later to become BR's Chief Economist) during the 1960s suggested that BR was capable of reducing its permanent way costs to a substantial degree. More recently, the select committee on nationalized industries[3] and the report of the Serpell Committee[4] have pointed to inefficiencies in the use of both equipment and personnel.

When inefficiency is substantial, falling average costs are not enough to maintain the railway monopolist's inherent advantage. The opportunity exists for a more efficient firm to set up in competition but producing at a lower cost. What prevents this happening is a second important characteristic of many railway assets. Embankments and cuttings, the rail formation and the platforms, etc., are fixed *in situ* – they are sunk, committed irreversibly to a specified market. Consequently potential competitors are faced with substantial risks to enter a particular market in this way. They face BR with equivalent infrastructure written-down or written-off and with the potential to eliminate its inefficiencies that provide the opportunity for a private enterprise company. Once entry is accomplished the inefficiencies of BR might quickly disappear leaving competitors with unamortized assets they are unable to transfer.

It is thus not feasible for the private sector to build new permanent way and terminals in competition with BR. There may be special cases which provide exceptions; for instance, where existing track and terminal capacity is saturated and the particular market still has considerable growth potential (the Victoria Gatwick airport service may be in this category). But even in these circumstances, it is most likely that BR will be able to add to its existing infrastructure at a lower cost than a potential rival could build new rights-of-way or terminal facilities.

If competition from new rail infrastructure is out of the question, private enterprise could take over existing permanent way (at book value) in competition with BR (or other private companies). But BR have eliminated some of the obvious spare capacity in the system established by competing rail companies in the 19th century to achieve precisely these economies of use. Consequently, the opportunities for competing rail services using alternative, existing infrastructure between common centres are few (London–Southend services are an exception).

Similar, but again limited, opportunities for increased competition exist where the permanent way carries multiple tracks so that track ownership can be divided. Although modern CTC makes it feasible to divide double tracks into lengths of single track with two-way operations,[5] more flexibility can be achieved where there are four running tracks with competing companies handling two each (and each having restricted running rights over competitors' lines). However, there is a limited length of quadruple track and the train-control, rail formation and stations would have to remain in single ownership. Although worthy of further investigation (especially where there is not too much mixing of freight, slow passenger and fast passenger traffic), it is probable that in many instances the additional complexities of operation would negate the increased efficiency achieved by competition.

State track, private trains

A more logical way to proceed would be to work with and not against, the constraints to competition inherent in the technology of railway systems. This approach would recognize that most large-scale effects are inherent in the permanent way, train-control and stations – precisely the assets irretrievably committed to a particular rail market once installed. In contrast the rail vehicles – locomotives, wagons, carriages – are mobile between markets and economies in their use are well encompassed by the market opportunities available. This distinction begs for wider recognition within the institutional framework.

By distinguishing the ownership of the permanent way from the ownership of the vehicles an opportunity presents itself for having competing trains running on shared track. In other words one would emulate a practice which is common in road and air transport; public sector buses (National Bus Company) compete against private coach companies on the state-owned motorway system and rival airlines (some in the private sector) utilize airports in separate and often state ownership. The last analogy is the more useful because of the scheduling and safety implications. Airlines arrange for access times to the terminal and runways and immediate air space; in effect, they rent this access. Translated into real terms, access to lines and terminals would be rented by competing train companies who would then sell services directly to the public.

Such a policy may sound distinctly different from that which we associate with railways in modern Britain but its strength lies in the fact that it represents a further development of what is now happening and what used to happen on a large scale until 1948.

Before nationalization in 1948, railways in Britain had developed quite complex structures reflecting in some cases a distinction between ownership of track and ownership of rolling-stock.

One example of this was the Cheshire Lines Railway which controlled lines between Manchester and Liverpool and between Chester and Stockport.[6] It was a statutory railway company under its own management but with parent companies (originally three and then two) represented on the Board. Its singular feature was that each year it handled millions of passengers without owning a single locomotive and millions of tons of freight without owning a single wagon. Locomotives were hired from another rail company and wagons came from a variety of sources including non-railway companies. (In the early 1930s there were something like 700,000 private rail wagons.)

The Cheshire Lines Railway disappeared as a separate entity in 1948, at the same time as much of the huge private wagon fleet was incorporated within the nationalized railway. For the private wagon fleets this at least was but a temporary demise: private wagons never disappeared entirely from the network (some specialist wagons were retained by private companies in 1948) and in recent years their role has grown very rapidly.

They now form a substantial component within the rail freight system.[7] In terms of tonne miles, private wagons carried 40 per cent of BR's freight traffic in 1982. If coal and coke tonnage, carried mostly in merry-go-round fleets running between collieries and power stations, was excluded, the private wagon proportion accounted for as much as two-thirds of tonne miles. Within this total, individual companies generate large flows of ore, cement, aggregates, oil as well as general freight and their investment in private wagons is substantial: oil and chemical industries alone have around £300 million invested.

Thus there already exists in the operational railway system a large private sector component and one that is based on a distinction between mobile and sunk assets. The next logical step would be for the private sector to extend into the motive power sector, purchase locomotives, employ or lease crews, and offer train services directly in competition with each other and with British Railways. Some of the large companies generating large volumes of traffic, might consider it worthwhile to operate their own freight trains, just as many now operate own-account lorries carrying road freight. But this would depend on their ability to utilize adequately the locomotives. The majority would probably prefer to hire the locomotive and train services (just as in effect they now do) but with the

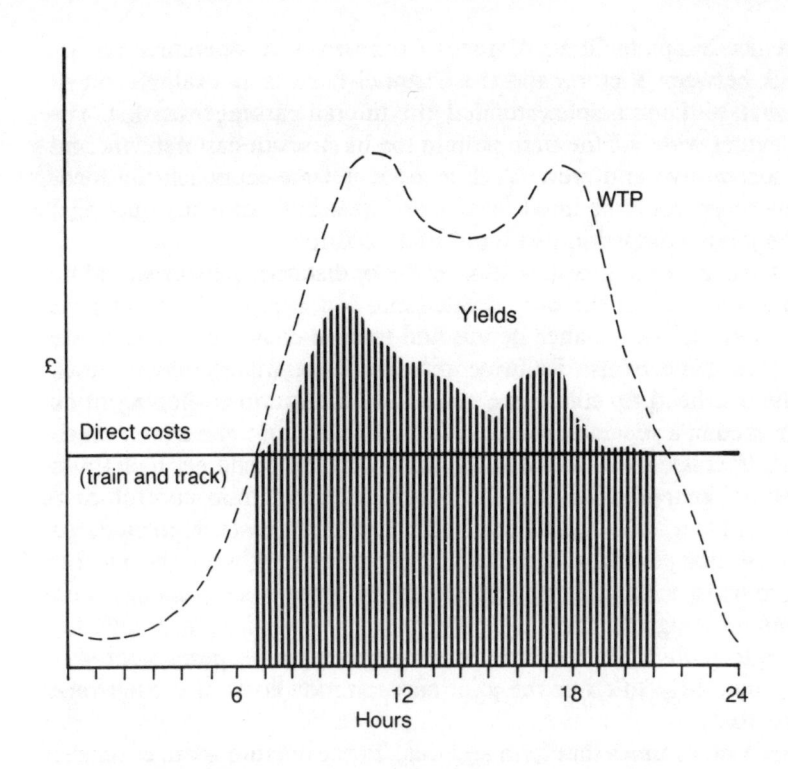

Figure 10.2 Bidding for the use of the rail right-of-way
The dashed line in the chart illustrates the aggregate willingness to pay (WTP) for a journey between two towns (at a specified quality of service) at different times of the day. Train operators are not able to expropriate the whole of this because of an inability to perfectly discriminate when charging. The yield to the train company from each service operated is shown by the vertical lines. The amount exceeding direct costs (the latter shown as constant per service) represents the maximum that the permanent way company can expect to extract as a contribution towards the joint and common costs of the right-of-way.

option of buying services from private hire-and-reward train companies.

Wagon hirers already exist and a number have combined to form the British Wagon Hirers Association. Included is the multi-national transport conglomerate, VTG, with a European fleet of 26,000 hire wagons, many of which operate over the BR network. VTG also operates in Europe large petroleum tank terminals and about 100 river-going vessels and an extension into railway locomotives would appear to complement its specialist transport activities. The provision of complete train services on a hire-and-reward basis might be particularly attractive to transport distribution companies like National Carriers or the new to Britain, aggressive, rapidly growing Thomas Nationwide Transport (with experience of chartering company trains in Australia).

The Venice-Simplon Orient-Express Company Ltd, operating private coach stock between Victoria and the Channel Ports is an example, albeit rather special, of the principle extended into the rail passenger market. The company agrees with BR the train path in the busy south-east network and hires the locomotive and crew. With a more flexible approach the locomotives and crew could be hired from a private sector company quoting a rate for the job in competition with the state sector.

This extension of the private sector in the operational railway would be facilitated if the assets of BR were divided into two groups. The permanent way, train control, maintenance depots and termini could be vested in one company (the name British Railways remains appropriate), which would also handle overhead functions like general administration.[8] Rolling stock could be vested in a separate, public sector company or companies, (which I shall refer to collectively as British Trains – BT). BR's charges to BT and private sector competitors would be based on direct train control cost, track wear and tear, and directly attributable terminal costs, supplemented by additional charges, broadly reflecting judgments of what the market will bear, to assist with covering joint costs. At times when passenger and freight demand is high the train companies would bid against each other for available train paths. The resulting rents accruing to the permanent way company would help to cover the joint and common costs of the network (see Figure 10.2).

The approach assumes that train services, if they operate at all, cover the marginal costs of operation. But there is a large social railway – services considered necessary for social reasons – which fail to cover their direct costs. These would exist alongside competitive services. But there is the danger that the Public Service Obligation (PSO) grant, paid to maintain social services, might be used to cross-subsidize BT's competitive bids for use of BR's system. This could happen, for example, where social and competitive services offered by BT used common rolling stock. To eliminate this possibility, one approach would be to fence in the competitive market to prevent misuse of the PSO grant.

This fencing-in is already taking place in BR's adoption of sector management. BR is now divided into five operating sectors: freight, parcels, London and South East passenger services, other provincial and intercity passenger services. Freight and inter-city have been set a commercial quasi-target and it is here that the privatization proposals outlined would apply more easily. Data in the Serpell Report suggest, for example, that only a small proportion of inter-city train miles (about 10 per cent) were failing to cover direct costs (Figure 10.3). With competition resulting in higher efficiency, it is likely that the total number of inter-city train miles covering these costs could be increased.

A substantial proportion of train miles in the London and South East network also cover their direct costs, some by a large margin. But there is a minor, but not insignificant, proportion making large operating losses. It is difficult to judge from the information available whether the spur of competition would radically alter this picture without a reduction of services. The size of the positive externalities attached to some of these services (reduced road congestion in London is one example) and the political implications, advises caution. For the time being at least, this sector is better considered, along with services in the provincial sector as lying outside the potential for developing commercially competing services.

For this large proportion of the present railway not susceptible to provision by direct competition, competitive franchising would provide a means of improving efficiency. The essence of the franchising idea is that services would be open for tender to be operated in a specified manner for a particular period. A distinction between track and trains is appropriate also when franchising the social railway. The expertise required to operate train services *per se* is different from that required for maintaining the permanent way – recognized in BR's existing corporate structure which distinguishes between operations and engineering.

With an extended role for the private sector, it will be important to ensure that the economies of an integrated railway system are maintained. These economies are realised through new technologies like British Railway's computerised wagon information system – TOPS – whereby the progress of each wagon (privately owned as well as BR stock) is monitored as it passes through the rail network. Private train companies, too, will need to have access to the TOPS information system. An integrated passenger timetable is another example; the present one includes more than a score of private, seasonal railways aimed at the tourist market (and for the most part run by volunteers). Professional, private sector services as they develop, will need to be incorporated in the system-wide timetable.

The suggested approach begs the question of the extent to which a more efficient railway system would be achieved. The report of the Serpell enquiry contains estimates which suggest that, by 1986, the financial performance of inter-city rail and rail freight could be improved by £84 million by the adoption of various cost-cutting measures. This figure is based upon improvements to services currently provided by these two sectors and reflects opportunities for reducing train costs by purchasing cheaper equipment (buying low-cost locomotives overseas was mentioned specifically); by the better utilization of both equipment and labour; and by savings in locomotive and rolling stock maintenance. One would expect private sector train companies to avail themselves of these opportunities and to force the pace of adoption by the state sector railway.

The benefits of competition extend beyond the savings pinpointed in the Serpell Report. Competition in services would have the effect of optimizing the price and quality of services offered. For the passenger railway, BR display a tendency to market a standard service with increasing emphasis on quality – speed, on-board catering, air-conditioning – manifest in the High Speed Train Services. It may have judged the market accurately. But

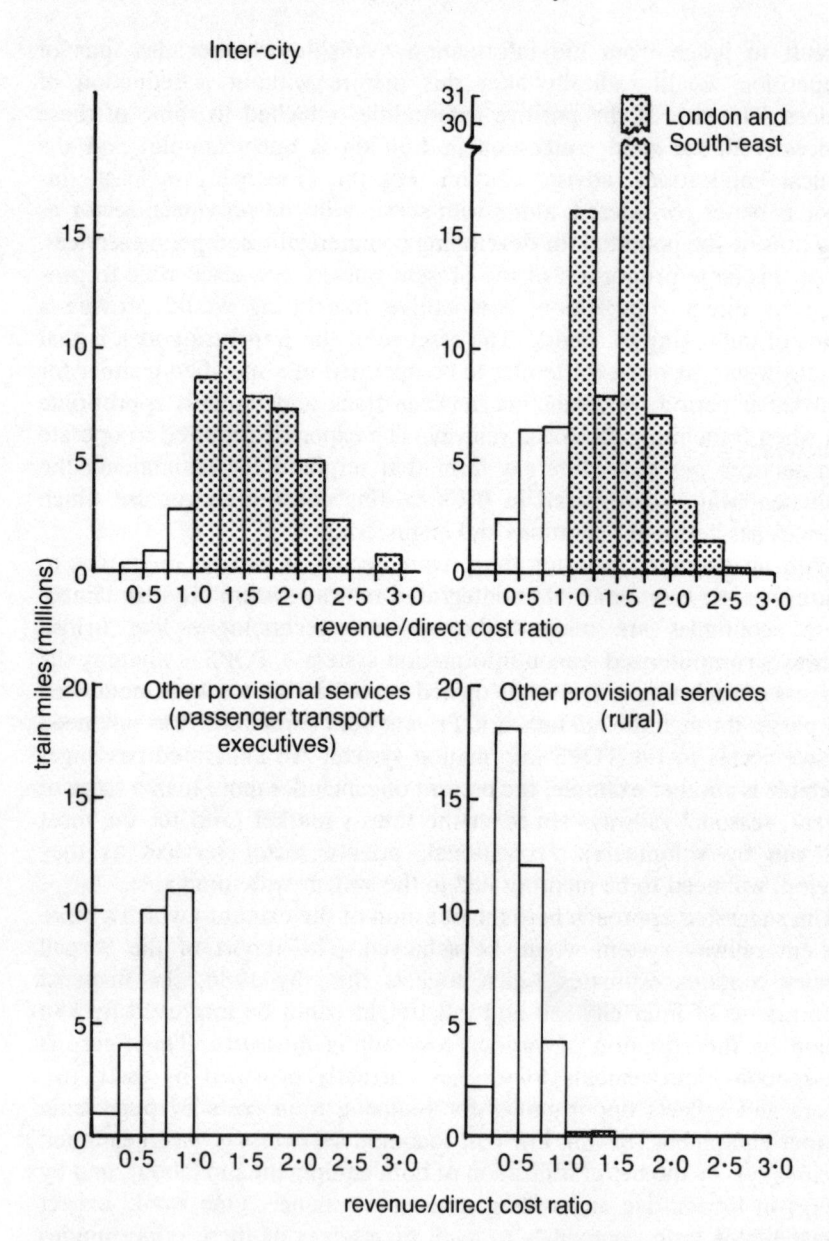

Figure 10.3 Passenger services

it is possible also that the market could support a wider variety of price/quality packages.[9] For example, the private sector may wish to test-market a lower standard of inter-city service based on the new rail-bus technology. Crew savings, lower fuel consumption, reduced vehicle depreciation and less wear and tear on the track could produce a lower ticket price acceptable, despite the slower, less comfortable ride,[10] to a number sufficient to support the service – the young, pensioners, and so on.

A further benefit of the suggested competitive model would be the provision of better guidance for investment in rail infrastructure and a reduction, if not the elimination, of the present arbitrary allocation of overhead and joint costs to the inter-city sector. Inter-city rail is expected to earn a surplus on direct and indirect costs equivalent to a 5 per cent discounted cash flow on certain defined capital assets. As Mr Alfred Goldstein, a member of the Serpell Committee, remarked in his Minority Report, the rationale of this test has not been satisfactorily explained. Under the proposed framework for competitive services, the contribution towards costs not attributable to the direct provision of a train service would come from track 'rents'. If these rents fail to cover renewal of infrastructure specific to a competitive sector, the market will have signalled an eventual withdrawal of these services. Conversely, where competitive bidding for train paths pushes up rents, expansion of track and terminus capacity will be called for.

Finally, one can speculate on the long-term structure of a competitive railway industry. We might expect an initial increase in the overall size of the freight and inter-city sectors. A wider variety of services and/or lower fares and charges should produce an increase in demand for rail travel. In the longer term, the character of the industry will depend also on the government's view on the size of the social railway and thus on the amount of infrastructure that the government is willing to support.

It is difficult to judge whether the public sector's involvement in freight and inter-city services would continue as at present. This depends upon whether there are economies or diseconomies of scale and scope in the provision of train services.[11] Large companies may be able to balance and match rolling-stock to different market demands rather better but at the expense of managerial diseconomies.[12] The most plausible outcome is that the state sector will maintain a substantial presence alongside a range of private sector firms – as they do in today's airline and bus industry.

Privatization and universities

Norman Barry
Source: *Economic Affairs*, January 1984, 4, 2, p. 56.

At one point in his article Graham Hallett says he began 'to wonder if we are discussing the same country'. After reading his account of my views I began to wonder if he had read the same article.

Mr Hallett claims I suggested that all the best university staff had taken severance pay or early retirement. This is not what I said. I simply hypothesized that the terms offered would only be attractive to the able. Because all those who have left the universities are competent it does not at all follow that all the competent have left, leaving only the second-rate. There are undoubtedly very many able academics, almost certainly a majority, who weren't attracted by the various inducements; but many were. Moreover, the prevailing institutional arrangements made it impossible for the less competent to be weeded out. If we cannot have any confidence in the proposition that this outcome was almost certain to occur, we can have no confidence in the basic propositions of elementary economic theory.

I did not cite Hayek in support of my views on privatization and the abolition of tenure. I cited both Mises and Hayek in my speculation (supported by Mr Hallett) that the understanding of government policy towards universities could be advanced by drawing upon the Austrian theory of the trade cycle. Although I am an admirer of Hayek's intellectual system I do not follow him slavishly on every policy detail. Anyway, the quoted comments were written twenty-four years ago, well in advance of the post-Robbins expansion. In his more recent writings, especially *Law, Legislation and Liberty,* Volume III, Hakek shows considerable sympathy for some of the more extreme implications of classical liberalism, as well as distaste for some contemporary consequences of the expansion of higher education. For a thinker who now believes that money should be privatized, the suggestion that higher educational institutions should be subject to genuine market principles should appear somewhat moderate, if not tame.

I did not necessarily endorse the views of Mr David Hurst, I pointed to the irony of a situation in which the only person threatened with dismissal during a time of alleged financial exigency was one who had dared to speak his mind. So much for tenure as a protection of free speech.

I did not recommend that all universities should be immediately privatized – though I do believe that this should be the (not too) long-term aim. Neither did I suggest that tenure be instantly abolished – though I think it should have been tested in the courts. Certainly, a start could be made by ensuring that most, if not all, future appointments should be for three (or five) years, as in Australia.

When Mr Hallett is not misinterpreting my views his own suggestions seem to be roughly in the right direction. Curiously, they are not very distinct from my own. The most important task is to penetrate the mists of obfuscation that surround discussion of higher education: no institution should enjoy the privileged position of immunity from rational criticism.

Privatization: let the market decide

Roger Buckland and E.W. Davies
Source: *Economic Affairs*, July/September 1984, 4, 4, p. 32.

Since 1979 over £2.5 billion in cash has been raised by government sales of equity – part of a privatization programme that has had a significant impact on the Public Sector Borrowing Requirement[1] and will continue to do so up to 1988 (and perhaps beyond). Indeed, in the fiscal year 1984–85 a critical assumption underlying the government's forecasts of revenue is the amount to be raised from the privatization of British Telecom.

What are the costs incurred in the process of flotation of equity in nationalized companies? Flotation is in many respects similar to the issuing process by which previously unquoted companies transfer or raise capital. The success or the efficiency of this operation has tended to be measured by the willingness of investors to take up the shares on offer – and to a lesser extent by the price realized. Controversy has arisen on the underpricing of the Amersham International issue. Experience suggests there is a natural bias in pricing new equity to provide for a significant element of discount to buyers, how much depending on market demand. The significance of this bias for large government privatization issues is thus that of a potential loss in receipts, which with British Telecom could be substantial.

The history of the Government's organization of privatization issues has been most decidedly mixed to date, despite relatively favourable conditions since 1979. It is clear that sales have benefited from a rising stock market, which made these issues of shares comparatively risk-free. We have examined the government's record in privatization issues over the past five years and have found that, in effect, the choice of methods of issue adopted has resulted in significant avoidable costs. But, given the methods employed, how different has been the government's experience from that encountered by strictly private sector issues? Our, and others', research suggests that shortcomings apparent in pricing new issues in the private sector require a re-examination of the government's marketing technique for privatization.[2]

Disposals of public assets have included the spun-off section of British Transport Hotels, the employee/management buy-out of National Freight Corporation, the return of the National Enterprise Board's equity stakes in companies such as Ferranti, Fairey or ICL, the continuing sales of council housing and forestry land-holdings. Of the £2.8 billion cash total for non-housing receipts nine sales of equity alone have produced £2.4 billion to date. We concentrate the analysis on these nine.

To accomplish the privatization objective, sales by the government of its majority shareholdings are involved in most cases: 100 per cent of Amersham International, 51 per cent of Britoil and of British Aerospace, 75 per cent (in two tranches) of Cable and Wireless, 49 per cent of

Table 10.1 Privatization issues, costs and discounts for buyers

Company	Method of offer	Net proceeds £m	Issue costs £m	Discount %	Applications multiple	10 Jan values £m
Amersham International	Sale	69.9	.21	*36%	×200	109.5
Associated British Ports	Sale	21.5	.37*	*27%	×34	47
British Aerospace	Sale	147.4*	2.63*	+14%	×3.5	234
BP (1 : 1979)	Sale	238.8	6.6	+9%	n/a	332.4
BP (2 : 1982)**	Sale	293.5	—	+7%	n/a	407.8
BP (3 : 1983)	Tender	542.5*	9.21*	−0.4%	×1.3	523.9
Britoil	Tender	539.8*	8.5*	−8%	×0.3/4	522.8
Cable & Wireless						
(1 : 1981)	Sale	220*	3.92*	+8%	×5.4	382.4
(2 : 1983)	Tender	262	13	−2.6%	×0.7	287
Total		2334.4	43.33			2846.8†
Average				10%		

Notes: *Does not account for undisclosed expenses met by the government, which may amount in total to some tens of millions.
**Here the government sold its rights to a 1 for 7 issue at 275p, for 15p each: thus each share represented 290p not subscribed by the public sector.
† Comparison of this value with that of the net proceeds (Table) suggests that nearly £½ billion has been lost here. But the difference in values would have been largely explained by the overall increase in share price during this period. For example, investment of the proceeds in the *Financial Times* all-share index would have produced a portfolio of shares worth some £3 billion by 10 January 1984.

Associated British Ports. The Government also initiated the sales of some of its minority stake in British Petroleum, which complete our nine major issues. The efficiency question is: how close do the Government's receipts from these issues come to the market's valuation of them; and could more money have been raised?

Two basic methods of flotation have been used: offers for sale, when the price per share is fixed in advance by the seller's advisors; and offers for sale by tender, where a striking price is set by buyers bidding for the shares buy at a price they hope to pay. Research for comparable private share sales (new issues by companies gaining quotations) shows that average discounts on new issues of shares run at about 10.5 per cent of proceeds. Offers for sale costs an average 9 per cent and tenders 7 per cent, while placings of shares amongst advisors' clients were most costly at 19 per cent.[3] There is also evidence that large companies command smaller discounts (6.7 per cent on average) for offers for sale by companies of over £1 million net assets in the 1960s and 1970s.[4]

To compare the government's programme with these standards we calculate the discount offered on their issues over the first week of trading: that is, the change in price from the issue price paid by the buyer to the market price one week after trading, corrected by general shifts in the equities market (measured by changes in the *Financial Times* all-share index). The discount columns of the Table shows that even sales of the already-quoted share in BP had a market value some 7–9 per cent more than the government raised for them. The average discount offered on the offers for sales was some 16.8 per cent ranging from the BP minimum of 7 per cent to the 36 per cent for Amersham International. In contrast, the issues by tender were very tightly priced. (We return to this average of −3.6 per cent.)

Privatization is under-priced

In the event the Treasury has been lucky to be in a position – so far – to exploit a bull market in equities for its privatization programme. The *FT* all-share index has surged upwards over the period, with few long or significant reverses. This typically lowers required discounts to an average 5 per cent for offers for sale.[5] By comparison some of the Government's fixed-price issues, for example, Amersham and Associated British Ports, were seriously underpriced. There is no evidence that such underpricing is unavoidable, but it is not uncommon in fixed-price share sales, where several days pass between price-fixing by advisors and the market's judgment. The fourth columns of the Table show the extremes of over-subscription experienced for the underpriced issues: again, not uncommon. The Treasury must have regretted the public scrambles for shares in Amersham or in Cable and Wireless, but those are not surprising alongside purely private sector issues as Pearson and Sons (49 times oversubscribed in 1969) or Martonair (107 times), which were also severely underpriced.

It is perhaps obvious that it is easier to sell shares in stable or rising equity markets. We can demonstrate this fact by reference to the market applications for new issues in the 1970s of ordinary shares by previously unquoted companies. Thus in depressed bear markets applications for new issues were on average 16.7 times the shares on offer, while 22 per cent of the issues were left with the underwriters. In contrast in stable/rising or 'bull' markets the oversubscriptions were almost twice as high, averaging 29.6, and only 5 per cent of the issues had to be taken up by the underwriters.[6] Thus bull equity markets might be seen as a prerequisite to successful privatization. It is here that the 1984 Budget, laying the foundations for an investment boom associated with phasing out capital allowances, may be interpreted in the light of its dependence on a buoyant stock market for the success of privatization. But the prospects for future sales are potentially more hazardous when privatization involves a forecast £2 billion for each fiscal year rather than in each government term – and particularly when a single sale, that of majority stake in British Telecom, involves £4 billion alone. Further, many future issues are singularly less attractive than those of the past: British Airways, British Leyland, Sealink, British Nuclear Fuels, National Bus, British Shipbuilders, as examples.

To make markets work – from the government's point of view – we have to come back to that −3.6 per cent discount upon offers by tender. Although we know that the tender method works in equity markets, it is not a favourite of the City, particularly of the institutions, because it thrusts the burden of uncertainty of pricing upon the buyer rather than the seller. Tenders produce proceeds closer to market value; they allow markets to work with many converging opinions, much like an efficient, *tâtonnement*[7] mechanism; they preclude the activity of stags – speculators who apply for new shares solely in anticipation of selling at the higher market price immediately after issue. We see the apparent ineptitude of the government and its advisers – high discounts, stagging – as symptomatic of a deeper problem: the lack of any consistent ability to forecast even short-term market conditions. It has been observed in the past that advisors' decisions are often quite properly denounced by the financial press, which faithfully pick up signs of success or failure in all market conditions. This is perhaps the most telling argument in favour of some kind of tendering system for all privatization issues, not only for those like BP whose value is already well-attested, or like Telecom, whose status as a utility leaves its stable value more on a par with the water companies (users of tenders for many years).

Yet in privatization so far tenders have been used only infrequently and their performance has not been – on the surface – encouraging. As Chancellor, Sir Geoffrey Howe vetoed a tender for Amersham; with Britoil and Cable and Wireless, though the prices were right by the market, much embarrassment was caused by tender flops. Yet a close examination shows these flops to be spectral. In both evaluation was difficult (for Britoil a collapse in the oils sector just before issue, for Cable and Wireless problems in Hong Kong), but the positions of underwriting institutions were crucial. These buyers of shares were paid fees to underwrite shares at the minimum tender price and have every incentive not to bid above that price, but acquire shares by virtue of their underwriting commitment. To date £32 million have been spent on underwriting privatization issues. In the event, the only benefit of these fees has been to turn these two tender issues into quasi-placings: why buy above the striking price, when by holding off one can acquire shares more cheaply – and, moreover, be paid for the privilege?

Through their domination of the underwriting process the crucial target buyers of privatized companies – the large financial institutions – have been able to turn the tendering procedure into a merry-go-round where they can choose when to get on and off. In the face of the uncertainty surrounding that crucial sale of British Telecom, the government may be driven to a fixed-price offer for sale, which would then be expensively discounted. If it uses the tender, it once again risks offering the institutions the chance to turn an underwritten tender price to their own advantage. It is time to be imaginative in the face of these market imperfections. At least the government should develop the tender method, with the recognition that the Treasury or Bank of England – independent of the intended final purchasers – are best able to underwrite such a form of sale. This would force the institutions into the sale ring of tenders, where they must compete for their shares on equal terms with every small investor and employee.

Such action should increase the government's (and taxpayers') revenues from the privatization sales without destabilizing the markets. If the government fails in this purpose, it risks a derailment of the privatization programme which could push next year's public sector borrowing requirement well over target and plunge the capital markets into gloom. And gloomy capital markets are no place to sell such companies as British Leyland or British Nuclear Fuels.

Anglican economics

Russell Lewis
Source: Economic Affairs, April/May 1990, p. 33.

Suppose that you were a business consultant retained by the Church of England to report on how efficiently it was running its operation. You would surely find it hard to resist the conclusion that it is in a state of terminal decline. The numbers look ominous. Over the last twenty years the Church of England has demolished 289 churches and closed another 926. Nor can this shrinkage be shrugged off as rationalization. It is not like a manufacturer scrapping obsolete premises and plant in order to modernize, because, as far as the worshippers are concerned, the older they are the more they appeal. The position is more like that of Woolworths when it was taken over and many of its shops were offloaded as surplus to requirements. The church buildings are being disposed of because their congregations are too small. Church membership has fallen steadily from 2.54 million in 1970 to 1.93 million in 1987 and the official estimate in the Churches' statistical yearbook is that by the year 2000 it will be down to 1.55 million. That estimate is based on more than mere pessimism. The assumption that the downtrend will continue rests firmly on the low rate at which new members are dribbling in. Candidates for confirmation are fewer than half what they were in 1960.

Of course statistics are not everything. It could be that the quality of religious life among those who have stayed the course is higher than before. The Christian Church has been through evil times in the past, for instance after the fall of the Roman Empire when Europe fell under the thumb of the barbarians, and a few devotees kept the flame of hope alive. Yet, as it turned out, the Dark Ages made way for the Age of Faith.

Or again it may be no fault of those who rule the Church of England that attendances are falling off. Maybe our time is akin to the eighteenth century when there was a general withering of belief in the things of the spirit, possibly in reaction against the zeal and cruelty of the preceding era of religious wars. Today we in our turn may be reacting against the quasi-religious fanaticism which has given our century the bloodiest, most destructive wars in history. Perhaps also the Church is a casualty of the post-war growth of state activity, especially in the fields of welfare, education and even marriage guidance, which have deprived it of many of its traditional tasks. Such explanations are made more plausible by the fact that it is not only the Church of England that is in retreat. The other mainline denominations, the Catholics, the Methodists, the Baptists and Presbyterians are also on the slide.

But that is just the point. It reminds me of the remark of Sigmund Freud that the Catholic church was a wholesaler while the Protestant churches were retailers of Christianity. I think he meant that Rome was nearer to the source of doctrinal supply while the reformed churches were closer to the customer. The same distinction can be made today but this time between all the big old churches, with an established brand image, the oligopolists in other words, which are losing market share and the new entrants in the field. For the market share of the Independent and Pentecostal churches which have come to prominence in more recent times is on the up and up. Doubtless West Indian and African immigration accounts for some of this shift. Even so the fact remains that the traditional churches have failed to win over these new recruits just as the Anglican church failed to capture the immigrants from the countryside to the northern manufacturing towns during the industrial revolution. As a result, so historians tell us, they fell into the arms of the Methodists instead.

Still more striking is the rapid recent growth of the non-Trinitarian churches, members of which have increased from 278,000 in 1970 to 418,000 in 1987 and are expected to double from their 1970 figure by the century's end. The most striking expansion (if we exclude the Moonies whose numbers are still negligible) is among the Jehovah's Witnesses and the Mormons. If the climate of opinion in our time is antipathetic to the churches, how do these oddballs manage to prosper in spite of it?

The answer has to be salesmanship or what the more religious-minded would call the missionary spirit. I don't happen to be drawn to their point of view but I have to admire the enthusiasm with which the representatives of these way-out sects go and knock on doors. I haven't had a visit from my trendy local vicar in all the years he's been in my parish. But many a time members of the Jehovah's Witnesses congregation have appeared on my doorstep, often very young and unsophisticated but obviously sincere in their urge to share their good news and save my soul. In fact the only person who ever tried to convert me on my annual holiday in France was a Jehovah's Witness only last year. She appeared with her little daughter and addressed me first in French and then in English in a strong northern accent. It turned out that she had emigrated there some years before and had since been regularly trundling her gospel round the holiday homes in her spare time.

Most of the people I've talked to have had the same experience. The exhortation 'Go into the highways and byways and compel them to come in' seems to have been largely lost on the Anglican clergy of today. The one exception is the very thorough follow-up to the last Billy Graham visit. But then isn't it typical that they still leave the front line missionary work to an outsider? The secret of the success of some of the smaller churches may be that they not only take recruitment seriously but encourage lay participation – in the drive to drum up new members their congregations are fully involved.

Among some of the Anglican clergy there is not merely a lack of salesmanship but a positive dislike of sharing their message with those who are not already in the club. I mean the sorts of vicars who refuse baptism of infants of parents who are not paid-up members or will not conduct a church wedding for those who have not been regular attenders of services in the past. Needless to say such an attitude flies in the face of the whole Christian tradition. Such exclusiveness is I suppose the trades unions' most important contribution to British life. It is so deeply ingrained that even in religious affairs, the mentality of our nation of closed shopkeepers is difficult to cast off. Perhaps such clerics inherit some remnant of the feeling of those early Welsh who refused to convert their Saxon enemies because they wanted to ensure they stayed heathen and went to hell.

The same comparative lack of enterprise appears to apply to missions overseas. Paul Johnson's *History of Christianity* describes the explosive growth of church membership in Africa where Christians of all denominations double every twelve years. Yet it is the independent churches which take the lion's share of new recruits. This was brought home to me last April just before Archbishop Tutu arrived to lead and give a multi-racial twist to the celebration of the city of Birmingham's centenary. I was introduced to two bishops from African federated churches who had come over to protest against the Tutu propaganda for sanctions against South Africa. Like most people I had always assumed Tutu to be the leader of South Africa's black Christians but it turned out that these two represented nearly three times as many African Christians as he did.

In the event, incidentally, the Tutu visit was a complete flop. The Archbishop's rallies were ill-attended and the whole exercise incurred losses of at least £200,000 which had to be borne by the Birmingham Diocesan Board of Finance. The Bishop of Aston, the Right Rev. Colin Buchanan, who was responsible, duly resigned. No doubt his inflated notion of the importance of Tutu in Africa, which didn't matter, inspired his overestimate of Tutu's appeal in Brum, which did.

There is a parallel with the African experience in Latin America. There in the course of a generation according to a new book *Tongues of Fire* (published by Blackwell) by that fine scholar, Professor David Martin, one in ten of the population has become an evangelical, most likely a Pentecostal. Many people tend rather unfairly to associate Pentecostalists with religious conmen like Jimmy Swaggart and the Bakkers. But Professor Martin believes that they and the other more way-out independent churches are giving the wretchedly poor of Latin America the same self-confidence and ability to cope with their changing world that the Methodists gave to the working class in England in the industrial revolution.

One reason for the lack-lustre performance of the Church of England both in the home and the export markets is that there has been a decline in the quality of the product it promotes. As I write we are celebrating the fifth centenary of the birth of Cranmer, whose prayer book was until recently considered by one and all to be the greatest treasure that Anglicans possessed. Yet this much-loved text which moulded the thoughts of churchmen for generations has for all practical purposes been abandoned in favour of the insipid Alternative Service Book – the worst exchange since the Widow Twankie accepted a new but ordinary version in exchange for Aladdin's magic lamp. The only rational justification given for this liturgical revolution was that it was more acceptable to worshippers, but there was in fact no serious attempt to test the consumers' response.

The truth of the matter was the ASB was foisted on reluctant churchgoers by the clergy – largely I believe because they fancied it would make it easier to carry out a merger with Rome. In the event it was widely condemned by Christian academics, poets and intellectuals. An analysis of correspondence columns in the heavyweight national newspapers by Dr David Brewer showed the clergy three to one in favour of the change and the laity three to one against. It was as bad as a motor car showroom cancelling orders for the Rolls Royce and offering a Lada instead. Could there be a better example of how the Church of England has acquired one of the characteristic weaknesses of a nationalized industry – that it is run for the benefit not of the customers but of the staff. The financial dependence of the clergy on their congregations has been gradually reduced. The Church Commissioners might almost have designed their central system of financial control in order to relieve the priesthood of the burden of pleasing their parishioners. Donations increasingly take the form of covenants which are paid regardless of whether the churches are empty or full (and since the repayment rises with every increase of income tax the Church has a vested interest in keeping personal taxes as high as possible). The vicar's remuneration is based not on his efforts but on a national scale. Even the traditional Easter offering through which congregations could express their appreciation of parish priest's work throughout the year is now in many dioceses collected and reapportioned among the priests of the area.

Since 1974 the Sheffield formula has determined centrally the distribution of priests throughout the land. Under that dispensation clergy are allocated to a specific population, a very Whitehall approach, which ignores the opportunities for making membership expand. It is a bit like the attitude of the French army towards armour in 1940. As De Gaulle pointed out, France's substantial force of tanks was rendered ineffective by the policy of stationing them in penny packets all along the front instead of concentrating them as the Nazis did where they could make a breakthrough. Like the French army facing Hitler, the Church has a Maginot Line complex and its outlook is defensive and defeatist. Bureaucratic control has made it inert. God's plan has given way to Gosplan. Democratic centralism has all but destroyed the structure of economic incentives and penalties through which individual priests were once encouraged to seek their own advancement by spreading the Word.

It is indeed ironic that, at a time when the nationalized industries are being radically restructured to meet the challenge of a more competitive world, the Church of England is growing more and more akin to British Rail, British Steel and the National Coal Board in their earlier, unregenerate form. Increasingly control has fallen into the hands of the Church House bureaucracy which, since James Callaghan surrendered the Prime Minister's free choice of bishops, now in effect fills vacant sees with those who conform with its policies. After the last Synod we can say with confidence that no new bishop will be appointed who does not support the ordination of women. Regardless of the merits of that issue, it is scandalous that the promotion prospects of worthy priests are limited because on this matter they do not accept the trendy, progressive view.

Yet this only illustrates the negative power which now holds the Church in its grip. It absorbs, drains and sterilizes the energies of its servants and members in a constant round of committees and ecclesiastical quangos. These bodies attempt to justify their existence by the issue of portentous but intellectually second-rate reports on secular affairs which they address with neither distinction nor authority but merely echo fashionable cant. Far from redeeming politics this process has instead tended to politicize the Church. The central Christian purpose of helping individuals to save their own souls for eternity has been ditched in favour of collective salvation through social action in the present. The Church has drifted almost unawares into supporting the leading heresy of our age – which is also the source of most of its woes. For many of its leaders behave as if they believe that political action can bring a kind of redemption here on earth.

All of which suggests that, for the Church of England, privatization is just what the doctor ordered or what Dr Runcie would order if he were wise. It should bodily shift responsibilities and resources away from the ecclesiastical mandarins and back to the parish priest. It must eschew the vanities of national posturing and return to the task of repopulating the pews. Such a 'U-turn' would set free many energies of private religious enterprise now dormant. Think how a takeover bidder would regard the Church of England today. He would not dwell on crumbling cathedrals and falling rolls. He would look instead at his sales force of 10,000 priests established on prime sites throughout Britain. And he would ask how quickly he could induce these highly-trained professionals to 'go into the highways and byways and compel them to come in'.

Notes

Privatization – by political process or consumer preference?

1. Among the more serious articles in the literature, see for example: J.R. Shackleton, 'Privatization: The Case Examined', *National Westminster Bank Quarterly Review*, May 1984; Michael Beesley and Stephen Littlechild, 'Privatization: Principles, Problems and Priorities', *Lloyds Bank Review*, No. 149, July 1983; Alan Peacock, 'Privatization In Perspective', *The Three Banks Review*, No. 144, December 1984.
2. *Cf.* Michael Forsyth, *Down Withced the Rates*, Conservative Political Centre, London, 1982.
3. *Cf.* Rhodes Boyson (ed.), *Goodbye to Nationalization*, Churchill Press, London, 1971.
4. 'Privatization', *The Free Market*, March 1986. The Ludwig von Mises Institute, Auburn University, Alabama, USA.
5. *Op. cit.*
6. *Cf.* Arthur Seldon, *Charge*, Maurice Temple Smith, London, 1977.
7. *Economic Affairs*, Vol. 6, No. 5, June/July 1986.
8. 4 June 1986.
9. *Cutting Back City Hall*, Universe, New York, 1980.
10. For example, M. Frazier, 'Scottsdale Slashes Spending', *Reader's Digest*, June 1978.
11. John Blundell, 'Privatization Is Not Enough', *The Journal of Economic Affairs*, Vol. 3, No. 3, April 1983.
12. Ibid.
13. *Los Angeles Daily Journal*, 30 November 1983.
14. *Op. cit.*
15. Ibid.

British Telecom – has privatization delivered competition?

1. Detailed analysis of the BT privatization and of the development of Oftel are to be found in my *Public Enterprise*, Wheatsheaf, Brighton, 1986.
2. *British Telecommunications and Mitel Corporation*, Cmnd. 9715, HMSO, London.
3. At the end of April BT's share price fell sharply from 280p to 238p when BT threatened to reduce its prices on trunk and international calls in line with price reductions announced by Mercury. This move by BT seemed to many to be premature.

BR – privatization without tears

1. 'Privatization: Principles and Priorities', *Lloyds Bank Review*, July 1983.
2. 'British Railways' Truck Costs', *Journal of Industrial Economics*, Vol. 13, 1964, 74–89.

3 *The Role of British Rail in Public Transport*, First Report, Select Committee on Nationalized Industries. Session 1976-7, HC 305, London, HMSO, 1977.
4 *Railway Finances*, London, HMSO, 1983.
5 Some of the world's busiest lines in terms of tonnages handled are single track (but highly specialized) railways.
6 For further details, see R.P. Griffiths, *The Cheshire Lines Railway*, Oakwood Press, Surrey, 1947.
7 For further information see *The Future of Rail Freight: an End to Uncertainty*. A Submission to Government by the Private Wagon Federation, London, July 1983.
8 There would be some divestment of administration and marketing to train companies.
9 More freedom of entry into airline markets has produced this effect. See Peter Forsyth, 'Airline Deregulation in the United States: The Lessons for Europe', *Fiscal Studies*, Vol. 4, November 1983 and David Starkie and Margaret Starrs, 'Contestability and Sustainability in Regional Airline Markets', *Economic Record*, September, 1984.
10 There might be a beneficial effect of smaller trains operating at more frequent intervals. See Alan Walters, 'Externalities in Urban Buses', *Journal of Urban Economics*, Vol. 11, 1982 for a discussion of trade-offs between vehicle size and service frequency.
11 Economies of scale are to be distinguished from economies of utilization (sometimes referred to as economies of traffic density). Economies of scope refers to the advantages of jointly producing multiple outputs, i.e., different types of services.
12 Recent studies of US railroads have suggested only limited economies of scale. R.H. Spady (*Econometric Estimation for the Regulated Transportation Industries*, Garland, New York, 1979), for example, concludes that there are managerial diseconomies of scale in rail transport.

Privatization: let the market decide

1 When proceeds of council house sales (£6.25 billion since 1979) are included, PSBR targets have been eased cumulatively by well over £8 billion).
2 *Company Finance and the Capital Market*, E.W. Davies and K.A. Yeomans, Cambridge University Press, 1975; and R. Buckland *et al.*, 'Price Discounts on New Equity Issues in the UK', *Journal of Business Finance and Accounting*, 8, 1, 1981.
3 The placing is a fixed price method of selling shares to brokers' clients: it avoids costly advertising but is restricted to smaller issues and could not be used for larger privatization issues.
4 Davies and Yeomans *op. cit.*, Chapter 4; and Buckland *et al.*, *op. cit.*
5 Davies and Yeomans, *op. cit.*, 48.
6 Buckland *et al.*, *op. cit.*, 91.
7 Literally, 'groping', when buyers and sellers manoeuvre to find the correct price which clears the market, before trading occurs.

11 Manufacturing versus services

Deindustrialization: myths and realities

Tony Baron
Source: *Economic Affairs*, April/May 1989, 9, 4, p. 17.

Currently, there is much concern being expressed about the deindustrialization of Britain. This concern is not usually expressed now in terms of a declining trend in the absolute level of UK manufacturing output. However, it is worth noting that UK manufacturing output did not regain its pre-recession peak in the second quarter of 1979 and its record high in the second quarter 1974 until the fourth quarter of 1987 and the second quarter of 1988 respectively. Instead the concern reflects the shrinking proportion of UK GDP accounted for by manufacturing output. In 1988 manufacturing output was 23 per cent of GDP compared with 27 per cent in 1979 and around 30 per cent in 1970. There is also concern about the long-term decline in the UK share of world trade in manufacturing from nearly 11 per cent in 1970 to 7.5 per cent in 1988.

At first sight this concern appears somewhat puzzling. Today agricultural output represents only 1.5 per cent of GDP and employs under 2.5 per cent of the total workforce. Yet before the first industrial revolution in Britain the land employed the bulk of the population and equally provided most of the GDP of the country. If the nation today can enjoy an ever-increasing standard of living through expanding activities other than manufacturing, why should there be any concern about the relative decline of the manufacturing sector?

There has been a steady increase in the share of the service sector as a proportion of GDP and employment since the 1950s.[1] This has happened in other major economies such as the US, Japan, West Germany and France. The growing importance of the service sector reflects greater specialization and innovation, and a tendency of other sectors in the economy to make greater use of the service sector. The relative cyclical stability of the service sector, relative to the manufacturing sector, may owe something to its immunity from changes in the exchange rate both nominal and real, as most of the products from the service sector (financial services excepting) are not typically traded in the international market.

Clearly the deindustrialization of Britain is a topic which raises much political heat and emotional reaction. Often an ill-defined spectre of deindustrialization is conjured up in defence of an ailing company or industry. At the same time the view is expressed that the country must have shipbuilding, electronics, heavy steel industries in order to be able to defend itself. This latter view is somewhat akin to the worries expressed by some Prussian and other continental generals in the 19th century that the migration to the towns would deprive them of a good supply of healthy peasants for their armies.

Nevertheless, leaving on one side the special pleading of trade unionists and some industrialists, a number of well-respected UK economists have argued the deindustrialization of Britain in the 1980s risks the long term health of the economy. In essence they believe that manufacturing is the mainspring of a modern economy and that the UK growth rate will suffer relatively to the growth rate of other OECD countries as a result of the process of deindustrialization.

The rapid build-up of oil production in the late 1970s and early 1980s is the factor most frequently cited as the cause of the deindustrialization of Britain. By the time oil production peaked in the mid-1980s, it was contributing 6 per cent of GDP and £11.5 billion to public revenues a year. Simply stated, Britain's good fortune in discovering oil in the North Sea and being able to exploit it in the aftermath of the two oil price shocks, generated a rise in the sterling real exchange rate above what it otherwise would have been and through the consequent loss of competitiveness resulted in deindustrialization. Other Western industrial countries, it is argued, had to industrialize more in order to pay for the increased cost of oil imports resulting from the oil price shocks.

For sterling the direct impact of rising North Sea oil production came through (a) the contribution of oil to the current account and (b) the value of oil reserves together with (c) sentiment effects of a petro-currency. The effect of (a) is, however, not clear given the heavy investment required to develop the North Sea and the redirection of resources in the economy away from manufacturing. Furthermore it is very difficult to disentangle the impact of oil on sterling from other factors. It is certainly the case, however, that sterling appreciated rapidly during 1979 and 1980 as North Sea oil production rose and oil prices increased.

However, at that time interest rates also rose sharply and there was clearly a sentiment effect arising from the change from a socialist to a Thatcherite government in 1979. There has been much academic debate about the relative strength of the factors which caused sterling to rise at the beginning of this decade. Forsyth and Kay for example have argued that sterling's real rate had to rise substantially in order to restore balance to the current account.[2] Niehans on the other hand has argued that North Sea oil was not a major contributing factor in the appreciation of sterling in the late 1970s and has suggested that the sharp rise in UK interest rates was largely responsible.[3]

The condition of the UK economy today makes an understanding of the processes at work over the last decade extremely important for current government policy. Are the fears of those who saw deindustrialization as a problem in fact coming true?

At the beginning of the 1980s there was much discussion about whether a relative decline in manufacturing industry caused by an oil-induced appreciation of the real exchange rate could easily be reversed once oil production started to decline. The fear expressed was that the pool of skilled industrial labour would diminish and that manufacturing companies would not be able to regain lost market share when oil production fell. The current overheating of the UK economy with domestic supply unable to meet domestic demand clearly leading to a large current account deficit, would superficially be seen to be a vindication of these fears.

Nevertheless, it would be wholly wrong to look at developments in UK manufacturing solely from the point of view of the rise in real exchange rate caused by North Sea oil. The 1980s saw many other fundamental shifts which have had substantial bearing on the UK industrial sector. These include major changes in the tax regime facing the corporate sector, privatization, the reduction of trade union power and, probably most significant of all, the movement from chronic high inflation to relatively low inflation. Looked at from the perspective of Austrian economics the sharp recession at the start of the 1980s was necessary to correct the malinvestments which had resulted from the inflation of the 1970s. Businesses, which were only profitable in times of high inflation, inevitably had to rationalize or restructure or go out of business completely. The early removal of stock relief by the first Thatcher government and the subsequent removal of investment allowances added substantially to the pressure on industry. For the first time in decades industry was faced with the fact that investment in fixed capital and stocks needed to be justified on fundamental economic grounds not by tax efficiency. The resultant shake-out in manufacturing was dramatic and further reinforced by privatization which again resulted in investment being undertaken for economic as opposed to social reasons. Thus the deindustrialization of the 1980s can in large part be seen as an extremely healthy process of removing inefficient business that would only survive in a cycle of accelerating inflation and depreciating sterling.

Far from slowing after the peak in oil production in 1985, growth in the UK has been maintained at high levels both by historic and international standards. The Table shows the UK's relative economic performance since 1985. The sharp fall in oil prices in 1986 coupled with the declining trend in UK oil production has been taken by the economy in its stride. Oil production in 1988 accounted for only 1.5 per cent of GDP and the dwindling of government oil revenue has not prevented the government

Table 11.1 Average annual growth rates, 1985-8

	%
UK	4.2
US	3.3
Japan	4.3
Germany	2.5
France	3.0
Italy	3.3
Canada	3.9

(Here it is worth noting that the lamentable state of UK GDP statistics has probably resulted in the under-recording of growth in recent years).

from running a very substantial PSBR surplus. With the devaluation of sterling in 1986 there has been a substantial increase in UK manufacturing output.

A recent study by the Bank of England shows that the trends in both total factor productivity and labour productivity have increased substantially in the 1980s compared to the 1970s.[4] In the case of the manufacturing sector, labour productivity has grown by 4.4 per cent on average in the 1980s, compared with 2.3 per cent in the 1970s.

The Bank of England is reported to have estimated that the supply side of the economy is currently capable of growing at 3 per cent per annum, somewhat greater than that possible in the 1970s. It seems that today's current account problem is not caused by supply-side constraints, but more by excessive domestic demand, caused largely by an inappropriately relaxed monetary policy in the first half of 1988.

In terms of the traditional measures of health in the manufacturing sector, factor productivity, labour productivity and real return on capital employed, it appears that the economy has responded well and in a manner consistent with the principles of Austrian economics. In particular, the major changes in incentives resulting from the variations in real exchange rate, taxation and the labour market have brought about a major reorientation of the British economy.

Manufacturing or services after 1992?

Peter Lawrence
Source: Economic Affairs April/May 1989, 9, 4, p. 14.

It is almost impossible to read an article on business without mention of the decline of manufacturing to only 25 per cent of GNP or having parliamentarians moan how the Petropound destroyed the industrial base in the early 1980s, and consequently every upward blip in the Sterling exchange rate is to be deplored. The balance of trade will never revert to equilibrium until young entrepreneurs invest in manufacturing instead of services and graduates go into industry rather than the City.

This view is coloured by nostalgia for the days when Britain became great as the workshop of the world making articles – ships and sealing wax and cheap tin trays. The colour is the rosy pink idealism which convinced the post-war Labour government to nationalize the commanding heights of the economy and sings with fervour of the dark satanic mills (hopefully employing thousands, but no longer polluting the air). There are several reasons why this view cannot be supported.

The total number of people employed in the manufacturing categories has fallen. In a competitive era it is ultimately either the low cost producer, including the lowest labour cost per unit, or the market leader who contrives to include the most perceived added value, who prevails. The huge factories of the nineteenth century employed in this century a growing proportion of ancillary workers, night watchmen, cleaners, maintenance men, costing and sales clerks and just 'fat'. The 'lean' industry of the 1990s finds it expensive to employ people permanently and buys in all these services from professional companies selling security or janitorial services, leases on full maintenance trucks, cars and equipment and under demand pressure, contracts in its labour. Computers have replaced the clerks and will help increasingly with design in drawing offices and maintenance schedules. To this extent employment in manufacturing has declined and services has increased. The tendency will continue as manufacturing is broken into its component stages and sub-contracted to single telecommuters or to specialized teams.

But it is a mistake to think that there has been a switch in employment to

Table 11.2 Standard industrial classification

Agriculture, forestry and fishing

Energy and water supply industries

Extraction of minerals and ores other than fuels: manufacture of metals, mineral products and chemicals

Metal goods, engineering and vehicles industries

Other manufacturing industries

Construction

Distribution, hotels and catering: repairs

Transport and communication

Banking, finance, insurance, business services and leasing

Other services (public, armed, law, education, medicine)

---

services. In 1881 employment in domestic service was 2 million and 1981 was 167,000. Nostalgia is wrong!

There is a gnawing feeling, born of personal observation, that not enough cars on the roads are made in Britain nor any other kind of hardware in the shops. Perhaps there is something in the British psyche which abhors the mass manufacture of cheap articles. The success of Rolls Royce, JCB and Land Rover demonstrates the ability of British market leaders to find niches in the world market.

The Russian Trade Minister recently said of British machinery: 'When told they are dear, I say that is good, they must be well made. But please remember that we may not want it to last twenty years without repair. We may prefer to throw it away after five and buy a new one.' Value engineering has not been happily adopted in Britain. Perhaps we are craftsmen at heart, not metal bashers, hence the success of such firms as Wedgwood and Burberry. Yet there is no question of our ability to market biscuits, alcoholic and soft drinks, or confectionery in the category other manufacturing.

Concern about the hollowing of British industry centres on the deficit, currently growing, in trade in visibles which is seen to be bad by mercantilists in the City, the media and the Opposition. There is also the folk memory of sterling crises, when the reserves fall to the point at which recourse has to be made to the IMF.

It will take time to build up industry to meet the demands of the 1990s. First, the managers have to feel sure that by the time it is installed a stop will not render it superfluous and the capital saved or borrowed for the purpose will not be lost or the interest unpaid. If there is a shortage of capacity, then it is far easier to fill it with imports to build the market for the day when the odds in extra profit on run production are better than even! If foreigners are keen to exploit our position in Europe for 1992, then their investment will help to fill the monetary gap. The return on our overseas investments (much of it in manufacturing) and the net invisibles surplus will also help. If all else fails, eventually sterling will have to fall in the foreign exchange markets.

But surely the whole concept of a UK balance of trade is out of date. By the end of the century there will be one monetary system, at least for international trade, in Europe. Who now worries about the Scottish balance of trade or whether Texas has a deficit? Unfortunately for nostalgia, Britain had a deficit in the late nineteenth century when the map was pink and manufacturing at its height. Does it matter if manufacturing, however defined, does not seem to offer the attractive reward to effort ratio that investment in services obviously does? If one believes in market forces it does not matter at all. If the buyer, whether British or foreign, can obtain the quality he requires and the delivery and payment terms most satisfactory to him from Korea rather than Britain, so that he can in his turn offer the article or service he supplies more effectively and profitably, then he will do so and should not be discouraged from doing so. It is for those who wish that British manufacturers should out-perform Korean to create the conditions that will convince entrepreneurs, British or foreign, that Britain is the best place to start a manufacturing business. If more growth is expected in consumption of services than in manufactures then it is there that the investment should be made, and employment in services will grow as a result. If British companies excel in the provision of international services, then the balance of payments will benefit.

But all business including manufacturing is a service. There is nothing innately better, economically more worthy, or more productive of employment, about building a factory, supplying it with machinery and producing parts in it with the machinery, than in raising the loan to finance it, drawing up the contracts, servicing the boilers, machinery and trucks, guarding the factory, feeding the employees, providing the computers or software, insuring it and so on.

The list of ten divisions into which industry is classified for statistical purposes (the Standard Industrial Classification) shows four which fit the description of manufacturing (see Table). Of these, mining and energy and water supply would not be so described by the average observer.

The important characteristic that all these categories have in common is that they need a customer who will keep coming back – unless they are a monopoly. Manufacturing is a service in another sense. Everybody is familiar with the concept of after-sales service. There is also service on delivery – just in time or however it is required, and service on application, showing the customer how to use the product to best advantage. In the search for added value, manufacturers have gone so far as to see the supply of goods almost as incidental to the service they supply. Selling, in restaurant terms, not only the sizzle of the sausage but also the experience of eating it.

For instance, a French cooperative of small independent lubricant producers states in its list of corporate objectives: 'We could have just been satisfied with the sale of oils but we have decided to take charge of the whole process of lubrication.'

They employ both commercial assistants and technical consultants. The former both sell the product and install lubrication systems. The latter visit the customers, inspect the equipment and carry out regular oil analyses on the spot. They advise the customer when to change the oil and when some part is wearing out. From this the cooperative has progressed to simplifying the hundreds of lubricants for different purposes to just a few grades to cover the main applications, which the customers can use with confidence, knowing that the cooperative will warn of any trouble before it happens. The economies in purchasing, manufacturing and stocking balance the extra costs of the service and have enabled the members not only to remain in business against the major oil companies but to increase sales by 30 per cent annually. They also suggest that the way forward for independent firms in their industry is to join their cooperative. For this an annual budget charge is made (not a royalty). Packaging design, sales training, product development and central marketing will be jointly developed, but each franchisee runs his own market. In this way a multinational business will be created by the use of that French invention, the 'groupement d'intérêt économique'.[1]

Another form of manufacturing as a service is own-label production. This is ancient in the textile industry where it has been commonplace for middlemen to put out to a manufacturer of one of the many stages on commission to dye his wool, weave it or have it made up into garments for him to sell. Nowadays every retailer thinks he is as good as Marks & Spencer and will find a manufacturer to make goods to his specification to sell under his label at a price fixed by him. This extends from textiles to processed food, cosmetics, generic pharmaceuticals and cigarettes, wine, paint, chemicals for motor manufacture, leather goods, watches and so on. There are contract packers who only fill aerosols for other manufacturers and others who fill tubes and tins. All these manufacturers are offering nothing but a service. They can lose the business overnight, another manufacturer takes over and ultimately the consumer will not notice the difference.

In Italy, a study on the cost of non-Europe, or the current cost of the barriers which should be swept away by 1992 reported that flexibility is a key factor which allows firms to obtain substantial efficiency gains, where product-specific economies of scale or plant economies of scale are not important. In some subsectors dynamic expert-oriented firms, such as Benetton, put out a large share of production to a great number of small production units, which provide the necessary flexibility and efficiency in production. The knitwear industry is organised in industrial districts which work as if they were a single firm with hundreds of small, independent, highly flexible production units. The fragmentation of this production system is counterbalanced by the concentration of commercial and marketing activities in a smaller number of firms, often of a very large size in turnover, which organize the whole system of production. This system has been at the heart of the excellent export performance of the Italian firms of the knitwear, clothing and wool sectors from the 1970s onwards. The Italian model is not widespread in Europe, although some countries like Belgium and France are moving in that direction. It sounds very like the pre-mill-weaving industry in England. The conclusions of the study are also interesting:

> The existence of a common European market has been a crucial factor for the achievement of economies of scale due to *commercial* and *marketing* aspects. These also represent strong barriers to entry for low cost developing countries. The main point is that in order to exploit these economies, it is not necessary to be a multi-plant firm. As we have already seen, sub-contracting, both at national and international level and 'putting out' systems can do the job probably more efficiently.[2]

If the market is to rule and the world to shrink to a global village, which it will, then it is ever less relevant to think of business problems in national or even regional terms. One must think of them in terms of the firm as a unit. What is the right strategy for a firm in a global industry?

The economy reflects the sum of these individual judgments, just as it does the sum of all the buying and selling decisions of its consumers. Major government or European Commission-led decisions such as more or less protection, quotas, higher or equal taxes and so on will help or alter the firm's strategy but if a company or entrepreneur has decided that he knows his business, that it is profitable and worth staying in, then a way will be found to succeed in it. The business may cease to manufacture here or there, emigrate to save taxes, labour costs or secure raw material sources, but as long as the managers want to go on managing it, a way will be found. If they do not, it will be sold or be liquidated. Family firms, the backbone of industry in Germany, France and Italy and recovering their force in the UK, remain in the van.

So will 1992 bring impoverishment to the UK, silence to the factories and more unemployment? Why should the abolition of border formalities and other obstacles to the free flow of trade and capital have any different result from any of the previous improvements in business communication, namely an increase in total trade and general prosperity? Just as the first railway was built in Germany in 1835, the year after the Zollverein swept away the plethora of customs barriers of the states which made up modern Federal Germany – how absurd to have a customs officer climbing aboard every ten or fifty miles – so will the Channel Tunnel in 1993 help to end British insularity. But to get a true foretaste, examine the United States.

Contrary to popular belief, it is a single market but it is not one market. It is too big for even the largest global business to attempt to supply from one extra-large plant either inwards for raw materials or parts or outwards for finished products. The freight costs are too high for most articles of a low or medium value to weight ratio to be handled in such a way. There are, at the minimum, five main geographical markets for distribution purposes, North East, South East, South West, Mid-west and West. These are frequently subdivided into thirteen or fourteen for purposes of sales management and there are of course fifty states, with varying local sales, income and corporation taxes. A company can find its market in its local geographical area, state or distribution area, or try to sell nationwide. The difficulty of shipping long distances has led to much toll-manufacturing, the putting out of conversion processes and private label packing, often without formal licensing, in many industries.

The development of the Coca-Cola syrup concentrate and the relationship between supplier and bottler is a good example. In order to avoid credit problems many companies use distributors who buy goods for their own account and sell on an agreed mark-up or receive a commission, very like the agents of European commerce but without their protected sole or exclusive status. One can also hire a sales force of manufacturers' 'reps.'

who are paid on commission and are responsible for chasing payment but do not take title. They usually specialize in a particular industry and carry a line of many products, often near-competitors. They may operate in a state or marketing area and they are more difficult to sack but can be hired very quickly.

As President Reagan declared in claiming credit for reducing unemployment, America is the land of small businesses. If the future is really the United States of Europe, it offers opportunities for all sorts and sizes of business and there is nothing to fear. The post-1992 Europe will have a population larger than the US and although distances are shorter, there are worse roads, more expensive airlines and at least ten languages. It is not necessary for every business, or any business that has already thought through its strategy to do something before 1992. The opportunities in the new European single market can be exploited by any well-managed business.

The opportunities are just as good in manufacturing as they are in services, provided it is remembered that it is also a service and not an end in itself. Governments and the European Commission should not try to distort the economy by artificially stimulating manufacturing by protection, whether of the UK or Fortress Europe. Nor should they obstruct the expansion of service industries. If we cannot have a level playing field, then let the gradient be gentle.

Manufacturing versus services – a false dichotomy?

David Liston, OBE
Source: Economic Affairs, April/May 1989, 9, 4, p. 19.

There appears to be something highly emotive about the terms service or services, particularly amongst the top ranks of British manufacturing industry. This shows up most clearly, perhaps, in much of the oral evidence given to the House of Lords Select Committee on Overseas Trade (the Aldington Committee), whose report was published in 1985. Of particular interest are the remarks of Lord Weinstock, when faced with the suggestion (attributed to the Chancellor of the Exchequer) that given a mounting balance of payment deficit, partially at least due to the decline in oil revenues, the slack could be taken up by the service industries rather than by manufacturing. Lord Weinstock chose to press the point to extremes:

> What will the service industries be servicing when there is no hardware, no wealth is actually being produced? We will be servicing, presumably, the product of wealth by others ... We will supply the Changing of the Guard, we will supply the Beefeaters around the Tower of London, we will become a curiosity. I don't think that is what Britain is about. I think that it is rubbish.[1]

A similar view, though in much more measured terms, was taken up in his evidence by Sir John Harvey-Jones, then Chairman of ICI, whose remarks were then expanded in the 1986 Dimbleby Lecture entitled 'Does Industry Matter?'[2]

Sir John rejects the concept that Britain has entered a 'post-industrialization' era, asserting, quite correctly, that such a concept is totally inappropriate to a country that was still exporting goods to the value of more than £50 billion per year. He also quoted an article which appeared in the Bank of England survey of 1985,[3] to show that, whatever the state of Britain's manufacturing industry, the UK invisible exports were also showing strong evidence of strain, to the extent that their share of world trade was actually falling. The precise figures, like all statistics in this field, were hotly disputed and drew instant and caustic comment from Sir William Clarke, the Director of the British Invisible Exports Council. He pointed to a major distortion in the published statistics which recorded transactions in international banking in net, rather than the very much higher gross, figures.

For all that, Sir John was entirely correct in noting that in a rapidly growing market for invisibles, the UK share of total world trade showed some marginal decline. It would have been very surprising had this not been the case.

Be that as it may, Lord Weinstock and Sir John Harvey-Jones sounded clear signals against prematurely writing off British manufacturing industry. Others, too, were quick to mount a high profile defence of manufacturing, which was, perhaps, long overdue. The Royal Society of Arts, with its Industry Year, the CBI, the Institute of Directors and many other individuals and institutes hurried to the defence of British manufacturing industry and sought, in particular, to drown with ridicule the notion that, however important the services might be, they could replace manufacturing as the main bulwark of the British economy.

There were, of course, many excellent reasons for mounting, and indeed, maintaining, a high profile in defence of British manufacturing. The statistics have often been quoted and need no repetition.

There has, undoubtedly, been some dramatic and sustained recovery in the last few years but for all that, manufacturing output had by the end of 1987 failed to reach the peak level of 1974.

The main reasons for the decline are as follows:

1 Changes in manufacturing and materials technology and in patterns of consumption, affecting particularly many of our heavy industries such as steel, coal, shipbuilding and power generation.
2 Obsolescence and redundancy of many existing plants and inadequate investment to replace the old with the new.
3 Intense and diverse competition worldwide, particularly from Japan and the newly industrialized countries of the Far East.

4   Weakness in the infrastructure of our national education with a consequent shortage of technical and managerial skills appropriate to a world of high technology.
5   Resistance to change both by management and particularly by trade unions.
6   Aspects of Government policy, both fiscal and monetary, which too often reflect adversely on manufacturing industry, particularly high interest rates and fluctuating rates of exchange.

It is easy enough to see why manufacturing was in need of defence by individuals and institutions both inside and outside government. What is less easy to understand is the way in which, in exploring the paths to salvation, the particular contributions of the services and the service industry should have received what appears, too often, to be derisory and often arrogant dismissal.

It could be, of course, that to the British mentality the very concept of service implies something menial or at least secondary, and by implication the service industries are thought to lack an essential gravitas to fit them for a pre-eminent position in the national economy.

There could also be a feeling of irritation, not unjustified, at the premature obsequies on British manufacturing from participants in the service industries, and particularly from those who write about them, at home and abroad. Gunter Pauli has commented: 'At the end, the key ingredients for creating wealth seem no longer to be land or capital, nor raw material; nor energy; nor even labour in its traditional economic sense. Today, it is becoming mainly technological knowhow and mostly in the service industries.'[3]

Table 11.3 UK private sector invisible earnings, 1986

Main UK net invisible earnings

	£million
Insurance	4260
Banking	2295
Other financial services	2281
Consultancy	1216

Major sectors in net deficit

	£million
Civil aviation	449
Tourism	646
Shipping	937

Source: BIEC.

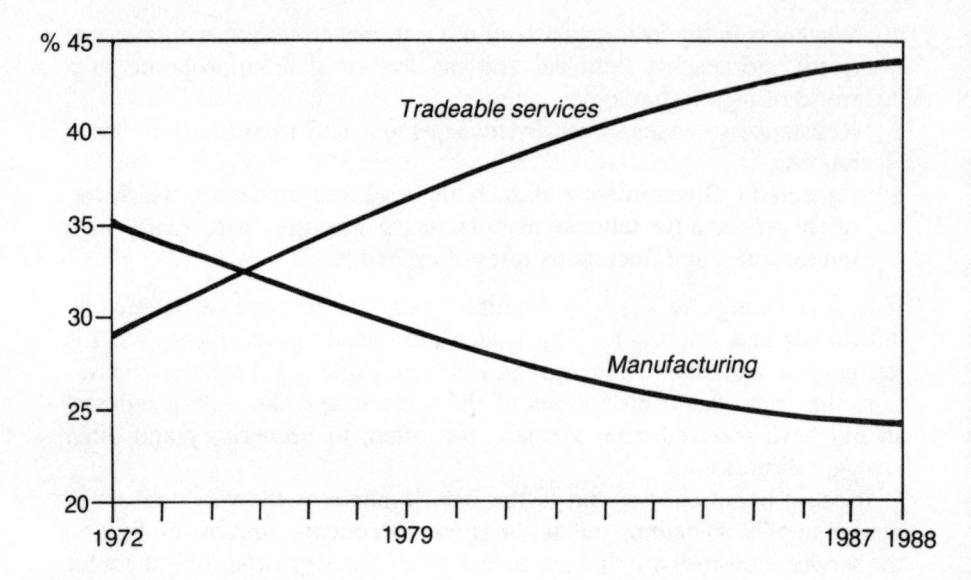

Figure 11.1 UK employment: manufacturing and tradeable services
Source: BIEC

Mr Pauli may or may not be, as described by Gaston Thorn, one of the ten most outstanding young people in the world; but his claims to personal pre-eminence are certainly not enhanced by extravagant language of this kind.

But it is true, unfortunately, that even after every allowance has been made for British attitudes towards service and for the personal prejudice of some individuals, there still remains a remarkable and widespread lack of appreciation of the scale and diversity of services and the service industries. As a result, there has been, at least until recently, very little understanding of their full contribution to the UK economy as a whole and in particular, to those very sectors of manufacturing industry whose representatives have been most vociferous in deriding them. For many of them must rely on the services for their technological support and growth. In an advanced industrialised economy such as the UK goods and services are interdependent and mutually supportive. It is to this particular aspect that the concluding paragraphs of this article are addressed.

Figure 11.1 and Tables 11.1 to 11.4, whatever their imperfections in detail, establish beyond reasonable doubt that invisible exports are, in fact, a most significant element within the total framework of the national economy.

The nature and scope of the individual sectors themselves refute the trivialization to which they have been subject. The main activities covered in the Tables – banking, insurance, financial services and the various aspects of brokerage and other city activities, not only form part of the very fabric of our commercial life, but have done so for many hundreds of years.

Exports of services are not limited to the City – they include engineering, professional and management consultancies, education of overseas students, transportation, intellectual property, telecommunications, fine art, real estate, films, books and videos. It is not a story of unbroken success, particularly in shipping, but on the whole the UK has performed well and the outlook is encouraging.

Even tourism, the butt for so many industrial leaders, has made an economic and social contribution to the economy far removed from its public image. The industry takes in hotels and catering, trade fairs, conferences and exhibitions, shopping and a huge range of entertainment and leisure activities. Between them they collect £5.5 billion per year from overseas visitors and, despite the huge growth in holidays abroad of UK citizens, (whose spendings are classified for official purposes as imports) tourism contrives in most years to achieve a degree of parity between income and expenditure in terms of balance of payments.

Most of what has been written above, together with the supporting statistics, has been concerned with service activities which operate as self-standing industries, many of them of very considerable size and trading, for the most part in overseas markets as invisible exports. There is, therefore, every reason to consider them as complementary rather than competitive with other national economic activities, such as agriculture, oil and mineral extraction and manufacturing industry. In so far as they have tended to grow both in earnings and in employment as other activities have declined, the service industries have tended to receive some overdue recognition for their enterprise.

Table 11.4 UK financial institutions – net earnings overseas, 1986

	£million
Insurance	4260
Banking	2295
Pension funds	638
Securities dealers	552
Export houses	350
Other brokerage	248
Commodity traders	223
Baltic Exchange	221
Investment trusts	188
Unit trusts	175
Stock Exchange	152
Leasing	50
Lloyd's Register of Shipping	24
TOTAL	9376

Source: CSO Pink Book, 1987.

No attempt, however, has been made in a short article of this nature to pursue the philosophical implications of the services as wealth-creators. Professor Dorothy Riddle of the University of Arizona has written and lectured widely on this subject, and established beyond reasonable doubt a correlation between service growth and national economic development world-wide.[5] She has noted that services – infrastructural, social and personal, business and trade, are found at their most vibrant in the most advanced economies of the world. She has concluded too that whilst even in low income countries some 40 per cent of GDP derives from the service sector, the percentage rises consistently through categories of development to some 66 per cent in advanced industrialized countries.

So far as the UK is concerned, we know from the work of Amin Rajan at the University of Sussex, that some 14 million people find work within the service sector, more than half of the total labour force – a figure which is still growing and has already done a good deal to offset the heavy decline in manufacturing industries.[6]

It is true that the figures for the service industries tend to be swollen by the externalization of many service activities, i.e. the hiving-off into separate operating companies (particularly in computer software, transport, catering and cleaning) of activities which formerly were contained within manufacturing companies.

For all that, the size of the total figures and their interrelation with other economic activities seems to reduce philosophical arguments on the role of services as wealth creators to largely a matter of semantics.

This is particularly true of the interdependence of the manufacturing and service sectors. In the City, which now contributes 14 per cent of the UK national output, it is clear enough that export loans, for instance overseas investment in land, buildings and stocks and shares, and the complex and sophisticated techniques of mergers and acquisitions, certainly depend for their success on the professional skills of financiers, accountants and lawyers. Equally, however, for the most part they have their bedrock within manufacturing – in production, exporting, marketing and corporate strategy.

Table 11.5 Current invisible transactions* of major OECD countries

	US $billions 1977	1986	1987
United Kingdom	+3.5	+12.5	+13.0
France	−0.6	+4.8	+4.7
United States	+16.8	+3.0	−1.5
Japan	−6.4	−7.0	−9.4
West Germany	−15.4	−18.0	−26.1

*Balance of services and total transfers (both private and official).

Table 11.6 Employment, 1978–88

	June 1978	Percentage March 1987	March 1988
Banking, finance, insurance	7	11	11
Transport	5	4	4
Hotels and catering	4	5	5
Other services	19	23	24
Total tradeable services	35	43	44
Manufacturing	32	24	23
Distributive trades	14	15	16
Public administration	9	9	9
Construction	5	5	5
Agriculture, mining etc.	5	4	3
Total employees in employment (000's)	22,273	21,084	21,466

Similarly, advances in banking procedures, such as service tills and automated clearing, rely on computing hardware and telecommunications. The revolution in securities trading and in the rapid recording of transactions relies (as so much else in the services field) on the rapid transmission of information and involves technologically advanced hardware, which itself requires frequent up-dating.

In the wider field of finance, both insurance and reinsurance are tied back to aircraft, ships, factories, power stations and ultimately to the products themselves. Similarly, in their overseas work architects, engineers and economic consultants draw for much of their expertise on equipment and materials from a well-founded construction industry at home, whilst the expanding activities of management consultants in particular could hardly exist without a substantial domestic corporate base.

Earnings from licences and patents owe at least as much to product development at home as to the sale of products manufactured abroad. Finally, within the field of the creative arts, the royalties of authors, musicians and artists are so bound up with the sale of books, cassettes, videos and similar products, that one cannot easily disentangle them from visible trade.

The general principle remains clear. It is not, as is often said, a case of manufacturing versus services. Much less it is the dawn of a post-industrialized era, either in the UK or in other advanced nations. It is not even a matter of service-led economy, but rather as Dr Riddle has said, a service-led growth, or perhaps more accurately an information-led growth. In such a situation, the national economy depends on the services for much of its technological growth whilst the services in turn (including banking, insurance and other professional activities) not only support the manufacturing industries, but also foster substantial and profitable industries on their own account. In this way, they create a new source of wealth for themselves, and from their activities generate additional wealth of many sectors of the economy.

The service sector is also productive

Walter Eltis and Andrew Murfin
Source: *Economic Affairs*, April/May 1989, 9, 4, p. 11.

From 1971 to 1986 United Kingdom employment in production and construction industries, mainly manufacturing, fell by over 3 million from 9,839,000 to 6,645,000 – a fall of almost one third. In the same period employment in the service sector increased by nearly 3 million from 11,754,000 to 14,441,000. Many have suggested that the shift these figures show of around 3 million workers from the production of goods to the provision of services is economically disturbing. There is a view that manufacturing makes a more fundamental and basic contribution to the economy than the various service industries.

The great classical political economists, Adam Smith, David Ricardo, Thomas R. Malthus and Karl Marx, all classified the output of goods as productive and the provision of many or most services as unproductive, but their fundamental assumption that commodity production forms the bulk of economic output was forcefully challenged by J.R. McCulloch in his *Principles of Political Economy* in 1825:

> The whole of Dr Smith's reasoning proceeds on a false hypothesis. He has made a distinction where there is none, and where it is not in the nature of things there can be any. The end of all human exertion is the same – that is, to increase the sum of necessaries, comforts, and enjoyments; and it must be left to the judgment of every one to determine what proportion of these comforts he will have in the shape of menial services, and what in the shape of material products.
>
> The manufacturer is not a producer of matter, but of utility only. And is it not obvious that the labour of the menial servant is also productive of utility?[1]

Most modern economists would applaud this passage.

McCulloch's proposition that the object of all economic activity is the creation of utility and that services provide utility just as much as physical goods is one which corresponds to the modern concept that all workers, in every sector of the economy, contribute to the National Income. This is the sum of the outputs of workers and salary earners who produce both goods and services, and it measures what the economy can provide for the whole population. Industry, agriculture and construction will contribute to utility insofar as people wish to consume physical commodities, and the service sector contributes to utility insofar as they wish to enjoy services.

Moreover most services are internationally tradeable, so they can be exported and the proceeds used to purchase the capital goods that are necessary for economic growth. As soon as trade comes into the argument the machinery, that must be invested in order to achieve growth, will often be produced overseas and this can be paid for by exporting goods or services. Countries can export services to pay for machinery if that is where their comparative advantage lies, and therefore obtain more and better machinery than they would if they had to make each item themselves. This means that anything at all that a country produces, be it a good or a service, will be productive in the classical sense so long as it is internationally marketable, since all marketable goods and services are capable of earning the currency that will pay for investment goods.

There are nonetheless survivals of the approach of Smith, Ricardo and Marx in the modern world, most notably in the Soviet Union, where much of the economy is still modelled on Marx's categories, which are entirely classical. In Marx, as in Smith, the investable surplus can only be created in the production of commodities, and in Soviet planning this has therefore received priority over the provision of services.[2] Retail distribution is regarded as unproductive and the amount of time that the Soviet citizens have to spend queueing to obtain their consumer goods is a feature of that society. In the economies that have broken away from the Marxist classical model, it is recognized that retail distribution is an indispensable element in the process by which an economy converts productive inputs into final utilities. The time that workers save by using shops that function efficiently is worth money to them, and it increases the time at their disposal in which to produce other goods and services. The services that distributors provide are often indispensable to the enjoyment and proper use of goods; this is especially the case with most consumer durables which require continual advice and repair facilities that are often provided by the original retailers. Such support for consumers from services is regarded as unproductive in the classical Marxist schema, so such resources are stinted to Soviet citizens (they were included in the Russian National Income accounts for the first time in 1986), but they have always been deemed to contribute enough utility to justify their existence in modern Western economies.

The view that only physical goods output is productive creates the anomaly in the Soviet Union that actors and actresses are productive in the film industry where solid substances, namely reels of film, are created, and unproductive in the live theatre, where they echo Adam Smith who insisted that 'players, buffoons, musicians, opera singers and opera dancers' are all unproductive.[3]

In the UK we moved towards a similar error, which led to comparable anomalies in the 1960s, when it was believed that manufacturing made a

Figure 11.2 Relationship between productivity and output growth in UK manufacturing and services, 1972–86

Manufacturing
Productivity growth = 0.029 + 0.638 (output growth) $R^2 = 0.552$
          (4.08)   (4.00)

Distribution
Productivity growth = −0.004 + 0.747 (output growth) $R^2 = 0.715$
          (0.72)   (5.71)

Transport
Productivity growth = 0.015 + 0.964 (output growth) $R^2 = 0.602$
          (2.29)   (0.17)

Communication
Productivity growth = 0.006 = 0.863 (output growth) $R^2 = 0.659$
          (0.73)   (5.01)

Banking, Finance
Productivity growth = 0.009 + 0.269 (output growth) $R^2 = 0.248$
          (1.18)   (2.07)

Note: employment is defined in terms of full-time equivalents.

more fundamental contribution to the economy than the provision of services, because Lord Kaldor – then taxation adviser to the Chancellor of the Exchequer – believed that increases in manufacturing output were associated with faster rates of productivity growth. This arose because increasing returns to scale were the norm in manufacturing industry, but not in agriculture or the service sector. In the belief that this was true, it was decided in the 1966 budget following Kaldor's inaugural lecture in Cambridge University on the 'Causes of the Slow Rate of Growth of the United Kingdom' that a new payroll subsidy should be applied to employment in manufacturing while service sector employment should be taxed.[4] This produced the welcome result for Oxford University authors that the Oxford University Press, which was then still a manufacturing company that printed its own books, was subsidized, while the Cambridge University Press, which merely prepared its books for the printers but did not print them, had to pay Kaldor's Selective Employment Tax which was directed specifically at service employees.

Kaldor's very favourable production function for UK manufacturing was based on Verdoorn's Law, which states that there is a strong positive relation between the rates of growth of productivity and output. With a higher rate of growth of output, both productivity and employment increase at a faster rate. Several simple equations have been used to examine these relationships (and Bob Rowthorn sets them out helpfully[5]), but the simplest is the Verdoorn relationship itself linking productivity growth and output growth.

Productivity Growth = A + B (Output Growth)

where A and B are constants. We have estimated this equation for manufacturing and for four branches of the service sector over the period 1972–86, and the result is set out in the box.

Kaldor originally suggested that Verdoorn's Law only applied to manufacturing, but the 1972–86 UK data suggests that it applies equally strongly to a good deal of the service sector.

In the equation linking productivity to output growth, Kaldor found B to be in the region of one half for manufacturing, indicating that each percentage point of higher output growth will be associated with an extra 0.5 per cent of productivity growth. In our results, B is 0.6 for manufacturing and between 0.27 and 0.96 in Retail Distribution, Transport, Communications, Banking and Finance. It therefore appears that over the past fifteen years Verdoorn's Law has indeed been in operation, but it is not unique to manufacturing.

In fact, the complete process by which raw materials are converted into finished goods in the hands of final consumers includes several stages which may or may not be performed by firms that appear to be in the service sector. Raw materials and other inputs may be moved to the places where manufacturing takes place, in ships or lorries that belong to a manufacturing company or by firms classified in the service sector. Plant and machinery may be owned by manufacturing companies or leased from firms in the service sector: the leasing of plant and machinery and computer hardware from service sector companies has become a growing practice in the UK in the 1980s. Workers may be given lunch in canteens staffed by catering workers employed by manufacturing companies, or by outside caterers from the service sector. Finished products may be marketed by manufacturing companies themselves (who sometimes own their own distributors, as in the oil industry), or they may be sold to service sector companies to handle all the problems associated with marketing and distribution. Some of the approximately 3 million workers who shifted from UK production industries into service employment moved in response to the tendency of manufacturing companies to devolve activities like these to specialist service concerns. The Manpower Services Commis-

Table 11.7 Employment shifts in the UK, 1971–86, thousands

	1971	1986	Change
Agriculture	421	310	−111
Production industries and construction	9839	6645	−3194
Marketed services	6952	8577	+1625
Non-market services	4802	5864	+1062

280 *Recent controversies in political economy*

Table 11.8 Employment shifts in the UK, 1971–86 (Expressed as a percentage of all employees in employment)

	1971	1986	Change
Agriculture	1.9	1.5	−0.4
Production industries and construction	44.7	31.1	−13.6
Marketed services	31.6	40.1	+8.5
Non-market services	21.8	27.4	+5.6

Source: These figures are taken from Employment Gazette Historical Supplement No.1, February 1987, for Great Britain on 1980 SIC. Marketed Services embraces order 61–3, 64/5, 66, 67, 71–77, 79, 81–5, 97–98; Non-Market Services are 91–2, 93–6 plus the Armed Forces. Self-employed workers are not included.

sion estimated in June 1987 that up to half the shift may be explained in this way.

It is actually an injustice to Adam Smith and his great classical successors to suggest that they were unaware of this difficulty. Smith classified workers employed in agriculture and industry as productive and also the merchants who traded and transported the goods that they produced. The unproductive were, in contrast, those who played no part in the process of converting physical raw materials into final marketed outputs. Smith's productive sector included a good deal of the present service sector, transport, distribution and much of the financial activity that supports manufacturing and construction.

A modern restatement of Adam Smith's argument would predict that no difficulties should arise from a shift of a country's economic resources from production industries into services associated with production such as retail distribution, transport and financial services.

The principal services which will play no part in this complete commercially productive process are those that are not marketed. These are invariably provided by the state because private sector companies have to market their products in order to cover their costs. Unmarketed public services provided by government have to be financed from either taxation or borrowing, and these will both put pressure on the private sector industries and services which market their output. Private companies will ultimately have to finance the taxes and borrowing that support general government.

The modern parallel with the classical argument is a division of the economy into a market sector which produces investable outputs, and services that can be traded internationally for investables. A third sector of the economy is a non-market general government sector which has to be supported financially (via taxes or the financing of debt) by the market sector.[6]

Examined according to these definitions, more than two-thirds of the three million UK workers who shifted from production industries and

Table 11.9 UK sectoral shifts expressed as a percentage of GDP 1971–86

	1971	1986	Change
Agriculture	3.0	1.8	−1.2
Production industries and construction	44.5	38.1	−6.4
Marketed services	35.8	40.5	+4.7
Non-market services	16.7	19.6	+2.9

Source: Figures derived from Blue Book Data. Marketed Services embrace Distribution, Hotels, Repairs, Catering, Transport, Communication, Banking, Finance, Insurance, plus half of other services. Ownership of dwellings is not included.

construction to the service sector from 1971 to 1986 went on to produce marketed services that are either complementary to manufacturing, or else tradeable for manufactures. Only approximately one-third, in fact just over one million workers, went from the production industries to the provision of the unmarketed public services that have to be financed by taxation or government borrowing.

The structural shifts between 1971 and 1986 are set out in the tables; Table 11.7 shows total employment shifts in the UK, while Table 11.8 expresses these as percentages of the labour force.

These shifts from manufacturing to the service sectors are considerably less when they are measured as shifts in real national income, because much of the increase in service employment that took place from 1971 to 1986 took the form of an increase in the employment of part-time and female workers, who are paid less than men on average.

It will be evident from Table 11.9 that the fraction of the UK national income that shifted from production industries and construction to the service sector between 1971 and 1986 was a relatively modest 6.4 per cent, and for the most part this went into the marketed services sector which grew by 4.7 per cent of the national income. The non-market services grew by 2.9 per cent of the national income, and the contribution of agriculture declined by 1.2 per cent.

The most significant structural shift that emerges is the relatively modest one of around 6.5 per cent of the national income from production industries and construction, which mostly went to the provision of marketed and tradeable services. There is no *a priori* reason to suppose that this involved any weakening in the ability of the UK economy to finance its necessary imports and to provide the capital equipment from domestic and overseas sources that is indispensable to economic growth.

The United Kingdom suffered a sharp deterioration in its trade in 1988 but there is no reason to suppose that this arose because of the modest shift of resources from manufacturing industry to the private service sector. A more competitive trade performance by both sectors will probably be needed to restore the balance of payments.

Why manufacturing industry matters

S. Bazen and A.P. Thirlwall
Source: *Economic Affairs*, April/May 1989, 9, 4, p. 8.

In 1955 Britain had 48 per cent of its workforce working in industry, making it one of the most highly industrialized economies the capitalist world has ever seen. The proportion is now 22 per cent and still falling. Total industrial employment has been contracting since 1966. Industrial output as a proportion of GDP has also declined rapidly, and industrial output growth has been very sluggish in volume terms. Does this industrial decline matter? Can other activities, namely service activities, compensate in terms of their contribution to employment, output growth and the balance of payments, or does the decline of industry jeopardize the whole functioning of the macro economy?

The first introductory point to make is that structural change is natural in the process of economic evolution. All countries were once at subsistence level producing primarily food and raw materials for subsistence needs. The diversification of economic activity became possible when agriculture became settled, and agricultural productivity improved sufficiently to produce a surplus of agricultural goods over subsistence needs to feed labour in alternative occupations. In Europe the basis was laid for the development of manufacturing and service activities in the seventeenth and eighteenth centuries. Agriculture and industry grew together but the proportion of total output generated by industry rose, while that of agriculture fell.

Side by side with the growth of industrial activities was the growth of services, many dependent on industry but others not. The proportion of total output generated by services also rose. In any economic system there is an interdependence between activities, but this does not mean that each has the same production characteristics and is equally important as far as the growth process is concerned. For example, agriculture and other land-based activities are subject to diminishing returns (since land is a fixed factor of production), while most industrial activities are subject to increasing returns. The growth of land-based activities will depress the level and growth of productivity unless there is technical progress to compensate, while the growth of industrial activities will automatically raise the level and growth of productivity. It is no accident that the explosion of living standards in the West during the eighteenth and nineteenth centuries was associated with the industrial revolution, and it is no accident today that divisions in the world economy between the developed North and the less developed South are associated with the proportions of resources devoted to industrial activities on the one hand, and land-based activities on the other. There is a very strong correlation across countries between the level of per capita income and the relative importance of industry, and also a strong correlation between the growth of GDP and the growth of industrial output relative to non-industrial output.

Shifts in the structure of production within countries are associated to a large extent with the rate at which the demand for different types of output grows as income grows (i.e. with the income elasticity of demand for goods) and with what countries choose to specialize in as far as trade is concerned. The income elasticity of demand for agricultural goods is generally less than unity (Engel's Law), while the income elasticity of demand for manufactured goods is generally greater than unity. Service activities tend to have more varied demand characteristics. Basic services such as marketing, distribution and transport have a fairly low income elasticity, while other services such as banking and finance and some more personal services, have a high income elasticity. Services tend to develop in sophistication as societies become richer, and a certain point comes when the proportion of resources devoted to industrial activities starts to fall. This does not mean, however, that service activities have the same growth-inducing effects as manufacturing, and it has been noticed historically that following the so-called 'take-off stage of development' associated with rapid industrialization, the growth of GDP tends to decelerate.

The decline in the relative importance of manufacturing in an economy is often referred to as deindustrialization. Deindustrialization, however, may be either of the positive or negative variety. A relative decline in the importance of manufacturing is quite consistent with a healthy manufacturing sector and overall economy, provided the sector continues to grow absolutely at a sufficient rate to maintain full employment and to contri-

Table 11.10 Trends relating to manufacturing and services

	1960	1979	1986	Change 1960–86
Share of manufacturing in total output (%)	32.1	24.9	21.8	−10.3 points
Share of manufacturing in total employment (%)	36.0	29.3	22.5	−13.5 points
Index of manufacturing output (1980 = 100)	77.2	109.5	104.7	+35.6%
Employment in manufacturing (000s)	8,996	7,253	5,243	−3,753
Employment in services (000s)	11,362	13,580	14,192	+2,830
Balance of trade in manufactures (£ million)	+1,552	+2,698	−8,055	−9,607
Balance on invisible trade account (£ million)	+173	+2,713	+7,607	+7,434

bute to exports in sufficient quantities to pay for a country's appetite for imports as it becomes richer and more specialized. This is positive deindustrialization. Negative deindustrialization, by contrast, is when industry languishes to such an extent that it starts to jeopardize the achievement of society's macro-economic goals. That is when deindustrialization starts to matter.

In the post-war years, Britain has experienced the most extreme form of deindustrialization of any country in the world, and since the mid-1960s, it has been of the negative variety. It has suffered the severest decline in the share of manufacturing employment and output in total activity; the slowest growth of industrial output, and the largest contraction of employment in manufacturing industry. Associated with these trends (and causally related, we believe) has been the slowest annual growth of GDP of any major industrialized country (averaging 2.7 per cent from 1950 to 1972, and 1.9 per cent from 1973 to 1986) and the slowest rate of growth of export volume. Most countries set themselves the macro-economic goals of full employment; faster growth; balance of payments equilibrium (as an intermediate objective); and stable prices. Negative deindustrialization on the scale experienced by Britain is not consistent with the achievement of these goals, and there is no evidence that service activities can adequately compensate. Let us take these goals in turn.

The current level of unemployment is appalling by any standards, and the unemployment record has worsened gradually through time. Employment in manufacturing peaked in 1966, and since then over four million jobs have been lost – two million prior to 1979, and over two million since the economic experiments of the Conservative government. In the 1970s, service employment rose to compensate, but since 1979 total employment has fallen by 1.35 million while unemployment has risen by 1.56 million. The expansion of service industries has not compensated for the decline in manufacturing. This is not surprising for two reasons. First, a part of the measured decline in manufacturing and the growth of service activity has been the result of a process of increased vertical integration within industry whereby tasks previously performed by manufacturing have been subcontracted to specialist (service-type) agencies. This, in itself, means that services cannot be regarded as a substitute for manufacturing, but are part and parcel of the process of change in industrial organization. Secondly, many services are dependent for their existence on manufacturing, and if the demand for manufactured output declines, so does the demand for services in a vicious spiral downwards. It is an interesting empirical question, which needs further research, how many service activities have an autonomous existence, i.e. can survive and prosper independently of manufacturing.

Turning to the growth of GDP, the close association across countries between the growth of manufacturing and the pace of economic growth has already been mentioned. There are two main reasons for this close association. The first is that the faster manufacturing output grows, the faster productivity growth in manufacturing tends to be. This is sometimes called Verdoorn's Law. This relation is associated with static and dynamic returns to scale, which characterizes manufacturing. Such a relation is not nearly so marked in the case of service industries, and appears completely non-existent in land-based activities. The second reason is that the faster manufacturing grows, the faster productivity growth outside manufacturing tends to be where there is disguised unemployment or low productivity. When labour is unemployed it tends to eke out a living on the fringes of the industrial sector (in the petty service sector), and when this labour is absorbed through industrial growth, productivity naturally rises. This is still a major potential source of growth in some European countries which have a much larger agricultural sector than Britain.

As far as the balance of payments is concerned, the contraction of the British manufacturing industry is starting to have devastating consequences. Traditionally, Britain ran a deficit on visible trade financed by a surplus on the invisible account (i.e. earnings from insurance, shipping and other financial services provided by the City of London). Within the (negative) visible account, there was a surplus on manufactured trade which partially (but not entirely) helped to pay for a deficit in food and raw materials (including oil). In the last ten years or so, the situation has radically altered for the worse. The surplus on trade in manufactures has gradually dwindled. In 1983, there was a deficit for the first time in British economic history, and now the deficit is a staggering £10 billion or more. At the same time, the surplus on oil is diminishing, and will shortly disappear. This leaves the traditional surplus on invisible account to pay not only for the deficit in trade in food and raw materials, but also for Britain's insatiable appetite for foreign manufactured goods. The situation is clearly not sustainable, since there is no evidence that the service sector can generate the export earnings to finance such huge deficits. The House of Lords Committee on Overseas Trade (1985) estimated that only 20 per cent of service activities are tradeable, whereas, of course, virtually all manufactured goods are potentially tradeable. Moreover, international trade in service activities is hotting up. Already, Britain's share of world exports of services has fallen from 12 per cent in 1970 to 7 per cent today, and the decline looks like continuing.

In the long run, no country can grow faster than that rate consistent with balance of payments equilibrium on current account, since no country (apart, perhaps, from the United States) can finance continual deficits without running into severe debt problems and/or speculative attacks against its currency. The latter makes all the harder the goal of price stability, which is also the reason why countries are reluctant to resort to currency depreciation to rectify balance of payments disequilibrium, even if this were an efficient balance of payments adjustment weapon. Britain's growth rate consistent with balance of payments equilibrium has been the lowest of any industrialized country since the Second World War. Current estimates put the rate at under 2 per cent per annum if the current £15 billion deficit is to be reduced to manageable proportions, even allowing for some currency depreciation. Such a low rate will not be enough to stop unemployment rising, let alone reduce it. The major cause of Britain's low balance of payments equilibrium growth rate has been the neglect of the manufacturing sector, which has both lowered export growth and raised the propensity to import manufactured goods.

If Britain is to escape the syndrome of slow growth and rising unemployment, a combined industrial and trade strategy is urgently required to halt the decline of manufacturing industry. On the industrial front, there needs to be a forward-looking policy which concentrates on investment in technologically progressive industries, combined with policies of skill training and education, so that British industry produces goods the world (and the British public) want. Investment incentives have an important role to play in this regard. On the trade front, subtle forms of export promotion and import substitution are called for which do not violate the Treaty of Rome and other agreements, of the type that many other European countries (and Japan) adopt. Britain is far too polite in international trade. With some imagination, there is no reason why Britain should not acquire again a comparative advantage in the production of goods that once made it the workshop of the world, and sooner or later the European Economic Commission will have to address the question of structural surpluses and deficits in the balance of payments of member countries, particularly as 1992 approaches.

The present indifference to manufacturing seems destined to vindicate Napoleon's jibe about Britain being 'a nation of shopkeepers'. Services have an important part to play in the economy, but they do not provide the growth momentum of the manufacturing industry, nor can they be relied upon to substitute for the loss of employment and tradeable output caused by the weakness of manufacturing. The British economy is slipping into a gross state of imbalance with regard to the division of resources between manufacturing on the one hand and services on the other. A healthy economy requires a healthy manufacturing sector.

Notes

Deindustrialization: myths and realities

1   Services in the UK Economy, *Bank of England Quarterly Bulletin*, Vol. No. 3, September 1985.
2   P.J. Forsyth and J.A. Kay, *The Economic Implications of North Sea Oil Revenues*, Institute of Fiscal Studies, 1980.

3   Jurgen Niehaus, *The Appreciation of Sterling Causes, Effects, Policies*, Centre for Policy Studies, 1981.
4   Productivity Trends, *Bank of England Quarterly Bulletin*, Vol. No. 1, February 1989.

Manufacturing or services after 1992?

1   Since 1985, the 'groupement d'intérêt économique' has been part of European Community law. Perhaps unfortunately, Airbus Industrie is the best known example. It is a legal entity able to sue for its money but otherwise a partnership of any number of firms or individuals, without separate tax status. Profits or losses are simply divided among the partners and they pay or claim tax allowances accordingly. Its ideal application is as a means of exporting for a number of small companies which cannot individually sell to, say, China. It is the sort of acorn from which the Muscovy or the East India Company grew and complements mergers and acquisitions as a means of stimulating economic growth. There are fewer egos to bruise, it is cheaper in time and legal fees, and it is capable of adaption to different circumstances.
2   Michael Breitenacher, Sergio Paba and Gianpaolo Rossini, *The Cost of Non-Europe in the Textile-Clothing Industry*, Final Report, Executive Summary, The Commission of the European Communities, December 1987, Vol. I, 487.

Manufacturing versus services – a false dichotomy?

1   *The House of Lords Select Committee on Overseas Trade*, Oral Evidence Volume II, 1985, Question 1381, 24 April 1985, 474.
2   Reproduced in *The Listener*, 10 April 1986.
3   Bank of England, *Services in the UK Economy*, Bank of England Quarterly Bulletin, Vol. 25, No. 3, September 1983, 408.
4   Gunter A. Pauli, *Services: the Engine of the European Economy*, European Services Industries Forum, undated, 87.
5   Dorothy I. Riddle, *Service-Led Growth*. Praeger Publishing, 1986.
6   Amin Rajan, *Services – The Second Industrial Revolution?*, Butterworth, 1987.

The service sector is also productive

1   J.R. McCulloch, *The Principles of Political Economy*, First Edition, Edinburgh, 1825, 406–7.
2   K. Marx, *Capital*, Three volumes, republished in 1974, Progress Publishers, for Lawrence & Wishart, Moscow.
3   A. Smith, *An Inquiry into the Nature and Causes of the Wealth of Nations*, republished, R.H. Campbell, A.S. Skinner and W.B. Todd (eds), 1976, Two volumes, as Vol. II of *The Glasgow Edition of the Works and Correspondence of Adam Smith*, 33.
4   N. Kaldor, *Causes of the Slow Rate of Growth of the United Kingdom* (inaugural lecture), Cambridge University Press, Cambridge, 1966.
5   The full implications of this approach are set out in: R. Rowthorn, 'What Remains of Kaldor's Law?' *Economic Journal*, March, 1975.
6   R. Bacon and E. Eltis, *Britain's Economic Problem: Too Few Producers*, Macmillan, London, 1976.

12 Europe

Demographic trends in the industrial world: Europe's declining population?

David Coleman
Source: *Economic Affairs*, June/July 1989, 9, 5, p. 6.

The industrial world is developing new demographic patterns which have major implications for their economies, politics and international relations. These new features can include the following: life expectation of 75 years or more, birth rates chronically low, actual or incipient population decline, age-structures where the numbers of the elderly approach or exceed the numbers of children, a fragmented family pattern and a small average household size, substantial and growing non-Western racial minorities. This combination has no historical precedent.

Many of these trends require changes in policy on pensions, employment, family support and possibly immigration. It is not all bad news. In the short run, current low fertility and slow increases in the number of pensioners until the turn of the century, are easing the pressure on public expenditure. But longer term trends in pensions will increase costs to taxpayers or threaten the maintenance of state pensions levels. Low fertility will lead to inflationary wage pressures following a shortage of young workers, while voting power will shift towards older people.

Europe, North America, Australasia and Japan have had below replacement fertility since the early 1970s. Hong Kong and Singapore joined this group a few years ago; so have all the Eastern European countries except the USSR, Poland and Romania. In the industrial world the current fertility rates of women are equivalent to a family size between 1.9 (with some minor exceptions) and 1.3 children. This rate is known as the Period Total Fertility Rate (PTFR) and an average value of 2.1 is required for long term population replacement (see Table 12.1).

This is an abrupt reversal from the high birth rates of the baby boom which peaked a quarter of a century ago.[1] Then, the trend was to earlier and more popular marriage than for centuries. Universal family planning permitted earlier marriage without the consequent penalty of larger family size. Consequent earlier child-bearing, shorter intervals between births, together with some increase in completed family size, greatly increased the size of annual birth cohorts. Now, average age at marriage is back to near the levels of 1950 and, as at that time, high proportions may remain unmarried. The big difference is the popularity of cohabiting couples. Almost one in four of all births today are illegitimate. It seems likely that the low level of birth rates today can be substantially attributed to delays in births rather than smaller than average final completed family size.[2] But although today's PTFR of 1.8 may exaggerate the decline of family size, there are good reasons for supposing that fertility will be permanently reduced, and less volatile, than in the recent past. Recent UK population projections have assumed that the PTFR will stabilize at 2.0.

The main justification for this assertion is that a large number of married women are now part of the workforce and there is every reason to suppose that they will stay there. 62 per cent of married women in the UK now go out to work (part-time as well as full-time), compared with about 10 per cent in the 1930s and only 20 per cent even in the 1950s. Low participation rates in the 1950s, together with the mid-twentieth century fall in age at marriage, enabled the post-war economic recovery to generate one last classic Malthusian fertility fling in the form of the baby boom of the 1950s and 1960s. But now the old relationship between fertility and economic growth has been upset by the rising contribution of women's wages to the domestic budget. Not only are many more married women working, thanks to the Equal Pay Act of 1970 the incomes they earn are more equal to those of men.[3]

The new relationship is complex.[4] Women's contribution to the household economy has become important, sometimes indispensible for the maintenance of living standards. This contribution is incompatible with frequent or protracted child-bearing. Because of opportunity costs, income growth may now make child-bearing more expensive, not more affordable as in the past. By the same token, marriage is now less advantageous or necessary for women and tends to be delayed or avoided. Some estimates put the opportunity cost of a two-child family up to about £120,000; estimates for the US tend to give more emphasis to the direct costs.[5]

As well as income, work gives independence to women. It promotes divorce and helps to insure against its consequences. The high risks are now well known. Divorce will end 32 per cent of marriages by their 25th anniversary in the UK, 54 per cent in the USA. An increasing number of family incomes and standards of living now depend on the wife's contribution. For these and other reasons it seems likely that the married woman's place is now permanently in the workforce. They have certainly shown more staying power there than men, on both sides of the Atlantic, in the shake-out of labour after 1979.

With fertility low, there is increased interest in consequences for the

Table 12.1 Fertility and population in EC countries

Country	PTFR 1985	Population 1988	Population 2020
Belgium	1.5	9.9	9.1
Denmark	1.4	5.1	4.8
FRG	1.3	61.2	51.5
France	1.8	55.9	58.7
Greece	1.7	10.1	10.1
Ireland	2.5	3.5	4.8
Italy	1.5	57.3	52.6
Luxembourg	1.4	0.4	0.4
Netherlands	1.5	14.7	14.7
Portugal	1.9	10.3	10.5
Spain	1.8	39.0	40.7
UK	1.8	57.1	56.6
All EC	—	324.5	314.5
Turkey	3.6	52.9	87.5

Source: United Nations 1986, Council of Europe 1987.

population of trends in mortality and international migration. Now that smoking is on the decline (less so in women) improvement in rates of survival has speeded up again after a hiatus in the 1960s, especially among the later middle-aged and elderly. There is little room left for improvement in infant or child mortality (where the lowest rates are now to be found in Japan, Hong Kong and Singapore). Young male adult mortality has remained relatively unchanged thanks to traffic accidents, homicide (1 per cent of deaths in USA) and more recently AIDS (especially in the USA, where there were 13,130 AIDS deaths in 1987).

In the industrial world, expectation of life at birth for males is from 71–6, for females from 75–81. Sweden and Japan both have female life expectancy over 80. Average male survival from birth in the Western world is projected to increase at least to 75 years and female to 80 by 2010. Falling mortality is now making a greater contribution to the numbers of elderly. Many more will survive to retirement and beyond – in increasingly good health. This means an expectation of retired life (from age 65) of up to 20 years; compared to 15 at most in the 1960s.

The demographic impact of AIDS is most difficult to predict. Much depends on whether it spreads among heterosexuals. There are already enough HIV infected cases (between 1 million and 1.5 million in the USA, 20–50,000 in the UK) to guarantee a major epidemic of deaths and because of the long survival of cases, a substantial claim on resources. But the rate of increase of new cases seems to be slowing.[6] The latest UK population projections incorporate the effects of AIDS for the first time, assuming for example that 1.6 per cent of men born about 1960 would die of AIDS, mostly before age 50, and that the epidemic will claim about 200,000 male lives, 100,000 of them by the end of the century.[7]

Little will be said about migration in this article. It is usually a minor component of national population change. However this is less true of the USA, Canada and Australia, and it is becoming less true of the UK as well. Since 1982 the UK has become a net importer of population, reversing its previous traditional position. This has resulted in the 1987-based population projections being 1 million higher for 2021 than the previous projections (54.4 compared to 53.3 million). It is now assumed that continued net immigration to the UK of 20,000 from the New Commonwealth, together with 5,000 from the Irish Republic and 20,000 from the EC and other foreign countries, will offset the net loss of emigrating British citizens. Net gain from migrants 1981–2021 will be 913,000 compared to the previous projection of 227,000, plus a second generation effect of 350,000 extra births.[7]

The most important effects are on total population and its age-structure. Continuing sub-replacement fertility will undermine, stop and eventually reverse population growth. Population size in West and East Germany, Denmark and Hungary is already declining. By 2025 these countries will have been joined by Belgium, Sweden, Italy, with the UK, Japan and others soon to follow. Partly because of the reversal of net migration trends and improved survival despite AIDS, the population of England and Wales is projected to remain buoyant, increase from 50.2 million today by a further 2.3 million by 2001 and 4.8 million by 2027. US, Canadian, Australian population growth, still robust today thanks to a more youthful population and high immigration, will depend more and more upon immigration.

Table 12.2 Population projections in selected countries 1985–2025 (millions)

Period	USA	Japan	Germany	France	Turkey
1950	152	84	50	42	21
1960	181	94	55	46	28
1970	205	104	61	51	35
1980	228	117	62	54	44
1985	238	121	61	55	49
1990	248	124	60	55	55
1995	259	127	60	56	60
2000	268	130	59	57	65
2010	286	133	57	58	76
2020	304	133	55	58	88
2025	312	132	53	58	92

Source: UN 1986 World Population Prospects.
Estimates and projections as assessed in 1984.
Population Studies No 98, New York, UN.

In consequence, there will be a considerable shift in the relative size of the major industrial groups of countries, with political and strategic as well as economic consequences. With present membership, EC population will decline slightly from 325 million today to 316 million in 2020. Eastern Europe will increase only slightly, from 113 to 122 in 2020. Japan is forecast to peak at about 133 compared to today's 123 million (see Table 12.2). The USA, assuming continued immigration, will just exceed 300 million by that time. But the Soviet Union, thanks mostly to its fast growing Asian Muslim populations, will exceed 400 million. These are only projections. They may turn out to be wrong. No one forecast the baby boom and no one forecast its end. But that boom is likely to have been a unique event. And the forecasts are reasonably secure in the short run, because then they depend primarily upon persons already born, and therefore on the more predictable mortality rate.

The age structure is determined primarily by the historical series of birth totals, to a lesser extent by trends in survival. Western populations have been aging all this century because of the long-term decline in the birth rate from high Victorian levels. In Britain, the proportion of over sixty-fives in the population has accordingly increased from 5 per cent in 1911 to 15 per cent today. Much of the bill for an aging population has already been paid. The proportion over age sixty-five in the stable population corresponding to today's fertility and mortality is not much higher – about 20 per cent. But long term trends are not the only things that matter.

The unprecedented volatility of fertility in the twentieth century – the birth dearths and baby booms – have had even more important short-term effects on the age-structure, temporarily overriding longer-term effects. For example, a worsening of the ratio of pensioners to taxpayers is an inevitable consequence of long-term population aging. But from the 2020s it will be made much worse by the entry into pensionable age of the large baby boom cohorts born in the 1950s and 1960s. They will not be balanced by any corresponding increase in the number of working age people. Instead these must be recruited then from the low fertility birth cohorts of the 1970s and 1980s and – probably – the 1990s.

As a result, Western age structures by 2030 will typically comprise 18–20 per cent aged under 15 (20 per cent in England and Wales), 19–24 per cent over age sixty-five (19 per cent in England and Wales). West Germany is already the first country ever where the number of children under fifteen has been exceeded by the number over sixty-five. That position will become normal. But after the 2030s, when the baby boom is queueing at the pearly gates, the demographic position will improve again.

In the short-run the industrial countries will enjoy a period of relative stability. The baby boom is now safely accommodated within the workforce. Until the end of the century future recruits to the pensionable age-groups will not increase much. Those now approaching age sixty-five were born in the period of declining fertility after the First World War, and therefore come from stationary or declining birth cohort sizes. Such growth as does occur to pensioner population comes from the (very expensive) older population over age seventy-five and especially over eighty-five, born to the increasing birth cohorts before the First World War. In addition to this all these age groups are growing because survival at older age is increasing. So general statements about rapidly increasing numbers of the elderly do not necessarily apply in the short-run. There is no current pensioner crisis in terms of total numbers, which in England and Wales will remain constant at about 9.4 million for the rest of the century.

These trends are common in varying degrees of severity to all parts of the Western Industrial World. In the USA the baby boom was unusually large and protracted (see Figure 12.1). The USA, unlike Europe, had a good war. Eastern Europe and the USSR have experienced general aging of their populations but no severe distortions caused by baby booms because they experienced no surge in individual living standards in the post-war years. Japan is a partial exception. Until the end of the Second World War it had much higher fertility than any other industrial country. From the middle 1940s this declined abruptly to reach a level similar to that of the rest of today's industrial world but generating *en route* a very different age-structure. Discontinuities in age-structure, caused by the abrupt decline and its later echo, produces bulges at different age-groups from those in the West. Starting from an originally youthful population, Japan now has the most rapidly aging population of any industrial country.

The problems of pensions and dependency, especially to pay-as-you-go state pension schemes, are now well known even to governments. Population aging has shaken the foundations of the welfare systems, set up especially in Europe earlier this century, from which earlier generations have benefited so much, and for which more recent generations will have to pay so much. Only Japan, the USA and the UK have taken steps to accommodate the problems of 2020 and beyond – which cannot be entirely resolved. The US has increased contributions to its partly-funded state pensions scheme and pushed back statutory retirement ages. The British Government's attempts initially to abolish, but now only to limit, the hugely expensive State Earnings-Related Pension Scheme (SERPS) is another example.[8] Now the other end of the problem – the immediate consequences of the low birth rate since the 1970s – is claiming public attention because of its threatened effects on the young workforce.

No one would have believed it would ever be possible to have too few teenagers. It is only a few years since politicians were fretting over youth unemployment and citing demography and the baby boom as one of the chief causes of their problems. The rapid reversal of the problem is a consequence of the volatility which universal family planning has given to fertility. Figure 12.2 shows the course of the numbers of persons aged 15–19, which can be forecast with confidence at least until 2005. It will be seen

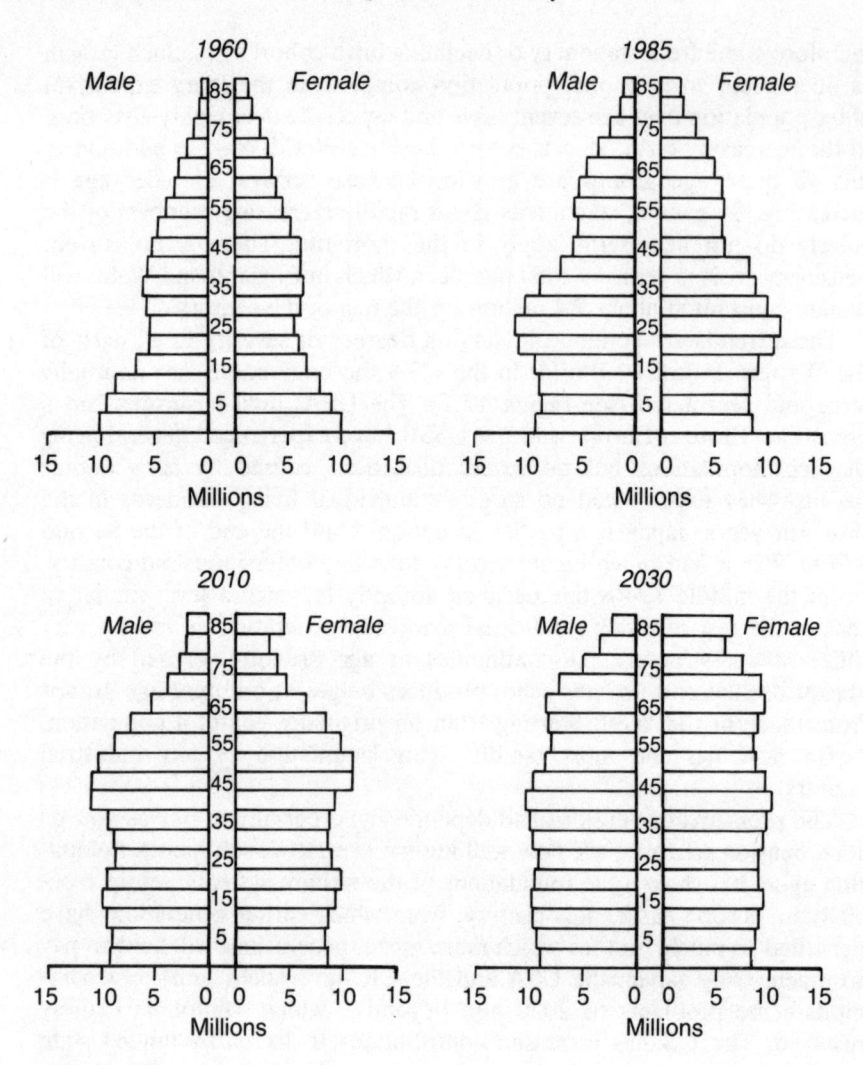

294 *Recent controversies in political economy*

Figure 12.1 The baby boom in the USA (US population–age pyramids)
Source: Population Reference Bureau, Inc., Washington, DC

that part of the problem arises through comparison with the immediately preceding cohorts which were inflated to unusually large size by the baby boom. We are in fact returning more to the position of the early 1950s and 1930s, which may help to put it into slightly more favourable perspective. According to the latest estimates, the numbers of 15–19 year olds will decline abruptly from 3.8 million in 1987 to 3.2 million in 1991 (a decline of 15.3 per cent). But the decline will end by about 1996 (3.1 million, a further fall of 5.3 per cent) if current fertility projections are justified. From then onwards, numbers in this age-group will increase again as a result of

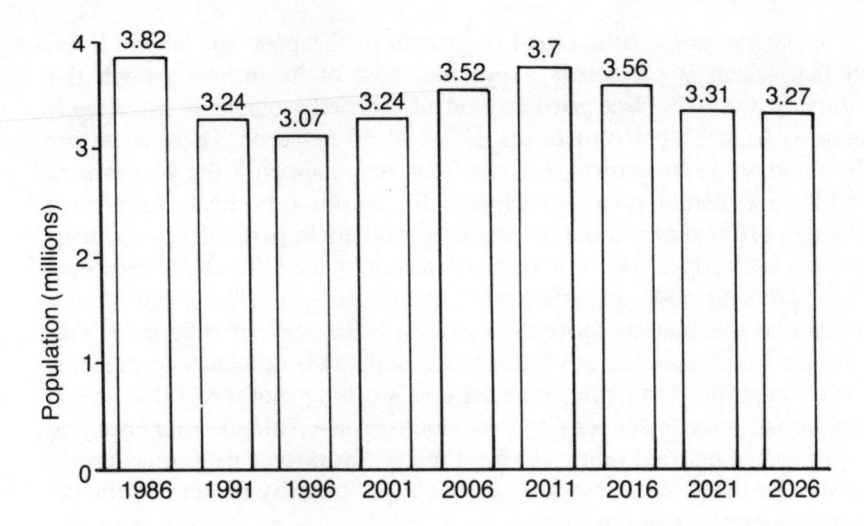

Figure 12.2 England and Wales population aged 15–19, 1986–2026
Source: OPCS Monitor PP2 89/1 to 4 year

the maturing of the larger birth cohorts of the present day, the offspring of the large number of baby boom mothers now approaching peak reproductive age. From then onwards numbers will increase again to reach 3.7 million by 2011, not far short of their present number.

What will be the consequences? Certainly the good old days when employers could take their pick of the young, including graduates, and impose more or less their own conditions for employment have gone. If new attitudes among youth and the need for skills are not firmly established by now, then market forces may ensure they cannot become established for the foreseeable future. But there are other sources of employment, which were somewhat neglected when there was such a glut of youth. Partly in order to deal with the now receding threat of unemployment, early retirement was encouraged in most industrial countries. But now circumstances have changed.

Rates of participation in the workforce of men over age fifty-five are now low and declining throughout the West. It no longer needs encouragement for demographic or unemployment reasons, quite the reverse. In any case pensioners now do much better than they did. One of the results of longer survival is that the debilitating diseases which cause disability as well as premature death are declining (although in the UK slower than elsewhere) leaving healthier and more active, as well as longer lived pensioners. Many would welcome longer employment, even if part-time. And their numbers will greatly increase, at least for a while, after the turn of the century. Retirement age itself has been reconsidered in the USA and Japan. Recent Government statements have hinted at similar measures in Britain.

The biggest single component of growth in the post-war labour force, and that which is projected to provide most of its further growth this century, is the workforce participation of married women. It has already increased from 20 per cent in the 1950s to 60 per cent. There is further substantial scope for growth. But that may only happen if the government provides a coherent policy of support for working mothers. At present child support in general, and for working mothers in particular, is the least generous in Europe. Such women are deterred by the difficulty of returning to their previous post, or holding it for a while part-time. European surveys suggest that this matters more than help with the costs of child care. This raises the wider question of whether such support is necessary to preserve or even raise the birth rate, especially as working mothers, other things being equal, have lower fertility than housewives. Without compensation, recruitment of married women to meet today's workforce needs may prejudice the size of the future workforce, as low-productivity Eastern European countries have long discovered.

Such issues were last raised by the Royal Commission on Population in its 1949 Report. In the long run there is a national interest in the number of workers and consumers of the future. If conditions have changed to increase the relative burden on those families that produce the citizens of the future, then it may be in the national interest to help them more than at present. It has been suggested that renewed immigration be reconsidered to balance the population account. The only likely source is the poorer countries of the third world. Economic and social arguments seem overwhelmingly against it. The social problems associated with assimilating the already large third world populations in most West European societies are already difficult enough. Present unemployment rules out the option at the moment. There is no need to perpetuate social problems and bad work practices by evading labour shortages with imported workers.

The challenges presented by population change can instead be met in other ways. Most usefully, these changes should concentrate attention further on the biggest problem still facing the British economy – its low productivity and high unit labour costs, despite recent gains. Liberalizing the pattern of retirement and recruitment of older people will not only help solve the temporary shortage of young recruits to the workforce; it will recognise the new realities of better health and longer survival and help resolve the pensions problem as well.

European Community or imperial superstate?

Norman Stone
Source: *Economic Affairs*, August/September 1989, 9, 6, p. 16.

Politicians often blow their own trumpets, but in the parliament of Habsburg Vienna, they did so quite literally. Before 1914, Germans, Slavs and Italians sat together in it. The various languages could all be officially spoken, but hatreds on lines of nationality were sometimes such that deputies tried to drown each other out – banging of desk-tops, hurtling of statute-books and, on a famous occasion, the blowing of a cavalry trumpet by a Professor of Law at the (German) University of Prague. He was protesting because a Ukrainian deputy was obstructing parliamentary business with a twelve-hour speech – in Russian, not a recognized language, but one that some Ukrainians regarded as the literary form of Ukrainian.

Of course that parliament – the Reichsrat – became unworkable, discrediting the whole liberal experiment in Habsburg Austria. Efforts to combine the Germans, Czechs, Poles, Ukrainians, Italians, Slovenes, Dalmation Croats (there were also some Serbs and Romanians, along with other much smaller minorities) in a parliament workable enough to pass a budget were a failure, and in 1914 it was all closed down; the Prime Minister just ruled by decree. The most famous expression in Austrian politics says it all: a cynical long-term Prime Minister, Count Taaffe, recorded to his financial adviser, Baron Sieghart, that 'I have no political ambition beyond the achievement, all round, of a state of supportable dissatisfaction'. The descendants of both men – the one a descendant of Irish mercenary officers, the other the outcome of Jewish emancipation – soon, incidentally, moved to England, where these things were so much better arranged.

It is perhaps unjust to take the Austrian imperial parliament as an example of multinational bodies. In the Habsburg monarchy of the later nineteenth century, national rivalries ran high for reasons that had nothing much to do with an unworkable constitution. In Bohemia or Slovenia, the Slavs had been recovering a language and an identity after centuries of being told that both were inferior to German; there were similar problems with Italians, with both Slavs and (in the Tyrol) Germans. As people required education, there were battles over schools and their language of instruction; there were battles as to which should be the language of civil-service memoranda, and hence over the nationality of civil servants. For a time, the working-class party was immune from these mainly middle-class quarrels, but in time they, too, divided, since skilled workers were usually German-speaking, resentful of Slavonic semi-skilled or unskilled migrant labour, and anxious to keep control of trade-union or Party jobs. By 1910 both socialists and political Catholics, representative of the masses, defied their own purported internationalism and divided into Czech, German, Slovenes and so on.

Yet, when the Austrian constitution was adopted in the 1860s, the hope had been that a parliament of several nationalities would somehow create amity and cooperation. At that time, even in Bohemia, there were several utraquists – men, usually of a Catholic but classical-liberal persuasion, who themselves had no difficulty in speaking the other nation's language, sympathized with its aspirations, and enjoyed friendships on the other side of the linguistic line. One such was Count Leo Thun-Hohenstein, who promoted education and, in 1890, very nearly brought about an agreement between Czechs and Germans. On the side of the linguistic minorities, there was often a great deal of fraud – forgery of historical documents, invention of linguistic peculiarities, and downright hypocrisy.

However, the effort to overcome national differences by a multinational parliament made things worse, not better. In the first place, the issue of language dominated everything, and the parliament's business would be endlessly obstructed even by small minorities because of it. The German deputies, some of them of Czech origin, regarded Czech, say, as a peasant dialect, not fit for use by educated people, discussing serious public business. Now, to solve the problem of nationality, the Habsburg monarchy devised endless schemes. The first answer was to set up bureaucratic posts. After all, if everyone were guaranteed a state pension, they might then prove to be ultra-loyal to the State. The number of bureaucrats in Austria became something of a European joke: there were nearly four million of them, in a population of fifty million – in comparison with the British million-plus, the German two million.

Habsburg Austria became the classic country of the civil servant with his masses of paper. Nationalization of everything in sight was a constant danger – education, hospitals, the railways, canals, water, city transport, utilities in general, and much of the armaments industry came under the State's control, at a time when State control in other parts of Europe was a very long way from such luxuriance. Armies of resentful small civil servants worked this cumbersome machine, complete with plans and schemes for bureaucratic streamlining which never got anywhere. Civil servants, badly-paid but tenured, set the tone for the last years of the monarchy. The counterpart was a level of taxation which could only be escaped through dishonesty; and every such tax payment needed to go through 25 different transactions. The State itself functioned badly because of this. There was not very much money to pay for the armed forces, for instance – armed forces with a formidable tradition, and of which Grillparzer's comment, 'In your camp lies Austria', was true. The Habsburg monarchy had been kept together by the military, and the military were genuinely multinational. True, if you wanted to 'get on' then German, the language of command, was essential, but there was plenty of room for other languages.

The armed forces of Austria were unique in Europe of the later nineteenth century because, as the population doubled and trebled, they got smaller, not bigger. In theory, universal liability to conscription was introduced in 1868. The population of military-age men then more than doubled up to 1914. However, the army which took the field in 1914 contained fewer units than the army which had fought Prussia in 1866. The reason for this was simple enough. By far the largest item in a military budget was food, clothing and housing. If the army authorities had taken in all of the conscripts capable of bearing arms, they would have spent way beyond their budget, and would have been unable to pay for equipment, artillery etc. The budget constrained by all of the spending on bureaucracy, was under £25,000,000 – less than the British Army's budget, even though the British Army, with six divisions, was about one-tenth of the Austrian Army's size. In such circumstances, the Austrian War Ministry could train only a third of the available conscripts.

By 1914, the Austrian army had even been reduced to abolishing its military bands, its greatest glory, in order to save money for the infantry. That the Radetzky March should have been sacrificed, in the end, for countless meaningless civil-service pensions was a powerful comment on the Habsburgs' efforts to devise a multinational structure, where proper devolution would have been the obvious answer.

Owls of Minerva fly out, as we all know, by night. What is very curious about the later stages of the Habsburg Empire is the intellectual output that emerged: in many ways, the worse, the better. Vienna 1900 now has the status of a cliché, I hope that Budapest 1900 will some day have a similar status, because it is just as interesting. The Austrian School of economists has lately been coming back to favour, as Marxists and Keynesians alike lose their power. Joseph Schumpeter, the last of them, grew up in Habsburg Vienna (serving for a brief and surreal moment at the Franz-Josefs-Universitat, Czernowitz which, in the remote Bukovina, is now in the Soviet Ukraine). In so many ways Schumpeter had the right answers: on the relationship of technology, the business cycle and inflation he can still be read with profit. Now, these bright Austrians seem to have been all the better at theory because practice in the Austrian Empire was so woeful; when, coming to this country or the United States later on, they had the chance to fit theory in countries that worked without the Habsburgs' baroque efforts in bureaucracy and legalism, they had an immensely powerful impact. In multinational Austria, your feet were clogged at every turn; the only way forward was to join the rush of people with degrees in administrative law, a concept that had virtually no equivalent in the English speaking world until the day before yesterday.

Austrian emigrants to this country, from Namier and Redlich to the refugees of the 1930s (such as F.A. Hayek), had a good idea as to what was right about English practice. Unsatisfactory as it often was, it worked, usually with informality. In many ways it was more stuffily conservative than the Habsburg monarchy: the House of Lords, for instance, was a great deal less progressive than the Austrian Herrenhaus, in which representatives of the cities, the universities, and the chiefs of the main churches (including Jews) were represented. But in England in which bureaucratic formality was kept to a minimum, and where parliamentary bodies were not required to do more than they were competent to do, acted as a magnet for sensible central Europeans. It is worth considering the implications of all of this nowadays, as we contemplate the possibility of a multinational Europe.

There have been very, very few cases of successful cooperation, within a single body, by people of different language and nationality. The United States contains many peoples, of course, but they have been anglicized as far as language is concerned. The Soviet Union also manages to combine various languages and peoples – over one hundred – but the methods of control are such that the formula can hardly be recommended. The one obvious case in which people of different nationality have worked together is Switzerland. Her history is in fact much more turbulent than legend allows (pace Orson Welles's famous aside, in *The Third Man*, to the effect that Switzerland had had five hundred years of brotherly love and produced the cuckoo-clock: the fact is that Swiss history has been quite bloody, and that the Swiss have produced a long line of distinguished contributors to French civilization, including Benjamin Constant, Voltaire and the scientifically-distinguished Monod dynasty). But in recent times, French, German and Italian speakers have cooperated well, and the country is the most prosperous in Europe. It is also an exception: in the first place, neutral, such that internal problems were never aggravated, as happened in the Habsburg monarchy, by external involvements. Otherwise, the story is not very encouraging. In Spain, there is to this day a sort of Northern Ireland in the Basque provinces, and Catalonia, until very recently, was an ulcer. In Belgium, the cumbersome bureaucratic devices by which Flemish and Walloon parts live together are extremely expensive, have led to large taxes, and are sometimes comic in their results. (In Louvain, ten years ago, I was once faced by a telephone operator who knew both French and English perfectly well, but who was forbidden to talk either in public service. In the end, once I started to talk German with a thick Glasgow accent, in the hope of being comprehensible in Dutch, she broke the rule; we both laughed for a long time.)

It seems to me to be simply a matter of common sense that different nationalities should not be compelled to cooperate in single bodies except for very well-defined purposes.

Of such cooperation, there are many historical examples in the later nineteenth century: free-trade areas do require collaboration in endless detailed and fussy matters, such as hygienic controls for animals, or railway-freight charges for various goods, or insurance-provisions. These are all detailed and complicated; sorting them out takes much good will. By and large, where there has been a will, there has also been a way. The German Customs Unions of the 1830s, the *Zollverein*, was one such. That body has been much misunderstood. J.M. Keynes remarked, quite wrongly, that it had led the way to the unification of Germany under Bismarck. On the contrary, it made that unification less necessary, and anyway did not prevent the southern and Catholic German states from declaring war on Prussia, their *Zollverein* partner, in 1866. The customs union existed to promote free trade within Germany (excluding Austria) and it had a central parliament, the Customs Parliament, to sort out the details. It worked uninspiringly, but it worked. When the German liberals tried to get a proper parliament to discuss the making of a liberal Germany in 1848, that was a quite different matter. That body, containing endless professors, usually of law, talked and talked in the Paulskirche in the old capital of the Holy Roman Empire, Frankfurt. The talking led in the end to three things, all of them preposterous for liberals. In the first place, eastern Europeans were declared to be a fit prey for Germany. Then, a decision was taken to build up a navy by street-corner collection. Finally, when the working classes began to make rude noises, the Prussian army was called in, and the King of Prussia, a militarist, was invited to be German Emperor. Far from *Zollverein*, even in a country with one language creating unity, *Zollverein* was a substitute, and unity still had to be created by force of arms.

There is a final point to make about international organizations. Where they are separated from any root in popular consciousness, their decisions are apt to become utterly unreal. The League of Nations is a classic case. In the 1920s, it might (like the United Nations later on) achieve small-scale progress in limited areas of international cooperations, such as the suppression of the white slave trade or the quiet exchange of populations between Bulgaria and Turkey. Once contentious large-scale issues came up, these bodies became worse than useless – providing the illusion of a solution. When War broke out in September 1939, the League of Nations discussed the standardization of level-crossings, and its only cognizance of the War came later on, when it expelled the Soviet Union for invading Finland.

Conclusions for the New Europe? History makes them, I believe, obvious. Cooperation between states and nations is inevitable, and thoroughly desirable. We all have things to learn from one another, and, at the time time of writing, I am thoroughly impressed by Germany, in particular. But let us not pretend that this cooperation needs to have anything very considerable in the way of a supra-national bureaucracy, in the manner of the Habsburgs. Let us not pretend that a multinational parliament is ever either popular or workable. Every single historical case of which I know – even including that of the very similar Sweden and Norway, which amicably went their separate ways in 1905 – indicates that language and nationality have to be treated as the most important given. The *Zollverein* was not glamorous. Its long-term president rejoined in the name, Baron von Itzenplitz. The good Baron dealt in nuts and bolts, and picked nits. But nits, as I was told in my first Cambridge supervision, are there to be picked; and if Europe forgets that lesson in small-scale international collaboration, it will overreach what it can properly do, and end up as a Habsburg cacophony.

1992 and beyond: market freedom or collectivist regulation?

Martin Holmes
Source: *Economic Affairs*, August/September 1989, 9, 6, p. 10.

In recent months the debate about the nature of the European economy after 1992 has come into sharper focus. On the one hand the proponents of a single market open for business, as the Department of Trade and Industry publicity envisages it, have stressed the benefits of a free market of 320 million potential customers liberated from economic regulations ranging from the abolition of exchange controls to the facilitation of a flexible labour market. The Bruges Group, established to support the Prime Minister's position as expressed in her much quoted speech in Bruges last September, fully supports the single market as the 'Thatcherization of Europe' to borrow Lord Young's phrase.

But on the other hand a quite different vision of the European economy after 1992 has emerged at first covertly but later more boldly. This school of thought favours the 'social dimension', supports protectionism to defend European industry and envisages a regulated collectivism to nullify the competitive effects of the Single Market. Jacques Delors first expressed such views in Britain at the 1988 TUC Conference where he was gleefully perceived as delivering the unions from the reforms of the past decade by Europe-wide socialist measures. At the same time Chancellor Kohl, in his Georgetown speech in Washington, stressed the limits of global market competition with a clear protectionist and even autarkic implication. President Mitterand, in his New Year broadcast to the French people echoed the same sentiments believing that European trade is among partners but other trade is against rivals. The ubiquitous M. Delors illustrated the point by the undisguised relish with which he imposed the European ban on American beef imports on the wholly unscientific and spurious grounds of hormone content. It was no surprise that, not to be outdone, Neil Kinnock told the BBC in March that the social dimension was the socialist dimension, a view which has prompted a swift Labour Party policy review of the European Community.

There is very little consensus, therefore, on either how far the single market will have evolved by 1992 or how far it will be sustainable given the collectivist opposition. Once again there appears to be a divergence as to how the Community is projected to develop and how it actually develops. The current debate is reminiscent of the early 1970s plans for 'European economic and monetary union by 1980'. Mr Heath spoke of little else. Predicting the European Community's future economic path is consequently fraught with uncertainty and in the wake of the Single European Act it is understandable that free market opinion should be alarmed as Sir John Hoskyns 'collectivized utopia' speech demonstrated. Without becoming unduly pessimistic it is possible that many of the economic and labour market achievements since 1979 could be put at risk, nullified by majority vote rulings from the community. One only has to consider proposals already on the collectivists' agenda to understand this threat – European minimum wage laws, workers on boards by law, and aspects of tax harmonization which raise prices and costs. For anyone who thinks that such threats are too general to cause undue concern, one recent proposal from the European Commission provides a bizarre and illuminating example. Fearful that the small imitation plastic food displayed in butchers' shops will be accidentally eaten by children the Commission is proposing to make all plastic food and fish illegal. This would include the six foot long plastic bananas and fish used by football supporters and would cost 30,000 jobs in the United Kingdom if implemented. No wonder the pessimists have doubted the future freedom of the internal market.

The greatest threat, however, probably comes from the emergence by stealth of a protectionist Europe rather than from the internal dilution of the single market. At the moment, the Community is careful to reassure the rest of the world that the completion of the single market will not be a prelude for increases in the CET (Common External Tariff). But the effect of the social dimension – if it is ever fully realized – will be to substantially raise labour costs considerably higher than those in Japan and the United States Pacific Basin. In such circumstances protectionist pressures would be overwhelming from both producers fearful of foreign competition and also trade unions wishing to preserve jobs. The result would be a mothballed inefficient corporate state arrangement similar to that which existed in Britain before 1979 and which still keeps the highly protected industries of countries such as Mexico and India from realizing anything but a fraction of their true potential. In the motor industry for example it is competition which has seen the revival of Jaguar and the Rover Group. By contrast, the strict protectionism of the Mitterrand Government regarding Japanese imports only damages the French motor industry by shielding it from rationalization.

Moreover there is a specific British fear about the emergence of protectionism which is less relevant in other EEC countries. More than its Community partners Britain has a diverse global pattern of trade and investments. British companies now invest more in the United States than Japan, and British ownership of American real estate has also overtaken the Japanese. Of Britain's overseas investments, 60 per cent are in the United States, 20 per cent in the European Community and 20 per cent in the rest of the world. Indeed the proportion of investment in the community has fallen in the 1980s from 29 per cent. Any anti-American,

Fortress Europe protectionism would be a self-evident disaster for the British economy. The balance of payments figures – albeit an inaccurate guide as a Treasury rightly points out – confirm this trading pattern. In the year up to September 1988, Britain had a balance of payments deficit of £13 billion with the European Community but a £10 billion deficit with the rest of the world. In itself this is no cause for undue concern as the purpose of exports is to pay for imports; providing that British trade is flourishing elsewhere, a deficit with Europe need not matter. But in a protectionist regime of an increased CET, the British position would become acute in structural terms and quite different from the current £14 billion balance of payments deficit caused by domestic overheating. Britain's export strength in the world market is dependent on the avoidance of a protectionist Fortress Europe.

In the same vein the protectionist nature of the CAP has proved deleterious to the British economy. The CAP is the very opposite of Thatcherism. It is the world's biggest protectionist organization outside the Communist bloc and recent reforms have barely scratched the surface of price fixing, subsidies, excessive bureaucracy, dumping and destruction of food, and a gross misallocation of economic resources. In a relatively neglected passage of her Bruges speech, Mrs. Thatcher said:

> The task of reforming the CAP is far from complete. Certainly, Europe needs a stable and efficient farming industry. But the CAP has become unwieldy, inefficient and grossly expensive. Production of unwanted surpluses safeguards neither the income nor the future of farmers themselves. We must continue to pursue policies which relate supply more closely to market requirements and which will reduce overproduction and limit costs. Of course, we must protect the villages and rural areas which are such an important part of our national life – but not by the instrument of agricultural prices.

As readers of previous issues of *Economic Affairs* will be aware, the CAP has not even helped the farmers (with a few exceptions) and has led to major distortions in world trade. The cost of CAP protectionism against the Third World is twice as great as the amount of EC aid. Up to 400,000 jobs have been lost in European manufacturing industry because of the removal of comparative advantage caused by CAP. In a year in which Comic Relief raised £16 million, the CAP will spend £90 million on the destruction of apples alone. And a £6 billion annual fraud involving both the IRA and the Mafia as beneficiaries has been acknowledged by both the Community's own accountants and in the House of Lords Select Committee report in March 1989.

The most damning analysis of the domestic economic damage of the CAP was produced in September 1989 by Mrs Sally Oppenheim-Barnes' National Consumer Council which reported that:

Whatever the high hopes and noble aims with which it was founded ... it has proved to be inefficient, to exploit consumers and to stand in the way of the development of a true Common Market. The drain on Community resources has prevented the development of the Common Market in other areas.

The NCC noted that the extra cost to the consumer in terms of artificially high food prices was £9 per week per household. But this figure rose to £13.50 per week when the cost of storage, dumping and physical destruction of food was taken into account. The CAP is a negation of the free market dictum that the object of production is consumption. Indeed it may be argued that believing in the CAP as presently constituted is incompatible with believing in the benefits of a free market. To advocate the single market as well as the CAP is as logically consistent as advocating that the earth is round in the morning and flat in the afternoon. CAP abolition must be the ultimate aim of any European Thatcherism, with agricultural policy repatriated to the national parliaments, a policy in line with Mrs Thatcher's Bruges commitment to national sovereignty. Similarly the preservation of such sovereignty is essential to the continuation of Thatcherite economic policy in Britain alone. The notions of a European currency, Central Bank, common taxation and attendant federalist bureaucracy can only diminish free market economics. Lord Young has argued with some justification that such federalism is separate from and alien to the 1992 Single Market. Nor, given the pattern of Britain's global trading relations, should EMS membership by easily countenanced. The 1987-8 attempt to shadow the deutschemark (and thus covertly join the EMS) ended in tears with a monetary expansion and consequent increase in inflation.

In conclusion, Britain's growing and internationally competitive economy will benefit from a successful implementation of a genuine European Single Market unfettered by regulations and collectivist nostrums. British membership of the Community is desirable to realize this ambition despite the political energy that now has to be expended in preventing backsliding to the social dimension or through the economic illiteracy of protectionism. But these threats to a market-oriented consumer-led Europe are real and the creation of the Bruges Group was necessary – if not overdue. Spreading the benefits of market mechanisms within and beyond the European Community – this must be the message of 1992.

The costs of the CAP

Kenneth Thomson
Source: Economic Affairs, August/September 1988, 8, 6, p. 6.

The direct costs and benefits of the Common Agricultural Policy (CAP), as applied to a single commodity market such as wheat, can be derived from standard economic welfare analysis. To protect a pre-determined support price on the market for domestic farm producers, the CAP operates first by imposing import levies on supplies from outside the EEC at (usually cheaper) world market prices. As has happened successively with many European Community agricultural commodities, domestic supplies increase both because of technological progress (partly induced by the CAP) and high (and guaranteed) prices, so as eventually to exceed consumption levels (depressed by the high domestic prices).

The internal market is also buttressed by a combination of intervention buying and storage of the commodity (or its derivatives, such as butter in the case of milk) by public authorities, and/or subsidized sales on lower-priced markets both within and outside the Community. In contrast with the system of deficiency payments operated in the UK before EC entry (and currently operated, with modifications, in the USA for grains), EC users and consumers of farm products are faced with increased costs on the high-priced internal market, unless they can switch to alternative unsupported commodities.

The cost of such a regime is clearly dependent on the amounts bought on behalf of the taxpayer through intervention, storage and subsidy, offset by any agricultural levy revenue. This amount is reimbursed by the EC taxpayer through the budget, and such costs have increased rapidly as surpluses have grown, and as declining world prices have required higher export subsidies. The Agricultural Fund of the EC budget has risen from around 12 billion ECU in 1980 (1 ECU equals about £0.60) to about 28 billion ECU in 1988. Even allowing for the addition of Greece, Spain and Portugal to the Community, and for the effects of inflation, this is a dramatic rise.

Despite many efforts and even more exhortations, EC budget limits have been under continual pressure, and the CAP has remained accountable for between 60 and 70 per cent of the total EC budget. With the burgeoning cost of the CAP, member-state contributions have risen correspondingly, with little scope for the introduction of further common policies on, for example, education, research and development or welfare, or even reduction in exchequer costs.

In addition to these obvious financial effects, economic costs are also borne directly by the EC consumer of foods containing the CAP-protected commodities. He or she must pay a higher price for such foods, and hence suffers a lower real income and distorted choice. Calculations of this cost are complicated by uncertainty over the alternative free-market prices, the raw material component of retailed food, and the probable response of consumers to lower food prices, but may be well above the cost to the taxpayer identified above, though not so visible.

To set against these costs, there is the gain to agricultural producers enjoying higher and more stable prices for their products. As with the consumer losses, there are considerable difficulties in estimating their size, but added to these is the leakage of immediate producer benefits to the suppliers of farm inputs through higher prices, notably for land, which as the residual fixed expense mops up the quasi-rent of support directed to farmers. The benefits are however large (of the same order of magnitude as the consumer costs), and moreover fairly widely dispersed amongst numerous producers and processors of farm products, despite well-recognized inequalities of distribution.

The net economic cost of such a commodity regime is clearly the sum of the taxpayer and consumer losses minus the producer gains, and the direct economic (in)efficiency of the CAP may be measured by comparing losses to gains. It has been estimated that on average each ECU transferred to EC farm producers requires about 1.40 ECU from consumers and taxpayers. At the margin, this ratio is likely to be much higher. In addition, there are costs imposed on third countries with whom agricultural trade is damaged, and recent research has also attempted to estimate the CAP's indirect economic cost by looking at its macro-economic effects on the competitiveness of the EC's manufacturing sector.

Various estimates of these gains and losses have been made over the years, using a variety of data bases and economic models. One set[1] of figures on the direct costs and benefits has been recently produced by a study team invited by the European Commission to consider the impact of CAP reforms which would substantially, though not completely, reduce the high level of protection existing in the mid-1980s. Specifically, reductions of 40 per cent in the producer price of sugarbeet, 20 per cent for grains, olive oil and milk, 9 per cent for pig and poultry products, and 15 per cent for beef and mutton were contemplated, though balanced by a 10 per cent import tariff on oilseeds and feed-grain substitutes such as corn gluten feed (which currently enter the EC at low or zero tariffs under a GATT arrangement).

This analysis resulted in the estimates for the Community (of ten) as a whole and its main members given in the Table. Several points of interest can be seen in these figures. First, the major gains and losses from the particular analysis considered (not an outlandish one) are experienced as producers and consumers, not as taxpayers. In other words, the less visible market or non-financial effects dominate the obvious financial or budgetary ones, and go a long way to explaining why the growth in the latter has not led easily to changes in the policy.

Second, although all the member states identified in Table 12.3 show net welfare gains from the reform considered, three smaller countries – The Netherlands, Denmark and the Republic of Ireland – show net losses, because of the relative importance of their agricultural sectors. Moreover, the net gains in some countries – notably France – are not very large. Together with the producer and processor interest groups adversely affected in the other countries (where they often form a powerful political force), there is therefore only limited pressure for substantive CAP reform.

Third, the size of the total taxpayer effect in the Table is considerably

Table 12.3 Gains in economic welfare through CAP reform, 1986, million ECU

	Germany	France	Italy	Britain	EC-10
Producers	−4,592	−5,784	−3,118	−2,436	−20,188
Consumers	+4,159	+4,137	+3,900	+2,431	+17,245
Taxpayers	+2,981	+2,460	+1,683	+1,071	+ 9,696
Overall	+2,548	+ 813	+2,465	+1,066	+ 6,753

Source: Table 6, page 14/23, *Disharmonies in EC and US Agricultural Policy Measures*, Commission of the European Communities, May 1988.

below the actual 1986 budgetary cost of the CAP, due partly to the less-than-complete policy liberalization analysed, and partly to the omission from the calculations of (a) the storage costs of previously acquired intervention stocks and (b) the regime costs for a number of CAP commodities too complex to model easily, primarily fruits, vegetables and wine. Thus larger figures than those above can be produced by extending the coverage of the analysis and the radicalism of the policy change considered.

These relatively straightforward considerations are complicated in the case of the CAP by many factors, amongst which are:

1 the depressing impact of growing EC surpluses on world market prices, so that the cost of export subsidies is raised. This again obscures the true effect of the CAP and increases the difficulty of imagining an EEC without the CAP;
2 the common financing of the bulk of the CAP through national financial contributions to the Community budget according to a formula related to VAT or GDP rather than agriculture. This cost-sharing reduces the taxpayer cost of national farm surpluses through the well-known 'free-rider' effect, especially at the margin. Moreover, the special UK rebate achieved by Mrs Thatcher, though beneficial in budgetary terms to Britain, weakens this country's interest in reform by exaggerating this effect;
3 internal EC support prices for farm products fixed by translating prices fixed in ECU into national-currency prices using the artificial green exchange rates which lag behind money market rates and require a system of monetary compensatory amounts (MCAs) as taxes and subsidies to prevent large cross-border flows. This system is now of mind-boggling complexity even to those close to the Commission which must operate and amend it, but still shows few signs of reform, mainly because it provides a useful private weapon for national farm ministers;
4 departures from the simple commodity regime outlined at the start of this article, including (a) quotas on milk and sugar production, (b) complex coresponsibility levies on the producers of milk, sugar and

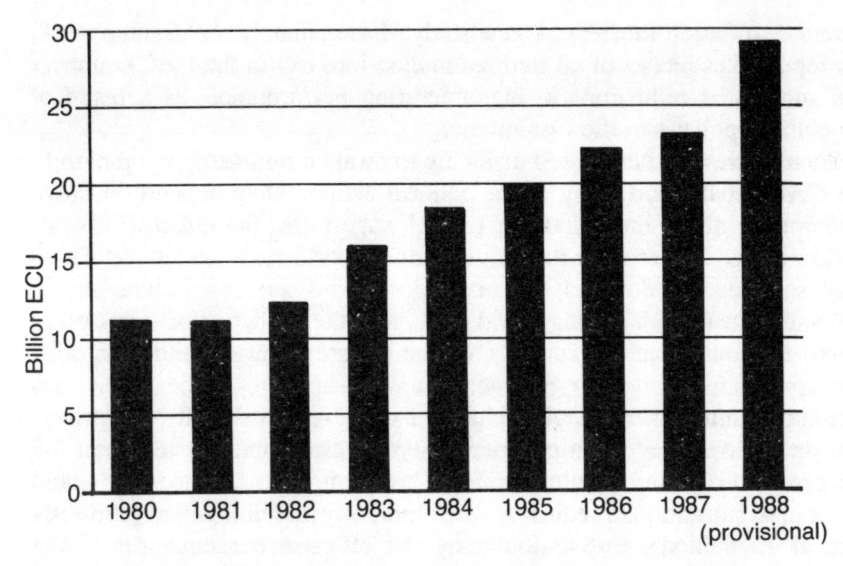

Figure 12.3 EC Agricultural Fund expenditure, 1980–8

Note: One ECU = 60 UK pence approx.

cereals, (c) variable premiums or deficiency payments on certain products, such as oilseeds, and beef and mutton in Britain, and (d) special arrangements for continued imports from outside the Community, such as lamb and butter from New Zealand, and sugar from French and British ex-colonies;

5   intercommodity relationships such as the use of cereals and oilseed cake in animal feedstuffs, and the competition between farm commodities for both productive resources and consumer expenditure;

6   the persistent and expensive (about 10 billion ECU in 1980, when last measured) remnants of national agricultural policy-making in the hands of the Ministers at the Agricultural Council. Indeed, precisely because loss of these remnants would radically alter the political weapons of the national Ministers, their elimination is strenuously resisted, and the full attainment of a Common Agricultural Policy – good or bad – seems to come no nearer. It remains to be seen whether 1992, with its far-reaching objectives, will be a powerful enough force to break down some of the barriers that remain.

A new element in the long-running debate over the CAP has concerned its consequences for the economy as a whole, particularly its effect on unemployment. Higher than necessary food prices, and diversion of scarce public expenditure, may have reduced the international competitiveness of the European manufacturing and service sectors, reducing waged employment and weakening the balance of payments (as well as missing a chance to reduce inflation further). A new study,[2] based mainly on German work, has reported estimates of up to three million jobs lost in the EEC countries and substantial reductions in manufacturing performance, as a result of agricultural policies in the Community.

Such figures are being used explicitly to awaken non-farming opinion to the CAP debate, and bring about political action. They depend on brave assumptions about the behaviour of real wage rates, the effect of liberalization in agriculture, and the adjustment of world trade to altered European supplies and demands for many goods and services. Labour-saving innovation in manufacturing world-wide, and the existence of many other macro-economic factors such as exchange-rate changes and non-tariff barriers against non-farm products would also have to be taken into account in considering a policy change over several years. It is surprising that drastic treatment of a productive sector responsible for less than 3.5 per cent of GDP and holding around 7 per cent of its labour force would result in so substantial a reduction of Community unemployment (currently around 12 million). But undoubtedly the off-farm consequences of the CAP deserve further consideration.

At first sight, it is easy to criticize the European Community's Common Agricultural Policy as a financial and economic monstrosity that should have been aborted or strangled at birth. Does not the CAP, in its efforts to support an industry which is bound to decline in relative if not absolute terms with general economic growth, account for a growing share of the real Community budget, in an era of general disapproval of public expenditure? Has it not failed to prevent the emigration of many millions of families from farming, and, even so, allowed farm incomes, measured as net value added per work unit, to fall in real terms? Does it not periodically threaten the cohesion of the Community itself, so that we see the farce of Prime Ministers haggling over mutton, soyabeans and cereals? Does it not poison trade relations with the United States and other trading partners, such as Australia, New Zealand and Thailand, with its arbitrary impositions of trading barriers in disregard of GATT provisions?

These feelings are natural, especially amongst those weaned on a diet of neo-classical economics. But clearly the analysis misses something, for the CAP goes on, ever more expensive, ever more complex, ever more crisis-ridden. This article, in addition to describing the conventional economic effects of the policy, has tried also to point to some of the complications, economic and political, that have defined the pattern of interests in the development of the CAP over the 30 or so years of the European Community, and should not be ignored in the quite proper pursuit of its reform.

The case for Britain joining the EMS

Nigel M. Healey
Source: Economic Affairs, February/March 1988, 8, 3, p. 30.

Ever since the demise of the Bretton Woods exchange rate regime in the early 1970s, fierce debate has raged in UK policy-making circles about the appropriate design of exchange rate policy. Should sterling be allowed to float cleanly? Or should the monetary authorities seek to peg its value through open-market operations (OMO) and short-term interest rate policy? If so, how flexible or inflexible should the peg be? And to what should sterling be pegged? The US dollar (the world's major grading and investment currency)? The deutschmark (the currency of the UK's largest trade partner)? Some weighted average of two or more currencies (such as the effective exchange rate index or an artificial currency basket like the Special Drawing Right)?

The tempo of this debate has been raised several notches by the apparently successful establishment of a regional exchange rate system within the European Community. As a Community country, the UK is automatically an associate member[1] of the European Monetary System (EMS), but since its inception in March 1979 successive UK governments have declined to lock sterling into the exchange rate mechanism (ERM) – the commitment necessary for full membership.

In Mrs Thatcher's third term of office, the tide now appears to be turning in favour of UK entry to the ERM. But the debate has become increasingly confused, invariably conflating two separate issues. The first is whether or not the external value of sterling should be systematically managed. The second is whether full membership of the EMS is the best way to achieve this management. I believe that recent developments have made an explicit, credible exchange rate target essential for successful macro-economic policy, and that the ERM offers a tried and proven means to this end.

Should the UK adopt an explicit exchange rate target? It is undoubtedly true that such a move would impose certain costs on the domestic economy, with the magnitude of these costs rising as width of target band (i.e., the band around the target rate within which the authorities would tolerate fluctuations) is reduced.

Direct controls (on capital flows, or imports) to influence flows across the exchanges lead to distortions and circumvention, which is growing ever-easier in a computer-linked financial world.[2] Direct controls apart, the authorities are then left with two basic weapons of exchange rate management: varying short-term interest rates in order to influence the relative attractiveness of sterling assets and liabilities compared with those denominated in other currencies; and OMO, the buying and selling of sterling by the authorities directly in the market – which reduces and boosts the UK

Table 12.4 Inflation, 1987

	Consumer price inflation (Annualized 12-month rate)	Wage/earnings inflation (Annualized 12-month rate)
	%	%
France	3.1 (to Oct 1987)	3.2 (to Jul 1987)
Germany	1.0 (to Nov 1987)	3.8 (to Oct 1987)
Japan	0.7 (to Oct 1987)	4.2 (to Oct 1987)
UK	4.1 (to Nov 1987)	7.8 (to Sep 1987)
USA	4.5 (to Oct 1987)	2.6 (to Nov 1987)

Source: *The Economist.*

money supply respectively. In essence, therefore, both weapons can be reduced to the same thing – subordinating domestic monetary policy to the requirements of exchange rate policy.

Such a sacrifice is often argued to be unacceptable, on the grounds that abandoning monetary policy to the vicissitudes of the international economy renders independent macro-economic policy in the UK impossible.[3] If, for example, inflation in the rest of the world were to soar above that in Britain, sterling would come under strong upwards pressure on the foreign exchanges and the authorities would be forced to relax monetary policy (by cutting interest rates and making open-market sales of sterling), in order to prevent the exchange rate appreciating. The result would be an upturn in UK inflation, which would continue to accelerate until it converged on the new, higher world average. Conversely, if inflation abroad fell well below that in the UK, the sharp tightening of domestic monetary policy required to defend the exchange rate might lead to an unwelcome dose of deflation and unemployment.

Such arguments might be convincing if UK inflation were well below that of our major trading partners, or if UK inflation were higher than that abroad and there exists a long run trade-off between inflation and unemployment. Table 12.4 shows that the first condition is sadly far from true; and, on the second, it is sufficient to note that macro-economic policy-making in virtually every major Western economy, including the UK, is predicated on the belief that the inflation–unemployment trade-off is a wholly short-term phenomenon.[4]

It is therefore difficult to argue that tying the UK economy to its lower-inflation competitors would involve an unacceptable loss of discretion in domestic monetary policy, given the Government's declared position that 'our ultimate goal should be a society with stable prices'.[5] Not only would an exchange rate target provide a firmer counter-inflation discipline than the government has been able to exercise through its medium-term financial strategy (MTFS), but it would also afford a sorely-needed anchor for inflationary expectations in the economy.

In the past this anchor has taken the form of pre-announced targets for broad money £M3, but the increasingly erratic behaviour of this aggregate, and its final abandonment as a target in the 1987 Budget, leaves the economy with no formal basis upon which to base its expectations of the future course of prices.[6] Although the Chancellor appears to be groping towards money GDP targets as a replacement, it is clear that the commitment to an exchange rate target – with its implicit promise to bring inflation into line with that in our major trading partners – would provide precisely the basis required.

Indeed, the Bank of England foreshadowed this possibility back in 1983, when commenting on the 1982 MTFS:

> Modifying and qualifying the monetary target leaves us so prone to a weakening of counter-inflationary resolve that there is need to reconstitute a published 'overriding constraint' or 'long-stop'. The obvious and indeed only remaining candidate for this vacancy, certainly in the United Kingdom, is the rate of exchange.[7]

The other important and more familiar argument in favour of systematic exchange rate management is to alleviate the havoc that volatile and unpredictable floating rates wreak on international trade. However sophisticated corporate treasurers become at manipulating forward and option currency markets, overseas business transactions can never be completely insulated from the dangers of see-sawing exchange rates. And much more damaging than short-term fluctuations have been the episodes of over- and undershooting[8] when speculative pressure has driven exchange rates to hopelessly unrealistic positions for extended periods. The horrific over-appreciation of sterling in 1980–1, when it soared to $2.45 and so reduced UK competitiveness by 60 per cent in a year, resulted in the 20 per cent contraction of manufacturing. Then in early 1985, sterling plummeted to $1.04, threatening a major resurgence in domestic inflation as imported raw material prices temporarily soared. As McKinnon warns: 'national monetary authorities can only ignore wide swings in their exchange rate at their peril'.[9]

Not only can systematic exchange rate intervention iron out short-term fluctuations, it can also ensure, through timely re- or devaluations of the target rate, that the long-term trend is consistent with underlying changes in relative competitiveness, rather than moving in a perverse direction. Of course, if the net effect of such intervention were simply to switch the realm of economic turbulence from the exchange rate to interest rates and monetary conditions, its value might be arguable. But experience suggests that speculative capital pressures feed on uncertainty.[10] Reducing that uncertainty through explicit exchange rate targets is therefore likely to result in interest rates being far less volatile than the gyrations of clean-floating exchange rates might lead the casual observer to suppose. More importantly, interest rates, on the average, may tend to be lower, since the uncertainty premium on interest rates that overseas investors require to hold sterling assets in a world of unpredictable and unstable exchange rates will no longer be necessary.

Dissatisfaction with the experience of floating rates after 1973 has not been limited to the UK. Within a decade of the breakdown of Bretton Woods, all but 37 of the 145 members of the International Monetary Fund (IMF) had readopted some system of formal exchange management, either pegging to the currency of their main trading partner (38 countries had pegged their currency to the US dollar) or to some basket of currencies. More recently, the notable exceptions to this trend, the US, Japan and Canada, have begun to show increasing interest in returning to an era of more orderly exchange rates. This change of heart has spawned the Plaza agreement of October 1985 (when the major central banks cooperated to reduce the overvaluation of the US dollar) and, most recently, the Louvre accord of spring 1987 (which committed the major central banks to maintain their exchange rates within undisclosed target zones). Although the latter agreement, publicly reaffirmed in both September and December 1987, has been put under increasing strain by the recent heavy downward pressure on the dollar, its significance lies in the explicit rejection of clean floating by the world's major trading nations. As Mr Nigel Lawson points out:

> The Louvre accord ... marked another important step forward. We agreed that ... the interests of the world economy would best be served by a period of stability ... Our objectives should be clear: *to maintain the maximum stability of key exchange rates, and to manage any changes that might be necessary in an orderly way.*[11]

It is often asserted that there are two special features of sterling which prevent the UK from following this international trend toward more systematic management of the exchange rate. The first concerns the status of sterling as a so-called petro-currency. The argument is that changes in the price of oil exert irresistible pressures on the UK's balance of payments and hence on the exchange rate. Worse, the same price changes have precisely the opposite effect on Britain's major oil-importing trading partners Germany, France, Japan and the US – so rendering unworkable any system which involves tying sterling to one or more of the industrial currencies.

But this objection has been grossly overstated. Oil production is now shrinking as a proportion of UK GDP, partly due to the fall in oil prices and partly due to declining production. Its share is now only 2.5 per cent compared to 6 per cent in 1984. As a result, sterling is increasingly less sensitive to gyrations in oil prices. In the first quarter of 1986, for example, the price of oil crashed 63 per cent while the trade-weighted value of sterling eased by only 3 per cent. Moreover, the Netherlands provides an excellent example of another nation which is also self-sufficient in energy and which has participated successfully in the ERM since 1979.[12]

The second argument concerns the international role of sterling as an investment currency. The fear is that foreigners' holdings of sterling are so large, and so volatile, that changes in exchange market sentiment can induce massive in- and outflows of this hot money which would swamp the ability of the monetary authorities to defend their target rate. Like the petro-currency argument, this worry is rooted in past history and has been receding in importance for many years. In the last decade or so, sterling has slipped from being the second to only the fifth most widely-held investment currency (after the US dollar, the deutschmark, the yen and the Swiss franc).

Faced with the growing difficulties of pursuing counter-inflation policy through domestic monetary policy alone, increasing dissatisfaction with the experience of floating exchange rates and the diminishing importance of the main arguments against active exchange rate intervention, it is hardly surprising that the Bank of England has been taking an increasingly *dirigiste* approach to sterling. Ever since September 1981, short-term interest rate changes have been taken with an ever-sharper eye on the exchange rate rather than the growth of broad money; OMOs have increasingly become the norm, rather than the exception. And the Chancellor and the Governor of the Bank have been key players in the various international accords on exchange rate cooperation discussed above.

However creaky the deals subsequently struck may be, such meetings of like-minded finance ministers are important because unilateral intervention by a single central bank is almost inevitably doomed to failure. Yet despite its growing enthusiasm for 'a more permanent regime of managed floating',[13] the government has to date curiously declined to avail itself of an already fully-operational system which would rally the resources of eight European central banks behind sterling – the EMS. The institutions and structures for inter-governmental consultation and cooperation are already tried and tested; and the eight years since its inception have provided plenty of time to appraise the performance of the EMS. Indeed, there have now been two Parliamentary enquiries. The first, by the House of Lords, concluded as long as four years ago that: '[full membership] is desirable given the Government's commitment to the British membership of the EEC ... and though exact timing must depend on general government policy, the balance of advantage lies in early, though not necessarily immediate entry'.[14]

The actual mechanics of the EMS are reasonably straightforward. Prior to its creation, several European countries operated an exchange rate system known as the snake. Under this arrangement, each currency was maintained within a range of plus or minus 2.25 per cent of its target rate, or central parity, against each other member currency; hence the system as a whole snaked along against outside currencies.

The EMS is essentially a revamped version of the snake. It was intended to improve on its predecessor in several ways. At its heart lies a new unit of account, the European Currency Unit (ECU), which acts as the reference point for all member currencies. The ECU is a basket, or weighted average

Table 12.5 European currencies

	Currency Units per ECU	Weighting in ECU (December 29th 1987)
		%
Deutschmark	0.719	34.8
French Franc	1.31	18.8
Pound Sterling	0.0878	12.7
Lira (Italy)	140.00	9.2
Guilder (Holland)	0.256	11.0
Belgian Franc	3.71	8.9
Luxembourg Franc	0.14	
Krone (Denmark)	0.219	2.8
Punt (Ireland)	0.00871	1.1
Drachma (Greece)	1.15	0.7

Source: European Commission: *Financial Times*.

of all European Community currencies,[15] that is, it consists of specified quantities of each of the member currencies. The precise quantities of each (the weights) are fixed according to each country's relative economic importance in the Community, although the actual weighting varies with movements in exchange rates (see Table 12.5).

Members are obliged to declare a central parity for their currencies in terms of the ECU. From these parities, the central banks work out the implicit cross-rates (deutschmark–lira rate, the deutschmark–krone rate), which then become the operational day-to-day targets; each cross-rate must be maintained within a band of 2.25 per cent either side of its target rate. If a particular cross-rate, say, the deutschmark–lira, moves to the edge of this permissible range, both the German and Italian central banks are required to intervene.

It might be possible for the lira, say, to move down against all other ERM currencies simultaneously, suggesting that the source of the pressure on other members' currencies is fundamentally Italian in origin. In this instance, the lira will also be moving against the ECU and much narrower fluctuations against the ECU are permissible. If this narrower ECU target band is breached (the outer limits are known as the divergence threshold), the offending member is required to make appropriate domestic policy changes to correct the situation. Since, for a currency moving in the same direction against most or all others, the divergence threshold will be reached well before the upper or lower limits of the cross-rates are approached, this prevents one member's domestic policies getting too much at variance with, and so imposing adjustment costs on, other members.

The central parities themselves may be changed only by mutual agreement, that is, the unanimous consent of all the finance ministers involved in the ERM. Such changes, termed 'realignments', have been made whenever the strains on the system are deemed unacceptable. By agreeing realignments in good time, the ERM has thus avoided the inflexibility which contributed to the demise of the Bretton Woods arrangement.

The other main improvements on the snake lie in the credit mechanisms which provide the support for central bank intervention. These are coordinated by the European Monetary Cooperation Fund (EMCOF). Under the guidance of EMCOF, participating central banks provide funds to one another for official market intervention. These credit facilities are available in unlimited amounts for up to forty-five days and on a quota basis for longer periods of up to five years. Debts and claims between central banks as a consequence of these transactions are recorded and paid in ECUs; thus the risk of a possible, forced realignment increasing the debt of a devaluing central bank is jointly borne by both debtor and creditor under this arrangement.

In a further attempt to foster the development of the ECU into a reserve asset, all EMS member countries (including the UK) deposited 20 per cent of their gold and dollar reserves with the EMCOF in exchange for the issue of ECUs. In time, it is intended that EMCOF will issue further ECUs unbacked by reserve holdings, so enabling the Community to increase directly the stock of international liquidity.

In view of the initially different economic policy priorities of the ERM countries – with Germany committed to curbing inflation and the other countries giving stronger emphasis to employment objectives – many early commentators were dubious about the prospects for the new system. But after eight years, and despite eleven realignments in central parities, important results have been achieved in reducing variability in both nominal and real exchange rates.

All the ERM currencies have fluctuated against one another less than against the US dollar and much less than in the period of floating rates before the EMS. These findings have been confirmed by studies by the Commission of the European Community, which concluded that 'the system has made a positive contribution to exchange rate stability',[16] by the IMF, which found that 'the exchange rate variability of the EMS currencies has diminished since the introduction of the system',[17] and by the House of Lords, which accepted 'the evidence that the EMS has contributed to greater exchange rate stability for its members'.[18]

At the same time, there has been a gradual convergence of the economic policies of the Community countries.[19] The average growth rates of monetary aggregates have fallen and their correlation increased. Inflation rates have slowed and inflation differentials have narrowed (see Table 12.6). The Commission also reports that 'nominal as well as real interest rates have shown a marked increase in correlation among the EMS countries'.[20]

That the EMS has provided the European zone of monetary stability which its architects intended therefore seems reasonably clear. The key question is whether it could offer the UK, now seeking a refuge for sterling

Table 12.6 Domestic credit expansion (DCE)

		Annual inflation (% average)		Annual narrow monetary growth (% average)		DCE[1] (% average)	
		1974–8	1979–85	1974–8	1979–85	1974–8	1979–85
ERM countries	average	10.7	8.9	13.1	8.8	15.9	12.7
	standard deviation	3.8	3.9	3.6	4.4	3.9	3.8
Non-ERM countries[2]	average	14.1	12.8	13.1	12.5	18.3	14.1
	standard deviation	8.2	11.1	7.1	14.2	8.9	9.8

[1] DCE = Domestic credit expansion, i.e., the change in the money supply domestically generated, rather than resulting from OMO in the foreign exchange market.
[2] Australia, Austria, Canada, Finland, Greece, Iceland, Japan, New Zealand, Norway, Portugal, Spain, Sweden, Switzerland, UK, USA.
Source: *The Economist*.

from the rollercoaster of open markets and an alternative anchor for counter-inflation policy, the same benefits.

One major worry from the UK's point of view is that, as a trade weighted index on which to peg the exchange rate, the ECU is not the most obvious choice, since it excludes both the US dollar[21] and the yen. There are two counters to this objection: first, that the process of European integration has radically shifted the trade patterns of the UK in favour of its Community partners in recent years, so reducing the force of this argument; and, more significantly, that the European Council Resolution of December 1978, which explicitly called for 'coordination of exchange rate policies *vis-à-vis* third countries and, as far as possible, a concentration with the monetary authorities of those countries',[22] looks increasingly like being put into practice in the light of the recent Louvre negotiations between the USA, Japan, Germany, France, Italy, Canada and the UK. Indeed, the entry of sterling into the ERM is likely to make the successful implementation and execution of a Community dollar and yen policy more, rather than less, likely. As the Commission has observed, 'where sterling is concerned, non-participation is particularly significant: it ... reduces the Community's weight in discussions on the shape of the international monetary system'.[23]

Although this is not the place for a detailed review of the reasons for the present travails of the Louvre accord, the refusal of the US to trim sufficiently its budget deficit is unquestionably at the heart of the problem. In other words, sterling's entry into the ERM might, by strengthening the bargaining position of the EMC bloc, facilitate ECU and sterling stability against the dollar; and to the extent that a firming up of the Louvre accord is prevented by squabbles between the White House and Congress over the budget issue, sterling will be unambiguously better insulated from the resulting turmoil if it is inside, rather than outside, the protective shell of the ERM. It is impossible to avoid the conclusion that, as an argument against full UK membership of the EMS, the absence of a Community dollar policy is now largely a red herring.

Policy coordination, although it has not been as rapid or as complete as many had hoped, has taken place. More significantly, this convergence has not been on some average stance; rather, policy in the ERM countries has been drawn towards the European centre of gravity in Bonn. Because of the West Germans' commitment to zero inflation, other member countries have either had to fall in step or resign themselves to regular devaluations – the lira, for example, has depreciated 40 per cent against the deutschmark since 1979 – although it is notable that even these other member countries have accepted smaller devaluations than purchasing power parity would have indicated (so that even here there is evidence of convergence). The UK government should welcome the challenge that this bias in the ERM throws down. Full membership of the EMS offers a workable means of simultaneously achieving both its declared objective of domestic price stability and stability in exchange rates.

The final argument in favour of full membership is the wider economic and political dimension. Entry to the ERM is fast becoming a test case of the UK's commitment to the long-term goal of economic integration. As the Community seeks to complete the internal market in goods and services and restructure its budgetary arrangements, the UK is likely to become increasingly isolated by its decision, originally accepted as purely temporary by all parties, to remain outside the system. As the Bundesbank reminded the Treasury and Civil Service Committee of the House of Commons: 'membership of the European Communities ... must be considered, as an undivided whole ... As a matter of principle, this precludes selective participation in EMS or other areas of Community membership'.[24]

In conclusion, the UK desperately requires a new anchor for counter-inflation policy and sterling requires a shelter from the turmoil of open markets. Full membership of the EMS would serve both these aims, while simultaneously facilitating progress towards wider international agreement on monetary relations by enhancing the influence of the system and cementing the UK's economic and political links with its Community partners.

The EMS has already proved that exchange rates can be successfully managed, and policies throughout Europe brought more closely into line. Full UK membership of the EMS would ease further progress towards wider international agreement on a more permanent system of exchange rate management, while the EMS would at the same time provide, as a free-standing, workable system in its own right, a valuable insurance policy against a further weakening of the Louvre agreement. Locking sterling into the ERM would also anchor market expectations, which have been left drifting by the abandonment of £M3 targets in March 1987 and, in the longer term, promote the goal of European integration by cementing the UK's economic and political links with the Community.

The argument against joining the EMS

Roy Batchelor
Source: Economic Affairs, February/March 1988, 8, 3, p. 35.

Many virtues have been claimed for the European Monetary System; the more sensible of these are invoked in Nigel Healey's presentation of the case for full UK participation. The EMS lays the foundation for a common currency in Europe. It facilitates the conduct of a concerted dollar or yen policy. It provides a stable environment for intra-European trade. It exerts a discipline on the monetary policies of the more inflation-prone members of the system. It serves as a focus for expectations about future monetary policy.

In view of the enthusiasm for reform of international monetary arrangements expressed at the recent IMF meetings, it should perhaps be added that the EMS also appeals strongly to the instincts of central bankers for order, intervention and 'cooperation'.

My own instincts are rather different. For one thing, I find it worrying that, on the several occasions when full UK membership has been seriously considered in public debate, the case in favour of membership has been quite different. In 1979 the idea was that control of British monetary policy should, after a decade of failure, in effect be handed over to the Bundesbank.[1] In 1985, when the Treasury and Civil Service Committee reported on the subject, inflation was under control, but British manufacturing was still smarting from the uncompetitive exchange rate of the early 1980s, and the main concern of the Committee was whether the UK could steal a march on the rest of Europe by entering the system at an undervalued exchange rate.[2] It would appear from rumours that the Bank of England has been informally targetting the £–ECU exchange rate, that the EMS is charged with filling the gap left by the sterling M3 (and M0 and M1) targets that were not adhered to. In short, full membership of the EMS has been repeatedly prescribed as a cure for whatever current ill afflicts UK economic policy.

I would argue against this band-aid (Elastoplast, not Geldof) view of EMS entry, and in favour of a more detached and strategic view of the role of the EMS. The EMS is one of several monetary arrangements into which the UK might enter. An alternative is, of course, a return to free-ish floating. All of these arrangements have benefits, and all impose costs. For an economist, the question of whether the EMS is a good thing for the UK should be an empirical one – namely, does it yield higher net benefits than all feasible alternatives? My particular concerns, elaborated below, are:

1   that the benefits of EMS membership, even to existing members, are small and possibly negative;
2   that while the usual cost attributed to the EMS – the loss of monetary independence – is phoney, the true cost of increased predictability in exchange rates – increased unpredictability in domestic interest rates and inflation – tends to be neglected; and
3   that the EMS is a second-best way of resolving current problems of monetary targetting.

Advocates of the EMS point to the low variability of exchange rates inside the EMS, relative to the variability of exchange rates between members of some control group of non-participants, as prime evidence of the success of the regime. The size of the claimed benefits varies, of course, according to what countries are included in the control group, but the finding of lower exchange-rate variability within the EMS appears fairly robust. But a reduction in variability does not necessarily entail a reduction in risk. Any recorded reduction in exchange risk is not necessarily attributable to the EMS. And there is little evidence that the reduction in exchange risk has been of benefit to trade or output in the EMS bloc.

What matters for trade is not whether exchange rates are less volatile, but whether they are less unpredictable. Since good estimates of the exchange-rate forecasts of market participants are available from the forward exchange market, it is straightforward to check whether exchange risk is in this sense lower inside the EMS. My own calculations[3] suggest that the EMS has had two offsetting effects on exchange risk. On the one hand, the errors in forward rate forecasts have on average been lower for bilateral rates inside the EMS than for rates outside it. On the other hand, the incidence of erratically high errors, at times of central rate realignments, has been higher inside the EMS. The fixed-but-adjustable nature of the EMS mechanism has effectively altered the distribution of unexpected rate changes in exchange rates in two distinct ways. On average, changes are smaller. But when changes do occur, they tend to be very sudden and very large. Whether this alternative constitutes a net reduction in risk is therefore hard to determine.

The next question is whether the low variability of exchange rates inside the EMS has been caused by the operation of the EMS system, or whether a similar degree of exchange-rate stability would have been observed even in the absence of the intervention mechanism. A test might be whether intra-EMS exchange rates have become relatively more stable, compared with those within a non-EMS control group, in the years after the establishment of the system in 1979 than in the years before 1979. The evidence is again ambiguous. There is little difference in the relative performance of the EMS bloc after 1979. On the other hand, since an informal exchange rate management system, the snake, was already operating before 1979, it could be argued that no significant change in relative risk should be expected.

The final question is *cui bono fuisset* – who has benefited from the reduction in exchange risk? The evidence of a large number of empirical studies is that volatile exchange rates have very little effect on the volume of trade.[4] Indeed, in the case of the EMS bloc, it is striking that the years of operation of the EMS have coincided not only with a reduction in exchange-rate variability but also with a sharp reduction in the growth both of trade and of output of member countries. Clearly, a number of factors unrelated to exchange-rate management have contributed to the recent poor economic performance of EMS economies. The boost to trade from tariff reductions is now spent. The European economies are suffering from the problem of adjusting to new trading patterns in the face of relatively inflexible labour markets. But part of the showdown in the European economy represents a cost imposed by having to maintain exchange rates within the EMS (below).

Traditionally, the trade-off between fixed and flexible exchange rates is presented as a choice between the gains to trade from exchange-rate stability and the loss to output and employment from the requirement that monetary policy be directed at a nominal (exchange rate) rather than a real target. The benefit in this calculus is rather slight. I would agree with Nigel Healey also that the claimed loss is even more illusory. The frustrating experiences of reflation in the 1970s have taught most governments that real objectives cannot be served in the long term by monetary policies, and that employment cannot be bought at the expense of high inflation and a depreciating exchange rate. The loss of monetary independence does not, then, constitute the true cost of pegging exchange rates – which does not mean that fixed exchange rates are costless.

A fruitful way to assess the potential costs and benefits of managed exchange rates is to regard fixed and floating regimes as alternative means of providing public insurance against the shocks which inevitably impinge on even the best-run economy in a large and ever-changing international trading system. The two exchange-rate regimes in effect force the burden of adjustment to external shocks onto certain groups within the economy, while insulating others. Under a fixed-rate regime such as the EMS, the benefits accrue to producers in tradeable goods industries, who are faced with less uncertainty about their real profitability. The costs of this insurance are borne by the public at large, who must suffer whatever offsetting policy shocks are necessary to maintain the exchange-rate target. Usually, these policies will involve increasing the volatility of domestic prices and interest rates, although some of the larger EMS members have preferred a rather different (and yet more costly) policy response (below). Under flexible exchange rates, on the other hand, the costs of insurance fall mainly on the producers of tradeable goods, who are faced with volatile exchange rates. Monetary and other policies can be directed at insulating the public at large from shocks which might otherwise hit prices and interest rates.

There are private market mechanisms which can also provide insurance against fluctuations in exchange rates, prices and interest rates. Forward exchange markets, indexation arrangements, and interest-rate futures markets serve such purposes. The question for exchange-rate policy should therefore be – in which of these devices is private market failure most severe? My own prejudice is that the tradeables sector is populated by highly professional businesses which can and do utilize an efficient forward market to hedge exchange risks. In contrast, the public at large is relatively ill-organized to deal with fluctuating prices and interest rates. I would therefore judge that monetary policy should be tailored to a target based on internal prices rather than to the exchange rate.

In practice, participants in the EMS have not operated within the system in quite this way. The two countries whose exchange rates have been constantly under pressure – France and Italy – have not used monetary policy to maintain their central parities. One of the most striking features of the EMS is that exchange-rate stability has been achieved without any convergence in national monetary policies on those of the dominant nation, West Germany. Instead, exchange rates have been maintained at artificial positions by controls on outward capital movements from the economies with depreciating exchange rates. The evidence can be clearly seen in the gap between internal interest rates and euro-rates for French franc and lira investments.[5]

Maintenance of exchange rates by means of capital controls avoids the costs of price and interest variability of a convergent monetary policy but leads to two potentially more serious objections. One is the micro-economic inefficiency caused by the artificially high internal cost of capital. This burden can be expected to lead to a sub-optimal rate of investment, and hence a lower trend growth rate. The second is the tendency for barriers to capital mobility to exaggerate the built-in tendency of the EMS towards deflation. In the absence of even an informal agreement to coordinate policy, individual countries within the EMS have little incentive to engage in reflationary policies, since these will suck in imports at the fixed exchange rate, and benefit mainly other members of the system.[6] On the other hand, if an individual country should choose to engage in a fiscal deflation, lowering domestic output and interest rates, it will not only cause deflation in the countries which supply it with imports, but the controls on capital outflows from the deflating economy will prevent any offsetting capital inflows into its trading partners.[7]

What incentives are there for the United Kingdom to join such an arrangement? The trend rate of inflation in the UK is already low, and stable. Trend growth appears to have risen since 1979–80. Manufacturing industry is recovering. If the UK plays by the rules, trend inflation may be reduced further, toward that of West Germany. But fluctuations around the trend will inevitably increase, as external shocks specific to sterling are accommodated. Oil is still important to the UK economy, and there is no doubt that unexpected fluctuations in the oil price will cause substantial changes in the international demand for sterling-denominated assets, at least into the mid-1990s. If, most improbably, the UK does not play by the rules, and reintroduces capital controls to, say, stabilize sterling in the face of a collapse of the price of oil, much of the impetus to growth of the past eight years would be lost.

Today's proponents of the EMS seem to fear that Britain's hard-won victory in the battle against inflation will be jeopardized if no monetary target can be found to replace the Sterling M3 target of past medium-term financial strategies. It is clear that some better target is required, and that none of the simple alternatives tried – M0, M1, M2, and the rest – exactly fits the bill. But confidence that the EMS will fit the bill is misplaced. An ECU target will not work. And there are better alternatives.

An ECU target cannot serve as a focus for expectations in quite the same way as a monetary quantity. One problem with the ECU target is that the ECU does not move in line with the effective rate of sterling. Targetting monetary policy on the sterling-ECU rate will not be consistent with external balance if the ECU-dollar or ECU-yen rates are trended. Another problem is that it is hard to infer future inflation from an exchange-rate (or interest-rate) target. For example, maintenance of an ECU parity in 1988 might imply a small fall in the rate of inflation in the UK. Maintenance of that same parity in 1980, when there was upward pressure on the real sterling exchange rate, would have meant a substantial rise in inflation.

The options for monetary targetting within the MTFS are well known. Several commentators have advocated a nominal income target as a focus for expectations. My own preference is for a move towards a target based on an index of types of domestic money weighted to account for the differing speeds with which they move in the economy. The point is that alternative quantity targets do exist, and either of these proposals would be preferable to a price (exchange rate, interest rate) target. At all events, the failure of the early architects of the MTFS to construct a robust monetary target is no reason for today's policy-makers to make the same mistake, and commit the United Kingdom to a system which offers few real benefits, and threatens to increase rather than reduce uncertainty about inflation.

The right road to monetary union

John Chown and Geoffrey Wood
Source: Economic Affairs, February/March 1990, 10, 3, p. 32.

When the EMS was established in 1979, it was a mini Bretton Woods System. Exchange rates were pegged, and there was provision for inter-country loans to finance foreign exchange intervention but, like Bretton Woods, there was no provision for moving to a common currency.

There are benefits and costs of having a common currency. One advantage is that it removes the risk of exchange rate fluctuations for those concerned with international trade and investment. This would increase the gains which could be brought by the abolition of barriers within the EC after 1992. The Delors report[1] suggests one route to that desirable goal, but there are costs as well as benefits to having a common currency. This paper sets out these costs, and shows that it is not possible to reach a firm conclusion on whether the EC should (on economic grounds – some may wish to advance political arguments) move to a common currency.

A large part of discussion of monetary union has been in a setting where there was a trade-off between inflation and unemployment. Low inflation would, it was believed, inevitably be accompanied by high unemployment. Writing in this context, Corden[2] saw two major problems for European monetary union: countries would be forced away from their preferred inflation/unemployment combinations, and some countries would become permanently depressed areas as a result of being forced to choose lower rates of inflation than they would without the fixed exchange rate constraint.

That difficulty has been removed by theoretical developments (it has been realized that the inflation-unemployment trade off was inevitably temporary) and the experience of the 1970s and 1980s. The way seems clear to monetary union. That does not, however, mean that a union should be formed. That you can do something does not mean that you should.

There is a small body of literature on the choice of optimal domain – the welfare maximizing area for a currency. Mundell,[3] writing implicitly within the trade-off framework, argued that the optimum currency area is the area of factor mobility – so long as factors, particularly labour, are mobile, there will be no need for exchange rate exchanges to alter real wages and hence the unemployment rate. He suggested currency areas should be small, because he believed labour to be rather immobile. McKinnon[4] made an opposing point. If a region were very open, so that a large part of what was used was traded, or potentially traded internationally, as this had its price determined internationally exchange rate changes might not change real wages. Indeed, wage bargains might well not be struck in terms of domestic currency. This, he suggested, implied that the currency area should be large.

Corden's next contribution was threefold. He developed the concept of a *feasible* currency area, and refined both McKinnon's and Ingram's arguments (see below). A feasible area is one which can have its own currency, and the associated possibility of exchange rate changes. It is not so involved in trade with some other country that it simply uses that other country's currency.

McKinnon's argument was essentially one for choice of currency domain on grounds of what would yield the greatest stability of the price level. When should one want fixed rates to import price level stability? The answer depends not only on the openness of the economy, as McKinnon conjectured, but also on the source of the disturbance. If the disturbance is a change in the foreign price level, then domestic price stability requires an exchange rate change. Only if disturbances are domestic is the effect of a fixed exchange rate stabilizing, via stabilizing the price of traded goods.

Ingram[5] argued from the experience of Puerto Rico that a pegged exchange rate encouraged capital mobility, and this prevented the emergence of the depressed areas which Corden (and others) feared. The argument is straightforward. There is decline in demand for the principal export of an area. Workers become unemployed. On seeing this, capital (free of exchange risk) flows in, and the workers become employed in a new industry. However, if the workers became unemployed because they had pushed up wages, then there would be no incentive for capital to flow in: so capital mobility would not remove this difficulty. As Corden observed, the source of the disturbance is crucial.

Those few points summarize the theory of optimum currency areas, so far as it goes. It is clear that what the theory comprises is not a framework within which a proposal for a monetary union can be rigorously appraised, but rather a set of points to be considered in the course of discussing such a proposed union.

On the basis of the above arguments, is there a case for urging that the EEC abandon the EMS, and move to genuine monetary union? Do the above arguments demonstrate that economic performance – growth, stability, inflation – would improve within the EEC as a result? The answer has to be no. All the countries of the EEC (with the exception of the Benelux countries) can produce economic stability without joining a larger unit. It is for this reason that it seems sensible to let a currency emerge rather than imposing one not knowing whether there will be net gains or net losses. If businessmen (and travellers) find that the benefits of using a foreign currency outweigh the problems, then one would emerge.

It is argued that a national currency will come to dominate the EC, if it is more stable in value than other currencies. When exchange controls come down throughout the EEC people could choose to use it and would probably do so fairly quickly for large transactions.

One problem with this scheme is that if a European currency does evolve by that route, it would raise the most awkward problems of sovereignty. For it would be a European currency issued by a central bank responsible to a national government. This would not be an economic problem; but many might think it unattractive politically. Observe for example the Dutch reaction to Nigel Lawson's Antibes proposal. To avoid this, we propose a two-stage scheme to encourage a European money.

We suggest here two ways to encourage the widespread use of the ECU (the European Currency Unit, a weighted average of all EC currencies) as a unit of account and a more cost-effective means of payment. Either proposal would, on its own, be helpful. The two, taken together (the order of events does not matter) would provide a powerful stimulus to eventual monetary union.

One step would be to encourage the use of the ECU as a unit of account, by use of the tax system. This would serve two purposes. It would increase the incentives for governments to lower inflation and thus improve the quality of their currency, and would increase familiarity with the ECU.

The complementary measures would encourage the use of the ECU as a means of payment. We discuss how this could be achieved by the issue of some ECUs in replacement for a modest amount of national currencies. As we explain, this need involve no net money creation, and might be a politically acceptable outcome of Nigel Lawson's competing currency approach.

The line of thought here goes back at least to Hayek's pamphlet on 'Choice in Currency' published by the IEA.[6] A UK resident is, since the abolition of exchange control, in practice free to transact business in any currency agreed with his counter-party, but is still forced to make his tax returns in sterling, the domestic currency. No country, with the possible exceptions of Brazil and Israel, gives full tax relief for the effects of inflation. At the time of Hayek's paper almost any UK business man or investor would have paid substantially less tax if he were permitted to compute his taxes under the same UK rules but converting every transaction into Swiss francs. His 'choice in currency' would (at the time) have been the Swiss franc.

There was little hope of having this concept enshrined in the tax law of the United Kingdom or any other country, with the possible exception of Switzerland. What was then a difficulty can now actually be turned into an advantage.

This 'inflation' point is important. It can be perceived most simply in the case of an individual investor. If he deposits £10,000 at 12 per cent he will earn £1,200 interest during the year. If inflation is 8 per cent the real return will be only about 4 per cent. Fair enough, before tax, but what if the interest is taxed at 40 per cent? Then:

Original Capital		£10,000
Interest	1,200	
Less Tax	480	720
Assets at year end		£10,720

This is £80 short of the amount he would need just to keep pace with inflation. He has paid £480 tax on a real return of only £400. In the UK capital gains are now indexed for inflation, but this does not help the fixed interest investor.[7]

There is a similar but technically more complex problem for companies. This mainly concerns inventory (stocks) and depreciable fixed assets. Assume a company carries £100,000 of inventory which is turned over rapidly. If inflation is 8 per cent at the end of the year the same volume will be worth £108,000 and this £8000 increase is in principle a taxable profit. This extra tax could be avoided by keeping accounts in a stable currency.

Similarly if the business buys a machine for £50,000 it will be allowed (in the UK) to write off 25 per cent of the cost against taxable profits each year. When the time comes to replace it, the cost may have risen to £80,000. The business must find the extra £30,000 out of taxed profits just to stay in the same place.

These problems are mitigated in the short run in several ways, and may not show up clearly in any one year. LIFO valuation may help stock valuations, while accelerated depreciation gives some relief on equipment. Before 1984 the UK tax system contained rough justice reliefs for inflation at the corporate (but not the shareholder) level. The situation is now reversed: personal capital gains (at least on equity securities) are indexed. Corporate profits are not.[8]

Bringing all these factors together is a complicated exercise, but the position can in fact be expressed very simply. Assume country A and country B have identical tax systems, making no explicit allowance for inflation and assuming that identical companies have to make up their accounts in both currencies.

Country A has zero inflation. The company starts out with a capital of SM (sound money) 1,000,000. It earns 20 per cent per annum, pays 40 per cent tax and is left with SM 120,000 which (we assume) it pays out in dividends. At the end of a period it still has a net worth of SM 1,000,000.

Country B's currency FM (funny money) starts off at par with the SM. Inflation is 7 per cent and purchasing power parity holds. After ten years (the time it takes for prices to double at this inflation rate) it has a book net worth of FM 2,000,000, but this increase in money value has to come out of after tax retained earnings. It may well in fact have earned the FM 1,000,000 extra but if so will have paid FM 400,000 extra tax.

Put differently, if it is to achieve no more than to preserve its real value, it must plough back 7 per cent per annum of after tax earnings. It may earn in FM, 27 per cent instead of 20 per cent, but this is only 16.2 per cent after tax. It can therefore only afford dividends of 9.2 per cent instead of 12 per cent, suffers a fall in net earnings by 23 per cent and faces an effective tax rate of 54 per cent instead of 40 per cent: all these changes are at a 'modest' 7 per cent inflation rate.

The European Commission's harmonization proposal concerning systems of company tax and of withholding tax on dividends was published on 1 August 1975.[9] It suggested a range of rates for corporation tax. The European parliament passed a Resolution on 8 May 1979, refusing to give a final opinion until the Commission produced proposals to harmonize the tax base: Parliament insisted that harmonization of the rates of corporation tax and tax credits must take place in parallel with the gradual harmonization of the systems for assessing companies' taxable profits. The years went by, and in early 1988, the Commission published a preliminary draft proposal to harmonize the tax base.[10] This has certain unsatisfactory features which have been discussed elsewhere. It has been argued that there is no economic need to enforce standard tax rates throughout the Community, and that enforced standardization might well result in a tax collectors' cartel, actually perpetuating high rates.[11] Market forces, competition policy between countries to attract investment and enterprise, are more likely to be effective in encouraging countries to converge towards the type of tax system best calculated to favour economic activity.

Although there is no need to fix tax rates at Community level, there are good practical grounds for seeking agreement on the Directive on the tax base. Assume this can be achieved, and make the not unreasonable further assumption that this is not on a full monetary correction basis; that is to say, correction for the effects of inflation would not be complete. The actual tax burden on this technically similar base will then be lower in a low inflation country than in a high inflation country.

At first sight this seems to be a problem, a defect in the approach of the base directive. We can turn a tax problem into a monetary opportunity. One simple measure would both correct this potential tax distortion and actively encourage the idea of common European currency. The Directive should provide that business enterprises could use the ECU as their functional currency for the purpose of calculating tax, as an alternative to the national currency.

Although it is unlikely that smaller enterprises would rush to take advantage of this concession larger businesses, particularly multinational enterprises trading within different member countries would do so in these countries where the interest rate-inflation rate structure was higher than the Community average.

This arrangement would have two major advantages. The first and most important is that it would severely reduce the benefits to the tax collector derived from running a higher rate of inflation. It goes back to the classic test of the distinction between good and bad measures of indexation. A good measure of indexation is one which puts the whole, and preferably rather more than the whole, of the cost of any inflationary correction on the inflation creating authority, namely the government.

The second advantage is that it would, by encouraging the widespread use of the ECU in high inflation member states, put pressure on these states either to bring their inflation down to the Community average or (which amounts to the same thing) to adopt the ECU as the *de facto* and possibly even the *de jure* currency of their country.

It is a mathematical truism that if everyone above the average seeks to get down to the average, the equilibrium position must be full convergence on zero inflation. As all the pressure for adjustment falls on the higher inflation countries this equilibrium is likely to be at a low level of inflation.

What of the shorter run? How can we encourage EC citizens to become familiar with a common currency? Such a common currency, the ECU, already exists, and is indeed actively traded. It comprises a basket of currencies, but as there are mechanisms for changing the composition of the basket it is at present not possible precisely to duplicate the ECU by holding a portfolio of national currencies. (There has in fact just been a change in the basket.)[12] To the extent to which this is possible, the currency has an interest rate structure and an implied inflation rate which can easily be calculated. Sophisticated borrowers and investors, including national governments, are already prepared to deal in bonds, and enter into contracts, in ECU.

About 20 years ago a paper by Alexander Swoboda analysed transaction costs in foreign exchange markets and showed that these varied strikingly with the amount of activity in the market for each currency.[13] In all the national markets he studied, the commissions for dealing in dollars were a fraction of those for dealing in other currencies.

Although a German wishing to buy French francs would do so directly, a Canadian or a Japanese might then have found it cheaper first to buy US dollars as a 'vehicle currency'. This involved two transaction costs rather than one, but the sum of two fees in high volume, liquid and competitive markets was materially less than the cost of a single transaction in a low volume, relatively illiquid, market. This phenomenon would be self-perpetuating: if a majority of market players preferred to use the vehicle route, liquidity and volume in the direct market would shrink and costs would rise. Correspondingly, increased use of the US dollar–French franc market by non-dollar participants would increase volume and reduce costs in that market.

Since that paper was written dealing costs in the wholesale markets have shrunk almost to vanishing point, and those trading in cross markets have actually enjoyed a revival. It is quite different in the retail and small business markets, where costs have actually risen. The traveller converting banknotes or travellers cheques from one currency to another will be charged about 1 per cent commission, but will lose much more on the spread. Lord Jenkins has calculated that someone starting with £100, visiting every EC country, changing his currency at each frontier, but spending nothing, would return home with £24.60. It is notorious that smaller businesses which cannot afford to employ a hawk-eyed treasurer to watch screens find that their banks book their foreign exchange receipts and payments at the wrong end of the day's range: a hidden transaction cost which may well exceed 1 per cent.

High retail costs are perhaps inevitable if every local office of every bank has to maintain an inventory of a wide range of currencies to meet tourist demands. Costs could be reduced if it became customary for travellers within the European Community to carry ECU denominated payment instruments with them on their travels. The British traveller then need only concern himself with the sterling–ECU rate of exchange. The German shopkeeper or retail banker would only be concerned with the deutschmark–ECU rate. In substance this was the position of the US dollar in Europe immediately after the war.

There is a 'critical mass' problem in getting this off the ground, rather similar to that facing early subscribers to the telephone, or more recently to fax. It may well happen in its own good time. Shopkeepers would then double-price their goods as is done (with national currencies) close to borders. Smaller businesses would be encouraged in their international activities if the ECU became the standard invoicing currency for cross-border transactions. Increasing familiarity with the ECU as a unit of account, produced by the tax proposal, would pave the way for a small, experimental, issue of ECU currency designed to reduce these costs and inconveniences.

Businesses can already contract and settle in ECU if they so agree. The 'traveller' part of this proposal presumes an actual means of payment in ECU. This raises the question of whether and by whom ECU 'bank notes' would be issued. ECU travellers cheques are already available. In principle any reputable organisation could issue ECU bank notes provided that the issue was 100 per cent backed by the appropriate mix of cash and short-term Treasury Bills or the equivalent in the various component currencies. This is a profitable activity, as the issuer would earn interest (at present just over 8 per cent) on the asset. This would cover printing and administrative costs with a very healthy margin. The Island of Jersey issues its own banknotes on just this basis. The profit is conveniently referred to as seignorage by analogy with medieval minting profits. The activity would be of negligible risk, so there is an effective private incentive there.

This raises the legal question of whether the ECU is money and what restrictions would in fact apply to a private issuer. In practice it is unlikely that private issue would be permitted or encouraged, although it might be tempting to try the experiment. Even if the ECU were not legally money the notes would surely be securities for regulatory purposes.

Free banking is not a practical possibility, while for governments a Community monopoly is politically unattractive. The best compromise is to permit national money issuing authorities, such as the Bank of England and the Bundesbank, to put their own ECU notes into circulation. They would then not lose seignorage on the replacement of their own banknotes by ECU notes issued by themselves. Central banks in high interest rate countries would obviously earn more seignorage by issuing domestic notes than by issuing ECU, and would, it might be thought, therefore be discouraged from supporting the initiative. This tendency would be more than counterbalanced as citizens of that country will have a stronger incentive to hold cash in the form of ECU. They will, in the presumed absence of exchange controls, acquire those issued by (and profiting) other countries if they are not available from their own central bank.

There will be pressure for a European Community organization to have exclusive right to issue ECU notes, appropriating the seignorage for *fonds propre*. This will be resisted as being in unnecessary breach of the principle of subsidiarity according to which the higher levels of government should be as limited as possible and should be subsidiary to those of lower levels. All policy functions which could be carried out at national levels without adverse repercussions on the competence and functioning of the economic and monetary union would remain within the competence of the member countries.[14]

Even if nothing is done at official level, the way would be open for American Express, the Eurocheque network and other issuers of travellers cheques.[15] A helping hand from them should obviously be encouraged, but there is no need to give them a monopoly. It may be that if they take the initiative, national governments will be encouraged, on revenue grounds, to make their own issues. That would be one incentive to governments to issue the currency. The main losers from the scheme would be governments which relied very substantially on inflation for revenue. There are now few (and small) in the EC.

It is of course important to ask whether such a scheme would be inflationary. To answer that we have to look at its impact on both money supply and money demand. If this currency rather than the domestic one were issued, with the stock of reserve assets left unchanged, there would be no change in money growth in any country in the EC, and hence no change in EC money growth – a meaningful concept with pegged exchange rates. What of demand?

This is more problematical. The currency could prove more attractive than that of high inflation countries, and less attractive than that of low inflation countries. Demand for the former would fall and for the latter rise, relative to existing supplies. There could thus be a temporary boost to inflation in high inflation countries, and a temporary squeeze on inflation in low inflation countries. It would be prudent to offset this perverse effect by action on the stock of domestic money – but the effect would surely be at most second order in size.

This approach would have the short-run advantage of facilitating travel and trade within the single market, without the need for any new mechanism, and without any material disturbance of broader economic policy issues. It would not be a single currency. Is it a step toward achieving one?[16]

If the ECU becomes an accepted means of payment for cross border transactions and a unit of account for tax purposes, the final move towards a common currency would become largely technical. Similar questions were addressed by the Royal Commission on International Coinage set up in 1868 to consider proposals made at a conference in Paris the previous year.[17] These would have involved adopting a 25-franc gold coin as an international standard unit. This had already been adopted by the Later monetary union of France, Belgium, Italy and Switzerland. All that was standing between us and membership was a transitional problem occasioned by the fact that the French 25-franc gold piece had a gold content of 0.83% per cent less than the sovereign. (The US Half Eagle of $5 would have needed an adjustment of nearly 4 per cent.)

The report dwelt on the cost saving to the business community, encouraging small business to export and the advantages of 'promoting commercial and social intercourse, and thus drawing closer the friendly relations between different countries'. The Committee agonized over the difficulties of adjusting salaries and rents and whether the change 'would be tantamount to a legal permission for every creditor to rob his debtor of 2 pence in the pound' and in the end caution won the day. (Against this, supporters argued that British travellers carrying sovereigns incurred losses because these were often accepted as being equal to only 25 francs, when their real value was 25.20.)

As long as the ECU remained a minority currency issued by national central banks there would appear to be no need either for a European central bank or even for the type of 'Federal Reserve System' proposed by M. Delors. If the ECU became the *de jure* currency of the Community the question of its issue would become important. But because we had secured convergence of substance in advance of convergence of form this would be a relatively minor economic problem as it was when Germany converted to a common currency in the nineteenth century.

Indeed, so far as the economics is concerned it would be immaterial whether ECUs were issued by national central banks (some of whose native currencies had diminished in use more severely than others) or whether one central bank was formed, perhaps with a federal structure, to issue it. The very cautious man might argue for national central banks – for the existence of potentially competing currencies would help check inflationary excess. The European optimist would urge a common central bank.

But in the event, by that stage Europe would be maximizing whatever the benefits were from whatever degree of monetary union turned out to be desirable.

The market would have been used in what Hayek (and Samuel Brittan) have argued is its primary role – a device for letting us by trial and error discover efficient solutions to problems.

Notes

Demographic trends in the industrial world: Europe's declining population?

1   D.A. Coleman, 'Population', in *British Social Trends 1900–1985*, Ed. A.H. Halsey, London, Macmillan, 1988, 36–134.
2   W. Brass, 'Is Britain facing the Twilight of Parenthood?', Ed. H. Joshi, Oxford, Blackwell, 1989 (forthcoming).

3   J. Ermish, *The Political Economy of Demographic Change*, London, Heinemann, 1983.
4   E. de Cooman, J. Ermisch and H. Joshi, 'The next birth and the Labour Market: a dynamic model of births in England and Wales, *Population Studies*, 41, 2, 237–68, 1987.
5   H. Joshi, 'The Cash Opportunity Costs of Childbearing: an approach to Estimation Using British Data', D. Barram Paper Series No 208, Centre for Economic Policy Research, London, 1987.
6   Department of Health/Welsh Office, *Short Term Prediction of HIV infection and AIDS in England and Wales*, Report of a Working Group, London, HMSO, 1988.
7   OPCS Monitor PP2 89/1, Population Projections: mid 1987-based, London, OPCS, 1989.
8   J.A. Kay, 'The Welfare Crisis in an Aging Population', in M. Keynes, D.A. Coleman and N.H. Dimsdale (eds), *The Political Economy of Health and Welfare*, London, Macmillan, 136–48.

The costs of the CAP

1   *Disharmonies in EC and US Agricultural Policy Measures*, Commission of the European Communities, May 1988.
2   *Macro-economic Consequences of Farm Support Policies*, Global Study Overview, Centre for International Economics, Canberra, 1988.

The case for Britain joining the EMS

1   Although the UK does not participate in the Exchange Rate Mechanism of the EMS, sterling is included in the basket of currencies that make up the European Currency Unit and the UK subscribes to the European Monetary Cooperation Fund.
2   The Government appears to have acknowledged the futility of direct controls to influence the exchange rate; the 1947 Exchange Control Act was suspended in October 1979 and finally repealed in the 1987 Budget.
3   For example, Milton Friedman, 'The Case for Flexible Exchange Rates', in *Essays in Positive Economics*, University of Chicago Press, 1953, for a classic statement of this position. David Laidler ('The Case for Flexible Exchange Rates' in M. Sumner and G. Diz (eds), *European Monetary Union: Progress and Prospects*, Macmillan, London, 1982) offers a contemporary restatement of the same arguments.
4   *Cf.*, for example, the Chancellor of the Exchequer's 1984 Mansion House speech.
5   Conservative manifesto, 1983.
6   *Cf.* Nigel Healey, 'From Monetary Restraint to Closet Keynesianism', *Economic Affairs*, Vol. 7, No. 4, April/May 1987, for a fuller discussion of the breakdown of £M3 targets in the UK.
7   J. Fforde, 'Setting Monetary Objectives', *Bank of England Quarterly Bulletin*, June 1983.
8   This terminology is borrowed from asset market theories which assume that prices in asset markets adjust more rapidly than prices in goods markets. Hence exchange rates, in the short-term, will tend to 'overshoot' or 'undershoot' their long-term equilibrium values following a shock to the system.

9   R. McKinnon, 'The Exchange rate and Macroeconomic Policy: Changing Postwar Perceptions', *Journal of Economic Literature*, 1981.
10 One classic example of this phenomenon was the episode in January 1985, when sterling fell to $1.04 following a statement by the Prime Minister's press secretary to the effect that the Government did not care about the standing of the pound.
11 Nigel Lawson, speech to the joint annual meeting of the International Monetary Fund and the World Bank, 30 September 1987, relevant extracts of which are reproduced in HM Treasury, 'Managed Floating', *Economic Progress Report*, No. 192, October 1987.
12 G. Zis ('The European Monetary System and the UK', *British Review of Economic Issues*, Spring 1986) makes the point that 'it necessarily follows [from the petro-currency argument] that no exchange rate system could survive unless all its members had identical patterns of energy consumption and production', which is a patently absurd proposition.
13 *Cf.* note 11.
14 House of Lords Select Committee on the European Community, *The European Monetary System*, 5th Report, Session 1983–4, July 1983.
15 The Greek drachma was incorporated into the ECU in 1984, the only time the currency weights have been altered since 1979; the Portuguese escudo and the Spanish peseta have yet to be included.
16 Commission of the European Community, *Five Years of Monetary Cooperation in Europe*, COM (84) 125 Final, Brussels, March 1984.
17 International Monetary Fund, *The European Monetary System: The Experience 1979–82*, Occasional Paper No. 19, May 1983.
18 *Cf.* note 14.
19 *Cf.* note 12 for a fuller examination of this aspect of the EMS.
20 T. Padoa-Schioppa, *Money, Economic Policy and Europe*, European Perspectives Series, Brussels, 1984.
21 *The European Monetary System*, Cmnd. 7405, HMSO, November 1978.
22 European Council Resolution, December 1978.
23 *Cf.* note 16.
24 House of Commons Treasury and Civil Service Committee, *The International Monetary System, Session 1985–6*, HMSO, 1985.

The argument against joining the EMS

1   *Cf.*, for example, the majority arguments in House of Commons Expenditure Committee, *Report on the Proposed New European Monetary System*, HMSO, London, 1979.
2   House of Commons Treasury and Civil Service Committee, The Financial and Economic Consequences of UK Membership of the European Communities: *The European Monetary System*, HMSO, London, 1985.
3   Presented in evidence to House of Lords, Select Committee on the European Communities, *European Monetary System*, HMSO, London, 1983.
4   Major studies are Bank of England, 'The Variability of Exchange Rates: Measurement and Effects', *Book of England Quarterly Bulletin*, September 1984; and International Monetary Fund, *Exchange Rate Volatility and World Trade*, IMF Occasional Paper No. 28, IMF, 1984.
5   K. Rogoff, 'Can Exchange Rate predictability be achieved without Monetary Convergence?: Evidence from the EMS', *European Economic Review*, 28, 1985, 93–115.
6   The importance of policy coordination is stressed in J. Melitz, 'The Welfare

Case for the European Monetary System', *Journal of International Money and Finance*, 1985.
7 This point is emphasized in P. de Grauwe, 'International Trade and Economic Growth in the European Monetary System', *European Economic Review*, 31, 1986, 389–98.

The right road to monetary union

1 *Report on Economic and Monetary Union in the European Community* ('The Delors Report'), 12 April 1988.
2 W.M. Corden, *Inflation, Exchange Rates and the World Economy*, 2nd ed. Clarendon Press, Oxford.
3 R.A. Mundell, 1961, 'A Theory of Optimum Currency Areas', *American Economic Review*, Vol. 51, 657–665.
4 R.I. McKinnon, 'Optimum currency areas', *American Economic Review*, Vol. 53, 1963, 717–27.
5 J.C. Ingram, *Regional payments mechanisms: The case of Puerto Rico*, University of North Carolina Press, Chapel Hill, NC, 1962.
6 F.A. Hayek, *Choice in Currency*, IEA, 1978.
7 Note that this point is quite separate from 'bracket indexation': moving tax allowances and thresholds in line with inflation.
8 Two other factors partly relieve this tax on inflation. A delay between earning profits and paying taxes means that inflation reduces the effective burden, while the falling real value of net debt (after deducting debtors and other monetary assets) gives a tax free benefit.
9 *Draft Directive Concerning the Harmonization of Systems of Company Taxation*, Brussels, August 1975 COM (75) 392 final.
10 *Preliminary Draft Proposal for a Directive on the Harmonization of Rules for Determining the Taxable Profits of Undertakings*, Brussels, 1988, XV/27-/88-EN.
11 John F. Chown, Company Tax Harmonization in the European Community, *Institute of Directors*, London, 1989.
12 Some of the technical defects could be removed by 'freezing' the basket. This is not of the essence of the present proposals.
13 Alexander Swoboda, '*Vehicle Currencies and the Foreign Exchange Market*' in Aliber, R.Z. (ed.) *The International Market for Foreign Exchange*, Praeger, 1969.
14 'The Delors Report', *op. cit.*, para. 20.
15 Since this article was written the Eurocheque member banks, meeting in Rome, have resolved to allow users to write cheques in ECU. The technical committee is instructed to work out details and report back to the May meeting. This is a welcome initiative. Transaction costs will be substantially reduced if travellers and occasional importers, as well as shopkeepers, hotels and other suppliers, maintain a ECU bank account against which these payments can be debited and credited.
16 This does not lead us to an all or nothing approach. The ECU could become the *de facto* currency of only part of the Community if that proves to be an optimal currency area.
17 *Report from the Royal Commission on International Coinage*, HMSO, 18 February 1868.

Index

Acquired Immune Deficiency Syndrome (AIDS) 290–1
Addison, J. 52–3
agriculture 85
airspace, congestion of 173–8; airline competition barriers 174; airline deregulation 174; airport competition 174; airport competition barriers 174; airspace competition 174; airspace competition barriers 174; European airspace 176
Albon, R. 116
Aldington Committee 269
Alliance Party 103, 116
Allied Lyons 206
American Express 331
American Medical Association (AMA) 153
Amersham International 249–52
Asda 206
Ashton, P. 124
Associated British Petroleum 249
Associated British Ports 249–51
Association of Futures Brokers and Dealers (AFBD) 69
ATE Management and Service Company 184
Atlas Copco/Desoutter merger 222
Austin Rover 145
Australia 9, 18, 39, 81, 102
Austria 4
Austrian School of Economic Thought 19, 23, 262–3, 298

baby boom (USA) 294
Badgerline/Midland Red West Holdings merger 222
Baker, H. 86
Baker, K. 102

Bakker, J. 255
Bakker, T. 255
Balance of Payments (UK) 9, 63–6, 281; current account 65
Baltic Exchange 273
Bangkok Metropolitan Transport Authority 184
Bangladesh 82
Bank of England 56–7, 65, 209, 252, 263, 270, 312, 314, 320, 331; Board of Banking Supervision 57; lender of last resort 58
Banking Act 1979 56
Barclays Bank 61
Barclays Development Capital Ltd 208
Baron, T. 260
Barrett, S. 3, 173
Barry, N. 247
Batchelor, R. 319
Bazen, S. 282
Beesley, M. 239
Beneficial Corp. 215
Berrill, Sir K. 67
Birmingham Diocesan Board of Finance 255
Bismarck 4
black economy 36–40
Blue Circle/Myson merger 222
Blundell, J. 226
Bosanquet, N. 75, 169–71
BP 250, 252
Bracewell-Milnes, B. 3, 78
Bretton Woods 310, 313, 315, 324
Brewer, D. 256
British Aerospace 249–50
British Airways 91, 145, 251
British American Tobacco (BAT) 206, 208–9

British Broadcasting Company (BBC) 36, 301
British Gas 221, 238
British Invisible Exports Council (BIEC) 270–2
British Leyland 251, 253
British Medical Association (BMA) 151–2
British Midland 175
British Nuclear Fuels 251, 253
British Pest Control Association 163
British Property Federation 118
British Rail 4, 239–47, 257; passenger services 246
British Rail Engineering Ltd (BREL) 239
British Rail Investments Ltd 239
British Shipbuilders 251
British Steel 145, 257
British Syphon 206
British Telecom 106, 245, 249, 252; privatization of 234–9
British Transport Hotels 249
British Wagon Hirers Association 253
Britoil 249–50, 252
Brittan, L. 235
Brittan, S. 63, 66, 333
Brook, L. 75
Bruges Group 301, 304
Brundtland Report, the 180–1
Brunner, K. 28
Bryan, R.H. 197
Buchanan, C. 255
Buckland, R. 4, 248
budget deficit 42
Bundesbank 65–6
Burberry 265
Burton, J. 52–3
Business and Technician Education Council (B/TEC) 107
business cycle 25, 29, 298
Business Monitor 208

Cable and Wireless 234, 238, 249–52
Calcutta State Transport Corporation (CSTC) 184–5
Callaghan, J. 257
Cambridge Economic Policy Group 27
Cambridge University 16, 278
Cambridge University Press 278
Canada 18, 81, 102
Capie, F. 56
capital market 46
capital transfer tax 82

Capital Transfer Tax (White Paper) 80
Carsberg, B. 234, 236–7
centralized traffic control (CTC) 240–1
Centre for Management Buy-Out Research (CMBOR) 204, 208
Chancellor of the Exchequer 278, 312
Channel Tunnel 268
Cheshire Lines Railway 242
Chicago Board of Trade 18, 20–1
Chicago School of Thought 43
Chicago University 22
Chiplin, B. 52
Chown, J. 324
Church of England 253–7
Citizens' Educational Advice Bureaux 92
Civil Aviation Authority, The (CAA) 175, 177
Clark, C. 3, 83
Clarke, K. 150
Clarke, Sir W. 270
classical Marxist model 277
Clinch River Breeder Reactor 86
closed economy 13
Coase, R.H. 177
Coats Viyella/Tootal merger 222
Cobbett, W. 83
Coca-Cola 268
Cocoa & Sugar Exchange of New York 21
Coleman, D. 288
Committee on Overseas Trade (1985) 285
common currency zone 63
Common Extenal Tariff (CET) 303
competition policy 203–25; independent acquisitions 208; leveraged acquisitions 203–9; privatization of 222–4; UK management buy-outs 205
Confederation of British Industry (CBI) 66, 270
Congdon, T. 2, 55, 66
Conoco 217
Conservative Party 49, 51, 62, 103, 116, 118, 126, 151, 154, 284
Constant, B. 299
construction industry, UK 276
Consumer Price Index 21
contracting-out 227
Cope Allman 206
Cornwall, J. 8
Cost of Living Adjustments (COLA) 43
Council for National Academic Awards (CNAA) 107

Cox, Baroness 102
Cross-Channel Ferries 222
currency depreciation 285
Curwen, P. 4, 234

Davies, E.W. 4, 248
Dawson, G. 36
Day, Sir R. 178
De Gaulle, C. 256
Deane, P. 8
Deficit Reduction Act of 1984 214
deflation 43
deindustrialization 260–87; employment in manufacturing 283; employment in services 283; invisible trade account 283; manufacturing industries 282–6
Delaware Supreme Court 212
Delors, J. 301, 332; the Delors report 324
Demsetz, H. 176
Department of Education and Science (DES) 107
Department of Employment 36–7
Department of Health and Social Security (DHSS) 159, 167
Department of Trade and Industry (DTI) 69–70, 220, 301
deposit insurance 56
Deutschmark (DM) 62–6
Dimbleby Lecture 270
Director General IV (DGIV) 221
Director General of Fair Trading 218
Douglas, Major 44
Duke of Edinburgh, HRH 112, 178
Dwek 206

East India Company 287
Economic Affairs 1, 5, 7, 9, 18, 22, 26, 32, 36, 46, 52, 55–6, 59, 67, 74, 83, 86, 91, 94, 97, 101, 106, 112, 114–16, 124, 131, 134, 136, 150, 157, 159, 169, 173, 178, 182, 191, 195, 203, 210, 218, 222, 226, 234, 239, 247–8, 253, 260, 263, 269, 276, 282, 288, 297, 301, 303, 305, 319, 324
Economic Trends Annual Supplement 63
Economist Intelligence Unit 75
Economist, The 311
education 83, 91–111; consumer sovereignty in education 97–100; parent power 91–4; privatization of schools 91–4; school curriculum 105; school grants 97–100
Education Act 1870 92
Education Act 1944 91, 96, 100
Education Act 1980 104
educational vouchers 99–100
Einthoven, A. 152
Elders IXL 206
Elders/Scottish & Newcastle merger 222
Eltis, W. 4, 276
Emap/Parrett merger 221
Emap/T.R. Beckett merger 222
Employment Act of 1980 51
Employment Act of 1982 51
employment and the real wage 10–12; real wage dilemma 11–12
Employment Gazette Historical Supplement 280
employment protection 50
employment shifts, UK 279
Engel's Law 283
England 76
enrolled general nurse (EGN) 135
environment 173–202
Equal Pay Act (1970) 289
Ericsson, L.M. 235
European Civil Aviation Conference (ECAC) 173
European Commission 177
European Council Resolution 317
European Court of Human Rights 88
European currencies; Belgian franc 316; Deutschmark 316; Drachma 316; French franc 316; Guilder 316; Krone 316; Lira 316; Luxembourg franc 316; Pound 316; Punt 316
European Economic Commission 286
European Economic Community (EEC) 64, 208, 288–336; aging of population 291–4; Agricultural Council 308; Agricultural Fund 305; arguments against the European Monetary System 319–24; arguments for the European Monetary System 310–19; basket of currencies 329; CAP reform 306; Common Agricultural Policy (CAP) 303–5; Common External Tariff (CET) 302–3; costs of CAP 305–10; European Currency Unit (ECU) 306–7, 330; Muslim population 292; 1992 and beyond 301–4; population of 288–96; racial

minorities 288; single market 301, 304; tax policy 328-9
European Monetary Cooperation Fund (EMCOF) 315-17
European Monetary System (EMS) 62-7, 304, 317-25; the snake 315
exchange rate mechanism (ERM) 310, 314-15, 317-19
exchange rate (UK) 63-6

Fair Trading Act 1973 219
Fairey 249
Family Practitioner Service 167
Federal Reserve Board 14, 19
Federal Reserve System 332
Federal Trade Commission 217
Ferranti 249
Fiji 82
financial futures 18-22
financial institutions, UK 273
financial markets, deregulation of 67-73
Financial Intermediaries, Managers and Brokers Regulatory (FIMBRA) 69, 71
Financial Services Act 1986 67, 72
Financial Times 100 18, 250
Financial Times 60
Fisher Act 1918 100
Foley, B. 26
Forestry Commission 193
forestry policy 191-5; tree planting 192
Forster, W.E. 92
Forsyth, P.J. 261
France 16, 18
Franz-Josefs-Universitat 298
free banking 331
French motor industry 302
Freud, S. 254
Friedman, M. 11-12, 22, 26, 29, 41, 45, 101, 117
Friends of the Earth 178

Gallup Poll 75, 78
Gamble, A. 107
Garvin, G. 186
Gateway supermarkets 206, 209
Gatwick Airport 177, 239-40
GDP 59, 125, 260, 281, 308
Gec-Siemens/Plessey merger 222
Geldof, R. 320
General Theory of Employment, Interest and Moiney 2, 9-10, 15, 27-8

Germany 5, 16
Gibson, Y. 151
Glynwed/Less merger 222
GNP 43-4, 159, 179, 263
golden parachute 210, 213-14
Goldstein, A. 247
Gordon, R. 25
Gower Report 70
Graham, W. 255
Grand Metropolitan/William Hill merger 222
Gray, J. 67
Green, D.G. 152, 157-8, 169
Green Economics 178-82; dangerous chemicals (Dieldrin) 180
Greenmail 213, 218
Greenpeace 178
Griffiths, Sir R. 150
Grosse 76
growth rates of OECD countries 263
Guardian, The 74

Hahn, F. 24-5
Hall, M. 55
Hallett, G. 247-8
Hansen, A.H. 40, 43-5
Hanson Trust 206
Harrod, Sir R. 120-1
Hartley, K. 134, 227-8, 231-2
Harvey-Jones, Sir J. 270
Hattersley, R. 178
Hayek, F.A. 248, 298, 326, 333
Healey, N.M. 310, 319, 321
health 83, 134-72; demand for enhanced insurance 148; how to pay for the NHS 159-69; lessons for the NHS 157-8, 169-71; NHS National Insurance rebate 144; NHS per capita funding 160; NHS policy review 136-9; NHS vouchers 139-41; opting-out 155-7; price of health care 158; training of nurses 134-6; two-tier health system 157; waiting lists 154-5
health care 152-3
health expenditure 137
health maintenance organizations (HMOs) 152-3, 168
Heath, E. 49, 51, 302
Heathrow Airport 175, 177
Helms, J. 86
Hicks, J. 9
High Speed Train Services 245

higher education 106–10
Hillgate group 91
Hillsdown/Pittard Garner merger 222
Holmes, M. 4, 301
Hong Kong Government 191
Hoskyns, Sir J. 302
House of Commons 318
House of Lords 49, 193, 298, 314, 317
House of Lords Select Committee (1989) 269, 303
Housing Act of 1980 117–19, 128, 130
Housing Act of 1986 118
housing, cost of 115–16
housing market 112–133; building land 115–16; job creation 124–31; mortgage interest tax relief 114; mortgage subsidy 131–3; private rented sector 118–19; reform of housing regulations 126–8; state distortions in housing markets 129–31
housing reform 124–31
housing subsidies 112–14
Howe, Sir G. 78, 81, 252
Howell, R. 37
Hoylake 206, 208
human capital 47
Hurst, G. 248

ICL 249, 270
income support 144
income tax 79
Income Tax Act of 1952 131
incomes policy 14
India 82
Industrial Revolution 180
infant mortality 290
inflation 22, 59–62
Ingram, N. 325
Inland Revenue 166
Inner London Education Authority (ILEA) 103–4
Institute of Directors 81–2, 270
Institute of Economic Affairs (IEA) 1, 70, 76–8, 124, 169, 232, 326
Institute of Economic Affairs Health Unit 170
Institute of Environment Health Officers 162
institutional reform 46–52
Interest Bearing Eligible Liabilities (IBELs) 56
interest rates 19

International Airline Trade Association 173
International Bureau of Fiscal Documentation 82
International Business Machines (IBM) 236
International Monetary Fund (IMF) 265, 313, 319
International Stock Exchange 4, 20, 273
International Television Network (ITN) 36
Invergordon Distillers 206
Investment Management Regulatory Organization (IMRO) 69
invisible exports 269–76
IRA, the 303
IS–LM analysis 9
Isoceles 204, 206
Italy 16, 267

Jaguar Car Group 302
Japan 16, 18
Jarvis, F. 98
JCB 265
Jefferson, Sir G. 236
Jehovah's Witness 254
Jenkins, R. 330
John Loughborough School 96
Johnson, P. 255
Joseph, Sir K. 110
Jowell, R. 75
Joy, S. 240
junk bonds 204

Kaiser scheme 84
Kaldor, N. 18, 25, 278–9
Kay, J.A. 261
Keynes, J.M. 5, 9–10, 15, 18–20, 27–8, 40, 42, 44, 62, 298, 300; Keynesian macro-model 41
Keynesianism 2, 7–31, 59, 61; hydraulic Keynesianism 8, 23–5; neo-Keynesianism 24; post-Keynesianism 8, 24, 44
King, A. 75
King, J. 162
Kinnock, N. 301
Kohl, H. 301
Korea 265
Kuhn, T. 23

Labour economics 32–54

Labour Party 49–51, 103, 106, 116, 119, 264, 301
Lachmann, L. 19–21
Lakatos, I. 7, 23
Lambeth Borough Council 230
Land Rover 265
Landlord and Tenant Act 116, 118
Last In, First Out (LIFO) 327
Lawrence, P. 263
Lawson, N. 2, 62, 80–1, 155, 313, 326
League of Nations 300
Leal, D.R. 195
Levačić, R. 26–7, 29
Leverage Buy-Outs (LBOs) 207
Lewis, R. 253
Liesner, H. 220
Life Assurance and Unit Trust Regulatory Organization (LAUTRO) 69, 71–2
Lipsey, R. 8, 26; theory of 'the asymmetry' 26
Lipworth, S. 218
lira, Italian 315
Liston, D. 269
Littlechild, S. 239
Liverpool, city of 37, 39–40
Liverpool University 38
Lloyd's of London 70, 142
Local Education Authorities (LEAs) 92, 102
London Business School 16
London, city of 130, 285
London Commodity Exchange (LCE) 18
London International Financial Futures Exchange (LIFFE) 18, 20
London Metal Exchange (LME) 18
London School of Economics 19
London Transport 91
Long Gilt contract 20
Loughborough University 55
Louvre accord, the 313, 317, 319
Lowndes Queensway 206
LSW proposition 25
Lucas, R. 22, 25
Lydall, H. 9

Madison, J. 88
Mafia, the 303
Magnet 204
Malaysia 82
Malthius, T.R. 276
Malthus, R. 289
managed data network (MDN) 236–7

management buy-in (MBI) 203, 207
management buy-out (MBO) 203–5, 207
management Japan 17
management UK 17
Manpower Services Commission 279–80
Mansfield and District Trades and Labour Council 36
manufacturing output 260
marginal efficiency of capital 16
marginal productivity of labour 41
Marks, J. 3, 94, 102
Marks and Spencer 102–3, 267
Marshall, A. 15, 41
Marshall Field 217
Martin, D. 255
Martonair 251
Marx, K. 11, 276–7, 298
Mather, G. 4, 222
McCrum, M. 91
McCulloch, J.R. 276
McGee, R.W. 210
McKenna, N. 3, 159
McKinnon, R. 312, 325
medical technology 161
medium-term financial strategy (MTFS) 312, 323–4
Mercury 234, 237–8
Messenger Newspapers Group 52
mezzanine debt 204, 209
micro-economics 15
Midland Montague *Monetary Bulletin* 59
migration 291
Militant Tendency 178
Mill, J.S. 23
Miller, R.C.B. 18
Minford, P. 3, 52, 123–4, 136
Minorco/Consgold merger 222
Mises, V. 248
Mitek/Gang-Nail merger 221
Mitel Corporation 234
Mobil 217
Momin Motors 187
Monarchy of Habsburg 297
monetarism 59–62
monetarists 22
monetary policy 28, 55–6
monetary union 324–33
money and banking 55–73; bank lending to the personal sector 60; broad money 65; City of Glasgow Bank 57; depositors' protection 57;

Index

Johnson Matthey failure 56–7; M0 60, 67, 320, 323; M1 59, 320, 323; M2 323; M3 62, 65–6, 320, 323; M4 60, 65, 67; monetary growth 59–62; secondary banking crisis 56; sterling 320
Monopolies and Mergers Commission 175, 218–22, 235
monopoly profits 34
Monsanto/Rhône Poulenc merger 222
Morrell, F. 98
Mundell, R.A. 324
Murfin, A. 4, 276
Myers, N. 179

Namier, Sir L. 298
National Advisory Body 107
National Air Transport Services (NATS) 175
National Association of Health Authorities 163
National Audit Office 193–4
National Bus Company (NBC) 241, 251
National Coal Board 52, 257
National Consumer Council (NCC) 304
National Enterprise Board 249
National Federation of Housing Associations 112
National Freight Corporation 249
National Graphical Association (NGA) 52
National Health Service (NHS) 3, 134–7, 139, 145–7, 150–63, 165–70
National Income 276
National Income Accounts 59
National Income accounts (Russian) 277
National Insurance 130
national press, the 36
National Trust 178
National Union of Mineworkers 52
National Union of Teachers (NUT) 91, 94
'natural rate of interest' 45
natural rate of unemployment 11, 45
Neves, Government of Kuwait/BP merger 221
new classical macro-economics 22
New York Coffee Sugar & Cocoa Exchange 22
Newcastle Commission Report 93
Newgateway 206
Niehans, J. 261

Noise and Nuisance Index (NNI) 177
North Sea oil 261
'Not In My Backyard' (NIMBY) 195, 198
nuclear waste policy 195–201
Nuclear Waste Policy Act 1987 197
Nugee Report 116

O'Driscoll, L.H. 229
O'Keeffe, D. 100
Office of Fair Trading (OFT) 70–1
Office of Telecommunications (Oftel) 234–5, 237
oil production 262
open-market operations (OMO) 310–11, 314
Oppenheim-Barnes, S. 303
Organization for Economic Cooperation and Development (OECD) 114, 158, 171, 261, 274
Orient-Express Company Ltd 243
Orski, K. 184
output growth, UK 278
Oxfam 180
Oxford University 16, 278
Oxford University Press 278

Paish, F. 120–1
Pakistan 82
Parry Lewis, J. 114, 131
Patten, J. 116, 118
Pauli, G. 271–2
Peacock, A. 226
Pearson and Sons 251
Peel, M. 124
Peel, R. 85
Pegler, 131
Pembridge 204
Pendleton, 162
Pepper, G. 2, 59
per capita funding of schools 94–7
Period Total Fertility Rate (PTFR) 288
Personal Social Services (PSS) 167, 172
Petropound 263
Phillips curve 22, 24–5, 44
Pigou, A.C. 24, 40, 44–5
Pitt, W. 85
Plessey-GEC 235–6
poison pills 210–12
poll tax 3
Poole, R. 228
Popper, K. 8
population projections (UK) 289

Porritt, J. 178, 181
preferred provider organizations (PPOs) 168
Private Automatic Branch Exchange (PABXs) 234-5
private health insurance 138, 163-5
privatization 226-59; issues 250; pricing 251-3; universities 247-8
privatization of hospitals 145
productivity 14
productivity growth, UK 278
property taxes 198
Public Accounts Committee 194
Public Sector Borrowing Requirement (PSBR) 249, 263
Public Service Obligation (PSO) 244

Question Time 178

Radio Suisse 175
Rajan, A. 274
rational expectations 28
Reagan, R. 14, 226, 233, 269; Reagan administration 14, 86
real balance effect 24
real wages and employment 40-6
Recognized Professional Bodies (RPD) 69
regional health authorities (RHAs) 145-6
registered general nurse (RGN) 135
rent control 116-24
Rent Act of 1957 127
Rent Act of 1965 120
Rent Act of 1974 120
Rent Act of 1977 117
Republican Party (USA) 86
Restrictive Trade Practice (RTP) 220-1
Retail Price Index (RPI) 238
retirement age 295
Ricardo, D. 11, 276-7
Ricketts, M. 120-2
Riddle, D. 274-5
Robbie, K. 203
Robbins, L. 248
Robbins Report 109
Robinson, J. 24-5
Robinson, R. 157, 171
Rolls Royce 265
Roth, G. 4, 182
Rothbard, M. 20, 226
Rothschild, N.M. 69
Rover Group 302
Rowley, C. 7-8, 22-6, 46

Rowthorn, R. 278
Royal Commission on International Coinage 332
Royal Commission on Popular Education of 1861 92
Royal Commission on Population 296
Royal College of Nursing 163
Royal Society of Arts 178, 270
Runcie, R. 257
Rutgers University 196

Sandman, P. 196
Sandor, R. 21
Sargent, T. 25
Say, J.B. 23, 44.
schools as self-seeking syndicates 101-6
Schumpeter, J. 46, 298
Schwartz, E. 2, 40
Scruton, R. 102
Sealink 251
Secretary of State for Trade and Industry 218
Securities and Exchange Commission (SEC) 215-16
Securities and Investment Board (SIB) 67, 71-3
Securities Association, the (TSA) 69
Seldon, A. 3, 74
Seldon, M. 3, 97
Selective Employment Tax 278
self-regulatory organizations (SROs) 67-8, 70, 72
Serpell Committee 240, 247
Serpell Report 244-5
service sector productivity 276-81
Shackleton, J.R. 106
Sheffield formula, the 256
Shiell, A. 134
Simons, H.C. 40, 43-5, 53, 81
Singapore 18, 82
Smith, A. 4, 15, 32, 276-7, 280
Snowdon, B. 7, 22
Social and Community Planning Research (SCPR) 75, 78
Soviet Union planning 277
Special Drawing Right (SDR)
Spicer & Oppenheim 131, 208
Sri Lanka 82
Stafford, D.C. 116
Standard Industrial Classification (SIC) 266
Standard and Poors 500 18
Standard Telephones and Cables (STC) 235

Index   345

Stanley Royal Mental Health Hospital 163
Stansted Airport 177
Starkie, D. 4, 239
state welfare 74–8
State Earnings-Related Pension Scheme (SERPS) 293
Steel, D. 74
Steele, G.R. 2, 32
sterling, value of 312
Stigler, G. 117
Stockman, D. 86, 89
Stone, N. 4–5, 297
Strong & Fisher/Pittard Garnar merger 222
Stroup, R.L. 195
Sufferers Campaign to Resolve the European Aviation Mess (SCREAM) 173
supplementary benefit 38
Swaggart, J. 255
Sweden 79
Swoboda, A. 329

Taff Vale Railway Co. v. Amalgamated Society of Railway Servants 49
takeovers 210–18
Tate, 162
taxation 74–90; capital gains tax 78; capital transfer tax 78; Development Land Tax 80; estate duty 78; ethics of 86–9; Investment Income Surcharge 80; National Insurance Surcharge 80; political taxes 78–82; progressive tax 81; Reagan tax 89; USA 86–9; wealth tax 78
Taylor, T. 112
Teal, R. 185
terms of trade 16
Thatcher, M. 3, 51–2, 75, 83, 106, 124, 191, 226, 232, 261–2, 301, 303, 308, 310
theory of liquidity preference 19, 21
Third World, the 180
Thirlwall, A.P. 282
Thompson, S. 203
Thomson/Horizon merger 221
Thomson, K. 305
Thomson Regional Newspapers/Century merger 222
Thorn-EMI 235
Thorn, G. 272
Thun-Hohenstein, L. 298
Tideman, T.N. 86

Times, The 107
Titmuss, 136
Tobin, J. 23–4
Total Operational Processing System (TOPS) 245
tourism 273
Trade Disputes Act 1906 49
Trade Union Act of 1984 51
trade union immunities 49
trade union power 46–52
trade union reform 49
trade unions 10, 32–6; closed shop 35, 50; in a free society 32–6; institutional reform 46–52; power 46–52; sponsorship of MPs 50; tenure of union officials 49; wage bargaining 33–4
trade unions and society 52–3
traded v. non-traded goods 280
traffic congestion 182
transport 182–91; electronic number plate (ENP) 189–90; electronic road pricing (ERP) 189–91; private and public provision 182–91; tolls 189; vehicle ownership 183
Treasury and Civil Service Committee 318–19
Treasury, the 251
Treaty of Rome 286
Tutu, D. 255

UK balance of trade 263, 265
unemployment 16, 22, 125, 284; involuntary unemployment 42; mass unemployment 41; voluntary unemployment 41
unemployment benefit 38
United Nations 291
United States of America 14, 102
University Grants Committee 107
University of Arizona 274
University of Buckingham 107
University of Essex 75
University of Nottingham 208
University of St Andrews 37
University of Sussex 274
University of York 75, 170
urban public transport 188
US Congress 318
US dollar 317
US Environmental Protection Agency 196
US Second Circuit Court of Appeals 210

US Treasury Bonds 18–20

Value Added Network Services (VANS) 236–7
Value Added Tax (VAT) 308
Veljanovski, C. 67
velocity of circulation 42
Velsicol Chemical Co. 202
venture capital markets 18
Verdoorn, P.J. 27; the Verdoorn law 27, 278–9, 285
Vinson, N. 115
Virgin 206
Vishnevskaya, G. 157
Voltaire, F.M.A. 299
vouchers 227
VTG 243

wage-illusion 42
Wallace, N. 25
Warburg, S.G. 69
Warburton, P. 2
Washington Times, The 227
Wealth Tax (Green Paper) 80

Webb, S. 36
Wedgwood 265
Weinstock, Lord 269–70
welfare state 85
welfare taxation 83
Welles, O. 299
West, E.G. 99, 103
Whelan, R. 3, 178
Whetstone, L. 4, 191
White House, the 318
Whitney, R. 152
Wicksell, K. 22, 45
Williams Act 210, 215–17
Wilson, T. 24
Witherspoon, S. 75
Wood, G. 324
World Bank 181–2, 188
Wright, M. 203
Wynarczyk, P. 7, 22

Yale & Valor/Myson merger 222
Yale University 23
Young, Lord 301

Zola, E. 80